The 111th New York
Volunteer Infantry

The 111th New York Volunteer Infantry
A Civil War History

MARTIN W. HUSK

McFarland & Company, Inc., Publishers
Jefferson, North Carolina, and London

LIBRARY OF CONGRESS CATALOGUING-IN-PUBLICATION DATA

Husk, Martin W., 1965–
The 111th New York Volunteer Infantry :
a Civil War history / Martin W. Husk.
    p.   cm.
Includes bibliographical references and index.

ISBN 978-0-7864-4552-3
softcover : 50# alkaline paper ∞

1. United States. Army. New York Infantry Regiment, 111th (1862–1865)
2. New York (State) — History — Civil War, 1861–1865 — Regimental histories.
3. United States — History — Civil War, 1861–1865 — Regimental histories.
4. Soldiers — New York (State) — Biography. 5. New York (State) — History —
Civil War, 1861–1865 — Biography. 6. United States — History —
Civil War, 1861–1865 — Biography. 7. New York (State) — History —
Civil War, 1861–1865 — Prisoners and prisons. 8. United States —
History — Civil War, 1861–1865 — Prisoners and prisons. I. Title.
II. Title: One Hundred Eleventh New York Volunteer Infantry.

E523.5111th .H875 2010   973.7'447 — dc22   2009045087

British Library cataloguing data are available

©2010 Martin W. Husk. All rights reserved

*No part of this book may be reproduced or transmitted in any form
or by any means, electronic or mechanical, including photocopying
or recording, or by any information storage and retrieval system,
without permission in writing from the publisher.*

Cover photograph: Brigadier General Clinton D. MacDougall
and staff, between 1861 and 1865 (Library of Congress);
background ©2009 Shutterstock

Manufactured in the United States of America

*McFarland & Company, Inc., Publishers
Box 611, Jefferson, North Carolina 28640
www.mcfarlandpub.com*

To my parents, Ford and Nancy Husk,
who encouraged my love of history,
and to my wife, Darla, and sons, Ryan and Sean,
who bless me every day with their love,
encouragement and support in all things.

Acknowledgments

As is often the case, an undertaking of this magnitude is never truly the work of just one person. It takes the love and labor of many people. This book is no exception. First and foremost I wish to express my heartfelt thanks to Bill Jacobs. His untiring efforts in uncovering resources and most importantly, his friendship, throughout the entire project made this book possible. It is a friendship I will always treasure.

I am also indebted to Marge Perez of the Wayne County Historian's Office, and to R. L. Murray and George Contant. Each gave selflessly of their time and energy to uncover material on the regiment and shared their private collections with me.

Many individuals donated cherished family letters, diaries, photographs, and service records. Their generosity helped give a face and a voice to the men of the 111th. They include the late Burke W. Drummond (Robert Drummond), who related fond memories of his grandfather; Norman and Rosemary Smith (Harry Smith); Marion Dudley (Newman Eldred); the late Francis Benton (James Dana Benton); Hallie Sweeting (Simeon Cooper); Don Chatfield (John Paylor); Bill Holmes and Lela Rose (Langdon) Hergert (Owen Spencer Langdon); Janet Caves (Luman Decker); Joe Flynn (Chauncey Smith); David Crane and George Contant (Thomas Geer); Charles Bennett (David Gibbs); Joe Weaver (Charles White); Sally Hall (Henry Jeffery); Ken Harris (Esek Hoff); Wesley Howell (Daniel Grandin); David Mohr (Reuben Myers); Jeff Lape (Philip Ira Lape); Ken Hoxie (Allen Hoxie); George Kimbes and H. Richard Taylor (Richard Warren); and David Gibson (Lewis Husk).

All of the individuals mentioned and the staffs of the following institutions were of tremendous help to me. Chris Anderson provided information on the regiment's actions at Gettysburg and constant words of encouragement. You are a true friend. Mary Gilmore, at Seymour Library, Auburn, New York, was instrumental in gathering information on Jesse Segoine and Lewis Husk. Mike Winey, at the U.S. Army Military History Institute, helped locate many of the photographs used in this book. The entire staff of the Library of Congress, Manuscript Division and Main Reading Room, assisted me on countless visits to find every book that referenced the 111th. Michael Musick, Bill Lind and Michael Meier, of the National Archives, Washington, D.C., endured constant requests for records relating to the regiment. Scott Hartwig, Gettysburg National Battlefield Park, provided access to his park's library and files. Donald Pfanz, Fredericksburg/Spotsylvania National

Military Park, graciously opened his park's manuscript collection. Chris Bryce, Manassas National Battlefield Park, combed the park's records for information on the regiment's time in and around Centerville. Bill Hamann and Steve Zerbe, Military Order of the Loyal Legion of the United States and Civil War Library, constantly sent information on officers of the 111th. Darrell Beauchamp, Gaston T. Gooch Library and Learning Resource Center, Navarro College, provided a copy of the diary of Manley T. Stacey. Robert Cox, curator, William L. Clements Library, University of Michigan, generously copied the diary of Daniel Hutchins. The Alabama Department of Archives and History provided a print of the battle flag of the 41st Alabama. Chris Calkins, Petersburg National Battlefield Park, was gracious enough to answer numerous questions about the siege. Bill Julien, National Guard Museum, Albany, New York, discussed the regiment's flags with me at length. Deborah Ferrell, Wayne County Historian, Wayne County, New York, provided material on the early days of Wayne County. Ted Alexander and Paul Childes, Antietam National Battlefield Park, provided access to the park's extensive library and microfilm collection of the *National Tribune*. Brenda Prather, Martin T. Olliff, Wayne Cox, and John Varner of the Special Collections and Archives Department, RDB Library, Auburn University, Alabama, provided copies of the wartime letters of Thomas Dadswell and the diary of Edward Holcombe. Laura Clark Brown, Wilson Library, University of North Carolina at Chapel Hill, provided the Drummond Papers.

The following individuals provided invaluable information from towns that sent their sons to war over 140 years ago. It is nice to know that the history of these men is being preserved. My thanks go to Robert Lowe of Palmyra; John Trass, Walworth town historian; Virginia Skully Hill, Ontario town historian; Robert Hoeltzel, Arcadia town historian; Carol Bailey, Lyons town historian; Diane Van Lare, Marion town historian; Helen Burgio, Macedon town historian; Mary Willers, Interlaken Historical Society; Peter Gabak, Peter Jones, Bill Meritt, and Stephanie Przybylek, Cayuga Museum; Mary Ann Kane; Cortland County Historical Society; and Thomas Eldred and Malcolm Goodelle, Cayuga County Historian's Office.

I also wish to express my gratitude to Norman Laser, a great teacher and friend who is truly missed; Cathy Sanky, for her research; Joe O'Hearns for providing much of the information on the city of Auburn; Ed and Sue Curtis for providing their knowledge of the Salisbury prison camp; and Chris Jordan, for locating photographs that are now part of my collection. Thanks also go to Greg Coco, John Lamphere, Roger Sturke, Anthony Gero, Mike Nusbaum, Craig Pfannkuche, Wayne Mahood, Dave Zullo, Kurt Kabelac, Tom Harris, Sal Alberti, E. D. Wilson, Michael Reid, and John Burns, a man who should have been a genius.

A special note of appreciation goes to my brother and fellow writer Steve Husk. I'm also indebted to my brothers Colin and Darin Husk, who pretended for years to be interested whenever I wanted to talk about the Civil War.

Finally, I must express my love and gratitude to my wife, Darla. You were both my most ardent supporter and harshest critic. This book would never have been possible without your constant love and support. And to my sons, Ryan and Sean. You've endured, not always quietly, trips to more battlefields than any other children I know. Thanks for helping me to understand that I can be both a jungle gym *and* a writer at the same time.

Table of Contents

Acknowledgments vii
Preface 1

1. Answering the Call 3
2. On to Harpers Ferry 17
3. A Regiment in Exile 29
4. Back to Virginia 39
5. Redemption in Pennsylvania 55
6. With Pride to Bristoe 79
7. Winter Campaigning 94
8. Overland Through Virginia 105
9. Marching to the Left 129
10. The Cockade City 139
11. Routed at Reams Station 151
12. The Siege Continues 161
13. The Last Campaign 179

Appendix A. "We Left Him at Salisbury" 203
Appendix B. Regimental Strength 211
Chapter Notes 213
Bibliography 237
Index 243

Any man who gives his life for a principle in which he believes is a hero; and in this great contest, no matter from whence they came or on which side they fought, they were soldiers.
—*Brigadier General Clinton D. MacDougall,*
Gettysburg, Pennsylvania, June 26, 1891

Preface

The idea for this book came about as I was researching the genealogy of my father's side of the family. His Dutch forefathers came to the New World in the late 16th century and later settled in what is now upstate New York. An obscure reference in one archive led me to Lewis Husk of Auburn, New York. He was a bookbinder by trade and a veteran of the Civil War. As I was working in Washington, D.C., at the time, it was a short walk across the National Mall to the archives where I located his military service records.

Tucked away in the back of the century-old folder containing the requisite monthly morning reports and regimental returns was a short, one-page letter. In elegant but faded script were penned the words that Major Husk was to be placed under arrest until a formal court-martial could be held. My first thought was to tell my father that I had stumbled across a little family dirt and leave it at that. However, curiosity got the better of me, and I needed to know the rest of this story.

The logical place to begin was with the official history of Major Husk's regiment, the 111th New York Volunteer Infantry. As I began my search, I stumbled across quite a few references to the regiment's service in the official records and located several articles written about its part in the battle of Gettysburg. However, I soon discovered that the regiment's service was not chronicled in one concise history. This presented a problem.

I ventured back to the National Archives and began reading through the boxed regimental records. They detailed the monthly and sometimes daily activity of the regiment. One packet of letters held the answer to my quest. It seems that during the siege of Petersburg, Major Husk was commanding a section of the picket line. Late one evening, a force of the enemy quietly slipped behind Union lines and made off with a large number of men from his regiment. For this, he was placed under arrest and brought up on charges. Fortunately, Major Husk was found not guilty on all counts and went on to command the regiment in the waning days of the war.

Case closed, just a side note to a war that is long over. But what about the men who were captured? What fate did they suffer? I began to dig a little more, and the more I found out about the 111th, the more I wanted to know. According to what I read at the outset of my research, they had acquitted themselves with honor at Gettysburg. But what about the other battles in which they participated? Did they achieve the same glory that they earned on two July days in 1863?

Despite my better judgment, I decided that a history of the regiment's service was needed. I began to darken the halls of the National Archives on a daily basis and became a regular fixture at the Library of Congress and the U.S. Military Institute at Carlisle Barracks. I solicited information from dozens of local historical societies in both Wayne and Cayuga counties, where the regiment was raised.

People were more than generous with their offers to provide what they knew about their ancestors who had served in the regiment, and I received a steady flow of diaries, letters, and pictures. Slowly the book began to take shape. As it did, a picture emerged of tremendous courage and sacrifice.

As I wrote, I had two goals in mind. First, let the soldiers tell the story of their regiment in their own words. Who better to provide a narrative of the exploits of the 111th New York Volunteer Infantry than the men, who for almost three years, stood the test of battle, endured countless marches under every conceivable condition, lived through the constant dangers of siege warfare, and languished in the hell-hole of a prisoner-of-war camp?

Second, the book would not be a recounting of the war or a social narrative of the times. It would have to be a history of the battles in which these brave men fought. Any mention of politics or war strategy is provided simply to offer context to the regiment's actions.

The episode that started this work, the capture of the regiment's pickets, would have to be covered outside the main text of the book. Too much research went into this part of the regiment's history to have it glossed over in a few chapters. The men who suffered through the experience deserve better. Therefore, an accounting of the imprisonment of the 83 men is provided in appendix A. It details what happened after the capture, where the men were imprisoned, and lists those who didn't live to see the end of the war.

Throughout the book, I used the soldiers' words exactly as they appear in their letters, diaries and manuscripts. Quotations have been modified only where clarification is necessary. I hope this book does justice to the sacrifices made by these great men.

Chapter 1

Answering the Call

> The President of the United States has called for 300,000 Volunteers for 3 years or during the war.... This appeal is to New York State — to each citizen. Let it come to every fire-side.... We cannot doubt that the insurrection is in its death throes ... a mighty blow will end its monstrous existence.... Present happiness and future greatness will be secured responding to this call.[1]

Just over 1,000 men resplendent in military dress stood in formation before the Western Exchange Hotel in Auburn, New York. An intense August sun beat down as dust from their recent march through town settled on the soldiers' new uniforms. In front of them was a raised platform, festooned in red, white and blue bunting. New York's governor Edmund Morgan and Colonel Jesse Segoine, along with other leading citizens from New York's Finger Lakes region, sat atop the dais and gazed with admiration upon the volunteers. Thousands of onlookers pressed in on the formation, searching for the familiar face of a loved one. They all listened intently as Governor Morgan delivered an eloquent speech on such an auspicious occasion.[2]

But what events transpired to bring these men to this place? What enticed them to answer their country's call for volunteers and to take up arms to defend her, even if it meant defending her to the death? Was it patriotism, fear of the draft, or the promise of a large bounty that lured them away from family and friends? It had been almost two months since the editors of the *Auburn Daily Advertiser and Union* printed President Lincoln's call to arms. Some in the district responded to the call with great alacrity while others were more reluctant. Whatever the reason, they now stood shoulder to shoulder on August 21, 1862, as their state's offering to the desperate appeal for men.[3]

The Civil War was in its second year and the prospects of a Northern victory seemed well within reach. In February 1862, General Ulysses S. Grant led his army into Tennessee and captured two important Confederate strongholds on the Mississippi River, Forts Henry and Donaldson. A month later, a small but important Union victory was won at Kernstown, in Virginia's Shenandoah Valley. Then, in the early days of April, General Grant snatched victory from the jaws of defeat along the banks of the Tennessee River at a place called Shiloh. April also saw the lower Mississippi River fall into Federal hands with the capture of New Orleans, as well as the reduction and surrender of Fort Pulaski on the South Carolina coast. When General George B. McClellan and his beloved Army

The Western Exchange Hotel, the second building on the left, was the site of the muster in of the 111th in August 1862 (from the collection of the Cayuga Museum).

of the Potomac began to drive up the peninsula toward Richmond, the entire North rejoiced as an end to the war appeared close at hand.[4]

But the sweet taste of victory quickly soured as setbacks on the battlefields began to mount and the Lincoln administration watched in desperation as a swift conclusion to the war slipped through its fingers. Early successes in the Shenandoah Valley were followed by defeat as the various Federal armies were beaten in turn and driven unceremoniously from the breadbasket of the Confederacy. Meanwhile, McClellan and his mighty army ground to a halt in the swamps and mire below the Confederate capital. With all of the recent setbacks, coupled with appalling casualty rates, Secretary of War Edwin Stanton soon realized that more fighting men would be needed in order to continue the war effort.[5]

Stanton had closed all recruiting offices when it appeared that the war would be over before summer's end. But now the North was desperate for men and the president was forced to make an urgent appeal for an additional 300,000 troops. Under the president's call, each governor was given a quota based on the population of his state. The quota was then passed on to the cities and towns; it became their responsibility to raise the requisite number of men. By order of Governor Edmund Morgan, New York was divided into military districts, coinciding with the already established senatorial districts used to elect members of Congress. Each district was responsible for raising a single regiment and establishing a training camp for the new recruits. New York's 25th Military District consisted of two counties, Wayne and Cayuga.[6]

Named for General Anthony Wayne of Revolutionary War fame, Wayne County is nestled in the rolling, fertile lands of the Western Finger Lakes region of New York State. Even before being officially designated as a county in 1823, the landscape was dotted with thriving communities. Palmyra was founded in 1789 and Newark two years later, while the city of Wolcott was named in 1810. Some of the county's earliest settlers were veterans of the Revolutionary War, who were given tracts of land for their service against the British. Others to arrive in droves were the workmen who helped build "Clinton's Big Ditch," the Erie Canal.[7] The workmen found the area to their liking and decided to stay on after the canal was complete. While agriculture was the mainstay of the county, where wheat and fruit were grown in abundance, a number of small industries began to take shape. There was glass manufacturing in Clyde, pottery in Lyons, and shipbuilding in Sodus for trading on Lake Ontario. According to the *Courier-Journal*, "small factories produced farm equipment and tanneries existed in almost every village."[8]

Religion played an important part in the lives of the county's inhabitants, who were predominantly Presbyterian. Despite the dominance of one faith, at least two different religions can trace their beginnings to Wayne County. First and foremost was Mormonism. It was near the village of Palmyra that Joseph Smith claimed he was visited by the angel Moroni who led him to the Book of Mormon. The first Book of Mormon was printed on the presses of the *Wayne Sentinel*. Hydesville saw the birth of what is now called Spiritualism when the Fox sisters claimed to have communicated with spirits. Neither of these religions took hold and their leaders were forced to leave the county.[9]

Like Wayne, Cayuga County owes its start to veterans who laid claim to land granted them for serving their newly formed country. Accompanying the one-time soldiers were groups of Dutch, French, Irish, German, and Scottish settlers. Officially adopted as a county in 1799, villages quickly sprang up throughout the region.[10]

One of the earliest settlements in Cayuga was Hardenbergh's Corners, named for Revolutionary War veteran James Hardenbergh.[11] Located along the Owasco Outlet, the tiny village quickly grew in importance and size. In 1805, the village was selected to be the county seat and its name was changed to Auburn. By the outbreak of the war, Auburn had been transformed into a major city, with a population of over 11,000. It contained four churches, a theological seminary, a female seminary, the state prison, an ironworks, a lumber and gristmill, and a brewery.

Auburn quickly became both the economic and industrial center of the county, laying claim to the Oswego Starch Company, which produced starch from corn grown throughout the county, and D. M. Osborne and Company, which introduced to the world dozens of innovative farming devices. Auburn also contained within its limits the Cayuga Chief Manufacturing Company, where Cyrenus Wheeler invented his famous drop reaper, and the Auburn Woolen Company. These products were shipped throughout the country on one of six different railroads whose tracks lead from Auburn.[12]

In 1862 as New York's 25th Military District, Wayne and Cayuga counties formed a war committee, tasked with producing a list of possible regimental commanders and other "prominent and active citizens selected throughout [the] district" to serve as officers in the new regiment.[13] With William C. Beardsley serving as its chairman, the committee met on July 10, 1862, at Port Byron, in Cayuga County. It established a quota of men that had to be raised in each county for the new regiment; Wayne County's was 461 while Cayuga County's was 539.

War meetings were held in almost every village, town and hamlet. Even the Honorable Theodore M. Pomeroy, the 25th District's representative in Congress, arrived from Washington to lend a hand in the recruiting effort. Great halls were filled to capacity with cheering crowds that listened to speeches and watched to see who would enlist in the new regiment. As each man stepped forward to place his name on the roll, the crowds cheered louder and louder. At one such meeting, Isaac Mulligan stepped forward and the crowd hushed. He stated in a loud voice that he would gladly enlist if only his wife would be willing to let him leave her side. An indignant Mrs. Mulligan then stood up and said, "yes, and if he won't enlist, I will put on his breeches and enlist myself."[14] The crowd roared its approval and Mr. Mulligan signed his name to the roll.

Others, like 27-year-old Simeon Sensebaugh, put their lives on hold to help the war effort. The proprietor of a meat market in Auburn, the local paper reported, Sensebaugh "enlisted in the Regiment last Saturday, sacrificing his business and family relations upon the altar of his country. He has opened a recruiting office at his market and announced he will pay $5 each from his own purse to the first 10 recruits to come forward before drafting is resorted to."[15] As a reward for his efforts, Sensebaugh was mustered in as a sergeant in Company C.[16]

During a war meeting in Sempronius, Theodore Pomeroy took to the stage and proceeded to whip the crowd into a frenzy. Many of the townspeople recalled being filled with the same patriotic fervor that consumed their forefathers as they marched off to fight the British nearly 100 years before. The euphoric townspeople raised almost $700 for the benefit of the recruits. At Union Springs a similar scene was repeated. The streets were thick with men, women and children. Speeches were made, a fife and drum corps played and the crowd filled the air with cheer after cheer. By the time the meeting ended, 15 men had enlisted in the company being raised by Silas Tremain.[17]

The towns and villages throughout both counties threw their full support into the war effort. But many in the 25th Military District were critical of the lack of support offered by the citizens of Auburn, who up to this point had done little to help raise men and material under this new call for men. The editors of the *Auburn Daily Advertiser and Union* asked, "Rich men of Auburn — What are you doing to protect your property and maintain your Government? Have you given the cause a single red cent? Echo answer, 'Nary red.'"[18]

In a speech delivered at the Car House, the one-time mayor of Auburn, Christopher Morgan, chastised the wealthy inhabitants of the county seat. He said, "Nothing but a score or 2 of bomb shells in their houses would arose them to danger. Are we waiting for Stonewall Jackson to come? Do we want England to interfere? What would Oswego Starch be worth with British shells whizzing thru Oswego factory? Are monied men deaf, blind and callous to the appalling dangers of the hour?"[19] According to the editors of the *Auburn Daily Advertiser and Union*, the speech had a thrilling effect, as "nine noble fellows enrolled their names" and one man offered to pay five dollars to each recruit.[20]

While the majority of the district's citizenry supported the war, a small minority sought to hamper the committee's efforts. These protestors went to the rallies with the intent of discouraging men from enlisting. Others showed their displeasure in different ways. The employer of John Sloan, a volunteer in the company being raised by Lewis Husk, refused to pay Sloan his due wages on his last day of work. The editors of the *Auburn Daily Advertiser and Union* took up Sloan's case. They write, "Such an instance of unparalleled disrespect should not go unnoticed. Employer will convey a favor on the community and save himself from perpetual disgrace and shame, by paying Mr. Sloan immediately."[21] Despite the paper's intervention, Sloan was never paid his due wages.

After signing the enlistment roll, each recruit was given a perfunctory physical examination. The doctors determined if each man would be able to withstand the rigors of military life. Each recruit jumped up and down, bent over at the waist, and had their eyes and teeth examined. The tests were merely a formality as few soldiers were ever turned away. Even James O'Hara, who was missing the thumb on his right hand, was allowed to join the regiment. An exception was 17-year-old Newman Eldred, who was thought too frail to be able to withstand the strain of campaign life. But after Eldred told the doctors that his two older brothers were already fighting, the doctors consented and allowed the young soldier to enlist in the regiment.[22]

On July 14, the war committee met in Port Byron and announced its choice for the man who would lead the sons of Wayne and Cayuga to war. While enlisting recruits to meet the district's quota, "General" Jesse Segoine was notified that he was selected to command the new regiment.[23]

Fifty-eight years old at the time of his appointment, Jesse Segoine's background was rich in military experience. At the age of 18, Segoine had enlisted in the 11th Regiment New York Artillery. Eight years later, he was honorably discharged from the artillery and in 1836, moved from New York City to Auburn where he set about reorganizing the Auburn Guards. In 1853, New York's governor commissioned Segoine a brigadier general and placed him in command of the state's 23rd Brigade. Segoine moved to Michigan in 1857 where he accepted a commission as major general, in charge of that state militia's Second Division.[24]

When rumors of war began to circulate throughout the country, Segoine returned to his native New York and took an active role in recruiting soldiers from counties in the upstate area. He helped to muster and train the 19th, 33rd, and 75th infantry regiments. But now he had a regiment of his own to recruit, a task that would take all his energy and skill. Assisting the new regimental commander was 42-year-old John Knapp. He was appointed Segoine's adjutant and helped with the administrative duties inherent in recruiting 1,000 men.[25]

The committee's selection for the position of lieutenant colonel went to Captain Clinton Dougall MacDougall of the 75th New York Infantry. According to the *Auburn Daily Advertiser and Union*, "this is a compliment, as we believe, to a brave and deserving young man; one in whom his old regiment had the most implicit confidence and who secured by his manly conduct the esteem and affection of his company."[26] At 23 years of age, MacDougall was elected to fill the position of captain of Company A in the 75th New York Volunteer Infantry when that regiment was being formed in September 1861. After being mustered into service, the 75th was shipped south to the Florida Gulf Coast. It was there on the night of May 12, 1862, that Captain MacDougall was mistaken for an enemy soldier by one of his regiment's pickets and was shot in the left leg. Granted a 60-day medical leave, MacDougall was at home recuperating in Auburn when he was approached concerning the position of lieutenant colonel in a new regiment then being formed.[27]

Colonel Segoine worked tirelessly and the regiment had on its rolls 400 volunteers by July 26. One reason for such a high number in such a short period of time was fear of the draft. No community wanted the stigma of having its quota of men raised this way. This fear manifested itself in the pages of the *Auburn Daily Advertiser and Union*. The editors encouraged all men to enlist lest the "odium of the draft be fastened upon Cayuga."[28] To ensure the "shame of conscription" was not associated with its city, the people of Springport voted to raise $5,000 to pay the volunteers of its town, 38 in all, who enlisted in the new regiment.

A second reason for such a large number of recruits was that many feared if they did not enlist soon they would miss out on the generous bounties being offered. As reported in the pages of the *Auburn Daily Advertiser and Union*, "all bounty stops on August 18th. U.S. and state as well as individual and town, and in case the regiment is not filled by that date, the draft will be resorted to, without bounty. Let this important fact be understood and people act accordingly."[29] In fact, the man who would be appointed as the regiment's second assistant surgeon, 25-year-old graduate of the Albany Medical College James Dana Benton, admitted freely his reason for enlisting: "It is not patriotism that made me take this course but I wanted to make money for my family."[30] The good doctor's pay in the army was more than he could make in private practice.

The bounty being offered by the United States government was $150. To further entice those motivated by money to enlist, Edward B. Morgan, the governor's brother, offered to pay $200 to the first company raised, $100 to the second and $50 to the third. The funds would

Above: Jesse Segoine. The 58-year-old Segoine was rewarded for his recruiting efforts with an appointment to colonel and command of the 111th (Alberti/Lowe Collection NYC).

Clinton Dougall MacDougall was the regiment's second in command at the time the regiment was mustered into service (Massachusetts Commandery Military Order of the Loyal Legion and the USAMHI).

be split among the men of each company. In addition to this money, the governor authorized the State of New York to pay an additional $50 to each man who would step forward and sign his name to the roll.³¹ An additional enlistment incentive was proposed by the governor. He offered to the first four regiments raised in the state under the president's call for men a regimental flag.³²

In late July, three officers from Company E, 54th Regiment National Guard began enlisting recruits for a company that would be part of the new regiment. On July 25, Captain Seneca Smith telegraphed Auburn, the gathering place for the new regiment, that he had raised the requisite 100 men needed to form a company. His men were described as "athletic, sinewy, powerful, full of spirit and ready to storm Richmond."³³ The *Clyde Commercial*, although disappointed that its hometown had not furnished the first company, was jubilant in its praise for Palmyra, where Smith's company was principally raised. "Old Wayne [County] has furnished the first full company for the regiment.... All honor to Palmyra and the gallant sons thus enrolled."³⁴

Surgeon James Dana Benton. He served as the assistant surgeon until he joined the 98th New York Infantry as its chief surgeon in March 1865 (Division of Military & Naval Affairs, NYS Adjutant General's Office, Albany, NY, collection at the USAMHI).

As Captain Smith's company, soon to be designated Company A, prepared to leave Palmyra for the rendezvous at Auburn, Second Lieutenant Samuel McIntyre paused to give a few brief remarks. In patriotic verbiage true to the times, Lieutenant McIntyre thrilled the crowd: "This is probably the last time you will see us all together as a company.... We go to defend your homes; see to it that our hearth stones are kept free from neglect and poverty.... It is for our country's sake rather than our own that we make this appeal. For ourselves we fear not death if it be our lot in the righteous cause we have espoused. 'It is sweet to die for one's country.'"³⁵

The town of Clyde did respond quickly and in no time at all the company then being raised by John Coe was filled. Knowing that some of his men were poor and enlisted for the bounty money, Coe offered to advance them the $200 in state and U.S. Government bounty money until they were paid. While this act of kindness surely taxed his resources, Colonel Segoine further depleted Coe's finances by ordering him to pay for the men's room and board in Clyde until the company was ready to leave for Auburn.[36]

Two of those enlisting in the Clyde company and collecting the bounty money were 42-year-old Philip Ira Lape and his 27-year-old brother Samuel. The father of five daughters, Philip signed his name to the rolls and was mustered in as a sergeant. Philip and Samuel were two of five brothers who served with distinction during the war.[37]

When they learned that George Smith was attempting to raise a company in Aurora, rivals Silas Tremain and Lewis W. Husk quickly traveled to Cayuga County. Each one wanted Smith and his men to

George Smith. Mustered in as first lieutenant, he was in command of Company K at Gettysburg where he was wounded on July 2, 1863. Smith was discharged for disability in November 1863 (courtesy of R. L. Murray).

join the companies they were raising. Through some clever negotiations, Tremain convinced Smith to consolidate their two companies. So on August 9, Smith and his 37 recruits joined Tremain and his recruits from Springport and formed what would become Company K.[38]

A bookbinder by trade, 28-year-old Lewis W. Husk had amassed seven years of military experience serving with the 49th New York State Militia. Despite his background, Husk did not rush to join the new regiment. "His wife and two young children were ties strongly binding him to domestic life that seemed almost impossible to overcome, and it was not till the summer of 1862 ... that he finally determined to leave the accustomed peaceful vocation to try the chances and hardships of war."[39] To reward his efforts on behalf of the regiment, Husk was made captain of Company G.

As more soldiers began to arrive in Auburn, they were placed in the barracks at Camp Cayuga, located on the east side of town along Moravia Street. With the addition of the new companies, the regiment's numbers soon swelled to capacity. The companies were organized and assigned a company letter, and each soldier was provided with a basic military uniform.[40] In a letter to friends, Thomas Geer of Company A wrote, "We got our uniforms all through knapsacks, haversacks, canteens and everything but guns and I think I have got enough to carry without them, But I suppose we shall have to take them when they come."[41]

While the enlisted men were issued their uniforms, the officers were obliged to purchase theirs. Surgeon James Dana Benton was surprised to find that he had to spend almost $70 for a sword, sash, sword knot, belt, shoulder straps that denoted his rank, spurs, and a saddle. The money he hoped to raise by enlisting in the regiment was being spent much too quickly.[42]

Lewis Husk, shown here as a lieutenant colonel, was the original captain of Company G. He commanded the regiment at the end of the war (author's collection).

On August 18, all furloughs were revoked and those saying their last goodbyes to loved ones were ordered to return to the regiment immediately and prepare to leave for the seat of war. Many of the men wanted to ensure they were remembered at home. Some, like Sergeant Casper Wallace of Company G, stopped at the Union Picture Gallery on Genesee Street to have their picture taken while in uniform. Corporal George Salisbury did more than just have his picture taken. In a ceremony held at the American Hotel, 26-year-old Salisbury married his sweetheart, Ms. Carrie Smith.[43]

Two days later, Captain W. G. Edgerton of the 11th U.S. Infantry arrived in camp to muster the regiment into Federal service. The men were drawn into line, inspected and then sworn into service as members of the 111th New York Volunteer Infantry.[44]

The companies were recruited from the following towns: Company A at Marion, Palmyra, Ontario, and Walworth; Company B at Clyde and Savannah; Company C at Auburn, Palmyra, Rose Valley, Victory, Montezuma, Summer Hill, and Sterling; Company D at Lyons, Sodus, Galen, and Williamson; Company E at Arcadia, Sodus, Williamson, Marion, and Palmyra; Company F at Port Byron, Auburn, and Weedsport; Company G at Auburn and Genoa; Company H at Auburn, Cato, Ira, Conquest, and Sterling; Company I at Moravia, Venice, Locke, Ledyard, Niles, Sempronius, and Scipio; and Company K at Union Springs, Springport, Genoa, Aurora, Moravia, Scipio, and Ledyard. Companies A, B, D and E were raised in Wayne County while Companies C, F, G, H, I and K were from Cayuga County.[45]

The men who formed the 111th came from all walks of life. Among the regiment's ranks were a bookbinder, a glassblower, a tile maker, and a watchmaker. There were a number of shoemakers, wagon makers, butchers, masons, mechanics, painters, printers,

George Salisbury (left) and George Bentley (right), both of Company K. Salisbury remained with the regiment for the entire war while Bentley left the regiment in September 1864 (courtesy of R. L. Murray).

coopers, blacksmiths and furriers. Craftsman and artisans were not the only ones answering the call. Major Seneca Smith owned a profitable mercantile business. Captain John Coe of Company B and First Lieutenant Samuel McIntyre of Company A were lawyers, and George Brown of Company E was mining for gold in California before the war. Sergeant Edward A. Percy of Company A and Corporal Daniel Hutchins of Company D were teachers. Filling the ranks were at least four students from the Cayuga Lake Academy. However, the majority of the men traded the life of a simple farmer for that of a soldier.[46]

The ages of the New Yorkers were as varied as their professions. At 58, Colonel Segoine was the oldest. One other officer, Captain Ezra Northrop of Company H, joined the good colonel in the 50 and over category. Seventy-one other soldiers were 40 years or older, including the chaplain, John N. Brown. While the youngest soldiers were reported as 18, it was rumored that a few of these boys, like Morris Welch of Company H, were actually 14.[47]

Colonel Segoine's new regiment represented a good cross section of those who immigrated to the United States in the middle part of the 19th century. Scotland was well represented by Lieutenant Colonel MacDougall, while James Conley, John Fahy and Nicholas Fitzgerald proudly represented the Emerald Isle. There were the Dutchmen, Gustavus Ritter and Leonard Vaninwager, alongside Germans Frank Schmidt, Augustus Donk and Henry Deitrick. The 41-year-old Schmidt was born in Florburg, Germany, and had served in the cavalry before coming to America. France was represented by Irving Jacques and Peter Dubois while Poland had at least one of its sons in the ranks, Franz Sielliskowski. Several members, including Richard Warren from Port Byron and Thomas Geer of Marion, were born in England. Even the indigenous Indian tribes of upstate New York were represented by Edwin and Barney Ten Eyck.[48]

The officers and noncommissioned officers of the 111th provided a mix of those new to military life and those with prior military experience. Besides the experience of the officers already mentioned, Captain Isaac Lusk of Company E had seen service as a first lieutenant with the 17th New York. Horace Hill, first sergeant of Company A, was previously discharged from the 13th New York in May 1861 for being a minor. Robert Perry, first lieutenant of Company F, had been a sergeant with the 75th New York. Daniel Hutchins had served with the 98th New York

Sergeant Thomas Geer, Company A. Contracted malaria during the Gettysburg campaign. Mustered out with the regiment in June 1865 (David Crane Collection).

but was discharged for disability due to illness contracted during the Peninsula Campaign.[49]

The most interesting case of prewar military service involved Captain Benjamin Thompson, commander of Company F. In 1853, at the age of 21 and suffering from severe tuberculosis, Thompson heeded the advice of doctors and moved to Florida. In 1860, the native New Yorker was forced to join a militia company under a law passed by the Florida State legislature that required all able-bodied men to drill one day a month. As the specter of war loomed over the country, his militia company was called into active duty and Thompson was faced with the real possibility of fighting for the South if hostilities broke out. Finding the situation altogether intolerable, he deserted his post in April 1861. After a harrowing journey made with several other "northern men" from his militia company, Thompson made his way back to New York.[50]

The editors of the *Auburn Daily Advertiser and Union* published a letter written by a father to his son who had enlisted in the 111th. Offering some fatherly advice, he counseled his son to "guard your life in battle, never falter in the presence of the enemy ... and be careful to faithfully obey your superiors in every particular, and to carefully observe the rules of the camp."[51] Besides the military advice, the father took steps to ensure his son's spiritual well-being. He instructed his son to "seek to learn the will and mind of God by close attention to his word ... and that you may shun every path of vice and walk in the road to virtue."[52] The paper's editors seconded the advice and recommended every new soldier read the words of wisdom.

Robert Tomlinson, Company D. He mustered in with the regiment in August 1862 and was promoted to first sergeant in March 1865 (Joseph P. Tomlinson Collection at USAMHI).

All was now ready for the departure of the regiment on August 21. At 3:00 P.M., and with the Auburn Coronet Band in the lead, the more than 1,000 men of the 111th regiment moved out from the barracks at Camp Cayuga and headed for the railroad depot at the corner of Garden and State streets. It was a typically hot New York summer day, and it did not take long before the regiment was shrouded in dust, the thousands of marching feet churning the dirt roads into a fine powder. "They marched us right down through the city," recalled Thomas Geer. "Dust my gracious you never saw such a time. Not even thrashing barley and hot, oh, me."[53] In fact, the heat and dust were too much for some as three men fainted along the line of the march.

Turning onto Genesee Street, the regiment was halted in front of the Western Exchange Hotel. The streets were "thronged with an excited people, the windows and doors crowded with women and children waving handkerchiefs and manifesting in various ways

Unidentified soldier of the 111th (Anthony Gero Collection).

the deep interest they felt on the occasion. The ranks of the noble volunteers were broken in upon by the wife who insisted upon a parting recognition from the husband, and by friends who pressed forward for the final shake of the hand."[54]

Governor Morgan rose to his feet and lifted his voice for all to hear. He complimented "in glowing terms the appearance of the regiment; the patriotism and devotion of the volunteers and the worth of its officers."[55] He asked Colonel Segoine to step forward and presented him with a national flag donated by the ladies of Auburn.

Colonel Segoine "responded in a brief and energetic speech."[56] He thanked the governor for his kind words and the ladies of Auburn for their generous gift. Segoine praised the men of his regiment for answering their nation's call to arms and also thanked the various religious societies located throughout both counties for their generosity in providing his men with items they would need while in camp.

Many of the community leaders brought tokens of appreciation to the officers who would lead their sons to war. The grateful citizens of Ira and Cato presented Lieutenant Frank Rich of Company H with a sword. Captain Tremain of Company K was presented with an "elegant sword, belt, revolver and case"[57] by the people of Union Springs. Lieutenant Laing of Company E was presented with "a beautiful sword, sash and belt ... the presentation address was made by James Galloway, and an appropriate response made by the lieutenant."[58]

After the ceremony was over, the regiment was called to attention. Colonel Segoine rode to the head of the column and ordered the men forward. With flag fluttering in the breeze, the New Yorkers marched off toward the depot, down streets crowded with cheering and waving relatives, wishing to catch one last glimpse of their loved ones. The men of the 111th reached the depot and boarded the coach cars of the New York Central Railroad, as the crowd of well-wishers swarmed around them. According to many, the men seemed to be "in the very best of spirits, laughing, joking and in high glee. They were anxious to get to work."[59]

The editors of the *Auburn Daily Advertiser and Union* commented that the New Yorkers were ready "to serve and save their country-as gallant and noble a body of men as ever took the battlefield. The 111th is composed of the very best men in this district. They go from a stern sense of duty to their country and they will discharge their obligation to their country in a manner that will reflect no discredit upon the district they represent."[60] With whistle blowing, the train steamed out of the station and the regiment was on its way to war.

Chapter 2

On to Harpers Ferry

> I wish I could give you a long description of the capture of 8000 prisoners at Harper's Ferry.[1]

By the morning of August 22, the regiment reached Albany, having passed through Syracuse the night before. At the state capital, the men of the 111th got off the train and paraded through the city streets, heading for the docks on the Hudson River. En route, the men enjoyed sandwiches and cold drinks provided by the admiring townspeople. After a short march, the men reached the wharf, where two barges and the steamer *Ohio* had been provided for the trip down river.[2]

Not long into the journey it began to rain. To make matters worse, the barges were recently occupied by horses and had not been cleaned before being pressed into service to ferry the regiment. The trip left a lasting impression on 23-year-old John Nostrant of Company G. "It rained most all the way up the river the boats were weat and dirty when the poor men wanted to rest themselves they had to lay down on the deck in water mud & horse tird. It made hard beginning I tell you."[3] As if that wasn't bad enough, the barges ran aground shortly after leaving Albany, resulting in a four-hour delay.

A few enterprising men had smuggled onboard a bottle of liquor and proceeded to get drunk. Having previously forbidden this type of behavior, Colonel Segoine placed the men under arrest. He also reduced Corporal Charles Hitchcock to the ranks. In a state of inebriation, Corporal Hitchcock was put under arrest after he grabbed the colonel by the neck and tried to choke him.[4]

Early on the morning of the 23rd, the barges arrived opposite New York City and dropped anchor in the middle of the harbor. Company F sent a delegation into the city to purchase a sash and sword for its captain, Benjamin Thompson.[5] From the barges, the regiment transferred to a steamer for the trip across the river to Amboy, New Jersey. The steamer was little better than the barges. According to Thomas Geer, who was trying to write a letter, "this boat wiggles so I can hardly follow the lines."[6] At Amboy, a train was waiting to carry the men on to Philadelphia.

Arriving in that city, "we passed by a window and received a handout from the window that was sufficient for us,"[7] remembered Newman Eldred. Fed and loaded aboard a train, the regiment headed for Baltimore. According to Eldred, "our field officers objected to the cars provided for our transportation, they being cattle cars. So the railroad company furnished second rate passenger coaches for us."⁸ Apparently not everyone was impressed with the life of a soldier thus far, for Corporal George Holliday of Company I deserted before he reached Baltimore.⁹

Colonel Segoine was ordered to report directly to the Baltimore headquarters of Major General John Wool, the 78-year-old Mexican War veteran who commanded the Union army's Middle Department. Wool instructed the colonel to reroute his regiment to the Union garrison at Harpers Ferry. Instead of joining the Army of the Potomac, Segoine would add the 111th to the forces already defending that important city.¹⁰

After leaving the train, the regiment marched from President's Street Station to a waiting train at Camden Street Station, along the same route taken by the Sixth Massachusetts the year before. The Sixth had been attacked by an angry Baltimore mob and shots were exchanged. The 111th was apprehensive, which was warranted since the only weapons in the regiment were the pistols and swords carried by the officers. Despite their misgivings, the New Yorkers arrived at Camden Street Station without incident. Sergeant Esek Hoff of Company K, a 28-year-old mason's apprentice from Springport, wrote to his wife Deborah that his march was different "from what there was on the 19th of April when the 6th Mass. went through. Well there might be when you look at the big guns on the fort north of the city."¹¹

For Newman Eldred, the trip to Harpers Ferry filled him with dread: "We passed over a rough and timbered country, inhabited with people who were more or less in sympathy with the South, some of them being vicious by nature, especially the poorer class. We expected nothing else but to be fired on from ambush at any moment. We naturally kept ourselves hid as much as possible from the enemy if any were lurking in the vicinity, not caring to be a target for even the poorest marksmen."¹² Passing Point of Rocks, a small town along the Potomac River, Sergeant Hoff "saw the place where the Rebs blasted off that little stream that carried away some of the track and landed in the [C&O] canal."¹³

Four days after leaving Auburn, the regiment arrived in Harpers Ferry, the one-time home of the United States arsenal. The town itself, located on the peninsula formed by the confluence of the Potomac and Shenandoah rivers, was dominated by Maryland Heights to the north on the Potomac side and Loudoun Heights to the south on the Shenandoah side. On the heights behind the town was Camp Hill and beyond that was the tiny hamlet of Bolivar. On the western edge of Bolivar was a ridgeline that ran almost from river to river, known as Bolivar Heights. The southern end of the heights ended abruptly at a steep prominence called Bull Hill.¹⁴

Southern forces first occupied Harpers Ferry in April 1861 and stripped the United States arsenal of all its valuable arms manufacturing equipment. The machinery was then shipped south to Richmond, where it formed the foundation of the Richmond Arsenal. The Confederates abandoned Harpers Ferry when Union forces under Major General Robert Patterson began to move against the city two months later. When Patterson's Federals arrived, they found the arsenal in ruins and the bridges spanning the Potomac River destroyed.¹⁵

After crossing the pontoon bridge over the Potomac River, "we got to the scene of old John Brown's exploits about noon and marched about a mile and ½ uphill all the way which was quite a march before breakfast,"¹⁶ recalled Captain Thompson. The 111th took up a position at Camp Hill where the rest of the city's garrison was camped, all under the command of Mexican War veteran Colonel Dixon S. Miles.[17]

The regiment's position at Camp Hill, close to 300 feet above the rivers, afforded the men a commanding view of the mountains surrounding the city. Directly behind their camp was a line of works that mounted almost 20 guns. The New Yorkers were tasked with guarding 12 of these guns. Directly to the regiment's right was an Indiana light artillery battery and to the left was the camp of a "small body of Maryland cavalry." Colonel Segoine took time to survey the fortifications on Maryland Heights, noting that there was "a battery of heavy guns of both Columbiads, and Parrot guns. A little lower down the slope of the same mountain, are two other light batteries."[18]

Once the regiment settled into camp, Colonel Segoine took the opportunity to write his wife a letter to inform her of his safe arrival at Harpers Ferry. "We arrived here all safe and sound and in good spirits at 10 o'clock this (Monday) morning. My boys are just getting their first meal to-day prior to pitching their tents on the hill in front of a fort ... the whole country about here is rocky and mountainous — scenery somewhat like the highlands on the Hudson River, and naturally healthy."[19]

Knowing that his letter would more than likely be reprinted in the local newspaper, the colonel took the time to ease the worries of those back at home, stretching the truth a bit. He wrote, "you may pass through the entire camp, and you will hear no loud or boisterous conversation, and anything like profane language is seldom heard, and if heard, is reproved by the officers at once. Permit me to say that while I am writing in my tent, I hear the sound of prayer and praise going up to the throne of grace, from neighboring tents in front of my quarters, led by our pious chaplain. Our Sabbath is as well observed here as is consistent with our military duties, so that pious fathers, mothers and wives need have no fears for their friends on that score."[20]

The regiment now numbered just over 1,000 officers and men. Six men had been left behind in Philadelphia and two more in Baltimore due to dysentery, along with a number who were too ill to travel when their comrades left Camp Cayuga. John Follett of Company D was one of those left behind in New York when the regiment took the train to Albany. Sick with typhoid fever, the 20-year-old from Lyons died at his home on November 18.[21]

The regiment's first night in Virginia was spent under the star-filled sky, as the tents had not yet arrived. "We got here Monday and had to lay on the ground the first night, but we were so tired that we slept first rate," recalled Simeon Cooper of Company G. "We got our tents up yesterday and it begins to seem a little more like living."[22]

By August 29, Colonel Segoine was ready to give the regiment its indoctrination into military life, issuing 16 general orders that ranged from naming the regiment's camp as Camp Beardsley to setting a schedule for washing and bathing. All of these orders were intended to give the civilians-turned-soldiers order and discipline. One of the most regimented aspects of a soldier's life is the daily schedule. It establishes when the men wake up, eat, conduct drill and go to sleep. General Order No. 2, issued by Segoine on August 29, had the regiment up at sunrise and drilling by 6:00 A.M. All told, the regiment would drill for over four hours each day.[23]

With camp established and a daily schedule in place, Colonel Segoine turned to the training of his regiment in the tactics of the day. To facilitate this, the colonel accepted the help of officers from another regiment to act as instructors. The drill being taught to the men of the 111th was *Hardee's Rifle and Light Infantry Tactics*. The first lesson to be learned was the School of the Soldier. The men were instructed on how to stand at attention (the "position of the soldier"), the basic facing movements, marching, the manual of arms, and the nine steps required to load and fire their new Springfield rifles.[24]

In addition to the constant drilling and marching, the men had to take turns manning the numerous picket posts that surrounded the garrison. The posts were about three miles from camp, along the roads and rivers leading into Harpers Ferry. Details from the regiment consisted of at least one company, sometimes more. On many occasions, the New Yorkers captured enemy soldiers, sometimes killing those who refused to surrender. On September 2, Lieutenant Edgar Hueston of Company G and a detail of men escorted a large number of prisoners to Washington.[25]

Life in Harpers Ferry was not all that bad for the men as they settled into their new roles as soldiers. To supplement their meager rations, the men purchased items from peddlers that came to camp selling everything from fresh produce to newspapers. Mail arrived regularly, and the soldiers even had the luxury of paying someone to do their laundry.

On September 3, the Federal garrison from Martinsburg arrived in Harpers Ferry. Sergeant Hoff saw long columns of "cavalry, artillery and infantry. They encamped in the hills all around us."[26] Along with the soldiers from Martinsburg came rumors that the rebels were going to attack the garrison at Harpers Ferry. Thomas Dadswell of Company A wrote to his father that "the news is now that old Jackson is a coming in both ways on up on us from east and from southwest."[27]

Dadswell could not have been more right. However, it wasn't just Jackson who was coming; the entire Army of Northern Virginia was on the move. To relieve war-torn Virginia, which had been beleaguered by more than a year of destructive fighting, General Robert E. Lee resolved to take the fight to his enemy's doorstep. The Confederate commander planned to drive his army into Maryland and beyond, where he hoped to supply his army with both material and recruits. Lee's bold plan called for the capture of the Union garrisons at Martinsburg and Harpers Ferry. This move would ensure that his army's lines of communication to the Shenandoah Valley remained open. His strategy called for the rebel army to split into four parts; three would move on the Federal garrisons, while the fourth would begin moving

Captain Edgar Hueston, Company K. Wounded at Spotsylvania, May 18, 1864, and at Hatcher's Run, March 31, 1865. He returned in time to be mustered out with the regiment in June 1865 (courtesy of R. L. Murray).

north toward the Pennsylvania border. Once both Martinsburg and Harpers Ferry were in Southern hands, the Confederate army would unite and continue to drive north.[28]

Three days after the arrival of the Martinsburg garrison, the 111th was ordered to take up a position along the heights above the town of Bolivar, facing west. Company F was on picket duty three miles away along the Shenandoah River, and did not join the regiment until September 7. The regiment was placed in the First Brigade with three regiments of infantry, the 39th and 115th New York, and the 65th Illinois, and one battery of artillery, the 15th Indiana Battery. The brigade was under the command of Colonel Frederick G. D'Utassy of the 39th New York, recently arrived from Martinsburg. With the 115th New York on its right, the new position offered the New Yorkers a commanding view of the valley below.[29]

After settling into the new position, camp life returned to normal. Everyday the soldiers posted guard, had drill, worked on building a line of entrenchments, and sent details into Bolivar for wood and water. This last task proved the hardest of all. In a letter addressed to the garrison's assistant adjutant general, Colonel Segoine complained that the 111th had neither horse teams nor wagons with which to haul supplies. When his men were detailed to Bolivar, they were forced to carry the wood and water back to camp by hand. Segoine's letter-writing campaign paid off, for a few days later, the regiment received two teams of horses and two wagons.[30]

On September 12, three companies of the 111th were ordered to move to Solomon's Gap, located about four miles north of Maryland Heights. In response to reports of enemy activity in the area of the vital mountain pass, the three companies, along with companies from the 39th and 115th New York regiments, were to help bolster the forces already there and prevent the enemy from easily moving over the mountain. When the New Yorkers arrived at the base of the mountain, a sharp skirmish was already underway.[31]

Union artillery sent shells screaming into the gap as the Confederate infantry of General Lafayette McLaws' division battled with the Union skirmishers under the command of Major Hugo Hilderbrandt of the 39th New York.[32] The men of the 111th watched helplessly as the hard-pressed forces under Hilderbrandt were pushed out of Solomon's Gap and off the mountain. As night fell over the field, the contest ended with the gray-clad infantry firmly in control of the field.

With no hope of recapturing the pass, the detachment was ordered back to Harpers Ferry. As if sensing the soldier's mood, a heavy rain began to fall as the New Yorkers made their way in the darkness. They marched over the Potomac River pontoon bridge, through the city streets and back to their works atop Bolivar Heights. No sooner had they broken ranks when the men were besieged with questions from their comrades about what they had experienced at Solomon's Gap.[33]

As the detachment from the regiment made its way back to Bolivar Heights, the Confederates were busy getting into position for an assault on Harpers Ferry the next morning. After pushing the Union skirmishers out of Solomon's Gap, the Southern brigades of William Barksdale and Joseph Kershaw made their way south along the top of the mountain leading to Maryland Heights. The Mississippi and South Carolina infantry halted when they encountered slashing and a line of breastworks manned by soldiers under the command of Colonel Thomas Ford. The Confederates were content to wait for the morning before resuming the attack.[34]

The pending attack at Maryland Heights was just a small part in the overall plan to capture the garrison at Harpers Ferry. General Lafayette McLaws was ordered to take two divisions and assault the fortifications atop Maryland Heights. General John Walker and his two brigades were to occupy Loudoun Heights, and General Thomas "Stonewall" Jackson was to move on the city with three divisions, by way of Martinsburg, and take up a position opposite Bolivar Heights. Once the Confederate force was in place, the city would be cut off and its fate sealed.[35]

Just after sunrise on September 13, the men of the 111th turned their heads to listen as fighting erupted on Maryland Heights. As the Confederates pressed the Union defenders posted behind breastworks, the New Yorkers sent details into Bolivar for water and wood. While lunch was being served to the regiment, the brigades of Barksdale and Kershaw were attempting to flank Ford's men. By the time the Union forces were being driven off the mountain, Colonel Segoine was drilling the regiment in the fields below camp.[36]

Close to 8:30 P.M., Colonel Segoine gave the order for his regiment to fall into formation. The men grabbed their rifles and accoutrements and hurried to take their place in line. At right shoulder shift arms, the New Yorkers made their way down Bolivar Heights, marched into Harpers Ferry, and took up a position to cover the pontoon bridge leading to the Maryland side of the Potomac. Although the men were aware that the enemy now occupied the heights on the opposite side of the river in force, they had an almost cavalier attitude about the whole affair. Most of the men brought blankets with them when they left camp, which they spread on the ground so they could get some sleep. According to John Paylor of Company D, they had a good time.[37] Later that evening, the regiment was again ordered to fall in and Segoine marched the regiment back to camp.

As the battle raged atop Maryland Heights, Confederate forces under General Walker seized Loudoun Heights without firing a shot. Walker placed his artillery to rain shot and shell down on the Union works along Bolivar Heights. Jackson used the cover of darkness to position his three divisions along School House Ridge, located in the valley opposite Bolivar Heights.[38]

Colonel D'Utassy issued orders notifying his regimental commanders of the obvious; the garrison was completely surrounded by the rebels. He instructed his regiments to cook three days rations and fill canteens. The First Brigade commander wanted the regiments roused at 4:00 A.M. the next morning and to be ready for the attack he felt was coming at dawn. Trying to instill confidence in his soldiers, he ended the order with "let our watchword and rally cry then be victory or death."[39]

True to the orders of the night before, the men of the 111th were roused at 4:00 A.M. on the morning of September 14 and ordered to man their trenches. They soon learned that General Jackson had given the garrison until 9:00 A.M. to surrender. "We had drawn our rations," remembered Newman Eldred. "I had just begun to eat mine as I heard a peculiar noise followed by the booming of a cannon. A piece of railroad iron came crashing through our camp from Loudoun Heights."[40] The skies were soon filled with whistling projectiles that began to rain down on Bolivar Heights. Although initially not having the exact range, the rebel gunners posted along School House Ridge soon found the mark and began a furious shelling of the Union position.

John Paylor remembered that the shelling caused "great excitement in camp. Some of the boys was almost scared to death."[41] This being their first exposure to artillery fire, the incessant pounding unnerved many of the New Yorkers. Paylor admitted being "nervously weak" from the falling shells. In an effort to save his men from the bombardment,

Colonel Segoine acted quickly. He ordered the men over the brow of the heights and into the trees that had been cut down in front of the regiment's position. Corporal Harry Smith of Company I recounted his experiences in a letter to his parents: "I had one man shot down close by my side & the bullets flew in all directions and over all the bursting shell & screeching of shot was terrible to a new soldier."[42]

The men hugged the ground in an effort to find some relief from the constant artillery fire. Newman Eldred lay as close to the ground as he could. "I could not say but the imprint of my body remained there still. I tried hard to get below the surface for everybody knows that self preservation is the first law of nature and a refuge that is impregnable to railroad iron was not to be sneezed at."[43] Shells began to fall among the regiment's tents, destroying one of them with a direct hit. Doctor Thomas Caulkins, serving as the hospital steward, narrowly escaped death when a cannon ball passed through the hospital tent he was occupying at the time.[44]

Caulkins was not the only one who had a brush with death at the hands of Confederate artillery. Surgeon Benton was in camp holding the bridle to his horse when the bombardment started. The mount, described as the best in the regiment, became unsettled by the crash of artillery and bolted away from Benton. The good doctor was left holding nothing but the reins. The horse ran out of camp and into the fields just outside of Bolivar. Benton and the horse's groom ran out of camp and down the hill toward town, through fields filled with exploding shells. The two were finally able to capture the horse, but not until after the saddle was lost.[45] Sergeant Hoff also had a close call: "Shells were screeching over our heads one of them came over in a few feet of where I sat."[46]

John Paylor, Company D. Nineteen years old at the time of his enlistment in 1862, Paylor was absent sick when the regiment mustered out in June 1865 (Don Chatfield Collection).

Others were not so lucky. Martin Van Buren Moore of Company A was in camp when the shelling began and hurried to seek shelter. As he was running from camp, a "shell from Loudoun Heights" exploded nearby, killing the 22-year-old instantly.[47] Moore had the unfortunate distinction of being the first of the 111th New York Infantry to die in battle during the war.

The Confederate guns continued to bang away throughout the day, relatively unopposed. They specifically targeted the Union guns posted at Camp Hill, which suffered terribly from the fire. According to Captain Thompson, "we had a battery of heavy guns high up on the side of Maryland Heights, which would have completely commanded the Rebel battery on Loudoun, but, instead of using the battery, our commander, ordered the guns rolled down the hill to save them from capture."[48] As the sun set that evening, the enemy guns fell silent. The bombardment had lasted almost five hours and exacted a heavy toll on the defenders of the besieged city.

Just before 8:00 P.M., fighting flared up to the south of the regiment's position. The Confederates were attempting to turn the left flank of the Union line in the area of Bull Hill, where the rebels advanced two brigades along an old road. The brigade under Brigadier General James Archer advanced up the right side of the road only to encounter a line of sharpened sticks and tree branches blocking the front of the Federal line. Archer's men spent the rest of the night trying to extricate themselves from the Union defenses. The North Carolina brigade under Brigadier William Dorsey Pender, on the other hand, fared much better. The Tar Heels managed to breach the Federal line and fight their way almost to where the Charlestown Pike intersected Bolivar Heights before retiring.[49]

An hour had passed since the fighting started when Colonel Segoine received orders from Colonel D'Utassy to move the regiment by the left flank and assume the position vacated by the 60th Ohio Regiment, on the right of the Second Brigade. Earlier in the evening the 60th had been ordered to the left flank to reinforce the area where Pender's Carolinians had broken the Union line. The colonel called the 111th to attention and had the men load their rifles. Segoine marched the regiment to the left, moving through the darkness until arriving at the designated location on the western slope and halfway down Bolivar Heights. He ordered the left and right companies to be sent out as flankers. The left company was to connect with the Second Brigade while the right company was to connect with the 115th New York.[50]

Colonel Segoine directed both Adjutant Henry Segoine and Major Smith to ensure that the flank companies were properly aligned. Before dispatching the officers, Segoine suggested that the two men dismount due to the nature of the terrain. While the adjutant heeded his father's advice, the major decided to remain mounted. The colonel then took up a position in the center of the regiment, behind the Color Company, and waited for word from the two officers.[51]

Colonel Segoine reported what happened next in his testimony before the commission investigating the surrender of Harpers Ferry:

> Suddenly we heard a clattering among the stones; you could see nothing; I supposed it was the majors horse floundering about the stones; but it turned out to be a body of the enemy's cavalry that made a dash at us and delivered a fire from carbines, as I supposed. I immediately ordered my regiment to return the fire; I repeated it about three times. I found they did not return it and I ordered the One hundred and eleventh regiment to cease firing. I looked about as well as I could; we could see nothing; I found one man dead lying pretty near me;

I could not tell who it was. I got some matches from one of the soldiers and rubbed and tried to make out the man's face but it was all covered with blood. I went on until I found 4 men killed and 1 very seriously wounded. I sent him to the hospital tent in our camp but he died before morning. That made 5 killed. I do not know how many were wounded, 9 or 10, mostly slightly wounded. One man was wounded in the breast, and another had a little finger shot off–some little things of that kind.[52]

When asked during his testimony if all the killed and wounded were from the 111th, Segoine stated they were. He could not tell how many of the enemy were killed and wounded until the next day. He further testified that "when they came into our camp [after the surrender] they told us we had killed 20 of them and wounded a number more."[53] Segoine had to take this information on faith, as he did not see any enemy casualties.

Among the regiment's killed was John Disbrow of Company D, a favorite among the men. Manley Stacey remembered him as "always kind and obliging ... he was always

Henry Segoine served as the regiment's first adjutant and was the son of Colonel Jesse Segoine (Massachusetts Commandery Military Order of the Loyal Legion and the USAMHI).

the first to do his duty, always volunteering, never having to be detailed."[54] The next day, Disbrow was carried to the bottom of Bolivar Heights, wrapped in a greatcoat and blanket, and buried under the shade of a large oak tree. Stacey carved a headboard for the grave just in case someone from home wanted to one day claim the body.

While not pleased with the actions of Captain Silas Tremain, the men of Company K had nothing but good things to say about First Lieutenant George Smith: "The boys all speak highly of Geo[rge] Smith (I wish I could say the same thing for their captain), they say that during the whole action at Harpers Ferry George was cool, brave, and intelligent as they could have wished, and that he was always in his place and just where he ought to be every time."[55]

The intense darkness had caused some confusion during the short fight. One soldier from Company F came to Captain Thompson after the firing ceased, claiming that his rifle would not fire. The captain examined the weapon and then extracted at least three bullets from the barrel, the first of which was put in upside down. Horace Acker of Company H was found dead out in front of the regiment's battle line. Apparently he became separated from his company and it is unclear whether he was killed by friend or foe.[56]

Sergeant Hoff had a very different account of what happened along Bolivar Heights that evening and did not believe for an instant that rebel cavalry attacked his regiment. In a letter to his wife, Hoff wrote, after a while some firing commenced on the right. I did not hear any orders to fire. Some of the boys said that the cavalry was on us. With that the firing became general and most of us shot ten to twelve rounds. I did not fire but four and loaded the fifth.... We then stopped. I was sent out as skirmisher ahead and when we stopped I came to the conclusion that it was only done to see if we would stand fire. Captain Meade made the officers see their mistake and have since made up some stories one of which is that we were attacked by the rebels but it will not work with me.[57]

Sergeant Hoff was not the only one to doubt the colonel's story of Confederate cavalry. Days after the battle, the *New York Times* ran a story that seemed to back Sergeant Hoff's account. The paper reported, "The 111th lost their killed and wounded by indiscriminate firing into each other, thru mistake."[58]

Newman Eldred's account of the "battle" also differed slightly from the official version as told by Colonel Segoine. Eldred remembered, "It must have been nine o'clock or more by this time. All of the sudden there came a blinding flash in front of our line. We were all alert in a moment and we got in line of battle as quick as possible. We began firing at will for we knew hardly a thing about military drill and didn't see anything to fire at but still kept firing till we were ordered to cease firing."[59]

The 111th remained in position near the foot of Bolivar Heights for the rest of the night. A sense of gloom settled over the regiment as the men contemplated their loss. Newman Eldred expressed it best when he said, "Indeed it was something new for us to behold a person laid low by a bullet and not only that but a schoolfellow and neighbor. We could realize what sad spectacles we would have to witness before we would be able to return to our homes."[60]

Colonel Segoine roused the men just before dawn on the morning of September 15 and the sight that greeted them on the plain below filled many with dread. "When morning dawned we saw a line of rebel batteries on the slight elevations in front of us, not half a mile away," recalled Captain Thompson. "Of course they were supported by infantry."[61] During the night, the Confederates had moved their batteries into position astride the Charlestown Pike, closer to Bolivar Heights. The rebels had also positioned batteries across the Shenandoah River, which were able to fire on Bull Hill. With these batteries in place, the rebels began their bombardment anew. But much to the relief of the soldiers in the 111th, the fire seemed to be concentrated on the southern end of the heights, where the Charlestown Pike intersected Bolivar Heights. Consequently, the regiment was only subjected to a light shelling.

Many believed, as did Colonel Segoine, that they were going to fight a tremendous battle that day for possession of Harpers Ferry. Yet as the New Yorkers braved the incoming fire and waited for the enemy infantry to advance, Colonel Miles and his brigade commanders were huddled together discussing their plight. Ammunition for the Union guns was nearly gone, relief from McClellan's army was not coming, and the rebels controlled the heights surrounding the city. The decision was clear. Miles would surrender the garrison.[62]

The Confederate batteries had only been firing for a little over an hour when word reached the 111th; a white flag was flying atop Bolivar Heights signaling they were being given up to the enemy. It had happened so suddenly that the New Yorkers hadn't even fired a shot. Soon after, Colonel D'Utassy rode along the line announcing the surrender and ordering his regiments back to the works atop Bolivar Heights. As Colonel Segoine later testified in front of the Harpers Ferry Military Commission, he believed that surrender was inevitable, but was sure they would at least make a stand before giving up.[63]

With heavy hearts, the men made their way back up the hill to take their place on the color line. Initially, Colonel Segoine ordered the New Yorkers to right shoulder shift arms. He was immediately informed by some of his officers that this was an inappropriate position for surrendered soldiers. Embarrassed, Segoine quickly rectified his error and ordered the men to carry their rifles at trail arms, with barrels pointing toward the ground.[64]

Many in the regiment resented being surrendered and chose to vent their frustration by smashing muskets against trees to prevent their use by the enemy. Captain Thompson had "never seen ten thousand men all terribly angry in my life but this once."[65] Nearing the top of the hill, the men noticed that one lone Union battery was still firing. It was later learned Colonel Miles had been killed while trying to silence these guns. No tears were shed over the loss of a man many believed to be a traitor to his country and who had reaped the benefits of his actions.

Upon reaching camp, arms were stacked and preparations made for surrender. While the officers conferred on procedure, the men ran straight for the commissary department and hauled off anything they could carry, whether they needed it or not. They had no intention of allowing the rebels to get their hands on the valuable food stocks.[66]

Colonel D'Utassy ordered his regiments to quickly strip all flags from their staffs and bring the colors to his headquarters. Here the flags would be stored in his private trunk for safekeeping until they could be returned to the regiments at a later date. This act saved the regiment's colors from capture by the Confederates.[67]

Word soon came down from brigade headquarters as to the proper procedures for the surrender. The regiment was drawn up in line, roll was called and muster rolls completed, and the statement of parole read. The soldiers then lifted their right hands and swore not to take up arms against the Confederacy until properly exchanged. The "proper exchange" would occur only when a sufficient number of Confederate prisoners were taken and could be "traded" for the New Yorkers.[68]

Around 6:00 P.M., and with the regiment's rolls in hand, Colonel Segoine and a correspondent from the *New York Tribune* accompanied Colonel D'Utassy as he went to see Confederate brigadier general Lawrence O'Brien Branch concerning the parole of his men. While Colonels D'Utassy and Segoine believed that their men would be allowed to enter a camp of instruction while waiting for their term of parole to expire, Generals Branch and Hill did not agree that this was part of the parole agreement. The two Confederate officers felt that soldiers awaiting parole were not entitled to take up arms in any manner. The group parted for the evening with no agreement having been reached, deciding instead to decide on this rather insignificant detail of the parole agreement the next morning.[69]

Dejected, the New Yorkers sat on the ground huddled in a large group. Captain Thompson took the opportunity to examine his captors. He noted that although the rebels were ragged and filthy, they had a certain air of confidence about them that showed through the dust and dirt. He also got the opportunity to see the man responsible for his regiment's present state, "Stonewall" Jackson. Thompson noted that the general did not appear as ragged as his infantry but was missing the majority of the buttons from his coat. The buttons, he explained to the New Yorkers, were given to the ladies of Maryland as souvenirs. Sergeant Hoff also saw the Confederate general and his staff as they rode by and noted they "were dressed very plain. They did not look like soldiers."[70]

George David of Company K would later write home to relate the appearance of the enemy: "The rebels are the most ragged set of beings I ever saw. Some of them are barefoot, some of them in their shirt sleeves." And like Captain Thompson, David was able to get close to General Jackson. "I had a fine view of old Stonewall. He is a smart looking man."[71]

The men passed an anxious night among their captors. The rebels had cannon loaded with canister pointed at the Union camp just in case the prisoners got any ideas of trying to escape. Although tensions were high between the two sides, there was some trading among the soldiers of the two armies. Newman Eldred traded a canteen full of molasses with a rebel private for a canteen of applejack.[72]

September 16 came early as the men were up by 4:00 A.M., making preparations to leave Harpers Ferry. Rumors swirled throughout camp about the regiment's final

Surgeon William Vosburgh. Served with the regiment for the duration of the war (Massachusetts Commandery Military Order of the Loyal Legion and the USAMHI).

destination. Some had heard they were to be sent to a camp of instruction, and all were against it. Others thought they might be heading back to New York. What they didn't know was that the regiment was ordered to Annapolis, Maryland, to be officially paroled. Still angry over the surrender and uncertain as to what was to become of them, the New Yorkers left their camp atop Bolivar Heights and marched through the dark streets of Harpers Ferry. Crossing the pontoon bridge that spanned the Potomac River, the New Yorkers began the long march for Annapolis.[73]

Left behind were the ten men wounded on the night of the 14th, along with a number of soldiers too sick to travel. Among their number was the grievously ill Lieutenant Colonel MacDougall. Under the watchful eyes of surgeon Vosburgh and Doctor Caulkins, MacDougall was still suffering from a bout of typhoid fever he contracted while serving with the 75th New York in Louisiana. The severity of his illness was no doubt caused by his reluctance to leave the men and go to the hospital while Harpers Ferry was under siege. He told one of his fellow officers, "I want to be with the men and it's unendurable to think of my going away from them when danger is near."[74]

Chapter 3

A Regiment in Exile

And we had all rather have fought to the last inch than to be as we now are.[1]

The men of the 111th were getting more tired as the minutes passed. Their line of march away from Harpers Ferry was littered with clothing and equipment thrown away by soldiers too tired and footsore to bear up under the weight. Despite the discomfort, some soldiers, like Corporal Smith, held on to their knapsacks. "We were allowed to bring away our knapsacks but we had to carry them & many threw them away after carrying them two days. I stuck to mine like a nailer & the last day we succeeded in getting a team to draw our packs."[2]

The march was difficult for those men whose entire military life to this point had been drilling in a garrison. This was their first taste of many hard marches yet to come, and the men were not pleased. Some complained the colonel was driving them too hard. John Paylor thought, "our colonel was very hard on us marching us as fast as his horse could walk."[3] Many dropped out of the ranks and did not make it to Frederick City, Maryland, with the rest of the regiment on September 17.[4]

While the men rested in the fields around the quiet little city, Sergeant Hoff could hear the booming cannons off to the west.[5] What they didn't know was that two armies were locked in a desperate struggle around a small town about 20 miles away called Sharpsburg that would culminate in the single bloodiest day in American military history.

Before the sun rose that morning, the Army of the Potomac launched an attack on the left flank of the Confederate line near the quiet country farm of David Miller. The initial attack succeeded, but the rebels were finally able to repulse the Federal assault. This back-and-forth lasted throughout the rest of the day, at places such as the West Woods, Cornfield, Dunker Church, and Bloody Lane. When the attack against the Confederate left proved fruitless, General McClellan ordered an attack on the center and then the right flank. Only the timely arrival of General A. P. Hill's infantry from Harpers Ferry saved the day for the Army of Northern Virginia. As the sun set on the bloody fields, over 23,000 men lay dead, dying, or wounded or had become prisoners of war.[6]

A few days after leaving Frederick City, the 111th arrived at Ellicott Mills, a stop on the Baltimore and Ohio Railroad. Here the tired infantrymen were able to rest, and those who had fallen behind on the march were able to catch up to the main body. Those who were unable to resume the march, for whatever reason, were granted permission by the surgeon to board a train and travel by rail to Annapolis. Among their number was Colonel Segoine. The regimental commander was suffering from a severe case of piles and was exhausted in both mind and body. It was the opinion of the surgeon that Segoine would not be able to remain with the rest of his men as they pressed on to Maryland's capital city.[7]

The march continued the next day under the same conditions as before. The main body of the regiment arrived at Annapolis on Sunday, September 21 and joined their comrades who had traveled from Ellicott Mills by train. Corporal Smith indicated the severity of the march in a letter to his father, in which he stated that when he arrived at Annapolis, half of the men in his company were sick and unfit for duty. Despite riding the train to Annapolis, Colonel Segoine's condition had deteriorated to the point that he was declared unfit for duty and given a 20-day leave of absence in which to recover. The command of the regiment fell to Major Seneca Smith.[8]

The stay in Annapolis would prove short but relaxing. After camp was established, the more adventurous men took advantage of the abundance and variety of local food to supplement their meager government rations. They ate peaches, sweet potatoes, crabs, oysters, chestnuts and persimmons. An amusing incident occurred one day when Newman Eldred went foraging for sweet potatoes. Busy digging in the dirt with a piece of sharpened board, he did not notice "a negro coming up behind me with a gun."[9] Eldred was informed that the slave was ordered by his master to shoot if he didn't leave the potatoes alone. Eldred jumped up and chased the slave back to his house, then went back to retrieve his bounty.

For the most part, the New Yorkers found the residents of Annapolis very hospitable. Many of the Marylanders opened their homes to the men of the 111th and provided them with food and a place to sleep. On one occasion, Sergeant Hoff and three of his comrades wandered to a local farmhouse when the weather turned rainy. They were fed supper and allowed to sleep on the kitchen floor. Sergeant Hoff thought his hosts were "good people, better than some we have seen before and since."[10]

While in Annapolis, the New Yorkers again speculated as to where they would wait out their term of parole. Some of the men heard rumors that the regiment was destined for the West to fight Indians. Others hoped that they would be sent to Camp Cayuga in Auburn, where the regiment was mustered. Letters received from home carried the hope that the men would be sent back to New York. To this end, a group of officers telegraphed William H. Seward, President Lincoln's secretary of state, to have him use his influence in getting the 111th sent home to Auburn. Still another possibility lay in the rumor started in Harpers Ferry that was still floating around camp, that the regiment was destined for a camp of instruction.[11]

None of their guesses held true. On September 24, the regiment boarded the steamers *John Tucker* and *City of Norwich*. Pulling away from the Annapolis dock, the boats steamed up the Chesapeake Bay and arrived in Baltimore about 3:00 P.M. The New Yorkers disembarked and marched to the railroad station. Sergeant Hoff remembered marching "through the city with a little different feeling from what we did some 4 weeks before and we could see the citizens talking together about our surrender."[12] Here the men boarded a train that would eventually take them to Camp Douglas in Chicago, Illinois.

Traveling in boxcars recently occupied by cattle was not a pleasant experience for the men. The trip was made even more difficult when many of the New Yorkers were stricken with diarrhea. This was a serious problem since no facilities were provided to address this affliction. So as good soldiers often do, the men made do with what they had and improvised. A hole large enough for a man to pass was made in the side of the boxcar. The soldiers had to grab the iron ladder attached to the side of the car, pull themselves through the hole, and climb to the roof. Once on top of the car, the men would walk to where the cars were coupled together and there relieve themselves.[13]

As the train traveled north, some of the men still held out hope that they might be heading home. But when they reached Harrisburg and the train turned west, the New Yorkers gave up all hope of spending their parole in Auburn. That night the train stopped in Altoona, where the "leaders brought baskets of food and coffee which we returned with thanks and cheers,"[14] recalled Sergeant Hoff. Once the meal ended, the journey west continued.

The next morning, the train stopped in Pittsburgh, and the men marched to the refreshment saloon where Newman Eldred and his comrades were treated to a dinner of "good bread, boiled ham, coffee and a peach, pear and a plum for desert."[15] After dinner was over, the men reboarded the train and the journey to Camp Douglas continued. All along the way, crowds gathered to cheer the troops. The spectators had probably gathered to cheer the Pennsylvania troops also aboard the train, but it must have lifted the New Yorkers' spirits to be made welcome at every town. Finally, on September 27, the regiment arrived at the "muddy nasty lousy ratty hole" that was Camp Douglas.[16]

Originally established on land owned by Stephen Douglas as a station for recruiting and instruction, Camp Douglas was serving as a prisoner-of-war camp when the parolees from Harpers Ferry arrived. The large number of Confederate prisoners taken at the capture of Fort Donelson earlier in the year had left the government desperate for space, so Camp Douglas was pressed into service. After the rebels were exchanged and sent south, they left behind a number of their sick and left the camp in a horrible state of disrepair.[17]

The camp was located on a little more than 30 acres of land. Divided into three divisions, the compound was surrounded by a six-foot-high stockade fence. The eastern division, or Garrison Square, contained the officers' quarters, post office, post headquarters and parade ground. The southern division, or White Oak Square, housed the enlisted quarters, hospital and morgue. The western division contained the prisoners' quarters, warehouses and the surgeon's quarters.[18]

The barracks were 90 feet by 24 feet and placed so that four of the buildings formed a square surrounding a courtyard area. The buildings occupied by the regiment, along with the 126th New York, were in the southwestern part of the camp. Sergeant Hoff described the camp as a great field of sheds that were comparable to "some of the Irish shanties present along the banks of the Erie Canal and smell about as stout."[19]

Soon after arriving, the men set about trying to make their barracks more livable, as well as sanitary. The buildings were scrubbed and painted, the bunks rebuilt, and mattresses cleaned and stuffed with fresh straw. But all the cleaning in the world could not prevent the diseases that had plagued the Confederate prisoners from running rampant through the regiment. Scores of men were stricken with typhoid fever. One of the first to succumb was Ansen Legg.[20] Living in Auburn at the outbreak of the war, the 21-year-old farmer enlisted in Captain Thomas's Company C. Legg was admitted to the hospital soon after his arrival at Camp Douglas, where he died on October 8. Before the regiment's stay in Camp Douglas was over, 14 more men would succumb to disease.

The number of men getting sick increased each day, and the hospital was soon filled to capacity. Regimental surgeons were overburdened and needed help, assistance that would come from home. When they learned their husbands and sons were confined at Camp Douglas, many wives and mothers traveled to Chicago. One such woman was Elizabeth Nichols. The wife of William Nichols of Company B, Elizabeth arrived in Chicago in October and immediately began caring for the sick men at the regimental hospital. She would stay with the regiment as a nurse until March 1863, when she was forced to return to New York to care for her own children, who had fallen ill.[21]

In early October, the *Chicago Tribune* published a copy of the Dix-Hill Cartel. This agreement, authored by Union general John A. Dix and Confederate general D. H. Hill, set forth the terms regulating the parole of prisoners. One of main provisions of the cartel was that soldiers serving their period of parole were not to perform military duty of any kind.[22]

The New Yorkers were quick to make their own interpretations of the agreement, especially the part about not performing any type of military duty. Corporal Smith believed that the officers could not "take up arms nor compel their men too, or to train, drill or do any duty wherein we assist the north in any manner we can until we are regularly exchanged. We can drill if we choose but our officers cannot compel us and if we should drill our officers are accountable not the men."[23] When Major Smith held regimental drills, some companies had very few men in attendance.

Asked by Captain Sebastian Holmes if he was going to fall out for drill, John Paylor said that he would only drill if the rest of the company did. Only 12 of his comrades drilled that day, and that number did not include Paylor. Captain Holmes lamented in a letter to his sister that there is "nothing to do but eat and sleep, the boys are getting very fat and lazy."[24]

The general condition of the camp and the likelihood of sickness further contributed to the lack of interest in drill. In a letter to his father, surgeon Benton described Camp Douglas as "two hundred acres of land, it is on the prairie and is as level as a house floor."[25] As a result, rainwater would collect and there remain, sometimes ankle deep, for days on end. Sergeant Hoff believed "the great curse of so many getting sick is on account of so much filth accumulating on the ground and privys and when it rains the water covers the ground all over pretty much."[26] When it rained, and it rained often, the camp was transformed into a vast sea of mud, buffeted by the cold wind blowing off Lake Michigan. Given these conditions, the men decided to remain indoors and not drill.

Tensions in camp were rising, and not long after the text of the cartel was published, things reached the breaking point. One night, a detachment from the 9th Vermont was detailed as camp guard, after having been issued faulty weapons. A group of soldiers attempted to run the guard but were turned away. Angry words were exchanged and rocks were thrown. What started out as a small band of soldiers quickly turned into a seething mob. The stockade fence surrounding the camp was set ablaze and barracks were put to the torch. Alarms in the city rang and engine companies responded to put out the fires. Members of the 60th Ohio threatened to burn the barracks of the 111th. To prevent this, details of 15 men from each barracks were posted around the buildings to ward off any would-be arsonist.[27]

Second Lieutenant Ezra Hibbard of Company A was sent into Chicago with a detail of 25 men to help bring back members of the 111th who fled camp during the fire. When he arrived in the city, Hibbard found a full-scale riot taking place. Bands of men armed with all sorts of weapons were running free through the streets. The lieutenant told his fellow officers that "the way the axes and knives flew there for a few minutes wasn't slow."[28] One soldier tried to shoot the lieutenant, but was stopped and hauled away in chains. Hibbard and his men were forced to fire several shots into the crowd to keep the rioters at a safe distance. The detachment finally returned to camp with as many men from the regiment as they could find.

A few nights later, members of the 39th New York burned their guardhouse. When the engine companies from the city arrived to extinguish the flames, some of the Garibaldi Guard threw rocks and stones at the firemen and drove them off. About 200 feet of barracks was burned, along with a section of stockade fence that the 111th had mended when first arriving in camp.[29] In all of the excitement, hundreds of parolees ran through gaps in the fence and headed straight for the city.

Running the guard became a daily ritual for the men of the 111th. Each night, Captain Thompson and his fellow officers had the unpleasant task of searching every saloon and brothel in the city for their men. The New Yorkers were herded back to camp, sometimes at gunpoint. Details from the regiment were posted as guards in front of hotels throughout the city. While the officers were allowed to enter, the privates and noncommissioned officers were not. Detachments from the 111th manning their guard posts made little or no attempt to stem the tide of men leaving camp. They couldn't even if they had wanted to.[30]

Taking the events of the past month into account, it is easy to understand why morale in the regiment began to decline rapidly. All discipline was gone, and the men seemed to be in an open state of rebellion. Surgeon Benton stated in a letter to his parents that if he had joined the regiment for patriotic reasons, he would have long since resigned. Simeon Cooper of Company G wrote to his father that he would rather "go back to Harpers Ferry again than to stay here."[31]

Evidence of the mounting morale problem within the regiment can be seen in the court-martial transcripts of Privates Jeremiah Collins and Samuel Adams, both of Company K.[32] Collins was charged with refusing a direct order from an officer of the 65th Illinois, a regiment also waiting to be paroled. The officer, Major John Wood, said that Collins refused to obey his order and then attempted to beat him with a piece of wood. When guards arrived to escort Collins to the guardhouse, he resisted and called upon those in his regiment watching to come to his rescue.

One of the onlookers was Samuel Adams. Adams declared that he and his comrades should attempt to liberate their fellow soldier from the jail and while doing so, burn down "the damned old camp."[33] But before he could put his plan in motion, Adams was arrested and hauled off to the guardhouse. Both Collins and Adams plead guilty to the charges brought against them. Collins was ordered to forfeit one month's pay and to serve 60 days hard labor, 15 of which wearing a ball and chain. Adams, on the other hand, would be given only bread and water and would serve 15 days in close confinement.

Morale had become so bad among the men and desertions so prevalent that special permission was granted by General Tyler, the commander of Camp Douglas, for the regiment to hold a series of regimental courts-martial. Instead of going through the trouble of holding a general court-martial as was done for Collins and Adams, the regimental officers could conduct their own trials. While the tribunal in a general court-martial was made up of officers from different regiments, the presiding judges in a regimental court-martial were officers from the offender's regiment.[34]

The majority of those being tried in this court were soldiers who had been arrested for desertion and brought back from Auburn. Although most of those on "french leave" were found, arrested and returned to Camp Douglas, there is at least one case of a soldier who managed to elude his captors. Private William H. Harris of Company H left the train on September 27 somewhere between Fort Wayne, Indiana, and Camp Douglas and was never heard from again.[35] Almost all of those found guilty of desertion were ordered to forfeit enough money to pay for the expense of their trial and transportation back to Camp Douglas. Other punishments included such things as wearing a ball and chain, being confined to quarters, standing on the head of a barrel, and wearing a wooden overcoat. Between the time the regiment left Harpers Ferry and the time it was exchanged and arrived in Washington in late November, 91 men deserted from the ranks.[36]

Whenever a soldier was absent from drill without permission, he was subjected to any number of punishments. On one occasion, about 15 soldiers were absent from dress parade. Colonel Segoine had the guilty parties line up in front of the regiment before their punishments were instituted. Among their number was a "half foolish fellow called the preacher," recalled Sergeant Hoff. "His name is Barney [Ten] Eyck That had been court martialled for abusing the officers of Company G."[37]

Another reason for the low morale was the insufferable quality of the food. Thomas Geer was so disgusted by the rations issued to him by the regimental quartermaster that he wanted to build a box out of hardtack and bacon and "bury him in it and let stay there until he gnawed his way out."[38] On one occasion, the men lined up to draw their usual ration of bread, only to find the loaves completely stale. Instead of eating the bread, the men divided themselves into two wings and held a full-scale bread war.[39]

The regimental quartermaster, James Trulan, also drew the ire of Sergeant Hoff. He recalled that the regiment only drew one ration on the trip between Pittsburgh and Chicago, and the men would have gone hungry had the people along the way not given "us all they had in their homes."[40] The good sergeant further complained that "sometimes we have bacon or shoulder that smell strong and some want a guard placed over it to keep it from crawling away."[41]

On one particular evening, Newman Eldred drew a ration of rice. The private sat down at the mess table and began to spoon what he thought was rice into a cup of milk. Sensing that something was not right, Eldred took the cup over to the light only to discover that his meal was crawling with worms. His messmates soon found their meals infested as well. They all ran over to the door and threw the wormy rice onto the ground.[42]

To supplement their meager government rations, the men would often go out to the surrounding farms to get fresh milk, sweet potatoes and any other type of food they could "forage." Some wandered into the city and purchased meat from one of the many slaughterhouses while others purchased items from the sutler store located at the camp. Here the men could purchase canned milk, tobacco, pies, apples, and just about anything they needed or wanted. One day when his shop was full of parolees, the store's proprietor made the mistake of referring to the men as the "Harpers Ferry Cowards." Enraged, the soldiers stripped the store of all its stock and reduced the building to a pile of rubble.[43]

In order to combat the growing morale problem in the ranks, Major Smith decided to take matters into his own hands. On October 10, the major issued General Order No. 30.[44] The order, read to the troops at morning formation, addressed the practice of using the parade ground as a toilet and singled out the declining state of the regiment's appearance and morale, as well as the fact that the use of profanity in the ranks was on the rise.

General Tyler took the added step of bringing regular troops into camp to restore order. Instead of relying on parolees to watch over each other, the regulars would guard the camp and institute strict discipline. The guardhouse was soon overcrowded with soldiers arrested for every infraction of the rules, from drunkenness to refusing to drill. With order restored, the terms of parole were made clear, and a strict regime of drill was instituted.[45]

With the restoration of military order came more privileges. Daily passes were issued, allowing the men to venture into the city. One of the most popular sites visited was the grave of Stephen Douglas. The view from the gravesite was spectacular and on a clear day, the men could see hundreds of boats out on Lake Michigan. John Paylor took advantage of his pass and hired himself out as a laborer on the docks, earning about 20 cents an hour.[46]

A particularly gruesome pastime involved shooting rats. Due to the poor sanitary conditions, partially on account of the prisoners who occupied the barracks before the regiment arrived, the camp had become overrun with rats "big enough to carry a knapsack." Sergeant Hoff wrote his wife the day after the regiment arrived at Camp Douglas: "You would have laughed to see the rats come out of their holes and look at the 111th regiment take possession of their mansions. Some of them I warrant did not like it. Some laughed and some showed their teeth in anger."[47] It was not uncommon for a wagonload of the beasts to be killed by the guard each night.

Rats were not the only vermin that infested the camp. Almost from the day they arrived in camp, the New Yorkers were besieged by lice. Nicknamed the Chicago Grays, or the Rebel Gray Back, the pests infested clothing, bunks, and even bodies. When asked by family at home if he had a comb to take care of the vermin, Geer asked them to "send a horse rake, I have seen lice in these barracks as large as a kernel of wheat."[48] The officers of Company K held an inspection and the entire company, except for five men, were found to be infested with lice. It was so bad that Sergeant Hoff could see the "little insects" crawling on the clothing of one of his fellow soldiers.[49]

When Colonel Segoine returned to the regiment on October 27, he had no idea that morale was so bad. Simeon Cooper recalled, "there was no great joy among the men at his return. He called the men all out in line on the day of his return and made a great speech to them and praised them at a great rate."[50] Segoine also returned the regiment's colors that had been given to Colonel D'Utassy at Harpers Ferry for safekeeping. He explained to his soldiers how he had gone to great lengths to ensure that the flags would be preserved and not captured by the enemy. But the men knew better. They knew that it was their brigade commander, not Segoine, who was responsible for the safekeeping of the colors. When Segoine had finished speaking, surgeon Benton remembered one of the "officers called for three cheers for the colonel, it was given very faintly, some whole companies not opening their mouths."[51]

Almost immediately upon arriving at Camp Douglas, Segoine began to tell his officers that the regiment would soon be exchanged and take their leave of Camp Douglas. The colonel based his assumption on the misguided belief that two great battles would soon be fought and enough prisoners captured to exchange the regiment. Yet he had no proof to back up his assertion and continued to spread the rumor anyway. Most of the officers saw right through the lies and lost all faith in their commander. Surgeon Benton summed up the regiment's feelings when he said he thought the "colonel was an old fool."[52]

Jerome Lattin. Mustered in as a sergeant in August 1862, Lattin was serving as captain of Company C when he was wounded at Petersburg in June 1864. He died of his wounds on July 13, 1864 (author's collection).

The rest of October and the beginning of November was spent drilling, holding inspections, and posting guard. During the second week of November, the 111th lost the services of two of its officers. Second Lieutenant Theodore Lampson of Company C and First Lieutenant Hasseltine Moore of Company D resigned their commissions and returned to New York. Promoted to fill Lampson's position was the regiment's sergeant major, Jerome Lattin. In Company D, Sergeant Augustus Green was promoted to fill the vacancy left by Moore.[53]

According to surgeon Dickenson Hopkins, Second Lieutenant Moore "has been ill during all of his term of service — I find that the severe diarrhea that has continually attended him has assumed a chronic form. His physical system being of that peculiar lax nature the least exertion in the way of drilling and marching prostrates him that it requires a long time to be able to do duty. He is consequently in my opinion wholly unfit for mil[itary] duty."[54]

Around the middle of November, the camp grapevine was alive with talk that all the regiments captured at Harpers Ferry would soon be leaving Camp Douglas to join the

Army of the Potomac in Virginia. Rumor became reality as, one by one, regiments began departing the camp. When the 115th New York left camp on November 20, its members were so disenchanted with their two-month stay that they burned their barracks to the ground.[55]

As the other regiments packed and left their prison home, word reached the New Yorkers that they would travel to Louisiana and take part in "General Banks' Expedition." To Sergeant Hoff, the expedition, which would advance along the Red River into Texas, was designed to "break up the rebel system of furnishing supplies from Texas, from the Mexican Ports, which have not been reached by our blockade."[56] Lieutenant Colonel MacDougall, who was in Albany at the time, actually saw the orders directing the regiment south. It was a matter of great pride to family members back home that their regiment would be associated with such an important venture. But the orders were changed before they reached the regiment. The 111th would go to Washington without the chance to cover itself with glory serving under Banks.[57]

Orders were issued for each man to cook four days' rations, fill their canteens, pack their knapsacks, and be ready to leave camp at first light on November 26. The regiment was divided into groups of 48 enlisted men, to be supervised by three or four noncommissioned officers and one commissioned officer.[58]

Colonel Segoine issued strict orders governing the orderly conduct of the men for the trip to Washington and the officers were to pay strict attention that the orders were observed. No one was to leave the train without his permission and whenever the train did stop and the men were unloaded, roll was to be called before the train continued on to the next stop. As with the trip to Harpers Ferry, the colonel forbid the New Yorkers from drinking any type of liquors. Segoine stated in the order that he "felt great pride in the orderly conduct of the men of his command and trust that nothing may occur to change that feeling of just pride into a feeling of shame and mortification."[59]

As the sun rose on the appointed day, Colonel Segoine marched the regiment one mile to the railroad station for the trip east. When the men arrived, they discovered there was no train waiting for them, and they were forced to remain until late in the day when a locomotive finally steamed into the station. Half frozen from the biting cold, the men boarded the cars and were on their way. Left behind were 15 comrades who succumbed to sickness and disease while at Camp Douglas.[60]

Arriving in Toledo, Ohio, on the morning of November 28, the men were given coffee and hardtack for breakfast before continuing the journey east. Sergeant Hoff was able to secure a Thanksgiving meal from a friend living in town and forgo the usual soldier's fare.[61] In a driving snowstorm, the train pulled into the station in Pittsburgh the next morning. The New Yorkers left the train and marched to the refreshment saloon where they were treated to a fine breakfast. After the meal, they reboarded the train and set off for Baltimore, which was reached the next day.[62]

When the New Yorkers arrived in Baltimore, they received a welcome surprise; Lieutenant Colonel MacDougall was there to greet them. The men were overjoyed to once again have the Scotsman among their ranks, and they welcomed him with open arms. Amid great celebration, the regiment climbed into old cattle cars for the trip south to Washington.[63]

The train arrived in the capital city on November 30 just as the sun was rising. The regiment left the train and marched to the Soldiers Retreat for breakfast. After the hearty meal, the New Yorkers were taken to barracks where they would stay until leaving the city. They quickly nicknamed their new home "No One's Barracks," due to the fact that troops were continually moving in and out. The men spent the remainder of the day seeing the sights of the city or just lying around the barracks writing letters.[64]

Sergeant Hoff, along with another member of Company K, traveled about the city. "Went up to the Capitol of our destructed country. It is a splendid edifice and one well worthy of our country."[65] John Paylor also went to see his nation's Capitol. "Then I went up to the capital & seen Washington monument & the Indian made of copper [atop the Capitol]."[66] But the casual life of the tourist did not last long. That evening, orders were received directing the men to be prepared to march at a moment's notice. It was time to get back into the war.

Chapter 4

Back to Virginia

The whole land is covered by ruins of camps and fortifications.[1]

The first day of December found the almost 700 men of the 111th marching through the streets of Washington. They crossed the Potomac River and entered war-torn Virginia. Surgeon Benton recalled in a letter to his father that "the country is a scene of complete desolation and not a spear of grain or anything of the kind is raised in the vicinity for miles around."[2]

When the halt was called, the men immediately fell out of ranks and began to establish camp, dubbed Camp Pomeroy in honor of their representative in Congress. Each company was divided into groups of 12 men, each group being issued a tepee-shaped Sibley tent. The tents were erected one next to another, with a company street to the front. The company officers placed their tents at one end of the row while the regimental color line was established at the other. The color line was where all regimental formations were held. This routine was followed until all ten companies were in line one next to the other. The tents of the regimental commander, lieutenant colonel and major were located behind those of the company officers. Once the tents were up and the company streets formed, the men were issued new Springfield rifles to replace those surrendered at Harpers Ferry.[3]

Colonel Segoine received orders four days into December to send details from the regiment out about two miles from camp to establish a line of pickets. John Paylor was relieved that it would be a short march, "but when we got there we thought it was 8 miles."[4] One of those selected for picket duty was Sergeant Hoff. He wrote to his wife, "Our duty consists of stationary posts about ten rods apart. We were the third lines of pickets from the front of the army which in front of us is General Sigel's forces. Where I was stationed was at headquarters of our divisions on the road that runs from Alexandria to Fairfax Court House. The duty was to examine passers and keep a guard across the road. My duty was to call out the guard and see about getting wood to keep up a fire."[5]

The next day, a steady rain began to fall. As the day wore on, the rain turned into a severe snowstorm. Surgeon Benton remarked, "Those knowing the climate say that so severe a one hardly ever occurs."[6] With no tents allowed on the picket line, the New Yorkers' only defenses against the weather were their blankets and a roaring fire. Despite the frigid, snowy weather and their distance from the enemy lines, the pickets had to remain vigilant. A few nights after the forward line was established, the evening quiet was shattered when a shot rang out from the picket line. One of the New Yorkers shot someone he claimed was a rebel spy. It turned out to be true, as the man had two sets of clothing: one set of civilian clothing and the other the uniform of a Confederate soldier.[7]

The New Yorkers soon found that standing picket was not all business. A few men from Company K left the picket line to go foraging and came back with a "pig that would weigh I should think about 20 pounds and we had one good meal." No one gave a second thought to stealing the pig, for as Sergeant Hoff put it, "a hungry stomach knows no conscience in this war."[8] On another occasion, Corporals Stacey and John Fishback decided to play a joke on an unsuspecting Virginian whose farm was located near their picket post. Corporal Stacey put on his best Southern accent and convinced the farmer he was a member of the 11th Alabama Regiment and had been taken prisoner by Corporal Fishback. They all had a good laugh at the farmer's expense.

It did not take long for disease and sickness that often plagued an encamped army to appear among the men of the 111th. Smallpox, varioloid, and typhoid fever were the most common sicknesses to sweep the camp. One of the first to succumb was Private John Johnson of Company D. The 44-year-old from Sodus was stricken with smallpox and sent to the hospital at Fairfax Seminary, where he later died. When William Stever of Company A died, his entire company turned out to bury their comrade and mourn a friend. "His duty as a soldier was well performed and his company will long remember his death with sorrow," recalled the *Auburn Daily Advertiser and Union*.[9] In the month of December, six men died of disease while eight were discharged for disability due to sickness. By the end of the month, 12 men were hospitalized due to severe illness.

To help combat the sickness plaguing the regiment, Lieutenant Colonel MacDougall called upon the people back home to lend a hand. He wrote complaining of the poor location of the regiment's camp, it being placed atop a high hill which was swept by strong gusts of frigid air. He remarked that those standing guard suffered terribly from the cold. MacDougall implored:

> [On] behalf of the soldiers now on duty in this regiment, I would ask people at home, who feel friendly toward us, to send what donations they can in way of buckskin gloves and warm winter vests. The government furnishes neither.... Our men suffer from want. Let them not forget while they are gathering around cheerful hearths these cold winter evenings, enjoying comforts of home, many brave men of Cayuga and Wayne are standing guard on the Potomac in forest and open field, with but few articles of warmth to protect them from rude winter winds.[10]

Around the middle of December, the New Yorkers received orders to strike tents, move about three miles south of Alexandria, and set up camp along Hunting Creek. Here the men moved into winter huts left behind by their previous occupants. Sergeant Hoff thought they made a "comfortable little hog pen not quite as large as mine at home. So you can see how soldiers can live."[11]

After setting up camp, named Camp Vermont in honor of a regiment from that state who had just vacated the camp, a daily guard schedule was created, picket posts were formed, and work parties joined in the task of throwing up a ring of fortifications surrounding the capital city. The men toiled with pickax and shovel in the frozen earth to build Fort Lyon. Captain Holmes was not happy that his men were forced to perform such menial work. The commander of Company D complained that his "boys did not enlist to shovel dirt."[12] Yet, despite such protests, the backbreaking work continued.

Colonel Segoine set up his headquarters in the home of an Episcopal bishop who fled when Federal troops first occupied the area in 1861. The rest of the regiment's officers made liberal use of the home's extensive library while pressing the dining room into service as their mess. Surgeon Benton remembered the house contained "everything but his most moveable valuables ... there is in the house an old piano made in Dresden which was probably considered as an elegant instrument when new."[13]

While at Camp Vermont, the 111th was temporarily brigaded with the 115th New York, the 4th Delaware, and the 25th and 27th Maine regiments as the 3rd Brigade, Casey's Division, XXII Corps. Colonel Segoine intimated that he would be made the brigade commander, but this did not happen. Colonel A. H. Grimshaw of the Fourth Delaware was given the command, and in the words of Sergeant Hoff, "a younger and of course a better man no doubt" than Colonel Segoine.[14]

On December 13, John Paylor listened as the faint rumble of artillery could be heard coming from the south.[15] Word soon spread like wildfire through the New Yorkers' camp of the fighting at Fredericksburg. The men waited anxiously for news of the battle, as many had family and friends fighting on the distant fields. Unfortunately, when word of the battle's outcome reached them, it was not good.

The new commander of the Army of the Potomac, General Ambrose Burnside, launched a series of attacks aimed at both flanks of the Confederate army. While meeting with initial success on the Confederate right flank, the attackers were eventually forced back. The attack on the Confederate left flank at Marye's Heights was a different story. Parts of three different Union corps attacked over almost a mile of open ground and were cut to pieces. When it was over, the one-day battle claimed more than 12,000 Union casualties. Thomas Geer was relieved when he heard that his brother Charles, serving with the 33rd New York, was only slightly wounded during the battle.[16]

Colonel Segoine's wife arrived at the regiment's camp along Hunting Creek for the holidays with New York's governor in tow. True to his word, the governor was there to present the New Yorkers with a regimental flag for being one of the first three regiments raised in New York under the president's call for volunteers. The flag was standard size: six feet, six inches by six feet. It was made of dark blue silk and emblazoned with the coat of arms of the United States. The coat of arms consisted of a bald eagle topped with two rows of stars, one for each state. Under the eagle was a ribbon containing the regiment's numerical designation, the 111th New York.[17]

Immediately following the ceremony the men were treated to a huge feast in honor of the holidays. They enjoyed sausage, beef, three types of potatoes, tea and applesauce. Captain Aaron Seeley of Company A bought oysters for his men in honor of the holidays.[18] At least on that day he was the most popular officer in the regiment.

Sergeants Hoff and Johnson McDowell obtained a pass to go into Alexandria on Christmas day, where they availed themselves of everything the city had to offer. In a letter to his wife, Hoff wrote,

> The city is about the size of Auburn I should think, some say larger. It is like all places pretty much, that I have seen South, dirty and nasty streets; some good buildings. The day seemed to me like Fourth of July; all the boys were firing pistols and fire crackers, and the Negroes were having a huge time. They were all drunk pretty much. The city was full of

soldiers and Negroes and there was considerable strife to see which could get the drunkest. I thought the soldiers took the lead as they generally do in all things. I got a dinner for Christmas, costing 25 cents. I also got some oysters to eat. I got back to camp about dark and we had a little liberty that night until 10 o'clock. Some of the boys had a great deal of fun. Songs and dances on the parade ground.[19]

December 28 started like any other day in camp: roll call, breakfast and an inspection. Company D received high praise from Colonel Segoine for having the best appearance and cleanest quarters of any in the regiment. Just as the sun was setting, the drummers beat the long roll and the New Yorkers grabbed their rifles and quickly fell into ranks. Company commanders distributed 40 rounds of ammunition to each man. Earlier in the day, the picket line around camp was attacked and driven in on the main line. Colonel Segoine had orders to take his men and reestablish the line.[20]

Chaplain John Brown strode to the front of the formation and led the men in prayer. When he was done, the New Yorkers marched off to the picket line. The regiment proceeded about four miles before Segoine called the halt and deployed the men in line. With no orders arriving, the colonel threw out a skirmish line and allowed the rest of the men to get some sleep.[21]

The New Yorkers passed a sleepless night in the cold winter air. Believing his men would not be out of camp long, Segoine did not think to have them bring blankets or tents. In the morning, John Paylor was ordered to go back to camp and bring blankets and rations for the men. The 111th continued to man the picket line for the next three days, even though the enemy made no more attempts to break the line.[22]

The New Year brought new orders for the regiment to move to the fortifications around Centerville, which were located about 15 miles west of the Capitol. Corporal Manley Stacey of Company D thought the order to move "put a damper on the boys, just got our quarters fixed up, this is the way with this war."[23] The men marched from Camp Vermont to Alexandria, where they boarded cars of the Orange and Alexandria Railroad. Guerrilla forces were operating in the area, and the train's engineer would not proceed until he knew his engine and cars would be safe. To appease the engineer, Colonel Segoine posted Company F in skirmish line ahead of the locomotive.[24]

Since the railroad did not go directly to Centerville, the regiment first had to travel to Union Mills, where it arrived in the early hours of January 3. Sergeant Hoff and his comrades "stacked our arms, kicked together some boughs and hay that lay on the ground, spread our blankets and then we lay down together."[25]

The next day, Companies D and H were ordered to march to Centerville to act as guard for a Massachusetts battery manning the fortifications around that city. Not long after the column started on the road to Centerville, the skies opened and it began to rain. The roads were quickly churned into a quagmire of mud as the New Yorkers plodded toward their destination. The two companies arrived by midafternoon and the men quickly erected their tents.[26]

A few days later the remaining eight companies of the 111th joined their comrades at Centerville. It was here that the 111th was brigaded with the 39th and 125th New York regiments. All three regiments had the distinct misfortune of being at Harpers Ferry. Besides the three regiments of infantry, the force at Centerville also contained two batteries of artillery.[27]

The camp at Centerville was established on the same ground the Confederates used for their camp the previous winter and was in plain view of the Blue Ridge Mountains and Thoroughfare Gap. Like the area around Alexandria, the countryside surrounding Centerville was one vast wasteland. There were forts and earthworks everywhere. Corporal Simeon Cooper wrote home that "old Virginia begins to look pretty desolate. There is not a fence left standing, nor a rail as far as I have been yet."[28] The only things remaining in abundance were the huts used by the rebels as their winter quarters. Unfortunately most were in a terrible state of disrepair and were deemed uninhabitable. Those in the regiment who could not make repairs or found themselves without one of the old huts were obliged to build one from scratch.

The sickness that ran rampant through the ranks while the regiment was camped along Hunter's Creek seemed to dissipate with the move to Centerville, although there were more common ailments. According to Sergeant Hoff, "the health of the regiment is the same as ever, a great many having colds."[29] One poor soldier, Martin L. Davis of Company H, was stricken with a different type of illness. Newman Eldred remembered his fellow company member this way: "He hadn't been a musician long before he was taken with rheumatism and he swelled up so a government shirt wouldn't fit him and he couldn't get a pair of government pants on him. He couldn't turn over alone for a long time. Some of the boys joked him by accusing him of blowing himself up. Let that be as it may if that was the only blowing up he ever got he was lucky."[30]

Around the middle of January, the garrison at Centerville received a new commander, Brigadier General Alexander Hays. A West Point graduate and Mexican War veteran, Hays had seen action early in the war, on the Peninsula and at Second Manassas, and he brought his reputation as a no-nonsense disciplinarian with him. Taking immediate steps to cut out the deadwood from the garrison, he instituted strict policies with swift retributions for infractions. The general would do everything in his power to make these men into the best soldiers in the army.[31]

Along with the move to Centerville, the New Year also brought a major upheaval in the regiment's officer ranks. Due to continuing complications with the illness he contracted during the march from Harpers Ferry to Annapolis, Colonel Segoine relinquished command of the 111th on January 3. His resignation was followed by that of his son,

Camp Pomeroy, the regiment's camp in Alexandria, Virginia, December 1862 (Massachusetts Commandery Military Order of the Loyal Legion and the USAMHI).

Adjutant Henry Segoine. Others tendering their resignations included Captains John Coe of Company B, Edward Thomas of Company C, the 50-year-old Ezra Northrop of Company H, and Silas Tremain of Company K. The junior officer ranks also saw their fair share of resignations. Leaving the regiment were Second Lieutenant Ezra Hibbard of Company A, First Lieutenant Jacob Van Buskirk and Second Lieutenant John Tremper of Company B, and First Lieutenant Andrew Soverill of Company E. Thomas Dadswell was sorry to see Hibbard resign as he was "one of our best officers."[32]

According to surgeon Vosburgh, Second Lieutenant John Tremper of Company B was suffering from "chronic bronchitis and that in consequence thereof he is unfit for duty." In his letter of resignation, Tremper asked that his request be forwarded on "at an early day in order to insure its speedy acceptance."[33] Colonel MacDougall endorsed the lieutenant's letter of resignation to General Hays, with a few remarks of his own: "I beg most respectfully to return the accompanying application for resignation of Lieut[enant] John Tremper, with the remarks that he has not done a days duty in three months, and when well was totally unfit to perform the duties of an officer. In my opinion it will greatly benefit the public service to have his resignation accepted."[34]

With the daily changes taking place among the officers, it was not long before rumors began to circulate around the camp that another officer would be put in charge of the regiment. Richard Warren of Company F wrote home that "our Lt Col [lieutenant colonel] is very well liked and it will create very hard feelings among both officers and men if their is another Col placed in command of the 111th."[35] The rumors proved to be false; Lieutenant Colonel MacDougall was promoted to colonel and given command of the regiment. Major Smith was promoted to lieutenant colonel and Captain Isaac Lusk of Company E was promoted to major.

Promoted to fill the position of adjutant was First Lieutenant James Haggerty while Irving Jacques of Company A made an amazing jump in rank from private to sergeant major. In Company B, First Sergeant Horace Hill was promoted to second lieutenant while First Lieutenant Ira Jones was promoted to captain in Company C. In Company E, First Lieutenant John Laing was promoted to captain, Second Lieutenant Augustus Proseus was promoted to first lieutenant and Sergeant John Brown was elevated to the rank of second lieutenant. The officer's ranks of Company H were filled with the promotions of First Lieutenant Frank Rich to captain, Second Lieutenant Rueben Myers to first lieutenant, and First Sergeant Edgar Dudley to second lieutenant. Like Company H, Company K received a new complement of officers with the promotion of First Lieutenant George Smith to captain, Second Lieutenant Adolphus Capron to first lieutenant, and First Sergeant Samuel Bradley to second lieutenant.[36]

A rumor spread like wildfire through Company A that Captain Seeley would resign, which was not received well by the men. According to Thomas Geer, "Capt Seeley, *we* think, is the best Capt in the regt [regiment]. If he resigns, I guess the whole Co [company] will."[37] The rumor may have started due to the fact that Seeley, commanding Company A, was next in line for the rank of major, yet was passed over for promotion. In the end, Seeley remained with Company A.[38]

Colonel MacDougall felt that it was in the best interest of the service that the resignations of certain officers be accepted as soon as possible. He felt that while most of the men were honest gentlemen and well liked among the men, they were totally unfit for command. Due to the fact that the newly commissioned colonel liked Captain John

Coe, MacDougall advised the captain to resign his commission before he was forced from the service. The exception was Lieutenant Jacob Van Buskirk. This officer was thought by all to be completely worthless in both moral character and military bearing.[39]

Born June 14, 1839, in Kintyre, Scotland, Clinton Dougall MacDougall came to America and settled in New York with his family at the age of 12. He studied law, worked as a bookkeeper, and was employed by a bank. After a short stay in the South, where he was recovering from ill health, MacDougall returned to Auburn in 1860 and went into the banking business with William H. Seward Jr.[40]

Colonel MacDougall took command of a regiment whose ranks were thinned by disease and desertions and that numbered only 540 men by mid–January. He set about instituting a rigorous schedule of drill and inspection, intended to raise both the morale and military proficiency of the regiment. Although a strict disciplinarian, MacDougall was well liked and respected by the officers and thought fair and honest by the enlisted men. He demanded great things from the men and they responded at once. The colonel ordered the men to ensure that their brass was polished, shoes and cartridge boxes blackened, and that they wear white gloves at all inspections and parades. MacDougall also convened boards of examinations to test the knowledge of the noncommissioned officers in drill and tactics in an attempt to weed out those not worthy to command his soldiers in the field.[41]

Clinton MacDougall, shown here as a colonel, when he took command of the 111th (Massachusetts Commandery Military Order of the Loyal Legion and the USAMHI).

In an order written to the regiment, MacDougall stated his desire to foster "that love of neatness and uniformity of dress, that cleanliness of person, that pride of profession, that gallant and military bearing at all times and in all places, but more particularly at parades and other occasions of ceremony which mark the good and faithful soldier and distinguish him from the common mercenary."[42] During one particular inspection, Corporal Smith recalled, "The Col [colonel] was very rigid & close in his inspection and sent several men to the guard house for not having everything right in regard to their cleanliness of person accoutrements and arms."[43] It became commonplace, and the men expected to be sent to the guardhouse when an inspection revealed the slightest imperfection.

Even though the schedule of drill and inspections was demanding, the men still found time to laugh. On one particular January day, the regiment spent the morning drilling by companies and spent the afternoon conducting battalion maneuvers. As the drill was coming to an end, First Lieutenant Robert Perry of Company B lost control of his horse. The mount ran out of camp, taking Perry along for the ride. Everyone in the regiment laughed themselves silly, and Corporal Stacey thought it was the "best thing I have seen in a long time."[44]

The 111th spent every third day on picket duty, with posts ranging from the stone bridge over Bull Run to Blackburn's Ford. Details from the regiment were also sent out under a flag of truce to the Manassas battlefields to dig up the partially buried bodies of Union soldiers when their families came to claim the remains. It was on one of those trips that a detail discovered a cache of over 300 weapons hidden in the underbrush. Knowing that there were guerrilla forces operating in the area, the same detail came out the next day with a wagon and carted off the weapons right under the nose of the enemy.[45]

In an effort to track down those absent from the regiment without leave, Colonel MacDougall sent Captain Lewis Husk of Company G to New York with a detachment from the regiment. The Federal government had proclaimed a general amnesty for all deserters, which lasted from the beginning of the year until April 1. If men returned of their own accord before the deadline, they would only lose pay for the time absent from their command. If captured after that date, they faced prosecution for desertion. Colonel MacDougall wanted to take full advantage of this amnesty to get as many men back into the ranks as he could. Captain Husk and his detail worked diligently and were able to track down and return about 20 men to the regiment.[46]

While in Auburn, Husk received another set of orders from Colonel MacDougall. The captain was ordered to raise a 16-piece band for the regiment. According to the *Auburn Daily Advertiser and Union*, "liberal offers are made to musicians for that purpose. We have some excellent players in this section [of the state] who might make it an object to communicate with Capt. Husk upon this matter."[47]

On the night of February 30, the booming of the camp's signal guns awakened the New Yorkers. Within three minutes, every able-bodied man was dressed, accoutered, and standing ready in the ranks as a steady rain fell. Under the command of Colonel Mac-Dougall, the regiment, along with the rest of the brigade, marched to Blackburn's Ford where it was thought that a guerrilla force might be trying to break through the Union lines at Bull Run. After two companies of the 111th were thrown out to the front as skirmishers, the rest of the regiment was posted directly opposite the ford while the 125th was posted to the regiment's left and the 39th to its right. Behind MacDougall's men was posted a battery of guns to further protect the ford.[48]

The New Yorkers waited in the cold, wet darkness. When no further attempts were made by the enemy to cross by 4:00 A.M., all three regiments were marched back to camp. David Pease of Company G noted that "some of the boys in the hospital that was sick and had been sick for some time got scart and jumped out of bed and put on their cloths and formed in with the rest to fight. There was two out of our company that had been home for some time and had done no duty that got so scart that they forgot to limp any more."[49] It was the colonel's view that it would be beneficial for his men if the regiment was turned out from time to time as a way of increasing proficiency and weeding out the undesirables.

Throughout the winter, Confederate forces continued to probe and harass the picket lines around Centerville, trying to find weak spots in the Union line. The New Yorkers were often awakened in the middle of the night by the long roll, calling the men to form ranks and march to an area of the picket line that was under attack. These affairs usually yielded no casualties, other than frayed nerves and loss of sleep.[50]

MacDougall's men were further bothered by the number of refugees traveling north, attempting to gain safe passage through the picket lines. The poor and hungry travelers, mostly women and children, brought news of near starvation conditions and food riots in Richmond. David Pease remarked that "they have to go back to look to Jeff Davis for their food. It is almost enough to breake ones heart to see them. They say the that the south cannot hold out much longer for everything is so clean that folks that are not in the army will all starve."[51] Yet despite the mournful tales, Pease and his comrades had orders to deny passage through the picket line and were forced to turn away the refugees.

Enemy soldiers were not the only threat to the safety of the men of the 111th. Constant rumors of supposed raids and attacks created a nervous air among the pickets.[52] Surgeon Benton remembered being ordered by General Hays to the picket line along the Warrenton Turnpike to attend to a wounded man. When he arrived, the doctor found George Gatesman of Company E laying on the ground with a wound through his left breast. Gatesman was returning from a patrol when a jumpy picket fired at him thinking he was the enemy. The private fell, crying out, "For god's sake don't shoot again."[53]

Newman Eldred woke one winter's night to the sound of the post's signal guns firing, only to find that the roof to his hut had blown off during the night. Much to his dismay, he found the interior of his hut, as well as his bunk, covered in about a foot of freshly fallen snow. Shaking off his blankets, he inadvertently covered his tent mate, Milton Seymour, with snow. Seymour jumped out from under his snow-covered blankets and angrily attacked Eldred, who was trying to get the snow out of his own clothes so he could dress. After fending off three such attacks, Eldred managed to throw Seymour out of the hut, get dressed and then run to take his place in line, only to find that the regiment had marched off without him.[54]

When not taking their turn on the picket line or performing assigned duties around camp, the New Yorkers occupied themselves in other ways. Since the middle of February, the ground around Centerville was covered in a blanket of snow. The temptation being too great, many snowball fights broke out in camp. During one such "battle," the regiment split itself into two wings and snowballs began to fly fast and thick. Colonel MacDougall personally led the left wing, and Corporal Stacey and his comrades in the right wing were forced to give ground. In the opinion of John Paylor, the "right wing got wiped out."[55]

Another pastime enjoyed by the men was gambling. They would bet on just about anything, often with large amounts of money changing hands. Gambling became so pervasive in the ranks that Colonel MacDougall was forced to issue an order forbidding the practice. One of the first to be arrested under the new regulation was Sergeant Lewis Dryer. The disobedient sergeant was reduced to ranks for his indiscretion.[56]

Letters for the regiment arrived at Centerville almost every day. Surgeon Benton remembered that the "rush for letters among the soldiers is only perhaps equaled by a bayonet charge on a battery."[57] The soldiers often wrote letters asking for items that would make their life a little easier. One of the most asked-for items was boots. The government-issued brogan had a tendency to wear out quickly, and the men were left either barefoot or with shoes that were totally unfit to wear. Sometimes the citizens of Wayne and Cayuga counties took it upon themselves to look to the needs of their sons. The citizens of Cato got together and sent a barrel of dried fruit and other items to Company H. The Genoa Aid Society did their part by sending bundles of socks and mittens to the New Yorkers.[58]

On a cold and rainy March night, Confederate guerrilla leader Colonel John S. Mosby embarked on one of his most daring exploits of the entire war. The rebel cavalryman headed for Fairfax Courthouse with the intention of capturing Union colonel Percy Wyndham, only to find that his nemesis had been called to Washington. However, Mosby discovered an even better prize in General Edwin Stoughton. Grabbing the general, the guerrilla and his band made their way safely through the Union lines. Captain Thompson remembered the entire event: The rebels "were all dressed as Union troopers and gave the countersign correctly. I saw the whole party myself and was as green as the rest."[59]

With the spring, and a return of better weather, came an increase in the frequency of drill, inspections and dress parades. Along with their regular activities, the men also conducted target practice, held skirmish drills, took part in running drills with their knapsacks, and held mock battles using blank cartridges. It did not take long for the 111th to become known as the best-drilled regiment at Centerville.[60]

One day, Colonel MacDougall marched the regiment about a mile out of camp and commenced to drill his men. As he was putting the New Yorkers through their paces, it began to rain quite hard. Not one to be deterred by bad weather, the colonel continued with the exercise. When the drill was over, MacDougall began to lead his men back to camp at a full run. Most of the men could not keep up and fell out along the way. One of those was the color sergeant. Before falling out, he handed the colors to Corporal Stacey. Stacey later wrote in his diary, "I took the colors just as long as I could move then gave to one of the color guard."[61] Those who made it back to camp with the colonel were rewarded with a ration of whiskey.

The constant drill and rigors of camp life were beginning to have an effect on the men. To Corporal Stacey, Second Lieutenant Erastus Granger made too many mistakes during drill and constantly made a fool of himself. Referring to the officer as "Lord Granger," Corporal Stacey vowed to "whip him if I ever live to get out of the service, putting on too much style for a fool."[62] Spencer Langdon of Company B had his own thoughts about the constant drill and military life: "This white glove business & scouring brasses will play out when we get into battle I don't think it whips the rebels. There is too much style put on in this army I hate the sight of military suit of clothes."[63]

Between March and April, the ranks were once again reshuffled due to more resignations and promotions. On March 6, surgeon Dickenson Stewart Hopkins resigned to accept the position of surgeon in the Fourth Delaware. Hopkins place was taken by 24-year-old Charles Frisbee. For some time, Lieutenant Colonel Seneca Smith had been suffering from extreme inflammation of the stomach and intestines. On April 3, his resignation was accepted on the grounds that the surgeon found him totally unfit for military service.[64]

A few days later, Smith stood before a sad regiment and read his farewell address. He would be remembered as a good and faithful officer. With the lieutenant colonel's resignation, the total number of officers leaving the regiment since the first of the year had risen to 12. In Smith's place, Major Isaac Lusk was promoted to lieutenant colonel, while the rank of major remained vacant until mid–July.[65]

After a careful examination, surgeon Vosburgh found Adjutant James Haggerty "laboring under Philthsis Pulmoralis and has been for the last ninety days and that in consequence thereof he is in my opinion unfit for duty and further declare he will not be able again to resume his duty."[66] Because of his condition, Haggerty was forced to resign. Taking his place as regimental adjutant was First Lieutenant Adolphus Capron of Company K.

Others were promoted to file several vacancies within the regiment. First Lieutenant Robert Perry of Company F was promoted to captain and transferred to Company B. Sergeant Howard Servis of the same company was promoted to second lieutenant. In Company C, Second Lieutenant Jerome Lattin was elevated to the rank of first lieutenant while in Company F, Second Lieutenant John Drake was promoted to first lieutenant to replace Perry.[67]

With all the upheaval in the regiment's officer ranks, Sergeant Hoff began to think for the first time about his own chances of becoming an officer. He wrote to his wife of his intentions of obtaining a commission: "I will tell you Deborah what I have not ever told you or even hinted. I think if I have any influence and could get some friends to work for me. There may be a chance for a Lieutenant in the company. This is what I wish Deborah and my desire is that I may get it but I must have someone to help me."[68]

Orders arrived on April 12 for the men to strike camp and be prepared to move. The New Yorkers cooked three days rations and packed their knapsacks. Cartridge boxes were filled and extra rations and ammunition were packed in wagons. Other than accoutrements and rifles, the men were only allowed to carry a change of underclothes, an overcoat and a blanket. All tents and extra equipment would be left behind under guard.[69]

Rumors flew around camp as to the destination of the regiment. Some thought they were bound for Fredericksburg to join the Army of the Potomac. Others, like Thomas Dadswell, were certain the regiment was headed south to take part in a different campaign altogether. In a letter to his father, he wrote, "We have got marching orders we have got to start to the south towards Vicksburg."[70] The men waited two days for the order to advance, but it never came. After all the packing and preparing was done, the New Yorkers were ordered to unpack their knapsacks and settle back into camp.

On May 4 John Paylor wrote in his diary, "Heard firing all day in the direction of Fredericksburg."[71] What Paylor and many others heard was the final action of the battle at Chancellorsville. On May 2, General Lee unleashed General "Stonewall" Jackson who attacked and drove in the right flank of the Army of the Potomac. Over the next two days, the Confederates launched a series of attacks against a defensive but larger Union army. The final outcome of three days fighting was a decisive Southern victory and one that would help shape the movements of their army in the coming months.

A welcome diversion from military life came when the regiment received visitors from home. Surgeon Benton's wife arrived in Centerville near the end of May and was treated to tours of the camp and horseback rides in the surrounding countryside. Mrs. Benton spent much of her time in the hospital talking to the sick soldiers, many of whom commented that it was nice to have a woman to talk with. Corporal Smith's father arrived in camp and was given the royal treatment by his son and other members of the regiment.[72]

Other prominent citizens made the trip from Auburn to see for themselves how the

111th was getting along in the field. One of those was John N. Knapp, the first adjutant of the regiment. Knapp was appointed as adjutant in July 1862 but resigned his commission before the regiment mustered into service the next month. A letter published in the *Auburn Daily Advertiser and Union*, written by a member of Company K, indicated the reason for Knapp's visit to the regiment's camp at Centerville. The "prevailing view in Auburn that Reg't [regiment] is not a first class reg't' behind in discipline, and never recovered from the infection and demoralization at Harper's Ferry and Chicago. With this conviction, J. N. Knapp came to [investigate] and expressed surprise to find us not only well fed and well clothes, in good health and spirits, and actually best drilled and disciplined of any regt in Dept. of Washington."[73]

At the end of May, newly promoted Corporal Geer reported that Colonel MacDougall took leave of the regiment. It seems that the colonel was thrown from his horse and bruised severely. While all in the regiment were concerned for their colonel's well-being, MacDougall's absence meant a welcome break from the usual rigorous drill schedule.[74]

The regiment received orders in early June for two companies from the regiment to be detached for a special duty. Companies B and C were selected and placed under the command of Captain Robert Perry of Company B, who marched his men about 16 miles southwest of Alexandria. Here Companies B and C would guard the Accotink Bridge on the Baltimore and Ohio Railroad. Camp was established atop a high hill on the estate of the widow Fitzhue, with a commanding view of the bridge.[75]

While the rest of the 111th was on picket duty near the end of June, reports came in of a large body of troops coming up from Bull Run toward Centerville. These soldiers belonged to Union general Oliver O. Howard's XI Corps. Corporal Smith wrote in a letter to his father that the XI Corps "came up and stopped on the fields south of Centerville and encamped completely covering those fields in all directions ... the next day the 1st corps came in and camped."[76] Over the next couple of days, the rest of the Union army arrived and set up camp around Centerville. Sergeant Hoff wrote to his wife about the arrival of the army: "We have not had much drill to do as the weather has been very hot and our attention has been taken up with looking at a part of the great Army of the Potomac as it moved along with its army trains of supply and ordinance stores. Imagine to yourself about as much again dust as you generally see at a state fair and then you can form some opinion. And so it is for miles as far as the eye can reach."[77]

The New Yorkers were awestruck by the sight. Many took the opportunity to visit friends and relatives serving in other regiments. Newman Eldred was returning from bathing after a tour on the picket line when he saw a group of soldiers approaching. He heard one of the soldiers say the name "wax," a nickname Eldred received as a child. Looking over the group, he recognized his brother, who was currently serving in the 147th New York. The two were reunited for the first time in over a year. Corporal Smith went to the camp of the 143rd Pennsylvania and visited with many friends he had not seen in years.[78]

When the II Corps arrived at Centerville, the battle-hardened veterans made a distinct impression upon the men of the 111th. Corporal Stacey recalled that they "were a rough looking lot of men. As soon as they halted, commenced to draw things, [we] had to put double guard to protect things."[79] The II Corps soldiers made an unfavorable impression upon Sergeant Hoff. "Some are lame and fat, some sick so that they have to wrap rags around them. Others have thrown away knapsacks and canteen and haversack.

And some even guns."[80] In turn, the New Yorkers made an impression on the II Corps soldiers. They called the men from Wayne and Cayuga counties "band box soldiers, with our white collars and gloves."[81] This term of derision was often given to soldiers who had not seen battle and whose entire term of service had been spent in garrison drilling.

With so many soldiers in one place, there were bound to be problems. One night, soldiers belonging to the II Corps broke into the sutler store of the Ninth Massachusetts Battery, which was also part of the garrison at Fort Hays. Before the stocks of the store were completely cleaned out, General Hays led a detachment of soldiers with fixed bayonets, many from the 111th, to stop the looting. Threatening to turn the camp's artillery on the thieves, Hays arrested all offending soldiers, whose number included several officers.[82]

On June 19, the men of the 111th were startled to see smoke rising from the mountains and hear the pounding of artillery. Reports soon arrived in camp of a "smart engagement between some reb cavalry and our infantry." According to Sergeant Hoff, "the principal part of the firing being I should think just at or near Snickers Gap and Aldie. The results we have not heard, only that we heard that the rebs had possession of the passes and our soldiers had driven them out."[83] Later in the day, a group of Confederate prisoners arrived in camp, guarded by a strong force of cavalry. The troopers stated that at least 300 more prisoners were taken in the engagement and sent on to Fairfax Station.

Having decided that the war had been fought far too long on Virginia soil, General Lee determined to try his hand at a second invasion of the North. The Confederate commander wanted to take advantage of his army's high morale to win a decisive victory on Northern soil that he hoped would win the war for the South. By the time the Army of the Potomac was concentrating around Centerville, Lee's army was nearing the Virginia-Maryland border along the Potomac River.[84]

One by one, the different Union army corps began to leave Centerville and march to overtake the Confederate army. The New Yorkers were beginning to feel as if they were destined to remain spectators in a war in which they desperately wanted to take part. To further compound their feelings of frustration, the men were ordered to draw rations, pack knapsacks, and be prepared to march to Bull Run Bridge on a routine drill. No sooner had the regiment arrived at the bridge when it was turned around and marched back to camp. For Sergeant Hoff, the entire affair was humorous. Thinking their men were being sent to fight the enemy, "the women in camp was some scared I reckon and there was some kissing and [hugging] one another goodbye and how ridiculous and laughable it was to think that we came back and they had shed their tears in vain."[85] Corporal Stacey did not share in the levity and summed up his feelings when he wrote, "The fact is we are getting tired of drilling, in the same thing, over and over again."[86] The men wanted to fight.

On June 24 the long-awaited orders arrived in camp. The 111th was directed to break camp at Centerville and march at once for Gum Springs. Tents were lowered, knapsacks packed, and extra uniforms and equipment packed away and stored at various locations in town. Whatever the men needed would be carried on their backs.[87]

After receiving word of the next day's move, Sergeant Hoff sat down to write a letter to his wife informing her of the impending move: "We had orders read to us on parade that we are to move at the shortest notice and that will be in the morning I think. We will go in the Second Corps General Hancock. So you see we are a part and a parcel of the great Army of the Potomac."[88] Hoff would rather that General George McClellan, not "Fighting Joe" Hooker, command the army, but was still hopeful of a Union victory.

The dutiful husband ended the letter by trying to comfort his wife, reassuring her that everything would be fine: "Deborah, brave all your troubles as a soldier's wife should, do all you can with a firm conscience of coming right toward Him who is absent. And have confidence in Him for he will always do that which He is not ashamed to tell when he gets home. To her he has always loved. Love and protect Edwin and blessings of your true and devoted husband will always be with you."[89]

The men were up well before sunrise on June 25. Ten days rations and shelter halves were issued to each man and final preparations were made for the march to Gum Springs. At 2:00 P.M., and with the sky threatening rain, Colonel MacDougall ordered the regiment forward and the men gladly left Centerville behind. Arriving at Gum Springs in a driving rainstorm late in the day, the old "Harpers Ferry" brigade joined the II Corps and went into camp. The command of the brigade was given to Colonel George Willard of the 125th and was designated as the Third Brigade of the Third Division. General Hays was elevated to the command of the Third Division.[90]

For the next two days, the New Yorkers marched in pouring rain and ankle-deep mud churned up by thousands of tramping feet. The first hours of June 27 found the 111th on the heights overlooking Edwards Ferry on the Potomac River. The New Yorkers found soldiers backed up for miles waiting to cross into Maryland. For Captain Thompson, the march was very difficult. He writes, "So crowded was the only road that led to the river and so slow was the motion of the troops ahead we could only march a few yards at a time and stand sometimes ten minutes in ankle deep mud waiting to take a step. Soon the men began to lie down and go to sleep at every halt and then at the command 'forward,' we officers had to wake them up and urge them along."[91] Finally, the men were allowed to stop for the night. But no sooner did they erect tents than the order to resume the march was given.

While their comrades were struggling through the ankle-deep mud and extreme darkness, Companies B and C were leaving their camp around Accotink and traveling north by train. Captain Perry received orders to move his men to Springfield, about a mile from the Potomac River. The detachment from the 111th was ordered to guard a camp of "contraband" and man the defenses around the capital city. Camp was established about one-quarter of a mile from Arlington House, the prewar home of General Lee. When they arrived, the New Yorkers noticed that the "negroes are busy as bees making a nice log city."[92] In a letter to the editors of the *Auburn Daily Advertiser and Union*, Doctor Caulkins boasted that he would eat his Fourth of July dinner in the Confederate general's house.

By 8:00 A.M. on June 27, the remaining eight companies of the 111th crossed the Potomac River and continued their march for almost seven more miles. Finally the halt was called and the New Yorkers were filed into a wheat field to get some much-needed rest. Later that afternoon the march resumed. The men passed through the towns of Poolesville and Barnesville before stopping for the night at the foot of Sugar Loaf Mountain.[93]

Before dawn the next day, the men fell in for a general inspection. In the darkness, officers checked rifles, accoutrements, ammunition and rations, and those deemed unable to keep up on the march were sent to Washington. With knapsacks slung across their backs, the New Yorkers once again took up the march. The rain had finally stopped falling and, despite the muddy roads, the day was rather pleasant. The march made a distinct impression upon Corporal Smith: "Nearly all the boys threw away their clothing and it was strung for many miles overcoats, blankets, blouses, dress coats, shirt, knapsacks."[94] After moving all day, the New Yorkers arrived at Monocacy Junction in the early evening and camped on the south side of the railroad. With some irony, John Paylor noted that they were in almost the exact location they had occupied the previous September after their humiliating surrender at Harpers Ferry.[95]

Late in the evening, rumors began to fly around camp about a new army commander. The reports were confirmed when it was learned that General George G. Meade, commander of the V Corps, had replaced Joseph Hooker as head of the army. Sergeant Hoff offered his own insight into the abilities of "Fighting Joe." In a letter to his wife, he wrote, "Still they say that Hooker is a good fighting man. And he is a good Corps commander. Further than that the opinion is among the men that he cannot handle a large army. But then common soldiers have no right to an opinion of their own."[96]

On June 29, one of the most severe marches in the history of the 111th began. Starting at 9:00 A.M., the regiment proceeded a short distance to the Monocacy River. The New Yorkers were amazed to find that General Hancock had posted one of his aides at the ford to ensure that each regiment marched on through the river without stopping, not allowing the men time to take off their shoes and socks. An angry Captain Thompson noted, "There were good fences and flattened logs upon which our men could have crossed almost or quite dry shod."[97] Crossing the chest-deep water with rifles and cartridge boxes held above their heads, the men continued on for another hour before halting and tending to their severely blistered feet.

The march quickly turned into a test of endurance. Men fell out at every step, overcome by the severe heat and exhaustion. Dress coats, blouses, blankets and even entire knapsacks littered the regiment's line of advance, thrown away by soldiers too weary to stand up under the weight. Newman Eldred recalled that "after a few hours of forced march in the boiling sun we were obliged to dump our knapsacks beside the road and with regret travel on feeling relieved of a great burden."[98] Every attempt was made by officers and noncommissioned officers alike to keep the men together and moving, but their efforts were futile. The 111th was soon scattered all over the Maryland countryside.

The severity of the march can best be summed up in the words of Captain Thompson:

> On, on we marched, the sun beating down with almost tropical power, the roads now a stifling cloud of dust and anon filled with cobble stones over which the footsore men were constantly stumbling. Men would fall out every few rods, declaring they could not go another step, but by coaxing and carrying their muskets for them, and more by keeping up a constant stream of funny stories and songs, we were able to hold them on for miles.... I commanded the color company and the colors could not halt, so I nerved myself and a few of my most resolute men to "see the colors through to camp."[99]

Unfortunately for him, the good captain could not quite muster the nerve needed for this day's march. As the regiment continued to move forward, he found himself unable to keep up with his men. He writes, "About eight o'clock I found myself unable to go further unaided and pressed forward to the adjutant, who was mounted, and supported myself for some distance by holding on to his horse's mane. At length I fell in the road unconscious and was carried to a house not far away, where I rested until morning."[100]

Stricken with chronic dysentery before leaving Monocacy Junction that morning,

Corporal Smith was finding it ever more difficult to keep up with the regiment. Sergeant Marcellus Mosher of Company I allowed Smith to ride his horse for a while and even tried to get him a place in an ambulance, but to no avail. The wagons were filled to capacity with men in far worse shape than Smith. "I succeeded in getting my gun and knapsack carried and then I thought I could keep up but I had to stop every few minutes,"[101] Smith wrote in a letter to his mother. After falling farther and farther behind, he finally gave up trying to catch the regiment and was forced to make a bed under a tree with fellow company member, George Peckham.

The next morning, Smith was taken with a severe pain and was forced to seek medical attention at a farmhouse in Carroll County, Maryland. The farm belonged to a Mr. Haines, "a strong union man, a friend to every soldier."[102] Here Smith spent the next two days trying to recuperate. Regrettably, the corporal was in such poor health that it would be six months before he could rejoin the regiment.

What was left of the regiment halted at Uniontown that night, a distance of over 30 miles from Monocacy Junction. Out of the 470 men who began the grueling march, there were only about 20 men left standing with the colors to answer the roll call. June 30 was a day of rest and recuperation for those with the regiment and a day to catch up to their comrades for those who had fallen behind on the march. After begging a meal from the "good Samaritan who lodged me,"[103] Captain Thompson continued his march and was able to rejoin his company at Uniontown.

Later in the day, the paymaster arrived in camp. Roll was again taken, and the men were mustered for pay. The strength of the regiment was recorded as 390 men, which according to Colonel MacDougall, "included men on extra duty, men detailed in commissary and quartermaster department, ambulance corps, and noncombatants generally."[104] The colonel counted the fighting strength of the regiment at about 350 men. No rations had been issued since leaving Centerville and most of the men had to scrounge through their haversacks or beg to secure food for breakfast. Lack of food was something that would plague the regiment throughout the entire campaign.

Chapter 5

Redemption in Pennsylvania

> This day I shall never forget it occurs to me.[1]

With the majority of the stragglers back in the ranks on the morning of July 1, 1863, the 111th was once again ready for another day of hard marching. At 9:00 A.M. orders arrived directing the regiment to Taneytown, where the men were ordered to guard the II Corps wagon train. Once again it appeared as though the regiment would be denied the chance to redeem itself for the humiliation suffered at Harpers Ferry. The New Yorkers had not advanced very far before several couriers galloped to the head of the column, carrying orders that directed the corps' wagon train to the rear and instructed the 111th to rejoin the rest of the brigade in preparation for the advance into Pennsylvania.[2]

Reunited with the rest of the Harpers Ferry brigade, the New Yorkers resumed the advance north, crossing the Mason-Dixon Line into Pennsylvania by late afternoon. As the sun began to set, Captain Thompson and the rest of the regiment "filed off the Taneytown Road just near Round Top into a piece of very broken ground covered with rocks, underbrush and a few trees. Without fire or lights we munched a few crackers and stretched our exhausted bodies on the ground for the night."[3] Sometime during the night, First Sergeant James Allen of Company H tried to commit suicide by shooting himself in the chest with a pistol. Instead of inflicting a mortal wound, the ball glanced off a rib and passed around his body before exiting his back.[4]

The evening tranquility gave the men time to speculate about what would happen come morning. Newman Eldred dreaded the coming contest, fearing that the next day might be his last. But one thought above all else gave him the strength to face his fears and that was being branded a coward. For Eldred, this was a fate worse than death. He remembered the last words his father spoke to him before leaving New York with the regiment. Gripping him by the hand, the senior Eldred cautioned his son not to get shot in the back. But not everyone was able to steel their nerves for the coming fight. Charles Todd and Robert Johnson of Company A chose to desert from the ranks rather than face the enemy.[5]

As the men of the 111th left Uniontown that morning, a battle was raging to the north in Pennsylvania. Against orders, Confederate general Henry Heth's Third Corps Division engaged the Union cavalry division of General John Buford along the heights west of the town of Gettysburg. The Union I and XI corps arrived on the field to reinforce

Buford's hard-pressed troopers and the contest quickly escalated out of control. Bitter fighting raged throughout the day, with more and more soldiers from both sides being thrown into the fight. General Meade's line was finally broken north of town and the soldiers driven back through city streets and onto the surrounding heights to the south. The rebels were unable to press their advantage and were forced to settle into position for the night. When the fighting ended for the day, the Union line was anchored on Culp's Hill and ran south from Cemetery Hill down Cemetery Ridge.[6]

Just before dawn on July 2, the 111th continued its advance north. After proceeding a short distance, the New Yorkers moved into a field to the left of the road. The regiment, along with the rest of the brigade, was assigned a reserve position at the east, or lower side of an orchard next to the road.[7]

In front of the 111th were the 126th and 125th, while the 39th was to its left. At the top of the orchard was the Abraham Brien house and barn, and to the right was a wooded grove owned by David Zeigler. Beyond the Brien homestead was Emmitsburg Road, a typical dirt lane bordered on either side by a rail fence, and beyond that, about a mile away, was Seminary Ridge. In the fields between the road and wooded Seminary Ridge was the Bliss farm, consisting of a house, a barn and numerous outbuildings. To the north of the regiment's position was the town of Gettysburg, occupied by soldiers of the Army of Northern Virginia.[8]

With the 111th in position, Colonel MacDougall dispatched two of his eight companies to join the brigade skirmish line. The picket reserve post was stationed at Emittsburg Road and the pickets were stationed out beyond the Bliss farm, almost three-quarters of a mile from the regiment's position. The New Yorkers traded shots with Confederate skirmishers who emerged from the woods at the edge of Seminary Ridge and from the southern end of town.[9]

The occasional crack of the skirmisher's rifle soon grew in intensity until a heated contest was under way on the Bliss farm. To bolster the skirmish line, Colonel Willard ordered the 39th New York forward, with colors flying. General Hays watched with growing concern as the right side of the line began to waiver, then give way under the Confederate fire. According to Colonel MacDougall, "the general rode down at a gallop mounted on his fine bay 'Dan,' with an orderly carrying his division flag, followed by his other orderlies. The line was at once re-established and never broke again. It was the first and last time I ever saw a division commander with his flag and staff on the skirmish line—they were targets for hundreds of sharpshooters."[10]

While the skirmishers continued to bang away, the rest of the men of the 111th were inspecting their equipment, getting some rest or searching for food, of which they had none. Just like the day before, the New Yorkers continued to suffer from a lack of rations. "There was a lull for a time," recalled Captain Thompson, "and by a diligent search of our pockets and haversacks we got coffee enough to give a swallow or two apiece to our regiment—but no food. We gave our belts a hitch and all who smoked indulged vigorously while we awaited events."[11] Sergeant Hoff informed his wife similarly that he was "short of rations with very poor water to drink."[12]

With nothing else to do, some of the officers wandered up to the top of the orchard near the Brien house, even though they had been given orders to stay out of sight. Captain Thompson spotted a soldier lying down behind a stump, firing at a distant horseman. Thompson watched through his field glasses as the sharpshooter fired a round from his telescopic rifle and felled the rider. "That shot brought a shell which fell in the regiment. Fortunately it did not explode but it created quite a sensation ... we found it had only gone through our bass drum and knocked a knapsack into a bundle of rags."[13]

The sporadic fire from the rebel artillery forced the New Yorkers to hug the ground for protection. Colonel MacDougall paced back and forth behind the regiment, reminding the men to stay low. A shell from the rebel guns burst directly over the regiment, sending fragments of iron raining down to the ground. One particularly large piece landed right between Wallace Fink and Martin Davis of Company H. Destroying a musket, the exploding shell showered both privates with dirt and debris. Wallace and Davis both jumped to their feet and began to wipe the dirt off their faces and from out of their mouths when Colonel MacDougall ran over and ordered the dirt-covered privates to lie back down.[14]

What started as intermittent shelling turned into a full-scale cannonade around 4:00 P.M. Advancing east across Emmitsburg Road under covering fire from their guns, two divisions of Confederate lieutenant general James Longstreet's First Corps slammed into the lines of Major General Daniel Sickles' III Corps. Longstreet was to take his two divisions, smash the left flank of the Union line and then drive up Cemetery Ridge, rolling the Federal army up on itself as it went. The rebels had reconnoitered the Union right flank earlier in the morning but were considerably late in starting the attack.[15]

But plans would have to change. Not long after the enemy had viewed his position and formulated a plan of attack, General Sickles had taken it upon himself to move his entire III Corps forward from the low ground north of Little Round Top to the high ground along Emmitsburg Road. Sickles had asked permission several times to make the move, but receiving no response, made the move anyway. The result of his indiscretion was to create a gap between the right of Sickles' corps and the left of Hancock's II Corps. The entire right flank of Sickles' line was severely undermanned; some portions around the peach orchard being held by nothing but artillery. It was in this area that the battle for control for the center of the Union line would take place.[16]

The men of the 111th smashed their bodies closer to the ground as shells crashed into the fields around them. Fortunately, the majority of the rounds fell to their left and rear. As they hugged the earth, many noticed that courier after courier galloped away from army headquarters located behind them at the widow Leister's house, carrying orders to various positions farther down the line.[17]

One set of orders arrived for General Hays. The message was from General Hancock, asking the Third Division commander to send one of his best brigades south toward the left flank of the II Corps, where it was needed immediately to plug the gap between the II and III corps. Hays immediately called for Colonel Willard. The general ordered Willard to "take you brigade over there and knock the h--- out of the rebs."[18] Ready or not, the men of the 111th were going into the fight.

Close to 7:00 P.M., the order to fall in was given and the men hurried to take their place in line. With ranks formed, Chaplain Brown climbed atop a stone wall in front of the regiment and began to speak. He knew his words of inspiration would have a profound effect upon the listeners, if only they could have heard him. Unfortunately, recalled the chaplain, "My voice was drowned ... by the louder and more eloquent voices proceeding from the throats of more than two hundred cannon."[19]

Once the skirmishers were recovered from the fields west of Emmitsburg Road,

Colonel Willard rode to the head of the brigade and shouted out the order to "fix bayonets; shoulder arms; left face; forward march."[20] To save time that otherwise would have been lost in maneuvering his regiments, Willard moved the brigade as it was positioned in the Brien orchard. The 125th, marching in front of the 126th, made up the right side of the column while the 39th, marching in front of the 111th, made up the left side of the column. Sometime during the movement, General Hancock joined Colonel Willard in conducting the brigade to its place in line.

As dusk began to settle across the field, the men from Wayne and Cayuga counties moved south along Cemetery Ridge, crossing fence lines and marching through fields pounded by exploding shells. Once the appointed place was reached, the 111th was fronted in an open field, behind and to the right of a row of artillery pieces, facing west toward Emmitsburg Road. The guns being worked at a feverish pace belonged to Colonel Freeman McGilvery, who had thrown together the makeshift line of fieldpieces in a desperate attempt to halt the Confederates pouring through the center of the Federal line.[21]

The area in front of the 111th was a flat, open field that sloped gently downward toward a swale about 200 yards away. According to Captain Seeley, the swale was "about 12 or 15 rods wide grown up to thick bushes and in some places were old stumps and large rocks or rough boulders."[22] Inside the swale was Plum Run, a shallow creek bordered on either side by generally marshy ground. On the west side of the creek, there was a large open field that rose gradually until it reached Emmitsburg Road.

Brigadier General William Barksdale and his brigade of Mississippi infantry had smashed through the III Corps regiments posted around the peach orchard. Urging his men forward, the Mississippian unleashed a devastating attack on the left flank of Union brigadier general Andrew A. Humphreys' III Corps Division, driving the Federals to the rear. Without stopping to realign his soldiers, General Barksdale turned his regiments to the northeast and advanced them toward Plum Run, where he spotted a gap between the two corps. He intended to drive his men straight into the gap and sever the Union line in the center. But the advancing Confederates had not gone far before a new line appeared to their front.[23]

With deliberate calm, Colonel Willard deployed his all–New York brigade. Placing guidons as the right and left flank markers, Willard formed the regiments as if "we were on parade instead of under a perfect storm of missiles from minie balls to bursting shells," recalled Captain Thompson.[24] He placed the 125th on the left flank and the 126th on the right. The 111th was positioned about 200 yards in the rear of and to the right of these two regiments to act as a reserve. The 39th was ordered to the extreme left and detached from the rest of the brigade to guard against an attack from that flank.

Standing in line of battle, the men of the 111th were able to see what was happening in front of them. Soldiers from the III Corps were streaming to the rear, shells were exploding all around, and three regiments from Barksdale's brigade, the 13th, 17th and 18th Mississippi, could be seen advancing through the swale toward them. While waiting for the regiment's turn to advance, Captain Thompson had to open ranks in Company F to "let four men carrying General Sickles, minus his leg, to the rear."[25]

Their flags waving and men cheering, the 125th and 126th began to advance. The men of the 111th watched in awe as their comrades pushed forward toward the swale and the oncoming Confederates concealed within. These two regiments came under heavy fire immediately as they began their deadly struggle with the Mississippians, leaving a trail of dead and wounded in their wake. Being in reserve, MacDougall's New Yorkers were ordered to lay down to escape the murderous fire being poured into the 125th and 126th. It was just a matter of minutes after the advance began that Colonel Willard excitedly rode up to Colonel MacDougall and ordered his regiment into the fight.[26]

When Barksdale made his initial advance against the Union III Corps, moving on his left was the Alabama brigade under General Cadmus Wilcox. But due to the nature of the ground and the numerous fence rails on the west side of Emmitsburg Road, Wilcox had to march his regiments by the left flank before he could advance them east toward the Union line. Consequently, there was a gap in the alignment of the Confederate line, causing the Mississippians to hit the III Corps divisions first. Now, after fighting its way across Emmitsburg Road, Wilcox's brigade headed straight for the exposed right flank of the 126th.[27]

Colonel MacDougall quickly put his regiment to action. The New Yorkers sprang to their feet, dressed their ranks and prepared to join the battle that was raging to their front. But not everyone rose to answer the call. While the regiment lay exposed to enemy fire, Sergeant John Lawrence of Company H was struck in the hip with a piece of shell.[28] The 30-year-old from Cato was carried from the field only to die almost three weeks later while on his way to a Baltimore hospital.

Moving double-quick and under heavy enemy fire, MacDougall advanced the regiment by the right flank so as to uncover his men from behind the 126th. Once clear, the colonel ordered the regiment to march by the left flank. Captain Seeley recalled that "during the movement to the right, we were under a heavy fire of shell and canister from the batteries of the enemy, commingled with the bullets of a triumphant horde of rebels who had forced their way up to the position previously held by others of our Union forces."[29] Captain Thompson remembered that almost as soon as the regiment appeared on the "open ground, we were met by a terrible storm of grape and canister."[30]

The 111th was still a little behind the two front-line regiments and was desperately trying to catch up. MacDougall guided his men around the right side of the swale and was then able to move in on the right flank of the 126th. The line, bristling with bayonets, was now three regiments strong. As the regiments advanced, men in the 126th began to cheer. The cry "Remember Harpers Ferry" swept like a wave through the other two regiments, who took up the cheer as they surged forward. The long wait to exact revenge for the humiliating capture at Harpers Ferry was finally at hand.

New Yorkers fell at every step, their ranks thinned by small arms fire and canister from enemy artillery put into action along Emmitsburg Road. Corporal Stacey would record in his diary later that night that at "every step one of our men would fall, awful sight, men all blown to pieces."[31] Several bullets struck the gun of Corporal Geer, destroying the weapon, tearing his coat sleeve and bruising his arm.

Officers screamed for the men to close ranks, trying hard to keep the lines dressed and moving. Soldiers stepped forward or moved toward the center of the formation to fill gaps in the line left by fallen comrades. Newman Eldred recalled that he was "loading and firing on the run."[32] The 111th advanced with the rest of the brigade and swept past the right flank of Wilcox's Alabamians, who were now heavily engaged with the hopelessly outnumbered but gallant First Minnesota of the II Corps' Second Division. MacDougall continued to push his men forward.

Postwar historian Lewis H. Clark describes the charge of the 111th in his book,

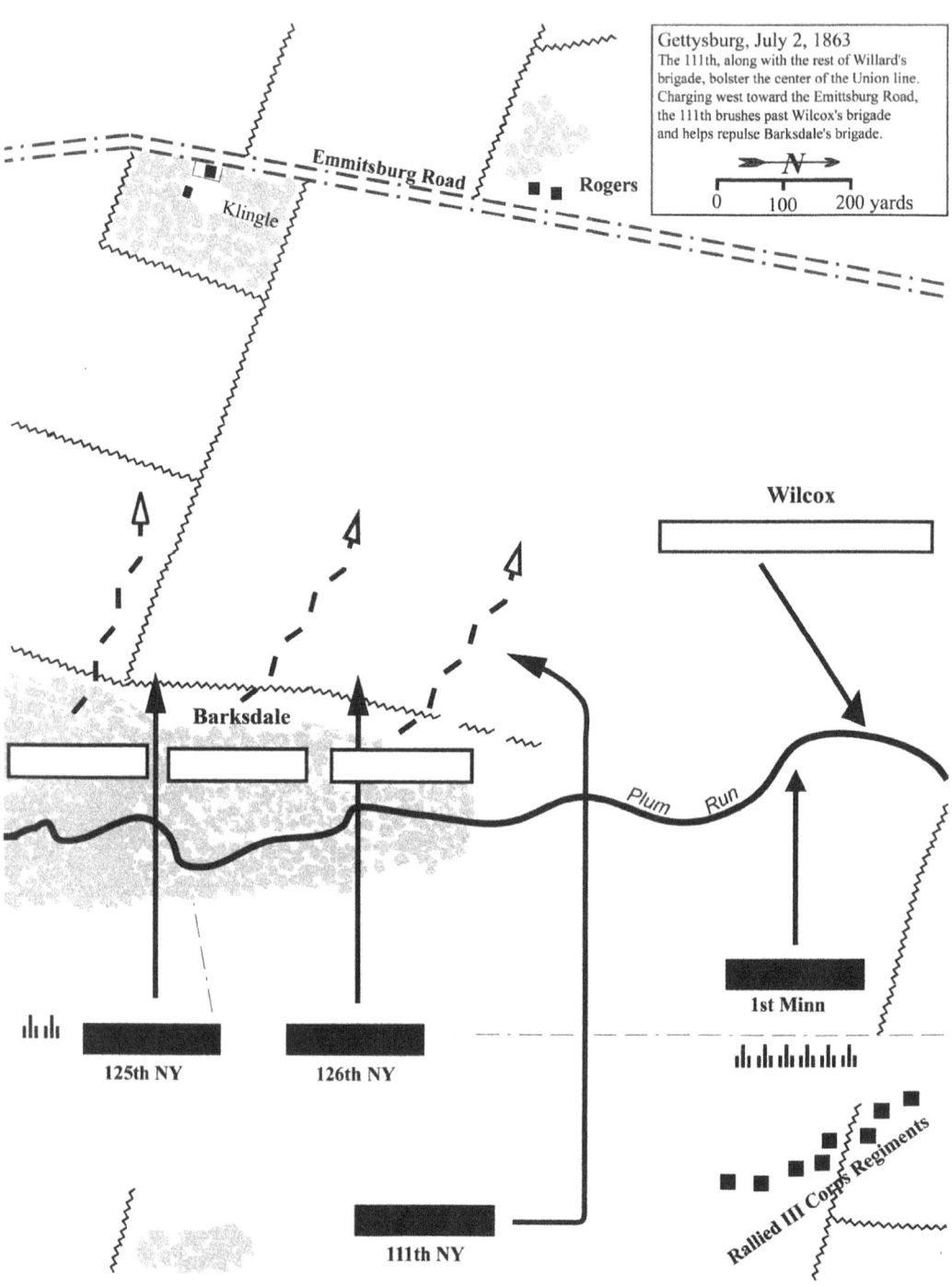

The 111th, along with the rest of Willard's brigade, bolster the center of the Union line. Charging west toward Emittsburg Road, the 111th brushes past Wilcox's brigade and helps repulse Barksdale's brigade (map by the author).

Military History of Wayne County, NY. He writes, "They advanced with firmness, the remembrance of Harper's Ferry tingling their nerves, and when the enemy were met it was with a sublime courage which rose above danger and made the One hundred and Eleventh irresistible."[33] Captain Seeley had a similar recollection of the charge: "At the command, the regiment with the brigade — not a man in the whole line faltering or hesitating for an instant — hurled themselves upon the advancing foe."[34]

The fighting was at close quarters as the men of the 111th drove the Mississippians off at the point of the bayonet. "The constant rain of missiles at this point was terrific," recalled Captain Thompson. "A large number of cannon at close range were pouring shrapnel and canister upon us without intermission.... Our brigade was a large one and, despite its losses, presented a long line of bright bayonets. As we neared the rebel lines their fire slackened and they began to give back. I have never seen soldiers who would stand and receive a bayonet charge. Their wavering inspirited our men."[35]

The torrent of shot and shell, along with the musketry, exacted a heavy toll on the color guard of the regiment. Chaplain Brown recalled that in the charge, the first color-bearer fell wounded and passed the flag on to someone else. This second man was struck down as soon as he grasped the staff. A third soldier took the flag from the dead man, but he too fell with a mortal wound. A fourth bearer took the flag and bore it aloft for the rest of the day.[36]

One of those color-bearers was Sergeant Judson Hicks. Carrying the national colors, Hicks was riddled with bullets, shot once in the head and twice through the body, and died instantly. No sooner had the colors dipped to the ground when Corporal Payson Derby of Company G reached out, grabbed the flagstaff, and raised the flag high into the air. But Derby, too, paid the ultimate price as he was struck down with a mortal wound. Some of the members of Company A tried to retrieve Hick's body, but all attempts failed due to the heavy volume of the enemy fire. Color Sergeant William Hart, carrying the regimental colors, was shot in the right leg, a wound that would require amputation. Another member of the Color Guard, Corporal Edward Riley, received a mortal wound when he was shot in the stomach.[37]

Casualties in the rest of the regiment began to mount rapidly, among both officers and enlisted men alike. First Sergeant Alfred Miller of Company A was mortally wounded when one ball passed through his ribs and entered his right lung and a second ball shattered his right forearm. Killed were two friends from Miller's hometown of Manchester, James Bump and William Tilden. The gallant Lieutenant Augustus Proseus of Company E was desperately trying to inspire his men, urging them to "stand firm, don't yield an inch."[38] No sooner had he uttered those words when an enemy bullet slammed into his head, killing him instantly.

William Brown of Company H was shot in the face while fellow company member Morris Welsh was killed when a piece of shell ripped through his thigh. Corporal William Birdsall of Company I went down when a piece of shell shattered his left arm. Captain George Smith of Company K was taken out of action, struck in the left elbow by a minié ball that traveled down his arm and lodged in his forearm. The captain's brother, Sergeant Horace Smith, received mortal wounds when bullets tore through his right shoulder and left leg. Sergeant Johnson McDowell of Company K, a good friend to both Esek Hoff and George Salisbury, was struck down with a wound to his leg.[39]

Colonel MacDougall was riding at the head of the regiment when his horse was shot out from under him. He fell hard to the ground but quickly mounted another horse. A few moments later, MacDougall again was thrown from the saddle as his second horse went down. Mounted for the third time, the colonel continued to lead the regiment forward.[40] Sometime during the charge, Henry Gifford of Company K lost his hat. The 19-year-old student from Cayuga Lake Academy was remembered fondly by his comrades. He fought "bareheaded and face blackened with powder, cool as a veteran."[41]

Corporal Simeon Cooper of Company G was struck down, grievously wounded. Writing to his father three weeks later, Cooper informed him, "I was shot through the right leg below the right knee and the bone fractured."[42] Taken to a battlefield hospital for treatment, Cooper was later transferred to the U.S. General Hospital in York, Penn-

Judson Hicks, Company A. Cousin of Thomas Geer, he was killed at Gettysburg while carrying the national colors, July 2, 1863 (David Crane Collection).

sylvania, in the middle of November. Here his wound slowly began to heal. But by the middle of December, the corporal took a turn for the worse. Chaplain Brown wrote to the elder Cooper on December 10, informing him that his son's "wound has not been doing very well and he has suffered a great deal." As the corporal's condition worsened, the chaplain again took pen in hand to inform those at home of Cooper's condition. "I wrote you a note two day's ago, and I now write again to say that your son is not doing well. He wishes me to inform you that he thinks his end is near, and that he would like very much, if possible, to see you."[43] His father would not make it in time; Cooper died on December 16 without seeing his father.

Suffering under a withering fire from both front and flank, the New Yorkers were finally stopped just short of Emmitsburg Road, close to where the III Corps line was located before being broken earlier in the day. Volleys from the regiment continued to rake the retreating enemy, who left a trail of dead and wounded to mark their path of retreat. The battered remnants of Barksdale's men were forced to seek refuge on the west side of the road. Among the Confederate casualties was General Barksdale himself. He fell with a mortal wound while urging his men forward, shot in the chest and in both legs.[44]

The regiment's position was fast becoming untenable. Advancing with its

Horace Smith, Company K. He was the brother of George and was killed at Gettysburg, July 2, 1863 (courtesy of R. L. Murray).

Henry Gifford, Company K. Captured at White Plains, Virginia, July 25, 1863, and died as a prisoner of war on June 25, 1864, at Andersonville (courtesy of R. L. Murray).

brigade farther than any other unit in the area, the 111th was beginning to take fire from the Union guns posted to their rear. Not long after the regiment stopped, Colonel MacDougall received orders from Colonel Willard to return the 111th to its original position. It was futile for the New Yorkers to stay on the open ground, exposed to such devastating fire, if they were not going to be supported.[45]

Under Willard's direction, the three regiments on line came to the right about and headed back toward the swale. The New Yorkers moved with a number of prisoners the regiments had captured during the charge and four pieces of artillery in tow. The 111th was still coming under heavy fire from the Confederate artillery and the handful of organized infantry on the west side of Emmitsburg Road. As he was leaving the field with his regiment, First Lieutenant John Brinkerhoff of Company G was struck in the belt plate with a piece of shell, rendering him unconscious. The lieutenant woke up almost two hours later and found himself all alone between the hostile lines. Moving under the cover of darkness, Brinkerhoff slowly made his way back up Cemetery Ridge to the regiment.[46]

As he tried to keep his company together during the move to the rear, Captain Thompson spied a "big, portly rebel captain, hugging the ground between two rocks." Thompson ran for him at once. The rebel pleaded to be left where he was, swearing an oath in God's name that he was wounded. Raising his sword above his head, the captain delivered a blow with the flat of his sword "across that portion of his person that was most prominently presented."[47] The rebel officer jumped up from his hiding place and ran toward the Union line as fast as his legs could carry him.

The 111th moved back into the swale and crossed Plum Run. Shells from rebel artillery exploded all around, sending pieces of iron and tree flying in every direction. One of those pieces struck the gallant Colonel Willard, tearing away his face and part of his head. The colonel fell from his horse, dead. Colonel Eliakim Sherrill of the 126th was informed of Willard's death and immediately assumed command of the brigade.[48]

The growing darkness, the broken terrain of the swale, and the constant storm of shells from the Confederate artillery caused the New Yorker's lines to become very disorganized. After being informed of Willard's death, MacDougall called a halt to allow the officers a chance to reform their companies before ordering the regiment forward again. Remnants of III Corps regiments had formed a makeshift line where the New Yorkers were positioned prior to their advance, and they heartily cheered the gallant soldiers from Wayne and Cayuga counties for their magnificent charge. Safely behind the new line, the men of the 111th threw themselves to the ground in complete exhaustion.[49]

While the rest of its brigade was struggling to reestablish the line along Plum Run, the 39th was locked in a desperate struggle with the remaining regiment from Barksdale's brigade. The 21st Mississippi had fought its way through the peach orchard but soon became separated from the rest of its brigade. The lone Mississippi regiment advanced through the Abraham Trostle farm, then attacked and easily overwhelmed Watson's Battery I, Fifth U.S. Artillery. The Mississippians were halted around the guns trying to regroup when the 39th charged. Catching the Southerners by surprise, the 39th was able to drive off the enemy, retake the guns and haul them off the field.[50]

After a very short rest, Colonel MacDougall was ordered by the new brigade commander to take his regiment back to the Brien orchard. The colonel's first reaction was to disobey the order, explaining that the move would leave the center of the Union line open and exposed to another attack. But after receiving a second order to move, Mac-

Dougall called the New Yorkers to attention and began marching the eight companies north along Cemetery Ridge. The column had not proceeded far when the colonel was approached by an angry General Hancock, "who with a stream of profanity which one might have expected from a drunken sailor, but not from a gentleman, demanded to know where we were going and who was in command."[51] MacDougall informed Hancock that he was following Sherrill's orders, who had directed him to return the 111th to the brigade's original position.

Enraged at finding the 111th marching away from where he had positioned the regiment just hours earlier, Hancock placed Colonel Sherrill under arrest. Sherrill pleaded his case, stating that he was following the last orders issued by Willard before his death: return the brigade to its original position. But the II Corps commander would have none of it. He ordered MacDougall to assume command of the brigade and return his regiment back to the area in front of the swale. According to Captain Thompson, the move back "was more for spleen than for sense."[52] Once this was done, a strong line of skirmishers was sent out into the darkness to protect the front of the brigade.

The weary New Yorkers took their place on the skirmish line and listened to the piteous cries of the wounded, some begging for help, some for water and others for death. About 30 minutes later, MacDougall received orders to march the brigade back to its original position below the Brien orchard. Skirmishers were withdrawn from the front and the column headed back to Zeigler's grove.[53]

The loss in men for the 111th in its first fight was appalling. Captain Aaron Seeley's Company A, the right most company in the regiment, had 37 killed, mortally wounded and wounded, while the next two companies to his left had 27 killed and wounded. The roll call that evening was sad, indeed. It would reveal that out of almost 350 men taken into the fight, a staggering 155 men had fallen as casualties.[54] To Colonel MacDougall, the loss to his beloved regiment was dreadful. But it almost broke his heart when he learned that the "lovable, gifted and brave boy, Sergeant Major Irving Jacques" was among the dead.[55]

Although it was shallow consolation for the friends they had lost, the men of the 111th could take great pride in the fact that the conduct of the regiment in its first fight was singled out in the official report by General Hancock. The II Corps commander wrote, "The Third Brigade ... made a gallant advance on the enemy's batteries to the right of the brick house, in which the One hundred and eleventh New York Volunteers, under Colonel MacDougall, bore a distinguished part."[56] The colonel would comment 28 years later, "When it is remembered that you had joined the corps but five days previous to Gettysburg, your conduct must have been marked to have thus attracted his attention."[57]

General Hays, too, had high praise for the regiment. The division commander related to Colonel MacDougall his pleasure with what the 111th accomplished during the fighting along Cemetery Ridge: "I saw your regiment, when they marched up in the face of the enemy's fire, and took their position. I know not how it could have been better done. It was one of the most brilliant things I ever saw."[58]

Back at the Brien farm, Colonel MacDougall formed the brigade as they were positioned that morning. Writing after the war, Captain Thompson remembered that "we cast ourselves down on the ground as thoroughly worn out and exhausted in mind, body, brain and stomach as men could well be."[59] Sergeant Hoff wrote to his wife that while "waiting patiently for the morrow I slept quite well although I thought of you when I lay down that night."[60]

For others, like Newman Eldred, sleep did not come easy: "As we lay there we could not help feeling bad for our comrades who had been taken away from us. We had been near and dear friends for so long. But we must not grieve, it may be our turn next."⁶¹ Those awake listened to the strains of patriotic music being played at the field hospitals located throughout the battlefield while others roamed the neighboring camps in hopes of finding some morsel of food.

Early in the morning of July 3, the New Yorkers were awakened by the sound of heavy fighting to the east. Fearing an attack, Colonel MacDougall ordered the regiment to fall in at once. What they heard was the battle raging for control of Culp's Hill, located on the extreme right of the Union line. When it became apparent that his regiment would not be needed, MacDougall gave the order to break ranks and the men were allowed to go back to sleep. The heavy fighting died down after a while but an intermittent fire was kept up until almost dawn. The New Yorkers would learn later that after hours of vicious fighting in the dark, the XII Corps was able to maintain control of the important hill and beat back a determined Confederate attack.⁶²

Morning dawned on July 3 with skirmishers west of Emmitsburg Road continuing their deadly work in earnest. During the night, Confederate sharpshooters reoccupied the Bliss farm and at first light, began to bang away at the Federal

First Sergeant Charles Cookingham, Company D. The 19-year-old was wounded at Gettysburg, July 3, 1863, and killed in the Wilderness, May 5, 1864 (Don Chatfield Collection).

skirmishers along Cemetery Ridge. The firing between the combatants grew hotter, causing Colonel MacDougall to order Companies F and G to join the skirmish line. Captains Thompson and Husk moved their companies about 500 yards west of Emmitsburg Road, where they took up a position behind a fence rail to the left of the beleaguered skirmishers from the 14th Connecticut. First Lieutenant Brinkerhoff watched as a "solitary tree (birch I think) was pierced by a 3 inch" solid shot as he moved across the field toward the skirmish line.[63]

First Lieutenant Marcus Murdock of Company I busied himself by distributing ammunition to replenish empty cartridge boxes, 60 rounds for each man. Parties were sent out to the battlefield to help bury the dead and to bring in any of their wounded comrades that were missed in the search of the previous night. Chaplain Brown and the regimental surgeons had labored long into the night trying to tend to the wounded. They also took special care to ensure that as many of the dead were taken from between the lines so they could have a proper burial.[64]

Fighting along the skirmish line was very onerous business indeed. The men lay upon the ground in the hot July sun seeking cover where they could find it. When an enemy weapon was discharged, the New Yorkers would look for the telltale puff of smoke and fire at that. The months of target practice the regiment received while camped at Centerville certainly paid off. The men were such good shots that some of the rebels captured later that day said that they thought they were up against a regiment of sharpshooters when the 111th was on the skirmish line.[65]

Captain Thompson writes that as he walked back and forth behind his men, he

> soon found that a group of sharpshooters were getting my range too near for safety or comfort. So I tried strategy. I would drop on my back in the tall timothy and lie still for a minute; then roll to right or left a rod or two and then get up and look after my men until some close shot warned me to drop again. I had the timothy heads cut off by bullets over my head a number of times. Finally I borrowed a rifle from one of my men took a shot at the sharpshooters who were devoting themselves especially to me. It was the only shot fired by myself in battle during the war, and it appeared to be effective, for there were three men in the party and I very soon saw two of them carrying the other man to the rear, and after that I had no trouble with the sharpshooter's bullets.[66]

By 7:00 A.M., firing along the skirmish line was beginning to intensify. It was at this time that General Hays decided to retake the Bliss farm from the enemy and eliminate once and for all the threat to his men. Captain Sebastian Holmes was ordered to take about 100 men from the 111th and bolster the skirmish line to support the attack on the farm. They watched as soldiers from the 12th New Jersey and the First Delaware attacked and captured the Bliss farm.[67]

Around noon, Companies F and G, along with Captain Holmes's men, were relieved from skirmish duty and ordered back to the regiment. Their place was taken by Company I under Captain Sidney Mead and a detachment from the 39th New York. Captain Holmes brought his detachment off the skirmish line and had the men gather behind the Brien barn. The captain was getting his men formed into ranks when Major Hugo Hilderbrandt of the 39th rode up and ordered Holmes away from the barn. The major needed to send his men out to the skirmish line but wanted first to form ranks behind the barn. When the captain refused, Hilderbrandt threatened to shoot him for disobedience. Faster on the draw, Holmes aimed his pistol at the major, who in a rage, wheeled his horse around and rode straight for Colonel MacDougall. Upon hearing the major's story, MacDougall called for Holmes to report at once. The captain related his side of the incident to MacDougall, whose only comment was to ask why Holmes had not shot Hilderbrandt, to which Holmes responded: "I should have been compelled to do so if he had drawn his revolver."[68]

Not long after the return of the regiment's skirmishers, General Hays and his staff rode up to Colonel MacDougall looking for a volunteer to carry important orders to the commander of the skirmish line at the Bliss farm. The colonel called for a volunteer but no one stepped forward. MacDougall called a second time for a volunteer, and when no one else answered the call, the "little slender red-haired Sergeant Hitchcock" stood up.[69] General Hays relayed his orders to the sergeant; have the commander of the skirmish line move his men back to a specified point and have them cease firing, after which Hitchcock was to burn the farm buildings. With the buildings destroyed, Confederate sharpshooters would no longer be able to use them for cover. Hitchcock gathered matches and some paper from an ammunition box and set off on his mission.

He kept low to the ground, moving double-quick across open fields, reaching the Bliss farm only to find a spirited duel still taking place between the opposing skirmishers. The enemy sharpshooters had been pushed out of the Bliss buildings but were still in the fields west of the farm, giving ground grudgingly. Hitchcock found Captain Samuel Moore of the 14th Connecticut and relayed his orders. Once the buildings were ablaze, Hitchcock started on his return trip back to his regiment.[70]

Just before reaching the safety of his lines, Hitchcock was met by General Hays, who stated that he could plainly see the buildings were on fire, but was concerned that the skirmish line was not in its proper place. He ordered the sergeant back to the farm to again relay the orders moving the skirmish line. Hays also recommended that, fearing for the sergeant's safety, Hitchcock remain at the Bliss farm rather than attempting another trip across the field. Again moving at the double, the sergeant reached the skirmish line unscathed and finding Captain Moore, conveyed the general's orders for a second time. The sergeant remained on the skirmish line for some time before he felt the urge to return to his regiment. Safely crossing the field for a fourth time, Hitchcock returned to his comrades in Company G.[71]

Maintaining that Colonel Sherrill was unjustly arrested the previous night, Colonel MacDougall led a delegation of officers to see General Hays to intervene on Sherrill's behalf. After hearing the evidence that Willard had ordered the regiments to return to their original position, Hays and MacDougall went to see General Hancock to plead the officer's case. The colonel explained to Hancock that Sherrill was carrying out the orders given by Colonel Willard before he was killed. Believing that he may have acted in haste, the II Corps commander released Sherrill from arrest and returned him to command of his brigade. But for Sherrill, this was the second stain on his military record; first the defeat at Harpers Ferry and now the arrest at Gettysburg.[72]

The morning wore on to the sound of musketry all along the Union line. Around 1:00 P.M., the regiment was posted at the lower end of the Brien orchard near a low stone wall that bordered Taneytown Road. Some in the regiment had managed to secure a supply of coffee and were busying themselves in the preparation of the much needed drink.[73] Captain Thompson was talking with Colonel MacDougall about the previous day's events, the general condition of the men, and, given the general inactivity of the enemy, the hope that they might be retreating.

Both officers continued their pleasant conversation when the quiet was shattered by the boom of a cannon in the distance, followed quickly by a second. "All at once, with the suddenness of the lightening flash, came a crash as of an earthquake and in an instant the whole hill was covered with ploughing shot and bursting shell"[74] recalled the captain. One group of coffee boilers was blown to bits right in front of the two officers. Both men fell to the ground, frozen with fear as hundreds of shells rained down on Cemetery Ridge. Colonel MacDougall was the first to regain his composure and yelled above the din that "it won't do for us to lay here; we must get [to] our place in line."[75]

In preparation for his attack on the center of the Union line at Cemetery Ridge, General Lee ordered over 130 pieces of his Southern artillery to bombard this point in hopes of sufficiently weakening the line and destroying as many Union batteries as possible. The Confederate commander believed that the strength of the Army of the Potomac's center must have been severely reduced over the past two days to meet the attacks launched against both of its flanks. Lee thought that a bold thrust with upward of 15,000 men would pierce the enemy's line and split their army in two. This notion might have been reinforced by the fact the General Ambrose Wright had penetrated the line on the evening of July 2 with his brigade before being forced to retire. But what Lee did not know was that General Meade was thinking the same thing. As Lee was preparing for his massive assault, Meade was taking steps to strengthen the center of his line.[76]

Colonel MacDougall received orders from Lieutenant David Shields, one of General Hays' aides, to advance the regiment to a stone wall that ran from north to south behind the Brien barn. Ranks were quickly formed under fire, and Mac-Dougall led the men double-quick, right shoulder shift arms, up the hill toward the front line. This move to escape the shelling proved futile as

William Boothwell, Company I. Mustered in as a corporal, he was killed at Gettysburg on July 3, 1863 (Massachusetts Commandery Military Order of the Loyal Legion and the USAMHI).

pieces of trees, fences, stones and shell fragments were flying in every direction. Several projectiles found their mark among the ranks of the advancing regiment, killing and wounding many. The noise of the cannonade soon reached a deafening pitch as Union gunners joined the fight.[77]

The New Yorkers made their way through the Brien orchard, shells exploding all around. Colonel MacDougall watched as "men were literally torn to atoms by shot and shell" right before his eyes.[78] Arriving at the Brien barn, MacDougall posted his men behind the wall, the regiment's right flank anchored on a lane that ran from the barn to Emmitsburg Road. A portion of its left flank overlapped and ran behind the right flank of the 12th New Jersey of the Second Brigade, which was also behind the stone wall. The 39th and 125th were placed to the rear of the 111th. The 126th was on the right flank of the 108th New York, which was to the right of the Brien house. In front of the 108th was Battery I, First U.S. Artillery.

Detailed to get water for his company, Newman Eldred found himself in the rear when the Confederate bombardment began. Suddenly, shells began to fall all around. Eldred had only enough time to fill a few canteens before he was compelled to scamper to safety. He writes, "It seemed to me that the heavens were on fire. Pieces of shells and different missiles that shells are loaded with, were thick as hail stones. The heavens looked like a continuous ball of fire. Shells striking the ground, dirt, gravel, stones and pieces of shell entirely blocked my way.... I was lost in the confusion."[79] Running a gauntlet of exploding shells and flying shrapnel, Eldred arrived at the spot where the regiment was located before he left to fill the canteens only to find a twisted pile of metal and wood that had once been a stack of rifles; the regiment was gone.

While Eldred was contemplating his next move, surgeon Benton, also separated from

Brien barn, scene of the regiment's fight on the third day at Gettysburg (Massachusetts Commandery Military Order of the Loyal Legion and the USAMHI).

the regiment, arrived at his side. Both men lay down behind a stone wall near Taneytown Road and decided that they needed to find safer surroundings. "Just as I rose to my feet to seek a different place or my company, a young soldier came running by wounded. His under jaw was torn off back to his ears."[80] Eldred took the wounded man's rifle and watched him continue running to the rear. With gun in hand, Eldred and Benton hurried through the rain of shells to the front, where they were reunited with the regiment.

To escape the relentless shelling, some in the regiment sought shelter in and behind the Brien barn. Colonel MacDougall quickly ordered Captain Thompson to drive these men away from the barn and back in line. The barn proved too tempting a target for the rebel gunners, as a shell exploded in the barn, loosening several boards, sending one crashing into the face of Captain Thompson and knocking him flat on his back. Others were not as lucky; the explosion killed several of the soldiers hiding in the barn.[81]

The men tried as best they could to find refuge from the shells raining down all around them, lying down behind the stone wall, placing their heads close to its base. One round landed near the colors, killing seven men and wounding many more. Another round exploded atop the rail fence around the Brien barn, sending pieces of wood in all directions. One of the flying shards pierced the arm of Sergeant Hitchcock. Leaving his place in line, Hitchcock found his way to a barn next to General Meade's headquarters and went inside. The sergeant was in the act of treating his wound when he was knocked head over heels across the barn. Dazed, and in a great deal of pain, the sergeant looked up to see that a solid shot had hit the side of the barn he was leaning against, dislodging several boards and sending him tumbling. He quickly left the barn for safer surroundings.[82]

Captain Thompson was lying down behind the stone wall with the men of his company when a shell landed on the opposite side. The resulting explosion flipped Thompson endwise out of line, pelting his face with dirt and pieces of stone, and temporarily blinding him. "So far as any memory of what passed for a time, I was entirely unconscious," recalled Thompson. "Yet my colonel says I came and reported myself wounded, wiping the blood from my face, and he told me to go to the rear. My company clerk, who was wounded soon afterward, in passing to the rear found me sitting against the body of an apple tree on the very summit of the hill, and the ground around me literally ploughed with shot. He led me down the hill to a barn near General Meade's headquarters and there I fully recovered consciousness."[83]

The constant pounding of the artillery began to unnerve many in the regiment. According to Newman Eldred, "the booming of the cannon, the screeching of the shells and the whistle of the bullets, it seems, would terrorize the stoutest hearts."[84] One of the officers on the left of the line was seen "lying prostrate on his face vainly endeavoring to shield his head from the death dealing missiles of the enemy, by holding an empty cracker (hardtack) box before it."[85]

First Lieutenant John Drake of Company F was lying near the colors when a shell exploded almost on top of him, killing Drake instantly. The recently promoted Drake was described by Captain Thompson as a "perfect gentleman, consistent christian and a most faithful officer, his loss was to me a personal bereavement."[86] Captain Holmes, less than 15 feet away from where Drake was killed, thought the rebel bombardment was "so hot I could not stand it there so I got up and went to the right and sat down in the door way of the barn."[87] The intense fire from the Confederate guns claimed Corporal William Burrad, and Privates James Griswold and Simeon Harmon, all of Company E.

Corporal Stacey was face down behind the stone wall when a shell exploded close to him, sending a large stone flying into his back. Corporal Geer was near the Brien barn when a man from another company decided to stand. The mistake cost the man his life when a shell took his head clear off. The decapitated body fell over Geer, covering him with blood and gore. Gustavus Ritter of Company D had both of his legs blown off during the shelling. His comrades carried him to the back of the barn, where "the cross eyed Dutchman" sat holding the bloody stumps of his severed legs until he bled to death. Sergeant Hoff was hit in the right shoulder by a piece of shell and was sent to the rear by Colonel MacDougall.[88]

Sergeant Levi White of Company I was with his company when a man to his right moved to another place in the line. "Thinking to better his condition, [White] took his place, while the soldier on the left moved into the position which had been occupied by Mr. White."[89] The sergeant looked over just in time to see the man occupying the position he had just vacated blown to bits.

After almost two hours, the fire of the Confederate guns began to slacken, and the enemy could be seen advancing through the smoke of their guns from the distant wood line. In a speech delivered at the dedication of the regiment's monument at Gettysburg in 1891, Colonel MacDougall recalled seeing the enemy lines appear in the distance: "It was a relief when the grey line was seen emerging from yonder forest. The crucial test of your courage was upon you; here you must stand and receive the shock.... The calmness and intrepidity with which their columns formed won your admiration. On came these brave men, as if marching in review."[90]

The shell-shocked men of the 111th looked on as the well-dressed Southern infantry advanced through the undulating fields, past the smoldering ruins of the Bliss farm, all the while being subjected to a horrific fire from the Union guns. Some members of Company I were still on the skirmish line and fled before the unstoppable wave of grey. Their own skirmishers advanced in front of the enemy's lines and a bullet from one of their guns found its mark in Colonel MacDougall. "Just as the charge commenced a sharpshooter of the enemy shot the lower bone of my left arm in two. I had it bound up and remained with my command."[91]

MacDougall's New Yorkers

Myron Van Winkle, Company E. He was wounded at Gettysburg, July 3, 1863, and died July 29, 1863 (Ruth E. Parker Collection at USAMHI).

5. *Redemption in Pennsylvania* 73

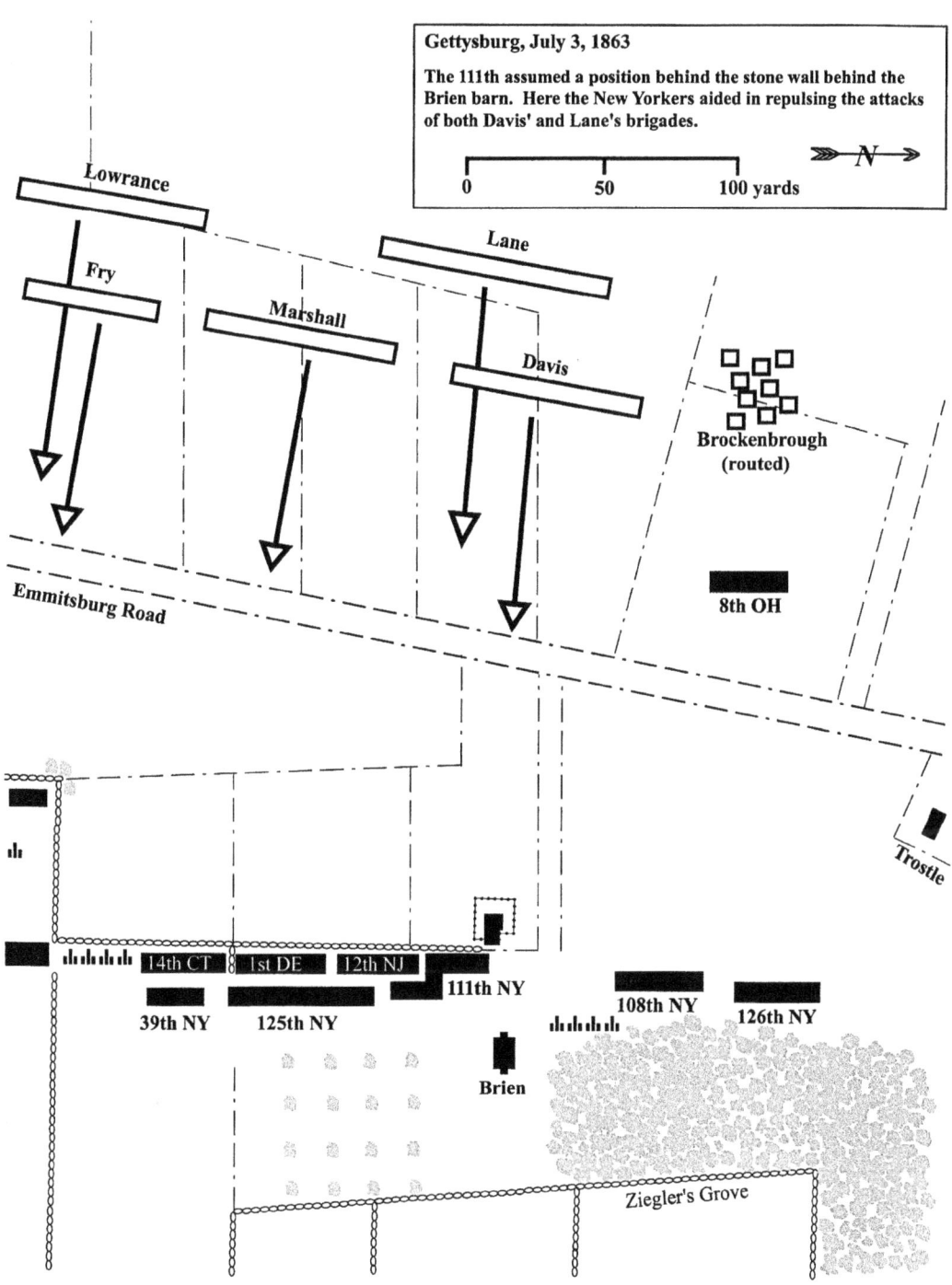

The 111th assumed a position behind the stone wall behind the Brien barn. Here the New Yorkers aided in repulsing the attacks of both Davis's and Lane's brigades (map by the author).

watched the first rebel battle lines reach Emmitsburg Road, and as the gray-clad infantry began to scale the fences, the Union line erupted in a wall of flame. The 111th, as well as the rest of the division, had been given orders to wait until the enemy reached the road before firing. When the advancing Confederates reached this spot, the New Yorkers jumped to their feet, delivering a devastating volley that cut into the already depleted ranks of the enemy.[92]

After the initial volley, the men of the 111th received the order to fire at will. "As the effect of each volley could be seen, the cheers and the confusion were wild." Captain Seeley noted that in the regiment, "not a man flinched, but every brow was knit and lip compressed with stern determination to win or die."[93] Corporal Geer and a few other members of Company A could "not be restrained and went off to the right and fired down the lane"[94] that ran from the Brien barn to Emmitsburg Road.

The Confederate infantry advancing directly at the 111th was the Mississippi and North Carolina brigade of Brigadier General Joseph Davis. These regiments had fought nobly along the railroad cut west of town on the first day of battle, but had paid a terrible price. Thrown into confusion by the initial volley, Davis's infantry was able to reform and valiantly press on. Their already thin ranks were once again being punished with artillery and small arms fire.[95]

The 111th was also suffering its fair share of casualties. Lieutenant Colonel Isaac Lusk received a severely bruised shoulder when he was thrown from his startled horse. MacDougall's orderly Henry Clark was hit in the leg just above the ankle and was helped to the rear by his comrades. Four color-bearers, as well as Lieutenant Erastus Granger of Company D, were struck down by enemy bullets on the same spot. Captain Meade of Company I went down with a gunshot wound to the right shoulder while Captain Holmes received a compound fracture to his right elbow. Second Lieutenant Samuel Bradley of Company K was shot in the left leg, just below the knee.[96]

The brigade also lost another commander. While behind the position of the 39th New York along the stone wall, Colonel Sherrill received a mortal wound in the abdomen. Sherrill was taken to the XII Corps hospital where he died on July 4, with no real chance to wipe the stain of arrest from his record.[97]

Despite the withering fire and losing scores of men, Davis's brigade continued to advance bravely. But the blasts from the muskets of the 111th were finally too much and the Confederates began to give way. Some survivors from the 11th Mississippi managed to take refuge at the rear of the Brien barn and began to fire at the New Yorkers at close range. But these men were either killed, driven off, or captured.[98]

One of those to see the Mississippians making for the back of the barn was John A. Thomas of Company K. In a letter written years after the battle, Thomas recounted what happened next: "The smoke had got too dense that I could not see the rebs directly in front of us but at my right a little in front I could see a squad of rebs coming up behind the old barn where there was not so much smoke & I turned & I fired my last shot at that squad."[99] No sooner had Thomas discharged his rifle than he was hit in the right ankle. Carried from the field by several comrades, Thomas was sent to a field hospital where his leg was amputated.

As Davis's line began to crumble, his men were replaced by the Tar Heels of Lane's North Carolina brigade. They too suffered under the tremendous fire being poured into them from the Union line. Some of the advancing North Carolinians managed to come within a few feet of the wall, while a few followed the example of the 11th Mississippi and took refuge in the Brien barn. Henry Gifford watched with alarm as some of Lane's men entered the barn. The still-bareheaded Gifford ran and reported what he saw to Colonel MacDougall. Under orders of the colonel, "flanking parties were sent out and the whole party captured."[100]

Sometime between the withdrawal of Davis and the attack by Lane, Lieutenant L. E. Bicknell of the First Massachusetts sharpshooters launched an attack on the Confederate left flank. Bicknell placed his men behind the fence rails bordering the lane leading from the Brien barn to Emmitsburg Road. His men were soon joined by the spontaneous charge of groups of men from the 126th New York. They poured volley after volley into Lane's flank, inflicting heavy losses.[101]

Not able to withstand the continuous musketry and artillery fire being hurled at them from their front and flanks, hundreds of the enemy in front of the regiment's position threw down their arms and asked to surrender. Others ran to the rear in hopes of escaping the terrible Union fire. In the words of Newman Eldred, "it was a trying time for those heroes in gray."[102] The carnage was terrible as the enemy finally ended their attack and fell back to Seminary Ridge.

About the time the Confederate attack was breaking up on the Union position, the men of the 111th surged over the stone wall and pushed toward Emmitsburg Road, collecting many prisoners along the way. Into the chaos of charging and retreating soldiers rode General Hays. Grabbing the flag of the 28th North Carolina, just captured by Captain Morris Brown of the 126th New York, the general rode along the front of the 111th and continued down the division line, dragging the flag in the dirt behind him as he rode. Hays was followed by two of his aides, each dragging a flag behind them as they rode. Amid wild cheers of celebration, Hays shouted, "so we wipe out Harpers Ferry!"[103] There was some irony in this act; the captured flag had as one of its painted-on honors "Harpers Ferry."

The men of the 111th brought in their prisoners, some 400 in all. It was noticed by the New Yorkers that many of their captives were wearing accoutrements with U.S. plates and were armed with Springfield rifles. When the captured rebels were forced to throw down their arms and accoutrements, they said that the equipment was what they had captured at Harpers Ferry and they had used it long enough. A rebel major was brought in on a stretcher by some of the men in the regiment and asked to be set down. He then propped himself up on one elbow to get a better look around. Upon being told that only a thin line manned the position, the Confederate officer uttered a feeble "my god" and sank back down on the stretcher.[104]

With the shock and adrenaline of fighting gone, the men of the 111th surveyed the scene before them. Newman Eldred was horrified by what he saw: "Pen cannot portray the awful sight upon the blood stained field. In our front sometimes 8 or 10 of the rebels lay in heaps. As you let your eye run over the field more than a hundred acres were covered with dead and wounded. In our front they were so thick you could almost jump from one body to another."[105] General Hays' aide, Lieutenant Shields, also saw the carnage in front of the regiment's position. "Around this house the dead lay in appalling numbers, and within and behind the house were many wounded and the dead who had crawled there for shelter, to die of their wounds."[106]

Captain Thompson returned to the regiment that evening and recalled years later the macabre scene. "The men lay in heaps, the wounded wriggling and groaning under the weight of the dead among whom they were entangled. In my weak and exhausted condition I could not long endure the gory, ghastly spectacle. I found my head reeling, the tears flowing and my stomach sick at the sight. For months the spectre haunted my dreams, and even after forty seven years it comes back as the most horrible vision I have ever conceived."[107]

The fighting was over now, except for the occasional crack of the skirmisher's rifle. For men of the 111th the grim task of counting the casualties and burying the dead awaited. Enduring the cannonade and repelling the charge of the enemy had cost the 111th another 27 killed, 11 mortally wounded, 51 wounded and 1 missing.[108]

In two days of desperate fighting, the officer ranks were left decimated. Out of 18 officers participating in the battle, only 9 were present for duty on the evening of the third, and 4 of them were slightly wounded. With all of the field officers out of action, the regiment was left under the command of Captain Seeley. Several companies were commanded by junior officers while two companies, F and K, were completely without officers and commanded by sergeants. In the two days of hard fighting, 3 officers and 55 enlisted men were killed outright while another 38 would succumb to their wounds in the coming days. Twelve officers and 136 enlisted men were wounded, a number of which would return to the regiment to fight again. With 2 enlisted men reported as missing, the regiment lost a total of 246 officers and enlisted men out of almost 350 taken into the fight, a staggering 70 percent.[109]

Two sets of brothers were killed during the battle. William Whitmore of Company E was shot in the head and killed during the fighting on July 3 while his older brother, Emmet, was mortally wounded the same day, succumbing to his wounds eight days later. The Wallace brothers of Company A suffered the same fate as did the Whitmores. Alonzo was killed during the charge on July 2, while the younger George was shot in the leg and lingered until he died on July 20.[110]

For Newman Eldred, the loss he felt was not solely for friends and comrades. At the first opportunity, Eldred went looking for his brother's regiment, the 147th New York. He recalled, "After the battle was over I went and found his regiment, what was left of them, and they told me he was dead, that he fell in the first day's fight and it was possible he was killed."[111]

In his official report, General Hays commended the men of Willard and Sherrill's brigade, saying that the "loss of this brigade amounts to one-half of the division. The acts of traitors at Harper's Ferry had not tainted their patriotism."[112] Indeed, the regiment had fought superbly in its first fight. The once-green New Yorkers helped to turn the tide of the fighting on the second day around Plum Run and played a major role in repulsing the enemy's charge on the third. Not much more could have been asked of or expected from a regiment in its first true test under fire. The division commander also singled out the actions of Second Lieutenant Edgar Hueston. For his "exemplary conduct in charge of posting and encouraging pickets,"[113] Hueston was appointed as an acting aide on Hays' staff.

With his arm bandaged properly, Colonel MacDougall returned from the field hospital to join the regiment. The colonel passed through the Brien orchard and saw General Hays lying under the fly of his tent. Hays called the colonel over and began to ask "Colonel Mac" about his arm. The two men were discussing the day's victory when an officer from General Alexander Webb's staff rode up to the general's tent. The aide stated that we was sent by the Second Division officer to collect the Confederate battle flags in Hays' possession that belonged to Webb. Responding in his usual fashion, Hays asked, "How in the h--- l did I get them if he captured them?"[114] He called on one of his aides to select half a dozen flags for the general. "Send them to General Webb with my compliments; we have so many here we don't know what to do with them and Webb needs them."[115]

The night of July 3 found members of the 111th on picket duty in the fields west of Emmitsburg Road trading shots with their counterparts posted in the woods along Seminary Ridge. Many in the regiment, including Lieutenant Brinkerhoff, "were on the open field all night the reserve carrying water to the wounded whether blue or gray."[116] Manning his picket post, Newman Eldred and his comrades discovered a wounded Confederate lieutenant who had been hit by artillery fire during the afternoon's fighting. The rebel officer proposed to split the biscuits that he had in his haversack with Eldred and his comrades. In the morning, the lieutenant was dead. Such acts of kindness between the one-time foes were not uncommon on that night.

The New Yorkers spent Independence Day lying flat on the ground in the pouring rain. They were trying to escape the skirmish fire and the occasional shell that was fired their way from the rebel batteries posted along Seminary Ridge. Despite this aggravation, the men of the 111th finally had something to be grateful for; they had food. This welcome sustenance did not come from the army's supply train, it came instead from a most unlikely source. They had spent most of the night rifling through the haversacks of the Confederate dead lying all around. They found plenty of fresh, unsalted beef and biscuits, enough for all to eat.[117]

Corporal Stacey and his comrades in Company D were worried about Captain Holmes: "5 of us took turns in watching with the captain, got him some breakfast & his wounds dressed, then brought him over to the 3rd division hospital on a stretcher. Doctors think his arm can be saved."[118] They also sent word to his wife, who arrived from Lyons to nurse the captain back to health. Holmes would keep his arm but would be discharged for disability almost a year later.

While those in the 111th posted along Cemetery Ridge only had to dodge the occasional bullet and shell fired their way, their comrades on the skirmish line were forced to endure a constant hail of bullets from the enemy videttes. One enemy bullet found its mark in Nathaniel North of Company K. Despite it being his birthday, Newman Eldred was posted on the skirmish line, firing at the distant enemy. A soldier from Company A took exception to the firing, thinking that if Eldred did not fire, neither would the enemy. The soldier threatened to shoot Eldred if he would not stop, but Eldred simply loaded his weapon and fired again. The soldier grabbed his rifle, stood and prepared to fire at Eldred when he was hit in the temple and killed instantly.[119]

The day passed with parties being sent out into the rain to help bury the dead of both sides. Details from the regiment collected the bodies that lay around their position and placed them together. A large trench, about seven feet wide and five feet deep, was dug and the bodies stacked in like cordwood, the top row being placed face down. Once dirt was thrown over the bodies, the process was repeated at another location. This duty was not without its hazards. A teamster from the regiment was shot and killed by a Confederate sharpshooter, the last casualty of the regiment during the Battle of Gettysburg.[120]

The next day, the men were ordered to get their rifles and equipment in fighting order. Rifles were cleaned and equipment ready for the march. With Colonel MacDougall out of action, Lieutenant Colonel Lusk prepared the regiment to move. With heavy hearts and thoughts of their comrades left behind, the men of the 111th slogged through the pouring rain down the muddy Baltimore Pike to the vicinity of Two Taverns, about five miles southeast of Gettysburg. Captain Thompson's "limbs and feet were so swollen that I could not get my shoes on, and I kept with my company by riding bareback on a broken down horse that we picked up."[121] When the march ended, the captain was taken to a house and placed in a bed. The good captain was deemed unfit for duty and was sent to an officers' hospital in Philadelphia to recover.

Corporal Geer took the opportunity to write his friends at home. He related the story of the death of his dear friend Judson Hicks, and told them that he was "very, very lonesome. We have got only 17 men with Co. A today. I am the only Marion boy."[122] Of Geer's three messmates, one was killed and two were wounded. The haggard remnants of the 111th remained encamped at Two Taverns until July 7, when it started with the rest of the II Corps in pursuit of Lee's retreating army.

Chapter 6

With Pride to Bristoe

Our regiment is now a pitiful sight.[1]

"We have been short of rations for the last two days … we started away this morning without anything to eat."[2] Sergeant Hoff wrote these words to his wife from Taneytown, Maryland, after a march of almost 20 miles in a steady rain. Here the men were issued their first rations in more than a week. Despite the rain, small fires began to pop up all around camp as food was cooked and coffee boiled.

The men were up and moving toward Frederick City very early the next morning. "At 5:30 A.M. ordered to strike tents and be ready to move," recalled Corporal Stacey. "Sat in the rain until 6:30 A.M., when we started for Frederick City. Oh what marching, awful muddy & the rain pouring down in torrents."[3] It was on the march that the New Yorkers received the happy news that Vicksburg, Mississippi, had fallen to Union forces under General Ulysses Grant. Edward Holcombe made note of the decisive Union victory in his diary with a simple passage, "Vicksburgh surrendered today thank god and take courage."[4]

Drummers beat the long roll at 3:30 A.M. on the morning of July 9 and the wet and tired New Yorkers took their place in line. The regiment pushed through Frederick City to waving crowds and the sound of bands playing. Pressing on, the regiment headed west toward the mountains, reaching the town of Burkittsville at dusk. Many, like Corporal Stacey, thought they would "stop for the night but we had to cross the mountain" at Crampton's Gap and proceed into Pleasant Valley before they could camp for the night.[5]

Not everyone could keep up with the regiment. Still suffering from the effects of the Gettysburg campaign, Newman Eldred had asked surgeon Vosburgh for permission to ride in a wagon at the start of the day's march. The doctor refused. Eldred recalled, "I made up my mind to fall out the first chance I got and follow on as best I could; if not die on the road."[6] When the opportunity presented itself, Eldred dropped out of the ranks, lay down under a large tree and was soon sound asleep. When he awoke, Eldred was greeted by fellow Company H member William Fynmore. The private had also fallen behind due to exhaustion.

Together, the two soldiers made their way slowly into Frederick City, where they soon went their separate ways. Eldred was invited into the house of a local family for dinner, where "as soon as I was through, they escorted me to a couch. I hesitated for I was lousy as a beggar and told them so but I had to sit and tell them of the great battle."[7] Taking leave of his hosts after hours of reliving the fight, Eldred reported to a local hospital. He spent a few more days in Frederick before being transferred with about 50 other men to a hospital in Baltimore.

One day, as he was bathing in Baltimore harbor, Eldred heard a familiar voice calling his name. "I could not believe my eyes. It was my brother whom I supposed was killed at Gettysburg, standing on the dock. I could not speak for a moment and then regardless of my nude condition I bolted for the dock and ran to meet and embrace him, my long lost brother Joe."[8] Eldred learned that during the first day's battle, his brother's knapsack was struck by a piece of shell. The resulting impact knocked him to the ground, causing his comrades to think he was killed.

The stay in Baltimore did Eldred a world of good. His improved health caused in him a desire "to go back to my own regiment where all the old friends and school mates were. I sent in my application to go to the front. Instead of sending me back to my old company they transferred me to Co. D 1st Reg't Veterans Reserve Corps as being unable to stand the fatigues of long marches at the front."[9] His days of fighting with the 111th were over.

The sun finally came out on July 10 and found the regiment moving west along the muddy roads of western Maryland heading with the rest of the army for the Potomac River. The pace of this day's march was not as hurried as the previous day, the regiment only advancing about six miles. After crossing Antietam Creek, camp was established for the night on the battlefield of the previous September. The men were moving before sunrise the next morning, and like the day before, little progress was made. By day's end, the New Yorkers found themselves in line of battle astride the Williamsport Turnpike, the main road leading into Williamsport from Hagerstown.[10]

Under cover of darkness, the Confederates had vacated their lines around Gettysburg on the rainy night of July 4. General Lee's plan for withdrawing from Pennsylvania called for his army to retreat to Williamsport, Maryland, where supplies sent from Winchester would meet his battered foot soldiers. With fresh provisions, the army would then cross the Potomac River into Virginia and move to the safety of the south side of the Rappahannock River. But when his infantry arrived in Williamsport three days later, they found the river had risen above its banks from all the recent rains. They also discovered that Union cavalry had destroyed the pontoon bridges left behind at the beginning of the campaign, the same bridges they intended to use if they needed to retreat from Pennsylvania. The Confederate commander would have to wait until new bridges could be built or the waters subsided enough to allow his soldiers to ford the river.[11]

Not one to let his army remain idle for too long, Lee set his men to work constructing a formidable line of fieldworks. With the left flank of the line less than a mile west of Hagerstown, the works were built to take advantage of the naturally rolling terrain as they ran south. The right flank, about a half mile from the Potomac River, ended on a hill overlooking the Clagett farm. Once complete, the soldiers of the Army of Northern Virginia waited for the Army of the Potomac to make an appearance.[12]

While Lee's plan was to cross safely into Virginia, General Meade intended to intercept the invading army before it had a chance to escape. To this end, Meade divided his army into three wings, each wing following a different path to Williamsport. It was here that the Union commander believed was the most likely crossing place for the Confederate army. He would trap the rebels against the river and destroy the Army of Northern Virginia once and for all. But heavy rains turned the roads into quagmires, slowing his columns. Meade also had to contend with exhausted men and animals, both being pushed to their limits. The final obstacle to Meade was an impatient administration in Washington that continually pushed him to attack. By the time the Army of the Potomac arrived outside of Williamsport, the rebels had already been there at least four days.[13]

As the regiment camped along the Williamsport Turnpike, a delegation from Auburn was making its way south toward Gettysburg. The party consisted of Charles A. Lee, Benjamin Snow, Solomon Meyers and Captain Edward Thomas, formerly commander of the regiment's Company C. These men brought with them a "liberal supply of lint, bandages, dried fruit and wine," along with other items provided by the Ladies Union Aid Society of Auburn, and intended for the wounded men of the 111th.[14] Along with the provisions, the delegation brought $600 in cash to purchase any additional supplies needed to ensure the comfort of their soldiers. Not long after the party left Auburn, the citizens of Ledyard and Aurora raised over $1,600 which they used to buy items for the wounded. The townspeople were able to fill five trunks with supplies, which they sent on to Gettysburg.

On July 12, the 111th advanced toward the enemy's lines and threw up a line of works. They labored to flashes of lighting as the heavens again opened and a drenching rain fell. To protect the front of the regiment, Lieutenant Colonel Lusk ordered a strong line of skirmishers to be posted. No sooner were the men in position than a lively exchange of fire began, neither side taking any casualties.[15]

The next morning, the works were abandoned and a slow advance toward the enemy's line commenced. The column halted within half a mile of the rebels, and the men were immediately put to work constructing another line of fieldworks. John Paylor's diary entry for July 13 best describes the day's activities: "We advanced our line of battle again. Going to dig rifle pits. Nasty day."[16] Although not happy with the continuous digging of trenches, Corporal Stacey noted in his diary that the "boys feel very well at the idea of having something to fight behind."[17]

At the same time the New Yorkers were laboring in the wet Maryland soil, General Meade was making plans to conduct a reconnaissance early the next morning. The purpose was to ascertain the strength of the enemy's position and determine where they could be breached. This reconnaissance was to include troops from the II, V, VI and XII corps. But while Meade was planning his movements for the next day, General Lee was conducting a movement of his own. His engineers had finally finished their work and the bulk of the Army of Northern Virginia was silently crossing the river on a makeshift bridge to the safety of the Virginia soil. The Southerners had escaped once again.[18]

The 111th moved into Williamsport on the morning of July 14, and the men got a splendid view of the abandoned rebel works. The joy of not assaulting a fortified enemy position was tempered with the knowledge that Lee and his rebel army had escaped. According to Corporal Stacey, "news came that he [Lee] had escaped & that we could have taken him as well as not, if we had only advanced. My god I am sick of this war, 150 mile walk for nothing. The boys all furious & swear they will not march a rod."[19] But march they did, this time to Falling Waters, a town on the Potomac River. Camp was established for the night, and the men drew three days' rations.

The next day's march began before sunrise. Passing through Sharpsburg, and heading toward the Potomac River, the column turned south onto the C & O Canal towpath and proceeded to within a few miles of Harpers Ferry. Some of the men took the opportunity to bathe in the Potomac River, washing off almost three weeks of dirt and grime.[20]

All the marching, coupled with the foul weather, had exacted a heavy toll on the men, not the least of which was Captain Frank Rich of Company H. Surgeon Vosburgh found Captain Rich to be "suffering from intermittent fever and has so suffered for the past sixty days and is wholly unfit for duty and in my opinion a change of climate is necessary to prevent permanent disability."[21] A few days later, Captain Rich was headed back to Cayuga County on a 30-day medical leave of absence.

The regiment remained along the Potomac River for the next three days, when Lieutenant Colonel Lusk led the 111th across the Potomac on a pontoon bridge into Harpers Ferry and then across the Shenandoah River and back into Virginia. The New Yorkers advanced up the steep slopes of Loudoun Heights, descended into the valley below, and marched south at an easy pace to Hillsboro where camp was made for the night. Here John Paylor was able to forage a lamb, a pig and some milk, a welcome addition to the usual fare of hardtack and saltpork.[22] Corporal Stacey marveled that the valley contained "blackberries by the bushel. Picked 3 or 4 quarts for my own use ... had berries in every style for supper."[23]

The march in the hot July sun continued midmorning the next day. All of the endless maneuvering gave Sergeant Hoff time to reflect on the failure to trap the Confederate army at Williamsport: "Lee no doubt is west of us. His object will be to cross the Blue Ridge through some of the gaps. We are within a few miles of the first one which is Snickers Gap. And we are to watch him I suppose. So that he can give us the slip again."[24]

After a few days of welcome rest, the pursuit of Lee's army began anew. The Third Brigade was assigned to guard the II Corps wagon trains, an onerous duty despised by all. The regiment passed through Woodgrove, Bloomfield, Paris, Linden and Markham Station before arriving at Manassas Gap on July 23. Here General Meade planned to surprise and attack the flank of the Confederate army. But due to a lackluster effort on the part of III Corps troops, the plan failed and, as Sergeant Hoff predicted, the rebels slipped out of the trap and got away.

The men were up before the sun on the morning of July 25 and had just enough time to cook breakfast before the command to fall in was given. Lieutenant Colonel Lusk led the column for White Plains, with the wagon train in tow. What had started out as an unusually cool morning rapidly turned into a typically hot July afternoon. The men suffered terribly from the heat and the line of march was littered with those unable to keep up with the regiment. After advancing almost 15 miles, the 111th reached White Plains and made camp for the night. Some of the exhausted men built fires to cook their rations while others simply fell to the ground and slipped quickly into blissful sleep.[25]

Sergeant Hoff ventured out of camp to pick from the numerous blackberry bushes that surrounded the camp. "I went down to a creek which run through the woods. There were two boys from our company with me. Henry Gifford and Abram Anderson. We marched through the brook and I got through first. I then went a few rods and I soon got my cup full just then the two came out and went to eating berries also. I came in camp and they have not come in yet. The supposition is that the guerrillas have picked them up and that to within 80 rods of camp."[26] Hoff was correct. Both Gifford and

Anderson were captured and sent south as prisoners of war. While Anderson would later be paroled, young Henry Gifford, remembered by his comrades for his bravery at the recent battle, would die less than a year later at Andersonville.

Warrenton Junction was the next destination for the Army of the Potomac. Finally relieved of the wagon train, the New Yorkers fell into ranks on July 24 and made their way southeast for the town located along the tracks of the Orange and Alexandria Railroad.[27] The day quickly turned hot and men began to straggle from the ranks. When the city limits were reached late in the day, the men straightened their tired bodies, dressed their dusty ranks and marched in step as if on parade. With flags flying and the regimental band playing, the 111th made its way through town as the curious townspeople looked on. The column continued a mile beyond the city when the halt was called and camp was established for the night. All the pomp and ceremony belied the fact that the men were suffering terribly. A large number of men had fallen out of ranks during the march; a few even died from the severe heat. Corporal Stacey recalled, "The roads were just lined with the poor fellows."[28]

The regiment remained in camp the next day. Rifles were cleaned, brass belt plates polished, uniforms mended and socks darned. But most importantly, the men were able to bathe for the first time since leaving Sandy Hook almost ten days before. Their filthy condition had left them vulnerable to the enemy of both armies, lice. Hardly a day went by that a soldier was not seen in camp scratching one part of his body or another, trying to get to the offensive critters. According to surgeon Benton, no one was immune from infestation. "I find that they range over the high in authority as well as the low. I have washed myself all over and found them the same day at night so friendly are they."[29]

While camped at Warrenton Junction, Corporal Stacey received welcome news. "Got orders to be ready to start for home this morning. Bully for that."[30] Stacey was ordered to Elmira for recruiting duty, where he would assist in raising and drilling new soldiers. After a leisurely journey of two days, Stacey reported to Barracks Number 1 in Elmira and began what would turn into a three month reprieve from field service. As Stacey was heading north, newly commissioned Second Lieutenant Warren Smith arrived in camp. Smith had served two years with the 13th New York Infantry as a private and was there to take command of Company F. That company had been without an officer since Captain Thompson was unable to stay with the regiment on the march away from Gettysburg.

After almost a four-day respite, the regiment fell into ranks and marched out of camp, continuing to chase Lee's army around the Virginia countryside. All of the marching and maneuvering accomplished nothing more than wearing out shoes, fatiguing the men, and adding more names to the rolls of the sick list. By August 2 the regiment stopped and set up camp along the banks of Elk Creek.[31]

Some of those absent since the battle of Gettysburg began to slowly return to the ranks. Among them was surgeon Benton. Leaving the Pennsylvania town on July 29 with "orders to report to my regiment with the least possible delay," the doctor procured a horse and saddle and, accompanied by Chaplain Brown, made his way south.[32] Along the way, Benton was stricken with dysentery and was forced to make several stops. Finding it increasingly difficult to go on, the good doctor received a pass to remain in Washington for ten days. After staying just eight, Benton felt well enough to continue his journey and finally caught up to the 111th at Elk Creek. He was aghast by the condition of the men, who were exhausted, poorly shod, and in desperate need of rest.[33]

On August 8, Brigadier General Joshua T. Owen arrived in camp to take command of the old Harpers Ferry brigade. Owen was a veteran of the bloody fighting on the Peninsula and a well-liked fighting general. The II Corps also received a new commander. Brigadier General William Hays, who commanded the corps since it marched away from Gettysburg, was replaced by Major General Governeur Warren of the V Corps. Warren assumed command of the corps with full knowledge that he would lead it until General Hancock's return.[34]

A week after Generals Owen and Warren arrived to assume their new commands, Colonel MacDougall arrived in camp, fully recovered, and ready to once again lead his regiment. He brought with him James Hinman to fill the long vacant rank of major. Hinman had served as a captain in MacDougall's old regiment, the 75th New York. He was actually appointed to the position of major on July 1 but had been unable to leave New Orleans and join his new regiment until now. The men in Company A wondered how Captain Seeley would take the appointment of another officer to the position that many felt he had earned and more than deserved.[35]

For his actions at Gettysburg, Sergeant Hitchcock received high praise from his division commander. In a letter to the governor of New York dated August 15, General Hays wrote, "I conceive it my duty to call your attention to the conduct of Sergeant C[harles] A. Hitchcock of the 111th Regiment of your state. His gallantry and daring were most conspicuous, in the different engagements at Gettysburg, especially on the 3rd July fell under my notice. A volunteer was demanded to go forward under a galling fire of the enemy to burn a house and barn. Sergeant Hitchcock answered the call, and accomplished his mission most successfully, but not to himself, as he was seriously wounded. I refer this to his immediate commanding officer who can answer for his previous good conduct and standing in his regiment, and request that your excellency, if within your power, will recognize his merits by conferring upon him a subaltern commission."[36] Hitchcock would get his commission but not for another three months.

August 21 caused many of the men to reflect on the events of the past 12 months. It was exactly a year to the day that the regiment mustered into Federal service in front of the Western Exchange Hotel. Since that time, the New Yorkers were unwilling participants in the siege and capture of Harpers Ferry, endured the hardships of Camp Douglas, gave their all at Gettysburg and marched all over the Virginia chasing the illusive Confederate army. Mustering over 1,000 men the previous August, the eight companies currently with the regiment could now only assemble 131 men for duty.[37]

On the last day of August, Colonel MacDougall received orders to have the regiment ready to march. The entire II Corps was directed to advance southeast toward the Rappahannock River in support of the cavalry, who were ordered to destroy several Union gunboats that had been captured by the Confederates several days before. The march lasted the better part of the day. Arriving at the tiny hamlet of Hartwood Church, the 111th set up camp in town while the rest of the corps ranged out along the river.[38]

In a letter to his wife, Sergeant Hoff described his new surroundings: "Hartwood Church is about like all places in this state that we hear of so much in the papers. It did once have a good brick church and probably half a dozen houses. Now the church has the windows knocked out and the walls inscribed with the names of innumerable soldiers that fight for the Union. Right over where the pulpit used to be is a large drawing of a charge of cavalry upon some rebs. All marked by a piece of coal. The floor has been pretty torn up I suppose to make someone a cup of coffee."[39] After three days of relative inactivity, the regiment marched the 16 miles back to camp, not sure whether the expedition was a success or failure.

Waiting in camp for Sergeant Hoff was a letter from his captain, George Smith, who was still at home recuperating from the severe wound he received at Gettysburg. Smith wrote, "He would not be with us in some time that is within two or three weeks."[40] To the dismay of everyone in Company K, the beloved captain was discharged for disability two months later, without ever returning to the regiment. While Hoff received his sad news, good news awaited Corporal John Fishback of Company D. The corporal was promoted to the coveted position of sergeant major.[41]

August was a very busy month for the two companies detached in the northern part of Virginia. Company C was in garrison at Camp Beckwith, in Lewinsville, while Company B reinforced the defenders holding Camp Rucker, in Falls Church. Each company scouted the areas around their forts continually, often times returning with horses and rebel prisoners. It was not uncommon for the two companies to be attacked at least once a month by Confederate colonel John S. Mosby and his band of guerillas.[42]

As the rest of the 111th continued regular camp duties along Elk Run, tensions were mounting in Tennessee. Union general William S. Rosecrans and his Army of the Cumberland were poised to march into northern Georgia. Standing in his way was Braxton Bragg and the Army of Tennessee. While his army was strong, Bragg was concerned that he would not be able to stop the invaders and appealed to Richmond for help. After much deliberation, it was decided that one corps from the Army of Northern Virginia would be sent by rail to reinforce their counterparts in Tennessee. The corps being sent to Bragg was Longstreet's First Corps, which began leaving Virginia on September 7.[43]

Orders to break camp along Elk Run finally arrived around the middle of September. Knapsacks were packed and tents struck as the 111th prepared to resume active campaigning. General Meade had received information of Longstreet's departure and wanted to take full advantage of Lee's weakened army. The army commander intended to fight a series of battles that would force the enemy back to their defenses around Richmond. The first step in his plan was to get quickly across the Rappahannock River.[44]

The hot and humid morning gave way to a driving rainstorm in the afternoon that transformed the dusty roads into ankle deep mud. After passing Bealton Station, the regiment halted and went into camp for the night. The 111th broke camp the next morning and headed west for the Rappahannock River. Ahead of the regiment was a strong column of cavalry, ordered to make a reconnaissance in the direction of Culpeper. The 111th crossed the river on a pontoon bridge at Rappahannock Station to the sound of heavy fighting coming from Brandy Station. Union cavalry were forcing their Southern counterparts out of the station, capturing three pieces of artillery and a number of prisoners in the process. As the sun set for the day, the 111th arrived at the outskirts of Culpeper.[45]

Here the men were able to avail themselves of the local hospitality. John Paylor "got some peaches. Had to pay 2 cents a piece" while his comrades secured potatoes and other delicacies.[46] After spending three leisurely days in camp outside of town, Colonel MacDougall was ordered to march his regiment along with the rest of the Third Brigade south toward Cedar Mountain. The 111th moved through Culpeper with flags flying, and the regimental band playing. All agreed that it had probably once been a beautiful city, although John Paylor noted that "many of the houses are deserted and things are torn to pieces."⁴⁷ The regiment pushed on until making camp on the eastern slope of Cedar Mountain. Picket posts were established just outside of camp along Crooked Run and the rebel pickets within sight just across the run.⁴⁸

The next day dawned rainy and miserable. All was quiet along the picket line when suddenly the Confederates made a dash for the regiment's line. The picket line erupted in a volley as Union cavalry charged across the creek and chased the rebel infantry back to their lines. As their infantry was falling back, rebel artillery opened a furious shelling and the Union cavalry was forced to retire. Things soon quieted down and the stalemate along Crooked Run resumed.⁴⁹

On the morning of September 21, Colonel MacDougall was once again directed to move his regiment south. Marching with the rest of the brigade, the New Yorkers moved to within a mile of the Rapidan River, where the regiment arrived and made camp. While the location of the regiment's camp changed, the duty did not. Picket posts were established along the river, within sight of their counterparts on the other side. Shots were traded back-and-forth but the regiment suffered no casualties.⁵⁰

While the men on picket duty were worried about being shot, surgeon Benton was worried about their health. According to the good doctor, the regiment was filled with ailing soldiers. "Many men have been made sick by the hard work & bad weather." Even the doctor himself was unwell. In a letter to his parents, Benton complained, "I have been having a touch of my old complaint the Ague for 8 or 10 days past brought on by the extraordinary exposure. I had a high fever last night and I have taken considerable Quinine to-day so that I think I shall break it up. Exposure to wet weather and sleeping on damp ground almost invariably brings on the symptoms of it."⁵¹

In response to the move west by Longstreet's First Corps, General Meade was directed by the Lincoln administration to send two of his corps to reinforce General Rosecrans's army in Tennessee. The two selected were the battered remnants of the XI and XII corps. When these units pulled out of line on September 25, the army commander had to adjust his lines to fill the gaps. On the left of the line was the I Corps, stretching along the Rapidan River from Raccoon Ford to Morton's Ford, facing south. Next came the II Corps, its left near Rapidan Station, the middle near the confluence of the Rapidan and Robertson rivers, and its right resting along Crooked Run. The VI Corps held the right of the line from Culpeper to Stone House Mountain, while the V Corps was in reserve at Culpeper and the III Corps was behind the VI Corps. The cavalry was posted at all fords and possible crossing points along the Robertson and Rapidan rivers to make sure they were in Union control for the move against Lee's army.⁵²

At the end of September, the 111th received orders to vacate its line along the Rapidan River and march north to Culpeper. The tired New Yorkers were trading shots with the Confederates across the river when elements of the VI Corps arrived to relieve them. The men of the regiment slung their knapsacks across their backs and began the movement north. Arriving about a mile north of the city early in the afternoon, Colonel MacDougall called a halt and ordered the men to establish camp. The regiment remained around Culpeper for the next nine days, posting pickets, drawing new clothing, and cooking rations. The men tried to get as much rest as possible for they knew that the relative quiet would not last long.⁵³

While the rest of the regiment was camped around Culpeper, Company C was busy fending off attacks from the enemy. On October 2, two companies of Lieutenant Colonel Elijah White's "Comanches," the 35th Battalion Virginia Cavalry, raided Camp Beckwith located at Lewinsville. Part of the Confederate cavalry, dressed as Union soldiers, allowed themselves to be stopped by pickets of the 16th New York Cavalry. The rest secretly made their way into camp and began to fire their weapons, causing "a general stampede among all the Yankees."[54] Lieutenant Patrick Welch was able to rally Company C and lead his men in a counterattack, driving off the enemy cavalry. But the raid was not without cost. Overall, 30 men and 60 horses were taken as prisoners. Company C had one man wounded and nine men captured. Of those nine, seven would die at Andersonville while prisoners of war.[55]

At the time of the attack, a four-man detail under Corporal Dewitt C. Bidlack was scouting out in front of the camp. When Bidlack and his party did not return at the appointed hour, everyone assumed them captured. But to the relief of the rest of Company C, Bidlack and his comrades returned safely to camp. Another member of the company to elude his captors was George Wishart. According to an account published in the *Auburn Daily Advertiser and Union*, Wishart was among the captured. He was "ordered by rebels to mount a horse, the horse stumbled, and he fell off. The Rebels were going at considerable speed, so Wishart quickly gathered himself up and skedaddled back to camp."[56]

Back at the headquarters of the Army of the Potomac, General Meade was busy planning a move against the Confederate left. What he didn't know was that his counterpart was readying his own infantry to strike the right flank of the Union army. The Confederate commander spent the better part of two days massing his troops at Madison Court House, located on the left of his line, for an attack on October 10. Lee's plan called for his cavalry to launch diversionary attacks along the Rapidan and Robertson rivers while his infantry crossed the Robertson River and moved against the right flank of the Federal army. If all went well, Lee would be able to crush Meade before he knew what hit him.[57]

The remaining eight companies of the regiment continued to hold the reserve position around Culpeper. In the early morning hours of October 10, the entire II Corps was ordered to move as rapidly as possible to the Union right in the vicinity of Stone House Mountain. A large force of the enemy was reported crossing the river and reinforcements were needed immediately. Arriving at the designated location, General Warren posted his infantry in line of battle on the right of the Culpeper and Sperryville Turnpike.[58]

Under pressure from the masses of Southern infantry moving against his right flank, Meade ordered the entire Army of the Potomac to fall back to the east side of the Rappahannock River. The New Yorkers retreated along the Orange and Alexandria Railroad and crossed the pontoon bridge spanning the river just below Rappahannock Station. Once across the river, the regiment proceeded northeast to Bealton Station, where camp was established for the night.[59]

The next morning, the 111th moved with the rest of the II Corps back toward Culpeper. Accompanied by a large force of cavalry, Warren's men were supposed to determine if the enemy had occupied the city with the intention of getting around the right flank of the Union army. They crossed the Rappahannock River, proceeded another two miles before setting into position. While the infantry remained in place, the cavalry continued toward Culpeper. The Northern troopers quickly discovered that not only had the rebels occupied the city, but they were also now on the same side of the Rappahannock

River as the rest of the Union army and were advancing on Warrenton. Just as General Meade had feared, Lee was trying to get around his right flank.[60]

The 111th remained west of the river until late in the afternoon of October 12, when orders finally arrived for the II Corps to rejoin the rest of the army. The regiment once again crossed to the east side of the river, the third crossing in two days. As the New Yorkers neared Bealton Station, they could hear the sound of what they thought was skirmishing coming from the station. It turned out to be the sound of the army destroying its huge stores of munitions. The army was falling back rapidly and the valuable stores could not fall into enemy hands. After a short rest, the regiment advanced to Fayetteville, which was reached in the early morning hours of the 13th. Positioning his regiment in line of battle facing toward Warrenton, MacDougall allowed the men to rest while waiting for orders to resume the march.[61]

After a few hours sleep, the retreat continued. Falling in behind General French's III Corps, the 111th moved along with the rest of the II Corps to Three-Mile Station, a stop on the Warrenton Branch Railroad. By nightfall, the exhausted New Yorkers reached the tiny hamlet of Auburn, where they bivouacked east of the city. Many of the men noted that Virginia's Auburn looked nothing like the city back home where they were mustered. Surgeon Benton described the village as consisting of just one house.[62] With pickets out, the exhausted men tried to get a few hours rest.

Late that same night, General Meade issued orders for the army to concentrate at Centerville. With the enemy turning his right flank, the army commander had to hurry his forces north and reform them on the heights east of the city. To ensure that the army could reach the city safely, General Hays' II Corps Division was tasked with the mission of securing Catlett's Station. Once this vital rail station was secure, the road to Centerville would be open for the rest of the army.[63]

The sun rose on October 14 to find the 111th trudging east along St. Stephens Road through a heavy early morning fog, heading for the bridge over Cedar Run. As the New Yorkers were crossing the run, the Confederate infantry of General Richard Ewell's Second Corps were advancing toward Auburn from the north and west. Besides the approaching infantry, the enemy's cavalry was already present in strength. General J. E. B. Stuart had been hiding with about 3,000 troopers and a battery of artillery less than a half mile east of Cedar Run.[64]

It was just after 6:30 A.M. when the men of the 111th heard the familiar booming of cannons coming from the hills north of Auburn. The seven guns of the horse artillery in position with Stuart and his cavalry were firing at the II Corps Division of General John Caldwell as it made its way through Auburn. Continuing their march, the New Yorkers soon found their line of march to Catlett's Station blocked by an enemy battery positioned astride St. Stephens Road. The column was halted and five companies of the 125th were immediately deployed to deal with the rebel gunners. No sooner had these skirmishers gone forward to clear the road when a line of dismounted cavalry skirmishers advanced from a wood line to the rear of the battery. Behind the skirmishers appeared a heavy column of cavalry, which charged straight for the hopelessly outnumbered companies of the 125th.[65]

Not able to withstand the overwhelming force of the charge, the skirmishers broke and ran to the rear. Watching the situation carefully, General Owen quickly reinforced his faltering skirmish line with the 126th, which went into action to the right of the road.

Behind the 126th Owen deployed the rest of the brigade in reserve. He placed the 111th, 39th and the remaining companies of the 125th to the left, or north side, of the road. Once the 111th was in place, Colonel MacDougall threw Companies A and H out in front of the regiment as skirmishers.[66]

The soldiers of the 111th watched as the enemy's cavalry charged headlong into the ranks of the 126th. The fast-riding Southern troopers were raked with a devastating fire that toppled many riders. After some severe hand-to-hand fighting, the cavalry retreated, taking their battery in tow. However, this unexpected skirmish had cost the Federals precious time. Owen quickly reformed his regiments, gathered his wounded and pushed on for Catlett's Station.[67]

The column arrived at the station, and a brief halt was given to allow the men some time to rest. While at the station, the II Corps commander received an urgent message from General Meade, ordering him to continue moving as rapidly as possible for Centerville. The enemy, wrote Meade, "may send out a column from Gainsville to Bristoe," another station on the rail line, in order to block the army's march to Centerville.[68] Orders quickly filtered down to Colonel MacDougall, who was directed to position his men as flankers on either side of the Third Brigade column. Their job was to protect the other regiments, keeping an ever-watchful eye out for the enemy. General Owen wanted no more surprise attacks like the one that morning at Auburn. As the rest of the brigade marched along the railroad tracks of the Orange and Alexandria Railroad, the New Yorkers were forced to march through fields thick with underbrush.[69]

Standing along the Greenwich Road, about a mile north of Bristoe Station, Confederate general A. P. Hill watched as the rear guard of Union general George Syke's V Corps crossed to the east side of Broad Run. These men were protecting the rest of Syke's corps as it retreated toward Centerville. Thinking these soldiers to be the rear of the Union III Corps whom he had been chasing all morning, Hill formed his lead division under Henry Heth on either side of the road and prepared to advance. The Confederate corps commander had Heth deploy his division with Kirkland's and Cooke's brigades in the front line while the remaining brigades of Walker, Davis and Archer were held in reserve. With the deployment complete, Heth began his assault.[70]

It was close to 2:30 P.M. and the exhausted men of the 111th were still struggling along on either side of the column. The faint crackle of musketry and the pounding of artillery could be heard coming from the head of the column. Colonel MacDougall was directed to move with the brigade to the south side of the tracks and advance along an old wagon trail that was bordered on either side by trees. The New Yorkers splashed across Kettle Run and continued to drive forward. After climbing a slight rise, the regiment found itself out in an open field atop a small ridge. To their left front, the New Yorkers could see several Confederate battle lines maneuvering in the distant fields. At the base of the hill, to their left, were the tracks of the Orange and Alexandria Railroad.[71]

The column was halted and the 111th was quickly recalled from its position on the flanks of the brigade. MacDougall had the men form ranks double-quick and the regiment took its place in line. Greatly fatigued from the long march, most were drinking what little water they had left in their canteens when a battery of artillery came up the trail at a dead run. The New Yorkers had to quickly break ranks or get run over. When the fast-moving artillery had passed, MacDougall quickly ordered the men back into formation.[72]

Meanwhile, Confederate major William Poague saw the long column of Union infantry suddenly appear atop the ridgeline a little more than a mile south of his position. The artillery officer quickly ordered the gunners of his battalion to stop firing on the retreating V Corps rear guard and train their sights on the regiments exposed along the ridge. Guns were pointed south, aimed, loaded and fired. The rebel gunners worked their pieces at a feverish pace. They sent round after round flying toward the unsuspecting Federals.[73]

The New Yorkers had just reformed their ranks when the first shells impacted the ground around them. In no time at all the air was filed with screeching missiles as the ground erupted under the endless explosions. Acting on orders to take possession of the railroad before the enemy could, Colonel MacDougall rode along the line shouting out commands. With rifles at the right shoulder, the regiment surged forward, advancing amid a hail of shells and bullets. The colonel noted that the "fire under which we advanced ... was more severe than that at Gettysburg, but fortunately ... their shots (mostly) passed over our heads."[74] Surgeon Benton watched as "we were on one side of the Rail Road and the Rebels on the other and both ran to gain it our boys got to it first."[75]

Arriving at the base of the hill, the colonel had the men lie down and take up a position behind the railroad embankment. Sergeant Hoff was amazed at the fire he and his comrades just advanced through: "How so many escaped as we did when we charged to get to the railroad is more than I can tell."[76] The 111th occupied the extreme left flank of the brigade, with the 125th to its right.[77]

Broken by scattered areas of dense stands of trees, the open ground in front of the regiment's position gently rolled up to Greenwich Road, about a mile from the station. In between the road and the station, the terrain was dominated by several small hills. These hills dwindled out a few hundred yards from the railroad and opened up to a vast plain, void of any cover. To the right of the regiment was Brentsville Road, which crossed the railroad at the station and led to Greenwich Road. The station itself consisted of the ruins of a few buildings, destroyed early in the war.[78]

To the right of Owen's Brigade were the Second Division brigades of Colonels Mallon and Heath, respectively. Heath's brigade was to the right of the station while Mallon's brigade occupied the section of the line where Brentsville Road crossed the railroad tracks, his left flank connecting with the right of Owen. Skirmishers from these two brigades were heavily engaged with skirmishers from Cooke's and Kirkland's North Carolina brigades. Despite the fact that Sykes was ordered not to leave Bristoe Station until the Second Corps came up, his men were already well on their way to Centerville when the lead elements of Warren's column arrived at the station.[79] With no assistance at hand, the II Corps would have to fight this battle on its own.

The New Yorkers lay behind the railroad embankment, watching as the Carolinians stopped chasing the V Corps rear guard and executed a right wheel to face this new threat along the railroad. Cooke's four regiments opened fire as they advanced toward the II Corps soldiers, all the while suffering under the destructive fire from the Union batteries posted on the ridge behind the regiment's position. Bullets slammed into the railroad bed, ricocheting in all directions. One bullet grazed the face of Captain John Laing of Company E.[80]

Just as at Gettysburg, the men of the regiment were ordered to hold their fire while the enemy closed on their position. Finally the command was given and the men of the

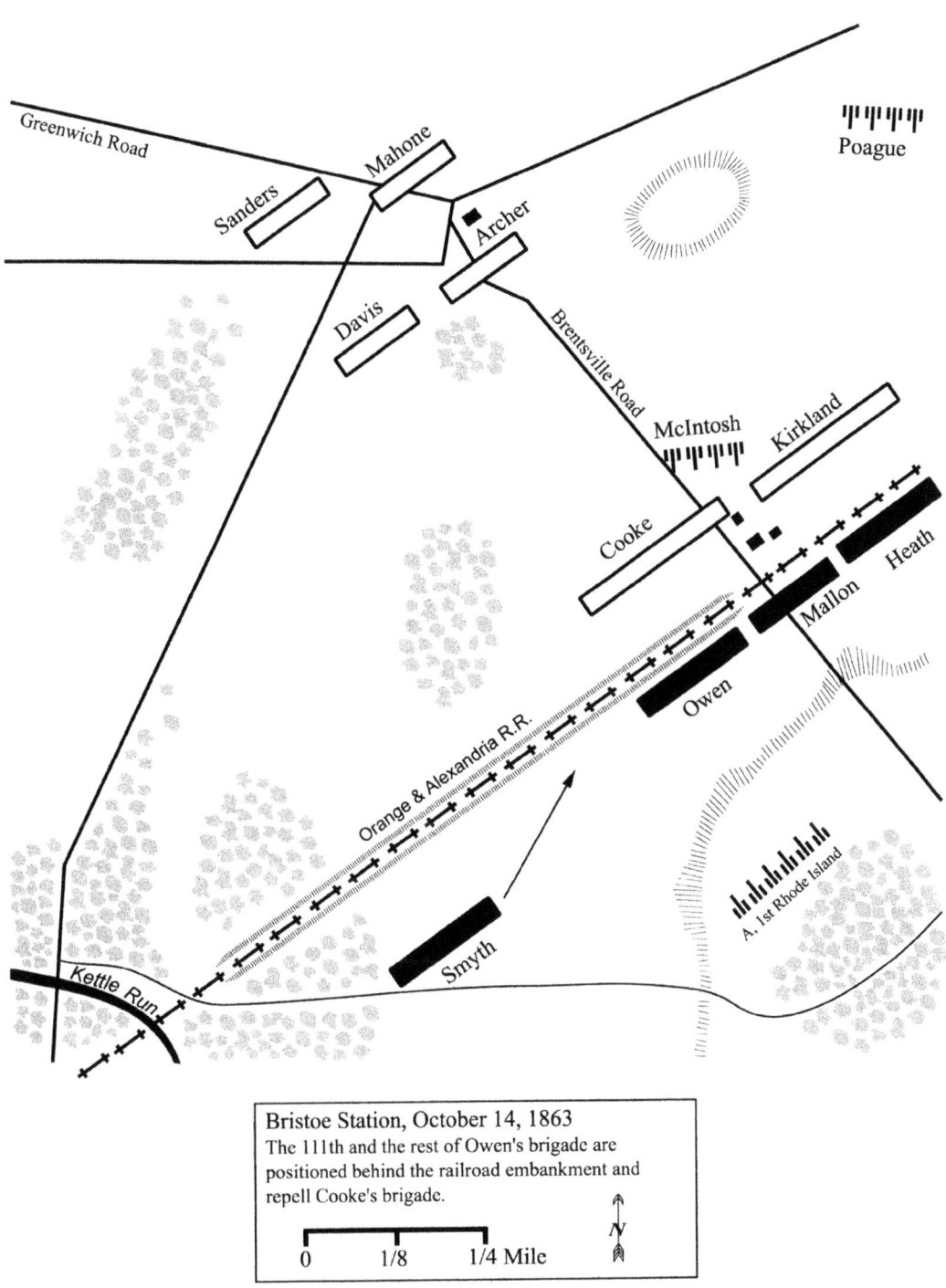

Bristoe Station, October 14, 1863
The 111th and the rest of Owen's brigade are positioned behind the railroad embankment and repell Cooke's brigade.

The 111th and the rest of Owen's brigade are positioned behind the railroad embankment and repel Cooke's brigade (map by the author).

111th leveled their muskets over the railroad embankment. The line exploded like a thunderclap as a perfect hail of bullets slammed into the Tar Heels. Comparatively safe behind the railroad, the New Yorkers, according to Colonel MacDougall, "laid the rebels thick upon the ground in front."[81] Battle smoke soon covered the field as Cooke's regiments returned fire.

While the battle raged, Sergeant Levi White of Company I decided that he could load and fire more rapidly by standing rather than laying behind the embankment. No sooner did he stand than a musket ball passed completely through his leg and hit Ebenezer Platt of Company K in the head, killing him instantly. Several of White's comrades came to his aid and carried him to the rear in a rubber blanket.[82]

The Confederates were suffering terribly from the fire being poured into them from the New Yorkers. Cooke went down with a severe wound and command of his brigade passed to Colonel Edward Hall of the 46th North Carolina, who quickly realized his men could not withstand the punishing fire any longer. Rather than ordering his gray-clad infantry to the rear, Hall foolishly ordered them to charge. The rebels gallantly struggled forward, leaving scores of dead and wounded in their wake. Finally stopped about 40 yards short of the railroad, the Carolinians began to trade volleys with the well-protected Federals. After about 20 minutes, and unable to withstand the combined small arms and artillery fire, the rebel line broke and fled to the rear in confusion. Many of Hall's men surrendered rather than risk running through the gauntlet of fire back to their lines. Those lucky enough to survive rallied at Greenwich Road.[83]

As the attack on Owen's brigade was ending, just after 3:00 P.M., Colonel Thomas Smyth's Second Brigade swung into line along the railroad to the left of the 111th. Smyth's regiments were settling into position just as the Confederate brigades of Carnot Posey and E. A. Perry rushed over the embankment and split his formation in two. Furious hand-to-hand fighting broke out all along the line. Fortunately for Smyth, the lead regiments of Union general Caldwell's First Division arrived on the field and drove the rebels back across the railroad tracks and into the woods beyond.[84]

For the next two hours, the men of the 111th lay behind the railroad embankment, watching as regiments from other brigades surged forward into the woods to their left, sparking brief firefights and bringing back scores of prisoners. A battery on the hill behind the regiment continued to bang away at the distant rebel battle lines. Around 5:00 P.M., the New Yorkers were listening nervously to the fight raging in the growing darkness off to their left, where members of General Caldwell's First Division fought off repeated advances by the enemy to turn his flank. Orders arrived for Colonel MacDougall to take charge of a group of skirmishers made up of men from the various regiments of the division. The colonel moved his men out in front of the Union line, and they were able to scoop up a number of prisoners and four pieces of artillery abandoned during the fight.[85]

The advantage of being posted behind the railroad embankment was reflected in the regiment's casualty list. Out of the almost 150 men taken into the fight, the 111th suffered only 2 men killed and 2 officers and 20 enlisted men wounded, with 2 men missing. Most of the casualties occurred when the regiment charged down the ridge to get to the railroad embankment. While both Colonel MacDougall and Lieutenant Colonel Lusk were slightly wounded during the fight, they were able to remain with the regiment throughout the battle. One of two soldiers killed was Private William Shimer of Company K.

Shot in the head, Shimer was described by his company commander as "a good and faithful soldier."[86]

Among the wounded was 19-year-old Corporal Joseph Deming of Company A. Hit in the thigh, Deming was carried off the field and loaded onto an ambulance for the trip to Centerville. Surgeon Vosburgh was able to remove the bullet and the corporal was transferred to an Alexandria hospital, where he arrived the next day. But Deming's condition continued to worsen. He wrote home asking that his father come see him soon, writing, "I have suffered almost everything."[87] With his father by his side, Deming died on October 21.

A cold rain set in as the regiment's officers passed along the line in the darkness, whispering for the men to be as quiet as possible. When the command was given, the weary New Yorkers slipped quietly away from their lines at Bristoe Station, leaving the field in the hands of the Confederates. The enemy's pickets were less than 300 yards away, and the fires in their main camp could be seen by the New Yorkers as they moved. The regiment crossed Broad Run and continued on to Centerville. Arriving outside the city in the early morning hours of the 15th, Colonel MacDougall placed his regiment in position facing west, back toward Bristoe Station. The men were utterly exhausted and those not detailed for picket duty threw themselves down in the mud and fell fast asleep.[88]

After seeing to the posting of his men, Colonel MacDougall had time to reflect on the actions of the previous day. His thoughts were put to pen in General Order No. 17. In it, he congratulated the regiment for the "new laurels won by it in the engagement of the 14th at Bristoe Station." MacDougall commended the men for enduring "long and tiresome marches for weeks and the exhaustion of a rapid march for hours as skirmishers on the flanks of the brigade, their courage and gallantry in charging through terrible fire to gain the position behind the R R [railroad] and then their steadiness in maintaining that position against the desperate charge of the enemy." He ended the order by stating that "every member of the 111th who performed his duty upon that occasion will in coming years look back with pride to Bristoe."[89]

CHAPTER 7

Winter Campaigning

It rained all day. Virginia is nothing but mud.[1]

Rain continued to fall in torrents and the men of the 111th huddled in their tents to escape the downpour. A detachment from the regiment, commanded by Captain Frank Rich, was sent to Bull Run for picket duty. Rich led his troops down to the run and took up a position around Mitchell's Ford. Confederate forces occupied rifle pits on the west bank of the stream and a lively exchange between the opposing pickets was soon under way. After two hours of constant skirmishing, Captain Rich's detachment found itself in dire straits as his men had exhausted all of their ammunition. Fortunately, a detachment from the 39th New York arrived just in time to relieve Rich's men. Despite the heavy exchange of fire, the detachment only suffered one casualty, that being Sergeant Henry Walker of Company K.[2]

Even as the men of the 111th continued to man picket posts along Bull Run, General Lee was putting his soldiers in motion. The Confederate commander knew that his battered army could not remain in such close proximity to the enemy without the proper supplies. Besides that, his men needed rest as badly as Meade's men did. With this in mind, Lee began withdrawing his army back toward the Rappahannock River, destroying the railroad as they retreated. By October 18, the two corps of the Army of Northern Virginia had established positions on the south bank of the river. Hill's Third Corps occupied the left half of the line and Ewell's Second Corps made up the right. Works were built on both sides of the river to guard the fords and the railroad trestle of the Orange and Alexandria Railroad.[3]

General Meade was also contemplating a move. But unlike his counterpart, the Union commander was receiving considerable pressure to act. Meade felt the dissatisfaction of the administration in Washington when the invading rebel army was allowed to slip unmolested back into Virginia after the battle of Gettysburg. To further compound the ill will pointed at Meade was his inability to keep Lee from turning his flank along the Rappahannock and his failure to follow up the defeat of Hill's corps at Bristoe Station. In fact, President Lincoln likened Meade's performance before the Confederate army at Williamsport to that "of an old woman trying to shoo her geese across a creek."[4] After several pointed telegraphs from Washington urging the general to act and attack the enemy, Meade decided he must leave Centerville and follow Lee back to the Rappahannock.

On the morning of the 19th, the men from Wayne and Cayuga counties left the safety of the fieldworks at Centerville and began marching west. After crossing Bull Run Creek at Mitchell's Ford and passing through Manassas Junction, the 111th headed for Bristoe Station. Early morning rain had turned the roads into mud making the movement all the more difficult. The exhausting march ended when the regiment arrived just outside the station around 11:00 A.M. Colonel MacDougall posted the regiment in line of battle facing west, with skirmishers out in front.[5]

Ranks were formed and the march resumed early the next morning, the column heading north toward Gainesville. The regiment reached the city, then turned west and proceeded along the Warrenton Turnpike. Late in the afternoon, the weary men marched into the small village of New Baltimore and made camp on the outskirts of town. During the day's march of 13 miles, the men were forced to cross the meandering Broad Run no less than three times. According to Sergeant Hoff, "there has been some rain lately making it up to our knees."[6] This caused great discomfort in the ranks as the frigid water was at least three feet deep, and the New Yorkers were forced to march all day with wet feet. Fortunately for Hoff and his comrades, "we had plenty of rails that we had good fires and went to bed alright."[7]

The next three days were spent maneuvering in the rain all over the Virginia countryside chasing the elusive rebel army, which was able to slip unmolested back across the Rappahannock River. All of the recent marching left many in the regiment to wonder what they were trying to accomplish. While surgeon Benton felt that the "object of the movement of our army up and back it is impossible to fathom,"[8] he was sure that the army would soon fall back to the defenses of Washington. In a letter to his wife written two days before, Sergeant Hoff once again prophetically anticipated the moves of the enemy: "The prospects of a fight this month are slim Lee has evidently fallen back across the Rappahannock and if we follow it will be slowly."[9]

Camp was established along Turkey Run, just south of Warrenton, and the men set about performing many of the chores that are often neglected while on active campaign. Sergeant Hoff, like many others, decided to make his situation a little more tolerable: "Today I have been stockading some of the tents. Mine I have made so that a person can turn around in. If an officer had a good place as my place was when it was new they would think that they was living like kings. We in my tent have some rails on the ground with leaves thrown over them. That is our bed with one blanket to spread over them."[10]

When it finally stopped raining, the weather turned cold and those unfortunate enough to be selected for picket duty suffered terribly. To help fend off the frigid temperatures, the men were each issued a ration of whiskey. Although the liquor did little to warm the body, it did do a lot for the spirit. At the end of October, the 111th was inspected by General Owen. John Paylor recalled that it was so cold, "we like to froze to death before they got through."[11]

Welcome news of promotions arrived while the regiment remained camped along Turkey Run. Nineteen-year-old Sergeant John Lockwood of Company F was promoted to first lieutenant to take the place of the gallant John Drake who was killed at Gettysburg.[12] A number of enlisted men were elevated in rank to fill the many corporal and sergeant positions that remained vacant due to battlefield casualties.

Even as the 111th remained idle in camp, the Federal cavalry did not. General Meade had the troopers riding up and down the Rappahannock River, desperately seeking a weak spot in the Confederate line. When none could be found, Meade decided to turn the enemy's right flank. With this in mind, the army was split into two wings. The right wing, consisting of the V and VI corps, would force a crossing at Rappahannock Station. The left wing, composed of the I, II and III corps, would advance on Kelly's Ford, cross the river, and drive north to linkup with the right wing. Once reunited, the entire army would move on Brandy Station and there defeat the enemy.[13]

Orders arrived in camp on the evening of November 6 for Colonel MacDougall to have the 111th prepare to leave camp the next day. All unnecessary equipment would be left behind; nothing was to hamper the men from moving as rapidly as possible. Unfortunately, the regiment would be without the services of surgeon Benton on this campaign. He was still suffering from intermittent fever and diarrhea which had plagued him since he left Gettysburg four months earlier. The doctor was "very fearful that it would become chronic and be very difficult to get rid of"[14] so he was sent to the Georgetown Seminary Hospital in Washington to recover.

When the appointed day arrived, the New Yorkers broke camp and left Warrenton behind, heading south for Warrenton Junction. Arriving there, the regiment followed the railroad bed southwest to Bealton Station and then tramped along backcountry roads toward Kelly's Ford. As the regiment neared the ford, the men could hear the distant rumble of artillery. A sharp firefight was taking place as advance elements of the Union III Corps fought their way across Kelly's Ford, capturing the valuable crossing site and a large number of prisoners in the process. The New Yorkers arrived at the river later that evening and established camp, with a strong line of pickets thrown out to the front. In the darkness, the New Yorkers listened to the sounds of heavy fighting as Russell's division of the VI Corps assaulted the Confederate works at Rappahannock Station, carrying the position and capturing over 1,600 men.[15]

The men of the 111th were up before the sun the next day, crossed the Rappahannock River and advanced slowly with the rest of the II Corps toward Brandy Station, where it was thought that the rebels would make a stand. As the regiment moved forward, the men received "news of 5th and 6th Corps movements, gave them three hearty cheers and a tiger."[16] While all were ready to meet the enemy, the advance was very uneventful, and the New Yorkers arrived at the station late in the afternoon. Camp was established and a strong line of pickets was posted out in front of the regiment's position. What the men did not know was that as they were slowly advancing toward Brandy Station, the Confederates were busy falling back to a line along the south bank of the Rapidan River. Any hope of quickly getting around Lee's right flank was now gone.

A few days into November, Corporal Stacey and his comrades saw the "first snow storm of the season. Put up tents in P.M. and passed away the day."[17] The New Yorkers were awakened just after 2:00 A.M. the next morning to be ready to march at a moment's notice. Tents were struck, knapsacks packed, and ranks formed. But as was usually the case, the men just stood around waiting for the orders to advance. It was 7:30 A.M. before the column got started, and the regiment only proceeded about five miles to the southeast before the regiment was halted for the day. Camp was made in a stretch of woods just outside Milton Mills, located along Mountain Run.

Believing that they would remain in camp for some time to come, the New Yorkers began to construct winter huts, many with nice stone chimneys. While he too began constructing winter quarters, Sergeant Hoff had little confidence that he would have the opportunity to get much enjoyment from his log home. In a letter to his wife, he wrote, "We encamped in the woods and I have been busy as we were at Warrenton getting up some sort of stockade to live in. We had just got in our log house over at Warrenton when it was up and away. Well I have commenced building again and maybe just as we get done we will have to leave it. So it goes."[18]

Pickets were posted about a mile from camp and a regular schedule of drill and regimental inspections was established. The paymaster arrived in camp around the middle of the month and each man was given two months pay. Over the next two weeks, life in camp was generally easy, and it was hard to tell that the 111th was on an active campaign or that the enemy was just a few miles away. The only disagreeable aspect to staying in camp around Milton Mills was the constant rain. It turned the parade fields and roads into seas of thick, red mud. But to Sergeant Hoff, there was at least one benefit to being in camp. For as he saw it, "if we are in camp we are not exposed to the bullets of the enemy."[19]

On November 17, Colonel MacDougall received a 20-day furlough to go home to Auburn to recover from extreme exhaustion. He would not return to the regiment until after the New Year. While the men were sorry to see the colonel go, some hoped he would use his influence to get the regiment transferred back to Auburn for recruiting duty. According to Sergeant Hoff, "he will no doubt make an effort to get us home where we can reorganize or do something with us."[20] Unfortunately, no orders arrived for the 111th to travel to Auburn; they would stay in Virginia with the rest of the army.

Once again, under great pressure from the Lincoln administration to destroy Lee's army, General Meade devised yet another plan to turn the right flank of the Confederate army. Much like the first plan that called for capturing fords over the Rappahannock River, Meade directed the entire army to make a lighting-fast move to seize the three lower fords of the Rapidan River. The II Corps would cross at Germanna Ford, the III and IV corps at Jacob's Ford, and two divisions of the I Corp, along with the V Corps, would cross at Culpeper Ford. The army would then occupy the lightly defended Orange Plank Road and Orange Turnpike, both of which ran behind the Confederate lines. If all went as expected, the army would be concentrated on the right flank of Lee's army before he could gather his forces to meet the threat. The enemy would then be forced out from behind his works and compelled to give battle in the open. November 24 was the day Meade planned to begin his winter offensive. But as is often the case with the Army of the Potomac, nothing ever seemed to go as planned.[21]

Orders for the 111th to break camp and move with the rest of the II Corps were issued on the morning of November 24. But the skies opened, flooding the roads, while rivers and streams overflowed their banks. It would be impossible for the army to move in this weather with any hope of success. General Meade had no other choice but to postpone the advance until November 26, Thanksgiving Day.[22]

Lieutenant Colonel Lusk had the regiment up before dawn on the appointed day and ready for the march. Each man was issued rations and 40 rounds of ammunition. With knapsacks slung, the 111th marched out of camp at first light, heading south for the Rapidan River. By midmorning, the II Corps column reached Germanna Ford, but was forced to wait for the missing III Corps. General French was supposed to cross upriver at Jacob's Ford and cover the right flank of the II Corps, but he was way behind schedule. General Owen used the halt as an opportunity break the news of General Grant's victory at the battle of Chattanooga: "Fellow soldiers and countrymen, on this bright morning, auspicious alike to our country and the world, I have the honor to announce that General Grant, that great man, has disastrously defeated General Bragg and that the arms of the western army are triumphant, and the rebel army is scattered to the winds."[23] The men gave three hearty cheers for their counterparts in the west.

The morning wore on and still no orders arrived. Corporal Stacey decided to spend his time preparing a Thanksgiving feast. But instead of turkey and all the trimmings, Stacey ate raw pork and hardtack and washed it down with brackish water from his canteen.[24] Late in the afternoon, Lieutenant Colonel Lusk was finally instructed to lead the 111th across the river and onto the Germanna Ford Road. The regiment only proceeded about two miles when the men were halted along Flat Run and camp was made for the night.

While General Meade was fighting a losing battle keeping his corps commanders on schedule, General Lee was preparing to concentrate his scattered forces and attack the Union soldiers crossing the Rapidan River. He ordered his Second Corps under General Ewell to march along the Orange Turnpike and Raccoon Ford Road and linkup with the right of Hill's Third Corps, which was posted behind Mine Run. With his army united, Lee would wait to see what his Union counterpart would do next.[25]

Shaking off the bitter cold, the men of the 111th were up before the next morning's sun and resuming their march down the Germanna Ford Road. After advancing about three miles, the column turned west along the Orange Turnpike. With General Hay's division leading the march, the 111th was heading for Old Verdiersville with the rest of the II Corps. Here, they would connect with the III Corps on what was believed to be the right flank of the enemy.[26]

By midmorning, the head of the column arrived at Robertson's Tavern, where a heated skirmish was already underway between cavalry from both sides. General Hays quickly deployed his division, with Carroll's brigade positioned astride the road, and Smyth and Owen posted to Carroll's left. Lieutenant Colonel Lusk ordered his men onto the skirmish line, who moved at the double and opened fire as soon as they were in position. Gunners posted along the turnpike worked their pieces feverishly, sending shells screaming into the Confederate line.[27]

The New Yorkers watched from their position atop a small hill as a strong Confederate battle line appeared to the front. More and more of the gray-clad infantry appeared, and it seemed that the tide would turn against the II Corps soldiers, who were holding their own without the absent III Corps. The New Yorkers had no way of knowing that the III Corps had taken the wrong road and were just then engaged with a division of the Confederate Second Corps two miles to the north at the widow Morris farm. Skirmishing between the combatants lasted throughout the day, with darkness bringing an end to the fighting as both sides settled into position. The men spent the night constructing a line of breastworks made of fence rails and dirt.[28]

Early on the morning of November 28, the New Yorkers were relieved by regiments of the First Division and ordered to the rear. Advancing through a miserably cold rain, the 111th had not gone far when their old beloved brigade commander, General Alexander Hays, approached the column and ordered his one-time soldiers to follow him.[29] The general marched the regiments to the right until they reached a high hill. From their perch, the men got a good view of the enemy works on the west side of Mine Run. While the New Yorkers were busy building earthworks during the night, the enemy had pulled back to a new, stronger line on the opposite side of Mine Run.

Informed of the enemy's move across the run, General Warren wanted to know if this new line had any weak spots that could be exploited in a direct assault. The II Corps commander ordered several regiments from each division to advance toward Mine Run to test the strength of the enemy battlements. From Owen's brigade, the 111th and the 125th were selected for the mission.

Lieutenant Colonel Lusk called his men to attention and ordered them forward toward Mine Run. Slogging through heavy woods and marshes, the two regiments quickly became bogged down in the swampy bottomland. The 111th was met with stiff resistance and came under heavy fire, bullets slamming into the trees all around. Visibility along the run was severely hampered by the dense growth of trees, and the regiment could go no farther. Without being able to ascertain the strength of the enemy's works, much less see them, the two regiments fell back to the safety of their own lines. Miraculously, the 111th suffered no casualties during the advance despite the lively fire from the enemy lines.[30]

The wet and tired men spent a long night trying to fight off the bitter cold. Fires were lit, but they did little to keep the men warm. The next morning, orders were received for the regiment to pull out of the line and march to the rear. Corporal Stacey echoed the sentiments of the regiment when he wrote, "We are in the reserve today, bully for that."[31] But Stacey's jubilation was short-lived, for an hour later the regiment was ordered to move with the rest of the II Corps to a position opposite the enemy's right flank.

At right shoulder arms, the New Yorkers plodded east along the Orange Turnpike. Arriving at Locust Grove, the column turned south and made for New Hope Church. Lieutenant Colonel Lusk's men could hear the ever-present crackle of musketry coming from the head of the column as elements of the First Division engaged enemy pickets around New Hope Church. After a miserable day of marching, the men were finally allowed to halt as darkness settled over the field.

The 111th, along with the rest of Owen's brigade, formed a line astride the Catharpin Road, which led into Verdiersville from the southeast. This new position put the New Yorkers less than half a mile from General A. P. Hill's entrenched infantry on the other side of Mine Run. Every so often, a rebel battery would fire, sending its missile into the brigade's ranks. With orders forbidding the building of fires and loud talking, the New Yorkers spent a sleepless night bundled up in their blankets and greatcoats fending off the cold. The frigid air was unbearable as the temperatures hovered around zero. All through the night, the ominous sound of axes and shovels being put to use could be heard coming from the Confederate line.[32]

When the sun rose on November 30, the men of the 111th got their first glimpse of the rebel works they heard being constructed during the night, and it filled them with dread. The rebels had built an imposing log and earth entrenchment fronted by abatis. Corporal Geer recalled, "The rebs had a bully position on the heights and dropped the timber on the side hill, threw them all down hill, and the devil could not have got through."[33] Beside the rebel infantry, numerous batteries were posted in the works and positioned to sweep the ground over which any attacking foe would have to advance. The

New Yorkers had seen firsthand at Gettysburg what happens to an assaulting army forced to attack over such open ground, and they wanted no part of it.

Orders were issued for the army to make a general assault at 8:00 A.M. The V and VI corps were to attack the Confederate left, the I Corps and one division of the III Corps would hold the center while two divisions of the II Corps and two divisions of the III Corps attacked the Confederate right. When the signal guns sounded, the regiment would fall in and advance across the open plain leading to the enemy's entrenchments. While making the crossing, the regiment would be exposed at every step to a murderous fire from musket and cannon.[34]

The New Yorkers were not at all confident that they could take the distant works. Many expected that they would not live through the day. Surgeon Benton, though not present, later spoke with many of the officers and was left with a lasting impression of the morning's events: "I talked with many officers and they described the scene before the expected charge on the Rebel works as a very affecting one as the chances of a man's coming out alive were as one in ten. There they stood in easy musket shot of the enemy having thrown off knapsacks and every other encumbrance to a double quick, officers bidding each other good bye making their wills and leaving tokens of affection for those at home."[35]

General Warren arrived at the front not long before the scheduled attack and surveyed the area over which his soldiers were ordered to advance. He quickly dashed off a note to General Meade stating that in his opinion the earthworks to his front could not be taken and that he was calling off the attack. The II Corps commander told Meade that he would only attack if ordered to do so, but "there will be no 2nd corps left."[36] Warren had no intention of squandering the lives of his soldiers on such a foolish venture. Meade rode to the II Corps position to see for himself why Warren balked at carrying out his orders. The two generals studied the distant works and discussed the chances of success. Meade saw no other option and conceded to Warren; he called off the attack.

When they received the news, the men of the 111th breathed a deep sigh of relief. Corporal Geer summed up the feelings of all when he wrote, "If our troops had tried to charge the Rebs in their entrenchments, it would have been good-bye Army of the Potomac."[37] Instead of an order to advance, Corporal Stacey and the rest of the regiment "got orders to build fires and cook dinner. This was a good thing boys about frozen." Later in the day, Lieutenant Colonel Lusk posted a line of pickets to the regiment's front, close to Mine Run. Corporal Stacey was one of those detailed. He noted in his diary, "Detailed for Picket or rather Skirmish. No Firing in Front of our lines, it is so Cold that men can not keep still, firing at such times is nothing but murder. Here we can plainly see the Johnies."[38]

The regiment remained in position opposite the Confederate works for the next two days, all the while listening as their enemy worked at improving their breastworks. Stacey wrote in his diary, "Got orders about 11 A.M. to be ready to receive an attack as they expect the Johnies to come over and see us today. Our boys throwing up breast works."[39] Despite the threat of attack, the day passed quietly along the line. Later that night, news arrived that the entire army was pulling out of line and heading back east. When he could find no way to force Lee from his position along Mine Run, Meade abandoned his plan to turn the rebel army's flank and chose instead to retreat.

A heavy line of skirmishers from Owen's brigade was left behind to cover the retreat of the II Corps. But due to "negligence of the officer charged with withdrawing the skirmish line,"⁴⁰ according to Corporal Geer, the men were forgotten and never received the order to withdraw. Taking notice of the retreating Federals, the Confederates sent a strong force forward to attack the rear guard. The rebel force quickly overpowered the Third Brigade's picket line, which included a detachment of 30 men from the 111th under Captain Sidney Mead. The entire group fell into enemy hands. In the end, only Captain Mead and six others would survive their captivity.⁴¹

The total casualties suffered by the Army of the Potomac in what came to be called the Mine Run Campaign numbered just over 1,600 in killed, wounded and missing, while the enemy suffered less. In addition to those captured during the retreat, the regiment suffered only one man wounded, Corporal Joseph Newton of Company A. Newton had just returned to the regiment after being wounded at Gettysburg and according to Corporal Geer, he was a marked man. "They seem to be bound to hit him."⁴²

As the sun rose on December 2, the 111th was crossing the Rapidan River at Culpeper Mine Ford. Lieutenant Colonel Lusk led his men across the river then up to the top of a slight hill. Here the men were able to cook a meager breakfast and get some much needed sleep. Later in the day the retreat east continued. Corporal Stacey found the pace very difficult: "Rather rough marching. Boys fell out often, the roads were lined with them."⁴³ At the end of the day the regiment found itself at its old camp at Milton Mills. In the words of John Paylor, "a happier lot of boys I never saw."⁴⁴

The stay in Milton Mills didn't last long, for two days later the men packed their knapsacks and left their winter quarters behind. The regiment marched about two miles south to Stevensburg, where a new winter camp was established in the open fields at the base of Dumpling Mountain. To surgeon Benton, Stevensburg was "like all Virginia towns, looks larger on the map than anywhere else."⁴⁵ The men immedi-

Byron Francisco, Company D. Wounded at Gettysburg, July 3, 1863, and captured at Mine Run, December 1, 1863. He sat out the rest of the war as a prisoner (courtesy of R. L. Murray).

ately set about constructing new winter huts and making their quarters as comfortable as possible. Bunks were built and chimneys added to the sides of the huts.

With active campaigning over for the foreseeable future, life in camp returned to normal. According to Corporal Stacey, "we are now drawing better rations & more of them. Looks more like living now than ever before. Boys all feeling well at the prospect of going into winter quarters. Now if the Johnies will only stay at home."[46] Arriving in Stevensburg the same day as the 111th was the regimental sutler. The New Yorkers were able to supplement their usual rations with delicacies only the sutler carried. John Paylor "bought a lot of tobacco and cigars and went a peddling. Made about $14, clear of all expenses."[47]

Just like the previous year, the regiment held a huge feast for the Christmas holiday. The New Yorkers enjoyed "soft bread and butter, cheese, fresh sausage, head cheese, mince pies, coffee, oranges, and apples."[48] The final entry in Corporal Stacey's diary for 1863 reads, "Christmas morning and in the Army, and what a way to spend it. Would give a small farm to be at home & call on the girls."[49] Unfortunately, Stacey would never see New York again. The day after Christmas, Stacey and First Sergeant Charles Catlin of Company D were fooling around with the sergeant's pistol, when the sidearm discharged. The bullet struck Stacey in the left eye inflicting a mortal wound. Members of his company collected $15 to have Stacey's body embalmed and sent home for burial.

January 1864 arrived with no change in the regiment's schedule. Everyday the men posted guard, conducted drill and sent fatigue details to cut wood, draw water, and build roads between the camp and Brandy Station. As another year of war began, the 8 companies with the regiment numbered 17 officers and 138 enlisted men present for duty.[50]

On New Year's Day, George Stevens of Company F died in the division hospital at Stevensburg, another victim of the ever-present disease and sickness that plagued the regiment. Two days later, a large contingent from the regiment turned out to bury their comrade. The brigade's band led the procession to the grave site, playing "Death March." Chaplain Brown said a few words over the coffin and led the group in prayer. With the brass band playing a mournful tune, Stevens was laid to rest in the Virginia soil. According to Sergeant Hoff, "sickness kills more than the bullet sometimes. I do not wish to be sick in the Army. I had rather run the risk of the bullets."[51]

With his company reduced to less than 20 men, Captain Thompson began to have second thoughts about staying with the 111th. He had seen the result of inferior recruits in his brother's regiment, the 39th New York, and was concerned that the same thing would happen in the 111th. He writes, "I had been a captain for a year and a half, had been with my company all that time, except for my hospital visits, and we had earned a reputation of which we had no reason to be ashamed. Now, suppose that state of New York should fill us up with such material as they had sent to the Thirty Ninth, was it right for me to risk and lose all I had gained with such a lot of bummers?"[52]

Thompson decided it was not worth the risk. He went to see General Hays, told the division commander how he felt and asked that his application for appointment to a colored regiment be accepted. Hays passed the application on, and Thompson was appointed major in the 32nd Unites States Colored Troops.[53] Thompson's move caused others in the regiment to consider their present condition. Orderly Sergeant Isaac Gardner of Company G was appointed a second lieutenant in the same regiment as Thompson. Esek Hoff, who had hoped to be an officer before now, figured he might as well try to get a commission in a colored regiment. In a letter to his wife, he wrote, "I might as well be a white man in a Negro regiment as a Negro in a white regiment."[54] Unfortunately for Hoff, he was not able to transfer and had to be content with remaining in the 111th.

At the beginning of February, a delegation of officers and enlisted men led by Captain Husk traveled home to Auburn to join Colonel MacDougall in raising recruits for their woefully depleted regiment. A year and a half of war had reduced the eight companies presently with the regiment to less than 150 men.[55]

The detachment got right to work trying to fill up the ranks. The officers and enlisted men were sent to various towns throughout Wayne and Cayuga counties, while Colonel MacDougall established his office above the Auburn post office. Signs went up throughout both counties imploring men to enlist. Bounties offered by both the federal and state governments helped sway many minds. New York offered to pay $300 to each new recruit, while the U.S. government offered $300 to new recruits and $400 to veterans.[56]

While the men of the 111th were content to let the rest of the winter in Virginia pass without firing another shot, the army commander did not share that view. In an attempt to take attention away from Union general Benjamin Butler's army then advancing up the York and James River peninsula toward Richmond, elements of the I and II corps were ordered to make a demonstration along the Rapidan River. The I Corps was to march to Raccoon Ford while the II Corps, under temporary command of General Caldwell, was to advance on Morton's Ford. Their job was merely to occupy the ground on the other side of the river for a day or two without bringing on an engagement with the enemy, then march back to camp. It was believed that this demonstration would discourage General Lee from sending any troops to help bolster the defenses south of Richmond.[57]

Morton's Ford, located at the bottom of a U-shaped bend in the Rapidan River, was dominated by a wooded ridge about a mile southeast of the ford. The rebels had constructed a crude line of rifle pits at the ford, with a more formidable line running along the ridge line, anchored on the river at each flank. From their position atop the ridge, the Confederate artillery and infantry had a commanding view of the river crossing. The better part of Ewell's Second Corps was located around the ford and any attacking force would find itself trapped between the river and the Confederate works.[58]

On the morning of February 6, Lieutenant Colonel Lusk led the 111th through a cold rain as it left camp at Dumpling Mountain. With three days rations in their haversacks, the New Yorkers marched with the rest of the brigade for Morton's Ford. Muddy roads and biting cold hampered the advance, and the New Yorkers did not arrive at the ford until close to noon.[59] General Owen was directed to select 300 of his best troops to storm the ford and capture the enemy's rifle pits on the opposite shore. The detachment, made up of 100 men each from the 39th, 125th and 126th, was quickly assembled and set off for the ford at a dead run, cheering as they advanced. Splashing through the waist-deep water under heavy fire, the detachment quickly overpowered their foe, captured the rifle pits without loosing a man, and secured the ford.[60]

With the crossing site secured, the 111th was ordered to move with the remainder of the brigade to the opposite bank of the river. Lusk led the New Yorkers through the frigid waters and along the road leading away from the ford. Advancing about three-quarters of a mile, the regiment took possession of a small hill, its right near the house of Dr. Morton. Skirmishers from the rest of the brigade were posted to the front and soon began to exchange fire with the enemy.[61]

Owen soon received word of a heavy force advancing against his front and left flank. He immediately sent word to General Hays requesting that reinforcements be sent to his aid at once. The division commander consented and sent Colonel Samuel Carroll's brigade, which was placed on the right flank of Owen's line. Not long after Carroll arrived on the field, Owen again received word of troops massing to attack, this time to his right. Just as with the early reports of enemy troop movements, Owen requested that more infantry be sent to his aid, which arrived just after 2:00 P.M.[62]

As the sun was setting, the New Yorkers watched as the Confederates finally launched their attack on the front and flanks of the II Corps line. The rebels came on with a yell, their lines dressed and flags waving. The 111th, its fire combined with the rest of the brigade, fired volley after volley into the advancing foe. The New Yorkers kept up such a steady fire that, despite being vastly outnumbered, the attack in their front ground to a halt. Darkness settled over the field, but that didn't stop the fight. Each side aimed at the muzzle flashes that silhouetted the opposing lines. Charles White of Company I had remained behind when the regiment advanced that morning and had a front-row seat to the fight: "It was a grand sight to see them fighting in the night. There firing looked like litening bugs and then to see the shells burst was grand."[63]

Just before 8:00 P.M., orders arrived for a general withdrawal to the north side of the river. The 111th was posted as skirmishers to cover the retreat of the Third Brigade. It was close to midnight when Lieutenant Colonel Lusk finally received orders to return his exhausted command to the other side of the river. Moving as quietly as possible in total darkness, the New Yorkers crossed back to the north side of the river and took up a position overlooking the ford. According to surgeon Benton, the men "lay down on the ground in their wet clothes," keeping an ever vigilant eye open for the enemy.[64]

It wasn't until the next night that the regiment abandoned the ford and marched back to its camp at Dumpling Mountain. Charles White, who had slept at a cavalry picket post the night before, joined the column on the march. He later wrote in his diary, "We started back for the olde campe just at dusk and after marching through mud knee deep most all the way and fording 2 or 3 creeks we arrived here about tired out and hungry enough to eat a raw dog or a piece of rotten beef. They gave the Boys whiskey just before we started back and about half of the boys got tight as bucks."[65]

When he wrote his report of the action at Morton's Ford, Lieutenant Colonel Lusk had nothing but praise for his men: "Throughout the whole affair the conduct of both the officers and men was such as to merit my highest approbation. Though suffering severely from cold, wet and fatigue they performed every duty and faced danger with a zeal and courage worthy of their reputation."[66]

CHAPTER 8

Overland Through Virginia

> The spring campaign will soon be upon us and in my opinion we have never seen any fighting which equal what is coming.[1]

Just as they had done during the previous winter, the men of the 111th spent most of their days in camp performing the usual mundane duties of the soldier. An entry from the diary of 21-year-old Second Lieutenant Horace Hill gives an excellent example of the daily routine of the regiment: "In camp all day performing the usual duties such as mounting guard, attending to police etc. spent the evening playing chess."[2] Hill's chess partner was surgeon Benton, with whom he would often play late into the evening. When the weather cooperated, inspections were held and dress parades put on for the benefit of the commanding general.

The New Yorkers were quite content to have all active campaigning ended for the winter. Sergeant Hutchins of Company D spent his idle time writing in his diary. He was fond of composing poetry based on popular songs of the day. One such poem was set to the tune of "Dixie" and expressed his wish to be home:

> I wish I was in old Wayne County
> My three years up
> And I had my bounty
> But I am away away away
> Down south in dixie.[3]

Yet camp life was not without its excitement. On February 11, the men of the 111th listened as firing erupted not far from their camp. The drummers beat the long roll, and the men hurried to take their place in line. Every man in the regiment was sure they were under attack. The regiment was just about to march away to the scene of the "conflict" when it was discovered that the firing was coming from a regiment of cavalry conducting target practice.[4]

Near the end of February, the regiment was drawn up in line with the rest of the Third Brigade in honor of George Washington's birthday, who "was first in peace first in war and first in the hearts of his countrymen." The artillery fired a salute and General Owens gave a speech that "kept the boys laughing most all the time."[5] Once the celebration was over, the New Yorkers marched back to tents to prepare for a review of the II

Corps to take place the next day. Uniforms were brushed, boxes and belts were blackened and rifles cleaned.

The next morning the regiment was called into line, and with ranks dressed, marched out to the parade ground. In attendance were Generals George Meade and Governeur Warren, Secretary of the Navy Gideon Welles, and many other dignitaries from Washington and family members from back home. Leading the review was a division of cavalry. Next came the II Corps' artillery, followed finally by the infantry: Richard Warren was awed by the spectacle and wrote home to his sister that it was a grand sight.[6]

While in Auburn, Colonel MacDougall wrote a letter to the assistant adjutant general of the Third Brigade asking that surgeon Charles Frisbee be ordered to stand before an examining board to determine his fitness as a surgeon. The colonel claimed that Frisbee's "attention to duty has been wholly neglected — He has sufficed himself to go looking so raggedy filthy and slovenly." The letter ended with MacDougall admitting that he was "positively ashamed to have him about my camp."[7] Frisbee was ordered to appear before the examination board in Washington and was able to do what MacDougall least expected, pass the examination with flying colors. The Medical Director's Office issued its finding on March 7, stating that Frisbee was determined to be "competent to fill the position of medical officer he now occupies in this army."[8] But by this time, the relationship between Frisbee and MacDougall was strained to the point that the board recommended the good doctor be removed from the regiment and assigned to another New York regiment. By March 23, Frisbee was gone.

Apparently, the appear-

William Stevens, Company D. The 18-year-old was promoted to corporal in April 1864 (courtesy of R. L. Murray).

ance and conduct of Frisbee indicated the early signs of mental illness. On May 7, 1865, the doctor was confined at Georgetown Seminary Hospital due to a mental aberration. He was reported to be a great deal of trouble to the hospital's staff and had a habit of wandering off the facility's grounds. Frisbee's service records indicate that on May 13, he was determined to be "insane" and was admitted to St. Elizabeth's Hospital in Washington.[9]

At the end of March, the Army of the Potomac underwent a major reorganization. Almost three years of fighting had thinned the ranks to such an extent that the once grand Army of the Potomac was a mere shell of its former self. Most of the veterans of many a hard-fought campaign were gone, replaced by conscripts, bounty jumpers and paid substitutes. To remedy this, the II Corps was consolidated into two divisions. The old III Corps was disbanded, its units consolidated, and added to II Corps as the Third and Fourth divisions. The 52nd New York, which included a detachment of the Seventh New York, and the 57th New York were added to the old Harpers Ferry brigade. This brigade became the Third Brigade of General Francis Barlow's First Division, and placed under the command of Colonel Paul Frank of the 52nd New York. Both Generals Hays and Owen were transferred to other commands within the II Corps.[10]

When it came time for General Owen to leave the Third Brigade, he delivered a farewell address to his old command. He said,

> Under the new arrangement of the troops of the Army of the Potomac, I am assigned, by the General commanding the Corps, to a command in which you are not included. I must, therefore, bid you adieu. You are endeared to me by your soldierly bearing and good discipline; your prompt obedience of all orders, and especially by your valor in battle. You have cause to be proud of your military record. Be as good soldiers in the future as in the past, and your new commander will have equal cause to be proud of you. Remember, the 2nd Corps always conquers, even though it has to pluck victory from the very jaws of death. When the war is over, and you return to your peaceful homes, your country will honor you as her brave defenders.[11]

The Union war effort also had a new leader. Ulysses S. Grant, who had amassed an impressive record of victories in the West, was brought to Washington to assume control of all Federal armies in the field. With him he brought his reputation as a tough fighter and as a general who gets things done. "There is no such thing as 'I cant' with General Grant," recalled Corporal Geer. "When he moves his armies *something* will be done. We think he is the *right* man in the *right* place."[12]

While the army was reorganizing, so too was the 111th. On March 9, Lieutenant Colonel Lusk was granted a leave of absence to recuperate from a bout of asthma that began during the march to Gettysburg. Lusk never returned to the regiment. He resigned his commission on April 2. Major Hinman was also granted a leave of absence. Hinman had contracted an infection in his left eye the previous October and had been fighting it ever since. With the prospect of losing sight in that eye, the major submitted his resignation near the end of the month.[13]

As winter gave way to spring, new soldiers arrived in droves as the recruiting efforts of Colonel MacDougall and his fellow officers back home in Wayne and Cayuga counties began to show results. During the months of March and April, the detail was responsible for enlisting over 200 desperately needed replacements. Once assigned to a company, the green soldiers were issued "guns and equipment knapsacks, haversacks, canteens, tents and all kinds of clothing necessary to fit a soldier for the field."[14] The new recruits also had to be instructed in the manual of arms, as well as company and battalion drill.

Harry Smith, promoted to first sergeant and in temporary command of Company I since Captain Meade's capture at Mine Run, immediately set about putting his recruits through their paces. He wanted to ensure that his company "can march and execute quite a number of different commands nearly as well as the old soldiers."[15] The new recruits spent a lot of time grumbling about all the drilling, and the old soldiers spent a lot of time laughing at their misery. Smith found much amusement in watching his new soldiers fumble with their weapons as he instructed them in the manual of arms, something it appeared would take them a lifetime to perfect. While many of these new recruits made fine soldiers, others were of questionable character and would prove harmful to the regiment in the upcoming campaigns. Smith was generally pleased with his recruits but observed that other companies had men that were "old, dumb, clumsy and everything else but fit subjects for soldiers."[16]

John Knapp was one of the new recruits First Sergeant Smith found himself drilling. The man, who almost two years before helped organize the regiment, now stood in the ranks as a private. Unfortunately, Knapp did not adapt well to military life. After a short stint with the Pioneer Corps, he was confined to the regimental hospital at the end of April with typhoid fever, "chronic diarrhea and chronic rheumatism in his feet and ankle joints."[17] After being transferred to several different hospitals, Knapp died in the U.S. General Hospital in Beverly, New Jersey, on October 11.

Corporal Geer also marveled at the quality of the recruits being assigned to Company A: "I wonder if we were ever as green as some of these new fellows are. If we was I dont see how the officers ever had the patience enough to learn us anything. Some of these new fellows dont know enough to know which end of the gun to take hold of to shoot. Some of them put the ball in first when they load and some of them never saw a gun until they came here."[18] The "greenies" were teased mercilessly. Pieces of their uniforms and equipment were stolen, and they were subjected to every type of name-calling. Many of the veterans tried to scare the recruits by telling them that men from the regiment were killed all the time on the picket line. Eventually, these men would be accepted into the regiment, but until that time, they would have to put up with the ridicule and abuse.

Arriving in camp at the beginning of March was a recruit named Franklin Lutes. Assigned to Company D, Lutes regaled his fellow soldiers with tales of his adventures prior to joining the 111th. At the beginning of the war, Lutes "helped to recruit a company for the 9th Michigan Infantry, but did not go with that regiment."[19] Instead he joined the navy and spent his time aboard various ships before being "detailed aboard the sloop of war *Adirondack*. I do not remember the exact date when I went to sea. After cruising a while, the first prize we captured was a schooner, the *Emma* of Nassau. She was laden with salt, flannels and shoes for the Southern Confederacy."[20] When his term of enlistment ended, Lutes went home to Michigan, "was drafted in the 8th Michigan Cavalry, but would not go as a drafted man. Came to Clyde, Wayne County, New York, in March 1864, enlisted in the 111th New York Volunteers."[21]

At the end of March, word arrived in camp that Captain Frank Rich of Company H was being dismissed from the regiment. He and an officer from the Ninth New York Heavy Artillery were being charged with rendering false and fraudulent accounts against the government.²² The charges stemmed from costs Rich incurred during the recruiting of Company H. The government felt his claims for reimbursement were unjust and took steps to have the captain removed from the service. But upon further investigation, it was discovered that the claims were correct and Rich was reinstated to the rank of captain. Unfortunately, the damage to his reputation was irreversible. With the stigma of the affair hanging over his head, Frank Rich resigned his commission April 1.

April saw the departure of yet another officer from the regiment's ranks. Suffering some time with a hernia, Captain Ira Jones received a surgeon's certificate of disability and resigned his commission.²³ His leaving was welcomed by the troops, for according to Wellington Hinman of Company C, "Capt. Jones received discharge, left in dishonor, hooted out of camp."²⁴

In Company K, politics among the officers were running rampant. There was considerable ill will between Lieutenants Edgar Hueston and Samuel Bradley, due in part to Hueston taking over the company after Gettysburg while Bradley was convalescing from his wounds. When Bradley returned to the regiment, he vowed not to serve under Hueston. The friction between the two spilled over into the enlisted ranks. Sergeant Hoff, himself hoping one day to become an officer in Company K, was put in the awkward position of choosing between the two officers: one who commanded the company and the other with whom he bunked. In a letter to his wife, Hoff lamented his situation: "Houston has got his tent done it stands close to ours. He asked me to tent with him ... it would not be policy for me to leave a tent I helped build and go in with Houston. And I shall tell Houston that I am thankful but will decline the honor. Bradley would think I was miffed at something when at the same time all would be on the square."²⁵ In the end, Hueston was promoted to captain while Bradley swallowed his pride and remained with the company.

After an almost year-long absence from the regiment, Company B left its camps in the defenses of Washington and joined the regiment at Dumpling Mountain on April 2. Company C did not join the regiment until the end of the month. The addition of two companies that were not worn out by constant marching and fighting and that still had many of their original members was welcome indeed. But with Colonel MacDougall and his detachment still in Auburn recruiting and with the positions of lieutenant colonel and major not yet filled, the regiment was dangerously short of officers. Including field and staff officers, the normal complement required for an infantry regiment was 33. In the coming campaign, the 111th would be commanded by Captain Seeley and would only be able to field 16 officers. While this may have caused great concern to Colonel MacDougall, Corporal Geer was not bothered in the least. "We live just well without them and we think we can fight just as well."²⁶

One of the many positions left vacant in the regiment was that of captain in Company D. Sebastian Holmes usually filled this rank, but the captain was still troubled by a wound received at Gettysburg that left his right arm severely mangled. In the opinion of surgeon Vosburgh, Holmes "will not be able to perform the duties of a soldier" and Holmes was forced to submit his resignation.²⁷

Drills and reviews were the order of the day. The 111th spent at least six hours a day conducting company, battalion and brigade drill. This, in addition to their usual duties, kept the men very busy. Sergeant Smith wrote to his parents that when he was not drilling his company, he was very busy completing his company's clothing books and filling out the morning and sick reports. Near the end of April, Colonel Frank was putting his brigade through its paces when General Owen and his staff rode along the line. The men of the 111th cheered like mad, waving and throwing their hats high into the air upon seeing their old brigade commander. Apparently Frank did not appreciate his troops cheering their old commander as, according to Wellington Hinman, he "looked pretty sour over it."[28]

Prior to taking over command of all Union armies, General Grant had identified a fundamental flaw in the way the war was being conducted. Whenever the armies in the east took to the field, the armies in the west were idle and vice versa. This lack of coordination allowed the rebels to rest and reform their idle armies while reinforcing those armies under attack. A perfect example of this was when General Lee was able to send his First Corps to Georgia the previous November while he faced the idle Army of the Potomac along the Rapidan River.

What the new commander in chief proposed was a simultaneous advance by all Union armies in the field, denying the rebels the luxury of shifting troops from one theater to another. The plan devised by General Grant for the coming spring campaign was quite simple. In the east, General Meade would advance with his Army of the Potomac south, his objective being to cross to the south side of the James River. General Benjamin Butler would advance with his Army of the James up the peninsula, applying pressure on Richmond from the south and eventually linking up with Meade. Finally, General Franz Sigel was to move up the Shenandoah Valley and drive for Staunton. In the west, General William T. Sherman would also put his army in motion and advance south through Georgia to Atlanta. All movements were scheduled to commence at the beginning of May.[29]

The focus of the Army of the Potomac was redirected as well. In the past, all operations centered around the capture of the Confederate capital of Richmond. It was believed that if the city fell, the Confederacy would be doomed. This logic was a holdover from the initial days of the war when the headlines cried, "On to Richmond." When Grant took command, he told Meade that the Army of Northern Virginia, not Richmond, was his objective. Wherever Lee went, that was where Meade and his army were to go. Destroying the Confederate army in the field, not the capture of Richmond, would end the war. The days of fighting and then retreating to the safety of the Washington defenses were over.[30]

General Meade's strategy for the upcoming campaign called for the Army of the Potomac to advance in two columns. The right column would be headed by the Third Division of the cavalry corps and followed by the V Corps and then the VI Corps. This column would cross the Rapidan River at Germanna Ford. The Second Division of the cavalry corps would lead the left column. Following the Union troopers would be the II Corps, the army's immense wagon train and the reserve artillery. This column would cross the Rapidan at Ely's Ford. The IX Corps, attached to the army as an independent command, and the remaining division of cavalry would cross at Germanna Ford at midnight and safeguard the rear of the army.[31]

For Meade's plan to succeed, the army had to be well underway before sunrise, when Confederate lookouts posted atop Clark's Mountain would have a clear view of the advancing columns. The army was to drive as quickly as possible through an area of dense forest and thick underbrush known as the Wilderness. To do this, the three vital arteries through the area, Orange Plank Road, Orange Turnpike, and Brock Road, had to be controlled. Once they crossed at Germanna Ford, the V and VI corps would occupy the Brock Road and Orange Turnpike intersection. The II Corps would advance on Chancellorsville, where it would control Orange Plank Road. With these valuable turnpikes in Union hands, the army could move swiftly through the Wilderness. Meade hoped to force the Army of Northern Virginia out from behind the strong line of works it had been occupying since the previous December by placing his entire army on Lee's right flank. It was this formidable line of works that the army faced the previous December and Meade had no intention of testing their strength again. If Lee retreated south, Meade was to follow closely behind. If not, he was to pitch into the rebel army at the first opportunity.[32]

The men of the 111th stood in formation with haversacks stuffed full with six day's rations, cartridge boxes filled with 40 rounds of ammunition, and extra rations and ammunition jammed into knapsacks. Shortly after 2:00 A.M. on the morning of May 4, Captain Aaron Seeley gave the order to march. To Sergeant Minard McDonald, a new recruit in Company H, the scene left a lasting impression: "Brigades, divisions, and corps were soon in motion, and in three grand divisions started toward the Rapidan ... long lines of infantry, artillery, and cavalry were soon moving in column toward the different fords."[33]

With the First Division in the lead, the 111th proceeded with the rest of the II Corps toward the Rapidan River. The march was difficult for many of the new soldiers of the regiment, including Sergeant McDonald. "Loaded down with ponderous knapsacks and surplus clothing which the veterans had learned to discard before starting on such a march, they soon became exhausted and fell out of the ranks, or painfully dragged themselves along until forced to unload a portion or all of their beloved extra luggage."[34] Scores of New Yorkers lined the roadside, too exhausted to continue.

Captain Seeley pushed the men on toward the Rapidan and crossed at Ely's Ford sometime after just after dawn. Advancing a short distance down Ely's Ford Road, the regiment arrived at the Chancellorsville crossroads close to noon. The column was halted and to the amazement of all, camp was made for the night. There was still plenty of daylight left and the New Yorkers wondered why they were wasting the opportunity to continue the march. Still puzzled at their good fortune, the men began to prepare their evening meal on the battleground of the previous year. Long after the war, Sergeant McDonald wrote, "Debris of all kinds — guns, old knapsacks, exploded shells and portions of skeletons — were seen upon all sides, and in many shallow trenches the elements had washed away the covering, and the ghastly sight of rows of grinning skulls met the gaze."[35]

Leaving the vicinity of the Chancellor House before sunrise the next morning, the New Yorkers proceeded south along Furnace Road toward Shady Grove Church. Here, the II Corps was to make contact with the V Corps, which at the time was advancing down the Orange Turnpike. Together with the rest of Frank's brigade, the 111th brought up the rear of the II Corps column. The day again turned hot, and "men dropped in the ranks by the scores and hundreds, but still the order, 'Close up! Close up!' continued to ring in our ears, as we plowed ahead with grim determination, straining every nerve and muscle,"[36] recalled Sergeant McDonald. Frequent rests were given, and bands were ordered to play to help lift spirits and give the men new energy for the march.

The head of the corps had passed two miles beyond Todd's Tavern and was nearing

Shady Grove Church when the advance was halted and a brief rest was granted. After waiting the better part of two hours, General Hancock finally received the order to countermarch and proceed immediately up Brock Road. He was to fall in on the left of General Warren's V Corps, then engaged with the enemy in the Wilderness along the Orange Turnpike. With instructions to guard the left flank of the corps, the 111th remained with the rest of Frank's brigade at the intersection of Brock Road and a road leading to the Catharpin Furnace Road. The New Yorkers rested in place as they watched the rear of their corps disappear into the dark woods.[37]

It was close to 4:00 P.M., and the 111th waited in reserve as the fighting on the right of the Union line intensified. The fight along the Orange Turnpike had escalated and now included elements of both the Union V and VI corps, while the rest of the II Corps was engaged at the Brock Road–Orange Plank Road intersection with A. P. Hill's Third Corps. General Grant had told Meade, "If any opportunity presents itself for pitching into a part of Lee's army, do so,"[38] and that was exactly what Meade was doing.

Before long a courier galloped up with orders for Colonel Frank to dispatch two regiments from his brigade and have them join the rest of their corps along Brock Road. Frank selected the 111th and the 57th and immediately ordered them to the battlefield. By 7:00 P.M., the two regiments were in position behind the earth and log fieldworks, to the right of Miles's brigade, on the southwest side of Brock Road.[39]

In the fading light, dense forest and hanging battle smoke, a brisk firefight broke out near the Brock Road–Orange Plank Road intersection, to the right of the New Yorkers' position. What started as two skirmish lines banging away to test the strength of each other's lines quickly escalated, and soon the Union skirmish line was in danger of breaking. The 111th and 57th were called upon to advance forward into the woods and help take pressure off the beleaguered Union skirmish line opposite their position. The New Yorkers were formed into line and nervously waited the order to advance. Stepping out in front of the regiment, Captain Seeley lifted his sword above his head and ordered the 111th forward. The two regiments crossed over the line of works and stumbled forward in the thick underbrush and growing darkness.[40]

The 111th had not gone far when the woods to the front exploded. "We received a withering fire that told us too well that our enemy was there in force to give us a warm reception," recalled Sergeant McDonald. "A perfect hail of bullets swept through the underbrush, fearfully cutting our ranks, and brave men were seen falling on every side."[41] The order to charge was given and the two regiments surged forward with a mighty yell into the morass of trees, brush and thickening battle smoke. As the incoming fire intensified, the regiment's advance ground to a halt. Captain Seeley gave the order to fire, and the men of the 111th aimed at the distant muzzle flashes, unleashing a ragged volley. Bullets slammed into the trees all around as the enemy, the 18th and 38th North Carolina, increased the volume of fire being poured into the two regiments. Both the 111th and the 57th tried valiantly to hold their ground but were forced to slowly fall back, leaving the dead and wounded where they lay.

One of the many casualties suffered by the regiment was newly commissioned Second Lieutenant James Snedaker of Company D, who was shot in the head and killed instantly while urging his men forward. The elder of two brothers serving in the regiment, Lieutenant Snedaker was a veteran soldier who served gallantly with the 27th New York Infantry from the first battle of Bull Run through the opening battles of the

8. *Overland Through Virginia* 113

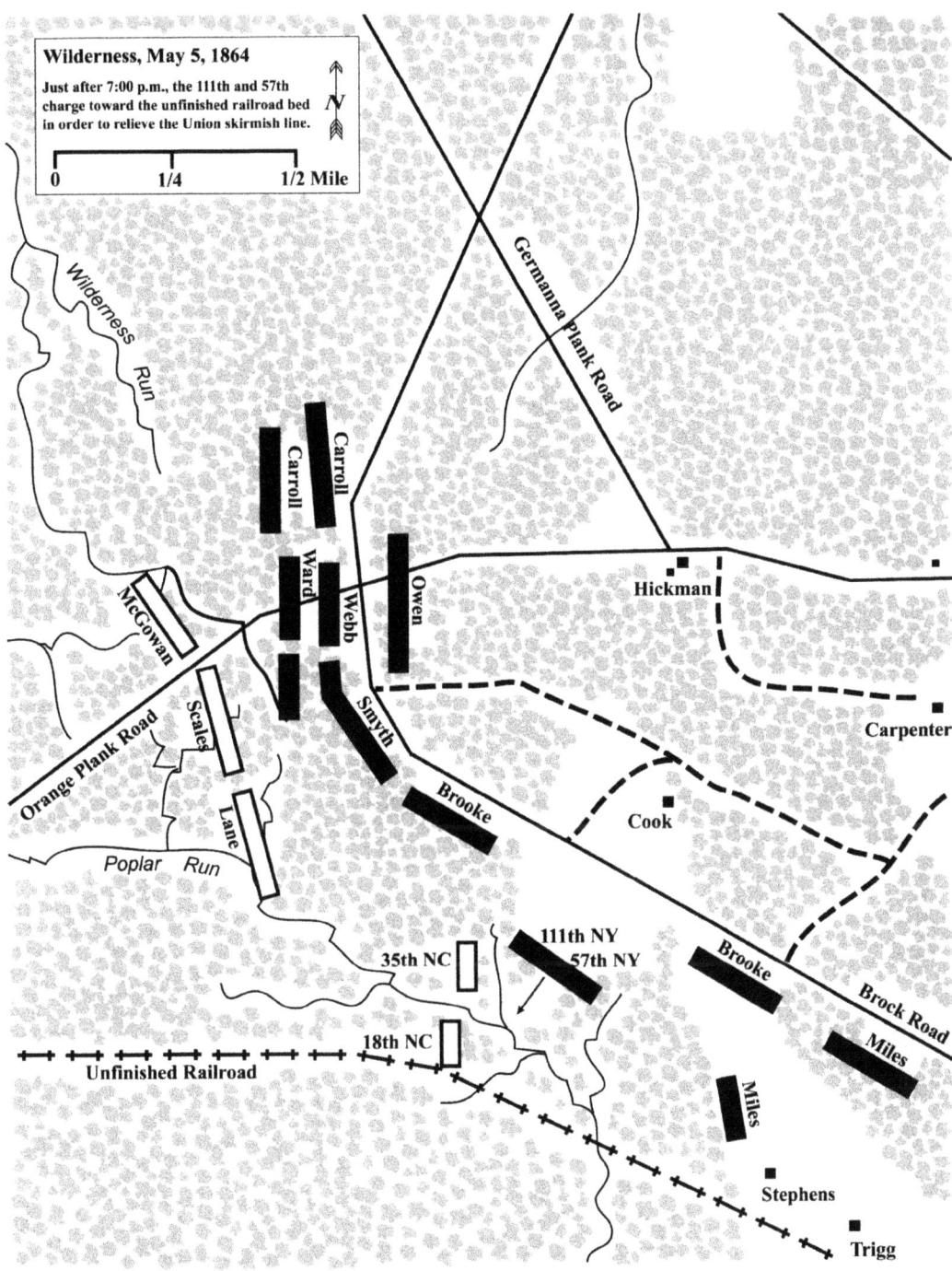

Just after 7:00 p.m., the 111th and 57th charge toward the unfinished railroad bed in order to relieve the Union skirmish line (map by the author).

Peninsula Campaign below Richmond almost a year later. His veteran leadership and bravery in battle would be sorely missed in the days to come.[42]

Captain Seeley was hit in the leg, but the wound was only minor and he was able to remain with the regiment. Warren Slocum of Company G was severely wounded when a bullet struck him in the head, mutilating the entire left side of his face. Corporal David Gibbs of Company C was virtually riddled with bullets. The 25-year-old from Victory was hit in the right leg below the knee, in the groin, and in the head, where the bullet lodged just above his left ear. Amazingly, Gibbs would survive his wounds and be discharged for disability in October.[43]

The charge was again attempted and again it met with defeat. According to Sergeant McDonald, "the rebel line was completely hidden from our view by the impenetrable thicket and the smoke that soon filled the whole forest. Only a sheet of flame from their guns marked their line-of-battle."[44] The two battered regiments retreated a short distance, reformed their ranks and readied themselves for another charge.

Pushing forward for the third time, the 111th and 57th advanced under a withering fire that further depleted their ranks. Lieutenant August Green of Company D was shot in the right hand and lost two fingers, while Lieutenant George Brown of Company E went down with a severe wound. Lieutenant Horace Hill was waving his sword above his head in an attempt to steady Company A when he was killed instantly, a ball slamming into his chin and exiting through his neck.[45] Losing men at an alarming rate and unable to see if his regiment's fire was having any effect

Albert Curtis, Company B. Captured in the Wilderness, May 5, 1864, and paroled in Wilmington, North Carolina, March 1, 1865 (courtesy of R. L. Murray).

on the enemy at all, Captain Seeley ordered the 111th to fall back to the works along Brock Road. While the 30-minute contest had failed to dislodge the enemy from their front, the attack had succeeded in relieving the threat to the Union skirmish line, but at a terrible cost to the regiment.

Around 10:00 P.M., as fighting again flared up along around the Brock Road–Orange Plank Road intersection, the rest of the brigade joined the 111th and 57th behind the fieldworks along the Brock Road. An anxious night was spent listening to the pitiful cries of the wounded out in front of the regiment's position. The days fighting had sparked fires in the dry underbrush that were now burning brightly. Those wounded who could not be moved from where they fell during the day burned to death in the spreading inferno. Sporadic skirmishing was kept up all night as the opposing pickets continued their duel, the crackle of musketry being added to the roar of the fire. Orders had already been issued for a general assault along the whole line to commence at 5:00 A.M., and many in the regiment viewed the morning's contest with dread. No one wanted to end up like those poor souls who were being consumed in the fires.[46]

The contest of the previous day had left both armies battered and weary. The VI Corps, on the extreme right of the Federal line along the Orange Turnpike, joined forces with the V Corps in facing Ewell's Second Corps. On the left of the line was the II Corps concentrated around the Brock Road–Orange Plank Road intersection facing Hill's Third Corps. Both sides were expecting reinforcements early in the morning. One-time commander of the Army of the Potomac, General Ambrose Burnside was supposed to be on the field with his IX Corps and move into the gap between the V and II corps. On the Confederate side, General Longstreet had returned from Georgia with his corps and was expected to move in behind Hill along Orange Plank Road. What each commanding general did

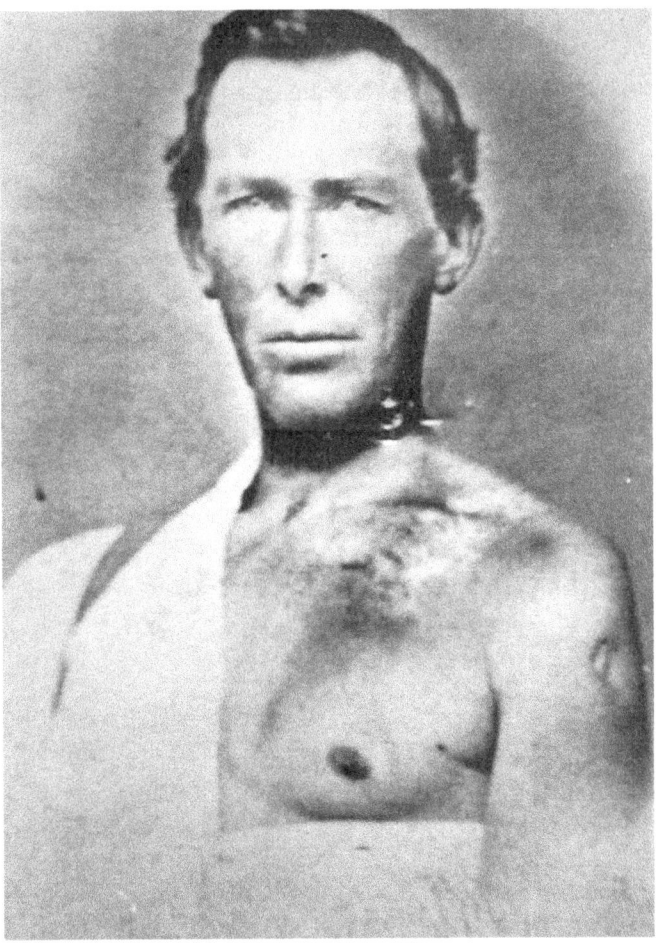

Martin Kilmer, Company E. He enlisted in the regiment in February 1864 at the age of 41. He was wounded at the Wilderness, May 5, 1864 (Massachusetts Commandery Military Order of the Loyal Legion and the USAMHI).

not know was that the other had planned an attack to begin early in the morning. General Meade's plan called for the VI Corps to hold the enemy in its front while the II Corps continued to press the attack against Hill's beleaguered rebels.⁴⁷

Early on the morning of May 6, just over two divisions of the II Corps attacked across Brock Road and slammed into the weak Confederate line. The rebel line was shattered and driven back down Orange Plank Road. Shortly before 7:00 A.M., and after listening for almost two hours to the battle raging to their right front, the 111th received orders to advance. General Barlow was to attack with his whole division, drive the Confederates from their position behind an unfinished railroad bed and force them back to Orange Plank Road. There Barlow would join forces with the rest of the II Corps and destroy the right flank of Lee's army. But due to a mix-up in the orders, Frank's brigade would make the assault alone.⁴⁸

Still suffering from his wound of the previous day, Captain Seeley deployed the regiment in line of battle and ordered it forward. Positioned on the extreme right of the brigade, the men of the 111th stepped over the line of works

Luther Rodgers, Company D. Killed in the Wilderness, May 5, 1864 (courtesy of R. L. Murray).

and drove across Brock Road into the woods already thick with the smoke of thousands of rifles and haze from the smoldering fires. Maintaining alignment was difficult as men stumbled through the thick underbrush, ranks becoming separated in the dense forest. To make matters worse, the ground was still strewn with the charred remnants of the previous night's battle. To Sergeant McDonald, "it was like stepping into hell."⁴⁹

The New Yorkers had not gone very far before they came upon the rear of Colonel

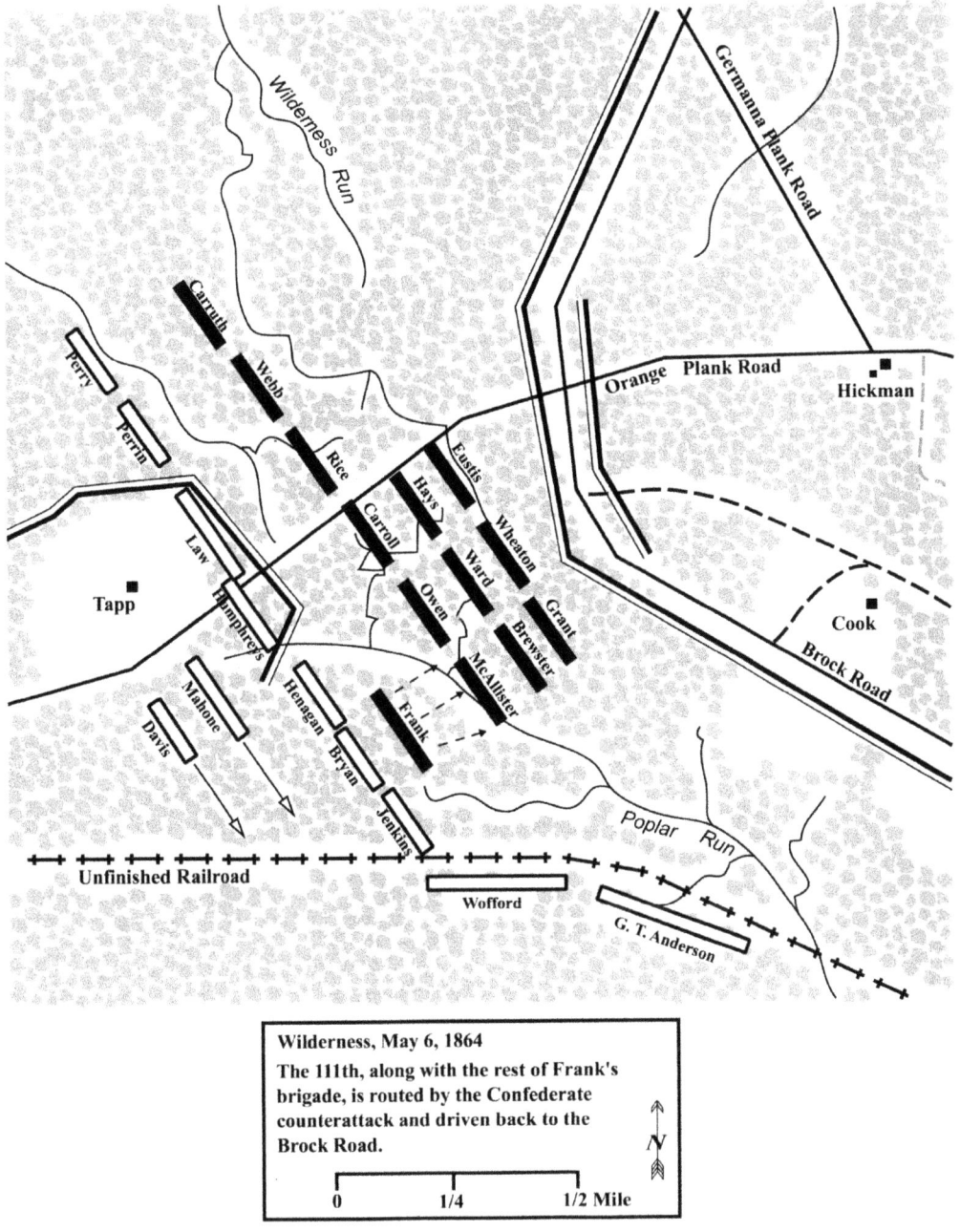

The 111th, along with the rest of Frank's brigade, is routed by the Confederate counterattack and driven back to Brock Road (map by the author).

Robert McAllister's brigade of the Fourth Division. McAllister's regiments were standing in line of battle, with a strong line of skirmishers posted to their front. Believing that his orders were to find the enemy and give battle, Colonel Frank asked McAllister to open ranks so that his men could pass through. When Colonel McAllister refused, Frank spurred his horse back to his command. The colonel placed the 125th in front of the brigade as skirmishers and ordered his regiments to guide around Colonel McAllister's left flank.[50]

Moving forward, the New Yorkers advanced deeper into the impenetrable forest. Before they knew what had hit them, the men of the 111th were stopped in their tracks by a devastating volley that cut into their frightened ranks. Captain Seeley steadied his soldiers and immediately gave the order to fire. The New Yorkers traded volleys with the unseen enemy, aiming at the muzzle flashes less than 40 yards away. Sergeant McDonald furiously loaded and fired as "swelling volumes of musketry rolled from right to left and left to right with a roar that was enough to strike terror to the stoutest heart."[51] What the men did not know, and could not see, was that they had run right into the better part of three Confederate brigades that had been attempting to get around McAllister's left flank.

Smoke hung in the trees obscuring visibility, and small fires again broke out in the woods around the 111th. A few at a time, men began to leave the ranks and head for the rear, unable to stand up under the ferocity of the Confederate attack. Officers and sergeants tried to stem the flow of men but quickly found their task impossible. The continuous roar of musketry was intensified by the thick woods, and the noise was almost deafening. "Crash followed crash louder and fiercer than heaven's artillery, and the deep forest, echoing its thunders, sounded as if the minions of hell itself had been loosened,"[52] remembered McDonald.

Lieutenants Patrick Welch and John Lockwood were both wounded as they struggled to rally their men. Sergeant Major John Fishback went down with a severe wound, and First Sergeant Harry Smith was cut across the back of his head by a bullet, the wound bleeding profusely. Benjamin Franklin Gould of Company I was hit several times, causing him to lose an eye and his left hand. Men were falling everywhere from the hail of bullets from the unseen foe.

The regiments on the left of the brigade line gave way and made a mad dash for the rear. With few officers left to rally the 111th, the New Yorkers' line buckled, then broke. The men raced as best they could for the safety of the rear. Sergeant Hutchins summed up the flight of the regiment in his diary: "We had to fall back and was flanked, when we retreated disorderly."[53]

Colonel McAllister's men tried to stop the retreat, but they were forced to open ranks and let the regiments through. The 111th eventually rallied with the rest of the brigade behind the Brock Road earthworks where

John White, Company F. The 25-year-old was wounded at the Wilderness, May 6, 1864 (Massachusetts Commandery Military Order of the Loyal Legion and the USAMHI).

the morning's attack began. The men were quickly formed into line facing the enemy, who seemed content not to press their attack. One of the first to break and run for the rear was the brigade's commander himself, Colonel Frank. Arriving behind the lines before most of his men, Frank was met by Colonel McAllister. When asked by the colonel where he was going, Frank said that he was taking his command way back to the rear to get more ammunition.[54]

By late morning, an eerie silence hung over the field. General Hancock took advantage of a lull in the fighting to realign his badly disorganized command. Regiments were rallied and lines were reformed in anticipation of the renewal of the conflict. It was close to noon when the 111th was moving south along Brock Road preparing to take up a position between the brigades of Brooke and Webb when General Longstreet launched a devastating flank attack on Hancock's weary infantry. Having just arrived on the field, the rebels quickly overwhelmed the confused ranks. Hancock's men fought valiantly but were forced to retreat, the shattered remnants falling back through the smoke and burning forest and rallying behind their fieldworks along Brock Road. Behind the protective cover of their earth and log entrenchments, Hancock's infantry was able to beat off the Confederate attack.[55]

Shortly before 4:00 P.M., a tremendous yell rang out from the woods to the right of the regiment's position. At least nine Confederate brigades began an assault on the Union position along Brock Road. The whole line was soon ablaze with small arms fire in an attempt to stop the gray tide. Fortunately, the Confederate attack fell closer to the Brock Road–Orange Plank Road intersection, the position the regiment had vacated around noon. The rebels managed to breach the line and drive the defenders away from their works, which caught fire early in the fight. Reinforcements soon arrived and the Confederate attackers were stopped and forced to withdraw.[56]

The men of the 111th waited behind the earthworks as the fires continued to burn in the woods all around them. Fighting had stopped, save the occasional pop from the skirmishers' rifles. Ammunition arrived from the rear and the men were able to fill their empty cartridge boxes. Laboring long into the night, the New Yorkers realigned their ranks and strengthened their breastworks. When roll call was taken that evening, just barely half of the men were present to answer to their names. In two days of severe fighting, the regiment lost 198 out of almost 450 men taken into battle.[57]

Counted among the missing was Albert Snedaker of Company D. The younger brother of James, who was killed on the first day's battle, Albert was captured while trying to help a wounded comrade from the field. Sent to Andersonville as a prisoner of war, he died a little more than two months later. Also captured was Augustus Donk of Company A. Unlike his comrade, Donk survived his captivity in Andersonville, was paroled, and was with the regiment when it mustered out of service a year later.[58]

Captain Seeley's wound was sufficient to warrant a furlough to go home to New York to recover. Never fully regaining his health, Seeley eventually resigned his commission without ever returning to the regiment. Captain Edgar Hueston of Company K received a slight wound to the right arm and was sent home to convalesce. In the two days of fighting, the 111th seemed to bear the brunt of the casualties in the brigade. While the 39th lost 136 officers and men, the remaining 4 regiments lost less than 100 men each.[59]

The two-day battle was costly to both sides. General Meade's Army of the Potomac had almost 18,000 men killed, wounded or missing while the Army of Northern Virginia lost almost 9,000. The battle of the Wilderness had set the tone for the rest of the campaign, proving surgeon Benton correct when he wrote that the battles of the coming campaign "will be fought to the bitter end and mercy will be a scarce article."[60]

Sunrise on the morning after the fight revealed smoldering woods littered with the debris of two days of hard fighting. Smoke hung low in the trees, giving the woods an eerie look. The smell of burnt wood mixed with the stench of burning flesh. Sergeant Hutchins remained behind the breastworks with what was left of Company D. In his diary he wrote, "We laid still all day in the breastworks. Very hot we had to keep our things all on & ready to move. We had to keep part of the men on lookout at a time & the rest could sleep with their things on."[61] Fellow company member William York was so tired that he was not bothered at all by the fact that he slept on Hutchins's gun all day.

Orders arrived for the regiment to be ready to move that night. In fact, the entire army was being put in motion. But instead of retreating to the defenses around Washington like the army had done so many times in the past, the army would move south. The V Corps would lead the movement down Brock Road, with II Corps following close behind. The VI and IX corps would proceed to Chancellorsville, by way of Orange Plank Road, then turn south. The march was scheduled to begin at 8:30 that night.[62]

The soldiers of the Army of the Potomac were not alone as they plodded wearily along the roads through the Wilderness that hot May evening. General Richard Anderson, placed in command of the Confederate First Corps after General Longstreet was wounded on the 6th, had orders to move his divisions away from the battlefield on the night of the 7th. Around 10:00 P.M., he pulled his battered forces away from the Union II Corps' front and marched his men along a road cut through the forest by the army's engineers. When he reached Catharpin Road, the Confederate infantry proceeded southwest. Once the head of the column reached Shady Grove Church Road, Anderson turned his men east. They crossed the Po River and took up positions just south of Laurel Hill.[63]

Although the New Yorkers were to begin the march during the night, the roads were so jam-packed with regiments from the V Corps that the 111th did not get underway until nearly dawn on May 8. Captain Perry, now in command of the regiment, led the 111th down Brock Road to Todd's Tavern, where it arrived sometime after 9:00 A.M. Turning west onto Catharpin Road, the column advanced only a short distance before halting. The New Yorkers set right to work throwing up a crude line of earthworks across the road, facing west. Work on the entrenchments stopped long enough for the men to draw five day's rations, then they went right back to work digging in the hot sun. As the men labored, the sound of fighting could be heard coming from their front. The lead division of General Warren's V Corps was clashing with Anderson's Confederate infantry around the tiny village of Spotsylvania.[64]

The order designating May 9 as a general day of rest for the army had no sooner been read to the weary New Yorkers when they were directed to leave the works at Todd's Tavern. This time the 111th would march without their comrades in the 57th New York. Earlier in the morning this regiment was detached from the brigade and ordered to escort the ambulance trains east to Fredericksburg. The regiment was selected personally by General Hancock for being a very reliable regiment and on account of the heavy losses it suffered during the battle of the Wilderness, which included the regimental commander, Lieutenant Colonel A. B. Chapman.[65]

The advance down Brock Road commenced around noon and the 111th marched with the First Division at the head of the II Corps column. Late in the day, the New Yorkers filed off the road and proceeded down an old farm lane, taking up a position near the Jones farm. Captain Perry posted a strong line of pickets close to the Po River and allowed the rest of the men to relax in place. Before long a rebel baggage train appeared on the opposite bank of the river, and some pretty sharp shelling commenced by Union artillerymen trying to hit the wagons. Rebel gunners quickly responded by throwing shells at the skirmishers along the river. According to Sergeant Hutchins, he "came very near being hit with a reb shell, it did not explode."[66] William Traver of Company C was not quite so lucky. He was wounded and taken to the rear.

Later in the day the regiments of Brooke's brigade left their position and marched off toward the Po River. Brooke had orders to drive his regiments south, cross the river and take possession of Shady Grove Church Road. About an hour later, Captain Perry was ordered to advance the 111th with the remaining brigades of the division to join Brooke on the south side of the Po. Once the entire division was together, they would march east in an attempt to get around the Confederates' left flank at Laurel Hill, where an attack was being planned for the next day.[67]

Wading through the knee-deep water and clambering up the steep banks on the opposite side of the river, the regiment advanced south along an old trail before striking Shady Grove Church Road. Here Colonel Frank reformed his brigade and resumed the advance. Crossing down river from the First Division was the Second Division of John Gibbon and the Third Division of David Birney. The New Yorkers proceeded east along the road toward Block House Bridge, where the road crossed the meandering river. The 111th arrived about a mile west of the bridge around midnight. Due to the depth of the water, the thick woods along the bank and the late hour, Captain Perry received orders to have his regiment fall out and make camp for the night. The river would be crossed early the next morning.[68]

When the 111th arrived opposite Block House Bridge, the only Confederate infantry in the area was Gregg's Texas brigade, about a mile away. Fortunately for General Lee, one of his cavalry units had spotted Hancock's men crossing the Po River and reported the information to the army commander. Aware of the threat to his left flank, Lee ordered the Third Corps Division of William Mahone to advance as quickly as possible west along Shady Grove Church Road. Once he arrived at Block House Bridge, Mahone placed his units on the opposite side of the river from the Federals and had them build a strong line of breastworks across the road. Close to midnight, the Confederate commander directed Henry Heath to march his division away from Spotsylvania Court House, cross the Po River below the Union II Corps and be ready to attack the Federal's unguarded flank the next morning.[69]

The early morning hours of the 10th were wasted as II Corps staff officers rode up and down the riverbank looking for the best place to cross the water, which was at least chest deep near the bridge. The 111th sat idle south of Shady Grove Church Road as other regiments from the division probed south toward Glady Run looking for an alternate crossing site. Close to midday, Generals Gibbon and Birney were recalled to the north side of the Po in order to aid in an attack at Laurel Hill on the center of the Confederate line, which was to coincide with the fighting along the Po River. General Barlow was now alone with his division south of the river.[70]

Word spread like lightening through the ranks that a large column of Confederate infantry was approaching from the southeast. Racing to meet the threat, the New Yorkers furiously began to throw up a line of works. With Brooke's brigade to their left, the 111th and the rest of its brigade constituted the extreme right of Barlow's formation.[71]

Around 2:30 P.M., Colonel Frank informed Captain Perry that the brigade was moving to occupy a line of works on the north side of Shady Grove Church Road. Along with Brooke, Frank's brigade was to cover the rest of the division as it withdrew to the safety of the other side of the Po River. Moving at the double, the New Yorkers crossed the road and occupied the works. No sooner had the 111th settled into position than the enemy's skirmishers were seen scampering through the fields to the front, firing as they advanced. The main Confederate battle line soon appeared behind the skirmishers and rushed forward with a yell. The regiment's line exploded with a tremendous volley that, along with the other regiments in the brigade, stopped the Confederate advance cold and sent the rebels reeling backward.[72]

As the fighting raged, a group of officers from the various regiments of the brigade went to General Barlow to demand that Colonel Frank be relieved from command due to drunkenness. The group asked that an officer other than one of them be appointed to command the brigade. But Barlow told the officers he was not willing to make a change in midbattle and informed them they would have to make do as best they could.[73]

The New Yorkers continued to load and fire as the gray ranks again surged forward. But the volume of fire began to slacken as their supply of ammunition began to give out. On the left, the rebels broke through Brooke's formation and pressed hard against the regiment's line. Then the woods were on fire, adding more confusion to an already desperate situation. Frank's entire line began to crumble, and Captain Perry was ordered to get his men to the north side of the river as quickly as possible. The flames, smoke and heavy fire from the enemy made the retreat a nightmare. First Sergeant Harry Smith found himself in quite a predicament: "I had to throw away my knapsack to get out alive, it was so dreadful."[74] Some of the men fired as they retreated while others ran as fast as they could to escape the pursuing Confederates, who were following close behind. The retreat quickly turned into a mad dash for the river.

In the confusion, a group from the 111th became separated from the rest of the regiment and instead of retreating, chose to remain and fight with members of the 52nd New York. They fought as long as possible before they were surrounded and forced to surrender. One of the captured was Sergeant Hutchins. In his diary he wrote, "I with a few of my Co [company] staid & fought with the 52 N.Y., by so doing I was taken prisoner & John Dearlove was killed. One of the rebels tried to rob me of my watch. I was taken to the rear by one of the 11 Miss [Mississippi], who treated me kindly."[75] Hutchins would languish in a series of prison camps before being paroled, returning to the regiment near the end of the war.

The scattered remnants of the regiment forded the river and reformed on the opposite bank. Captain Perry no sooner put the men in line and began to move them back to their works near the Jones farm then the Union artillery opened a furious barrage on the pursuing Confederate infantry. Suffering under a rain of shot and shell, the rebels were stopped short of the river and driven back toward Shady Grove Church Road. In the short but desperate contest, the 111th suffered 3 killed, 14 wounded, and 15 captured.[76]

Once the old Harpers Ferry brigade returned to its works near the Jones farm, General Barlow relieved Colonel Frank of command. His conduct at the Wilderness was inexcusable, his retreat from the Po had left Brooke to fight it out almost by itself, and his obvious intoxication during the afternoon's battle left the first division commander with no recourse but to strip Frank of his duties. Control of the Third Brigade fell to Colonel Hiram Brown of the 145th Pennsylvania from Brooke's brigade.[77]

However, the day's events hadn't been all bad. Elements of the II and VI corps had been able to breach the center of the Confederate line and hold it for a time, convincing Generals Grant and Meade to plan a massive assault for the early morning hours of May 12. They intended to assault an area of the Confederate works that jutted out like a finger from the rest of the works. Here the works formed a salient or "Mule Shoe." The entire II Corps would advance and strike this point. When the II Corps made its attack, the rest of the army would advance and attack the rebel works to their front. Grant and Meade hoped to keep the enemy occupied on all fronts so that at least one of the attacks would succeed.[78]

In a driving rainstorm on the night of the 11th, the regiment withdrew from its position near the Po River and made its way with the rest of the II Corps to the center of the Union line. The ankle-deep mud and absolute darkness complicated the movement. Around midnight, the wet and exhausted men of the 111th arrived in the vicinity of the Brown house where their division was forming for the next day's attack. General Barlow deployed his division with the regiments of Brooke's and Miles's brigades in the front line while Smyth's and Brown's regiments made up the second line.[79]

Regimental commanders were given strict instructions to ensure their men did not cheer or discharge their weapons until reaching the enemy works. Surprise and speed were essential to the success of the attack. Once all troop dispositions were made, the men lay down in the mud and water to get a few hours' sleep. One member of the 111th who would not be advancing with the regiment in the morning was Samuel Fuller of Company I. His best friend, First Sergeant Smith, had seen to it that the 19-year-old Fuller was assigned to the Pioneer Corps, as "it is half dangerous as with the co [company]."[80]

To get to the Confederate position, the 111th would have to pass through an almost mile-long field bordered on either side by woods. Between the regiment's position and the enemy were three distinct ridges. The fields adjacent to the Brown farm were located along the first ridge. Here ran a line of works that were captured from the enemy on May 10. Atop the second ridge, a half mile away, was the Landrum house and a strong line of pickets. Along the third ridge were the main Confederate works, an incredibly formidable earth and log fortification. To make matters worse, the rebel works were fronted by an almost impenetrable line of abatis.[81]

Just after 4:30 A.M., Captain Perry called his men to attention, ordered them to fix bayonets, and led the 111th forward into the predawn darkness. An intermittent rain continued to fall and a heavy fog made viewing the distant rebel works impossible. After crossing a shallow creek, the New Yorkers crossed the first ridge and made their way down the other side. A scattering of shots told the men that the advance elements of their column had overrun the Confederate picket line near the Landrum house. By the time the regiment reached the top of the second ridge, all alignment in the ranks was lost and the formation became one giant mass of men.[82]

The tangle of abatis was encountered at the bottom of the second ridge. A detail of pioneers preceded the column and had chopped a passage through the obstacle, allowing the New Yorkers to pass through without too much difficulty. A deafening cheer rang

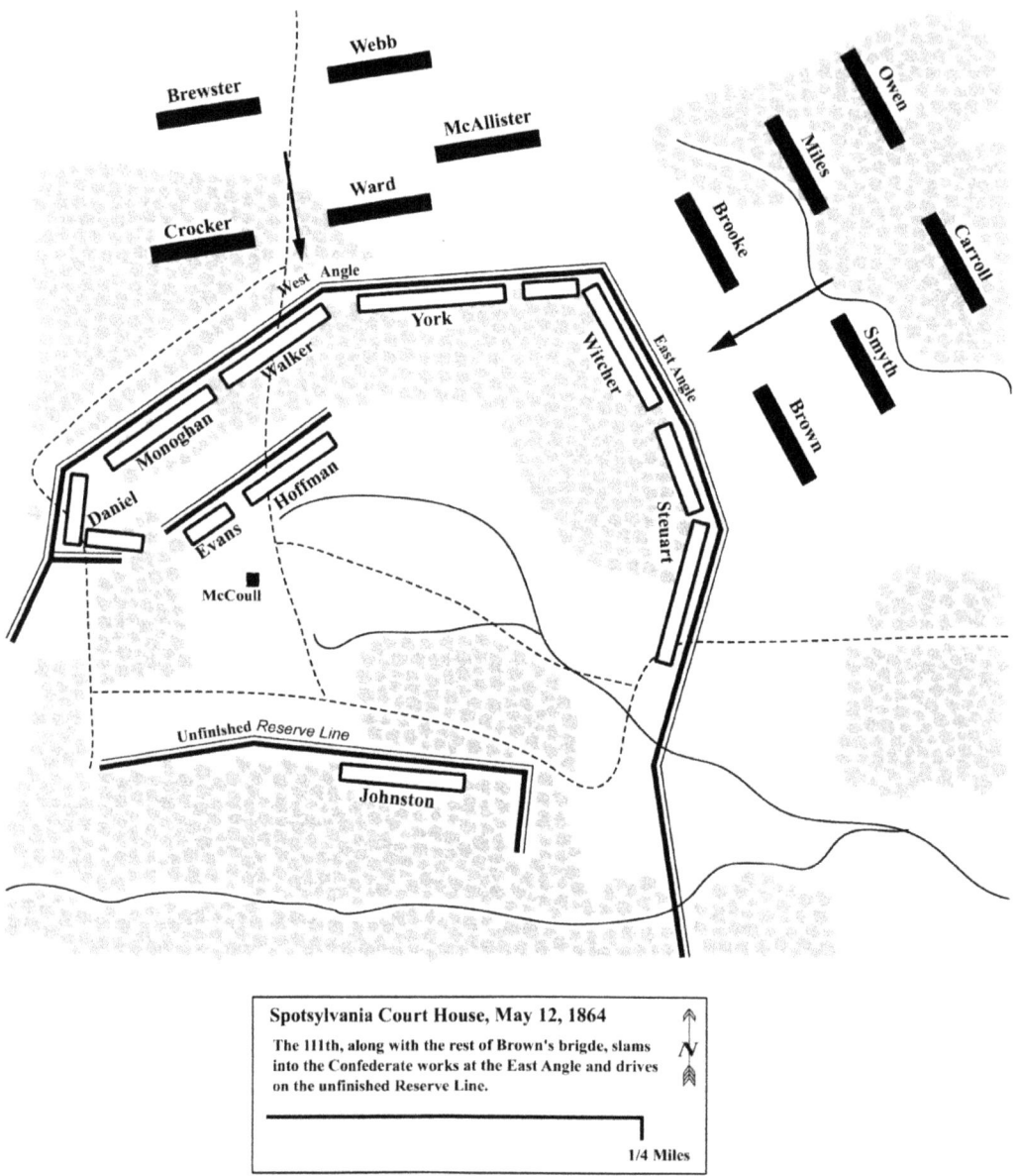

The 111th, along with the rest of Brown's brigade, slams into the Confederate works at the East Angle and drives on the unfinished reserve line (map by the author).

out from the head of the formation as Brooke's and Miles's regiments made a dash for the Confederate line. The New Yorkers' formation began to veer to the left, and the brigade hit the section of the works held by George H. Steuart's Virginia and North Carolina brigade, at the east angle. Captain Perry led the men forward with a thunderous yell, and they swarmed over the works. The enemy could only offer token resistance as they were reeling from the overwhelming force of the attack. In fact, most of the rebels seemed to be just waking up as the New Yorkers arrived inside the works.[83]

As the 111th was scaling the works at the east angle, the divisions of Birney and Mott slammed into the top of the salient. They also met with scant opposition as they gobbled up most of Confederate general Edward Johnson's division, including the general himself.[84]

Firing as they advanced, the New Yorkers continued to press forward, their ranks intermingling with the regiments around them as all resistance in the salient was quickly eliminated. Thomas Templeton of Company G was mortally wounded, First Lieutenant Reuben Myers of Company H received a slight wound while First Sergeant Harry Smith received his second wound of the campaign. In a letter to his sister, Smith wrote, "I was wounded or bruised by a grape shot that went through my pants just above the ankle and struck me a glancing shot across the right foot bruising pretty bad."[85]

About an hour into the attack, the men of the 111th found themselves advancing toward an unfinished reserve line of trenches about half a mile to the rear of the main Confederate works. Suddenly, a thunderous rebel yell rang out and a devastating volley ripped through the regiment's ranks. Confederate general John Gordon arrived on the field with his three brigades and launched a vicious counterattack aimed at driving the attackers out of the works. Fighting raged along the reserve line for only seconds before the unorganized mass of Federal infantry was forced to retreat. The men ran a gauntlet of fire to reach the safety of the breastworks at the east salient. Sometime during the melee at the reserve line, the newly promoted brigade commander, Colonel Brown, was captured.[86]

Officers and sergeants quickly formed the men of the 111th into a crude battle line on the opposite side of the breastworks, and Captain Perry ordered his men to commence firing. The regiment blazed away at the Georgia brigade of Colonel Clement Evans located on the other side of the earth and log fieldworks. Both sides held their ground as the firefight raged at almost point-blank range.[87]

After more than four hours of continuous fighting in the rain, casualties were starting to mount while ammunition began to run dangerously low. Union artillery posted near the Landrum house pounded the enemy to the regiment's front, adding more confusion to the already hellish conditions. Between 8:30 and 9:00 A.M., reinforcements from the VI Corps arrived and General Barlow was able to pull his exhausted men out of line and reform them behind the Second Division regiments of General Gibbon. Even though they were out of the main fighting, what was left of the 111th was immediately put to work building a new a line of works that ran from the apex of the salient back toward the main Union line.[88]

The men of the 111th labored under a heavy rain building the works, all the while being forced to dodge artillery shells and small arms fire. Wellington Hinman arrived from the rear leading mules loaded with ammunition to replenish empty cartridge boxes.[89] Even as night approached, the fighting raged unabated. Wounded comrades left behind inside the salient were in danger of being hit not only by Confederate fire, but by their own artillery as well. By the early morning hours of the 13th, the firing all but stopped as if by mutual consent. Both sides were utterly spent after almost 23 hours of continuous fighting. The lull in the fighting allowed what little Confederate infantry remained inside the salient area to pull back to a new line about a mile to the rear, leaving the salient in Union hands.

With rain still falling, the weary soldiers of the 111th spent most of the 13th improving their positions, carrying the dead and wounded to the rear, and replenishing their ammunition. The operation of the previous day did not go as the commanding generals had hoped. Even though the II Corps was able to bag nearly 3,000 prisoners and a number of artillery pieces, it came at a cost of over 2,500 casualties. Hancock's corps, while meeting with early success, found itself driven out of the salient and fighting the rest of the day on the opposite side of the field works from the enemy. The attacks of the V and IX corps did little to provide assistance to the II Corps. General Warren threw his V Corps divisions against a well-fortified Confederate line at Laurel Hill while General Burnside half-heartedly carried out his orders to attack the Confederate right.[90]

Not long after hearing of the casualties from the battle of the Wilderness, Colonel MacDougall abandoned his recruiting detail in Auburn and immediately set out for Virginia to join the 111th. The War Department was not pleased with his decision but more than understood: "Col. C. D. MacDougall having improperly left his station on recruiting service, will, under the circumstances, proceed to join his regiment in the army of the Potomac."[91] MacDougall arrived at Spotsylvania late on the 13th to find a regiment that looked nothing like the one he left three months before. His men were exhausted and filthy, their clothes stained and torn. Casualties from over a week of constant fighting and marching had reduced the ranks by half. A testament to the horrors the regiment had endured was the casualty figures for Company I. Starting the campaign with 5 sergeants, 4 corporals, and 42 privates, the company was reduced to just 21 men.[92]

On the evening of the 13th, the V and VI corps were moved to the left of the Union line with the intent of striking the enemy's right flank. Unfortunately, the Confederates discovered the movement, and reinforcements were sent to bolster their right, causing General Meade to call off the attack. Two days later, General Hancock ordered Barlow's and Gibbon's divisions to the left to further extend the Union line to Fredericksburg Road. The march was made in a driving rainstorm, over muddy roads and through swampy fields. By late morning, Hancock's men were in position, in the vicinity of the Ni River.[93]

At some point during the day, the regiment's picket line was attacked, at the cost of one man wounded and three taken prisoner. Among the unfortunate captured was Daniel Grandin of Company E. Along with the two other members of his company, the young father of two from Pultneyville arrived at Andersonville sometime between May 24 and 25. Grandin immediately sought out other members of the regiment and shared a tent with Adrian Contant, who had been captured at Mine Run the previous December.

In camp less than a month, Grandin took ill. Writing shortly after the war, Contant described his tent mate's fate: "He was taken sick about June 20th, 1864 and grew rapidly worse and that on or about June 28th or 29th 1864 he died — that I cared for him as well as I could during his sickness, and was with him when he died."[94]

The rain that fell on May 15 continued into the early morning hours of the 16th, when the skies finally cleared and the sun shown brightly. General Barlow took advantage of the weather and held a general inspection of the First Division. The next day, Captain Husk arrived from Auburn with much needed reinforcements for the regiment, including the detachment that traveled to Auburn in January. Husk assumed command of the 111th, and Colonel MacDougall assumed command of the Third Brigade, which had been without a leader since Colonel Brown's capture on the 12th. Captain Perry went back to his company and took command from First Lieutenant Philip Ira Lape, who had led Company B with skill and bravery since the campaign opened. To further bolster the officer ranks in Company B, John Smith was promoted from private in Company A to second lieutenant and transferred to Captain Perry's company.[95]

As the battle raged in the salient on the 12th, the Confederates were frantically building a new line of works about a quarter of a mile behind the reserve from which the 111th was driven. When the rebels pulled out of the salient in the early morning hours of the 13th, they fell back and occupied this new line. Based on the fact that the enemy had reinforced the right of their line on the 13th to face the V and VI corps, General Meade believed that this part of the Confederate line was weak. The commanding general intended to again send in the II Corps to try and pierce the enemy's center. But the men of the 111th were soon to find out that the line was anything but weak.[96]

In order to be ready for the attack on the 18th, the 111th was forced to make another exhausting night march. First Sergeant Smith recalled, "We had marched most of the night very slowly and secretly to get in position."[97] After what seemed like an eternity, the regiment finally reached the fields adjacent to the Landrum house, where General Barlow was forming his division. Colonel MacDougall's brigade and Colonel Smyth's brigade, now under the command of Colonel Richard Byrnes, made up the front rank of the division, with MacDougall on the right and Byrnes on the left. The regiments of Miles's and Brooke's brigades made up the second rank of the attacking column.

Shortly after 4:00 A.M., Union artillery opened a furious cannonade in preparation for the coming attack. At half past the hour, the order to advance was given, and Captain Husk led the men of the 111th forward. The regiment made its way down the gently sloping ridge and headed up the other side for the works at the salient. It gave the men little comfort to know that they were about to fight for the same ground they had battled and bled for just six days before. When the New Yorkers scaled the works and entered the salient, they were met with a horrifying sight. The area inside the Confederate works had become one vast graveyard of partially buried bodies. After a week of being exposed to the elements, the stench from the decomposing remains was overwhelming.[98]

Confederate artillery opened up with canister on the advancing regiments as soon as they landed inside the salient, tearing gaps in their lines. The regiment pressed forward, crossing over the reserve line and driving for the new Confederate fieldworks. "We went brigade after brigade under the most terrible & terrific fire of shell, shot, grape and canister. O the havoc & carnage was dreadful,"[99] remembered First Sergeant Smith. The regiment's ranks were again hit hard. Both Captain John Laing of Company E and Lieutenant Edgar Hueston of Company K, who had recently returned from home, were disabled with wounds. Lieutenant Charles Hitchcock, the fleet-footed messenger at Gettysburg, went down with canister wounds in both thighs.[100] Smith, hobbling along due to the wound he received during the attack on the 12th, was knocked to the ground when a piece of canister glanced off the bone in his right leg. The advance was finally halted about 100 yards short of the enemy works when the New Yorkers encountered an impenetrable line of abatis.

Seeing there was no hope of advancing through the obstacle, General Barlow ordered his regiments to lie down and return fire. The only fire coming from the rebels was from their artillery; the infantry remained hidden behind their works and did not fire a shot. With no hope of breaching the morass of trees and branches, the attack was called off. Captain Husk was directed to move the 111th to the rear as rapidly as possible. Making their way back over the reserve line at the double-quick, the men reached the salient and took shelter on the opposite side, all the while enemy batteries blistered the New Yorker's ranks with canister. Throwing themselves down in the mud, the men huddled behind the earth and log barricade as the firing died down, then finally stopped.[101]

Making his way to the rear, First Sergeant Smith stopped at the creek near the Brown house. In letters to his sister and parents, Smith wrote that he

> washed my wound & emptied my shoe of blood tied my handkerchief around it and started on, I got a little over a half mile further I gave out and set down to rest it pained me very much. When I tried to go further it was impossible. Some others came along with another wounded man from my brigade & one of them cut me a crotch for a crutch & then helped me along a few rods when an Ambulance Sergt. of 6th Corps came along & seeing my pitiful state, got off his horse and helped me on and he walked about 2 miles out of his way leading his horse before I got to the 2nd Corps hospital.[102]

Surgeon Benton was able to find Smith a place to lie down until he was transferred to Fredericksburg later that night. Smith was eventually sent to Washington to recover, where he was discharged for disability in March 1865.

During the day, the 111th sent detachments out onto the skirmish line. Each side traded shots over the now-abandoned earthworks at the salient. One of the enemy's bullets found its mark when Captain Perry was hit in the left shoulder by a musket ball. The captain was taken to the Georgetown Seminary Hospital in Washington where the doctors were able to save his arm. Unfortunately his military career could not be saved, and he was forced to resign his commission in October.[103]

Later in the evening, Captain Husk received orders from Colonel MacDougall to pull the regiment out of line and move with the rest of the II Corps back to the left of the Union line and assume a reserve position behind the VI and IX corps in the vicinity of Anderson's mill. Behind the main line the men were finally able to clean their clothes and equipment and get some much-needed rest.

During eight days of almost continuous fighting, the regiment had been fortunate to escape with rather light casualties. Starting with the advance over the Po River on the 9th and ending with the disastrous assault through the salient area on the 18th, the regiment suffered 16 men killed or mortally wounded and 37 officers and men wounded, while 20 men were reported as missing. Just two weeks before, the 111th broke camp at Dumpling Mountain and marched toward Ely's Ford 450 officers and men strong. Now after almost 14 days of continuous marching and fighting, the regiment numbered less then 200.[104]

CHAPTER 9

Marching to the Left

> We have been fighting and marching now 22 days and when we stop it is not to rest but to build earthworks to protect us from the shell of the enemy.[1]

In yet another attempt to draw the Confederates out from behind their strong line of entrenchments, Generals Grant and Meade decided a little bait was in order, in the form of the battered II Corps. General Hancock would march his weary foot soldiers south toward Richmond in the hope that General Lee would send a portion of his army to intercept them. When this happened, the rest of the Army of the Potomac would descend on the Confederates, destroying that part of Lee's army before it could be reinforced. If, on the other hand, General Hancock could advance unmolested and get between the Confederates and their capital, Lee would be forced to abandon his line and fall back to protect Richmond.

One way or another, the Army of Northern Virginia would be forced to give up its defensive position around Spotsylvania Court House. The generals wanted to fight the rebel army out in the open where the full weight of the Army of the Potomac could be brought to bear against the rebels. Unfortunately, this opportunity proved elusive at both the Wilderness and Spotsylvania.[2]

With their division at the head of the II Corps column, the 111th silently pulled out of its line at Anderson's mill shortly before midnight on May 20. Wellington Hinman was still on detached service and traveled with the II Corps wagon train. In his diary he wrote, "The train broke camp and followed on after the troops who had gone a little before in a southeast direction, marched all night."[3] The route of march took the men toward Guiney's Station, then on to Bowling Green, which was reached the next morning. Charles White took time to reflect on the city as the regiment made its way through town: "One of the pleasantest towns I have seen in VA [Virginia] but strong secesh. The girls would stick there heads out of the windo and look up there nose at us as we passed."[4]

The 111th continued advancing until it reached Milford Station. Here Captain Husk rested the men as the cavalry escort fought with members of James Kemper's Virginia brigade for control of the bridge over the Mattapony River. Initially being repulsed, the Union troopers were able to reform and route the rebel defenders, clearing the bridge for Hancock's infantry.

With the important crossing now in Union hands, the II Corps column was able to resume its advance. Barlow's division crossed first, followed by the rest of the corps. The 111th was halted about a mile southwest of the river and set to work constructing a line of breastworks. Gibbon's Second Division occupied the left flank of the corps, Barlow's First Division was on the right flank and Birney's Third Division was held in reserve. During the night, the New Yorkers listened anxiously to the sound of heavy cannonading off to their right, wondering what the next day had in store for them.[5]

Hancock's corps was not alone as it marched along the back county roads of Virginia the morning of June 21. After receiving word that a large force of cavalry and infantry was moving around his right flank, Lee began to put his army in motion, just as Grant and Meade had hoped. Lee ordered Richard Ewell to move his corps south, in the direction of Hanover Junction. Instead of attacking Hancock's lone corps, the Confederate commander was moving to place his army between the Federals and his capital. Earlier in the day, the Union V and VI corps had also pulled out of their works and began to head south, following the general route taken by the II Corps. Once he was certain that the entire Army of the Potomac had vacated the works in his front, Lee ordered the rest of his army to abandon their lines at Spotsylvania Court House and hurry south to connect with Ewell.[6]

On June 22, while the rest of the Army of the Potomac was rapidly trying to catch up with the isolated II Corps, the men of the 111th waited behind their earthworks, sweltering in the intense heat. Corporal Geer took the opportunity to write a quick letter to his friends back home. He echoed the sentiments of many in the regiment when he noted that "we have been building breastworks and are waiting to be attacked."[7]

Just before dawn the next morning, the men of the 111th left the safety of the fieldworks behind and continued their march south, heading for the North Anna River. The rest of the Army of the Potomac, which had caught up to the II Corps during the night, followed close behind. By early evening, the river was in sight, and General Hancock deployed his Corps with Gibbon on the left, Barlow in the center astride Telegraph Road, and Birney on the right. Captain Husk led the 111th in the fields between the Fredericksburg, Richmond and Petersburg Railroad on their left and Telegraph Road to their right.[8]

The North Anna River was spanned by two bridges: one for the railroad and the other for Telegraph Road. The Confederates had built a small redoubt on the north side of Telegraph Road Bridge (Chesterfield Bridge) and a strong line of works on the southern end. The rebels had also built a second line of works south of the river to protect the railroad. The six regiments of John Henagan's South Carolina brigade manned the bridges, with four of his regiments on the northern bank while the other two regiments manned the works on the south side. As soon as he saw the approaching II Corps column, Henagan ordered his soldiers to prepare for battle.[9]

It was close to 6:30 P.M., and with skirmishers out, the New Yorkers listened to their artillery open a furious shelling of the enemy redoubt. Shot and shell rained down on the fort, one shot exploding an enemy caisson, sending smoke and burning debris high into the air. With cannons booming, the men of the 111th looked on as regiments from Birney's II Corps Division advanced under a severe fire from the rebel line, thankful that they were not the ones making the attack. Birney's men swept over the fields in front of them, captured the redoubt and a large number of prisoners. Those of Henagan's defenders who were not killed or captured, jumped into the river and swam to the safety of the opposite bank.[10]

Early the next morning, the 111th stood in line of battle as regiments from Birney's division attacked across the river and captured the works opposite Chesterfield Bridge. With the south bank secure, the rest of the II Corps joined Birney on the other side of the river. The New Yorkers continued to advance adjacent to the railroad, closing to within almost 600 yards of the second line of works. A halt was called and the men busily set to the task of constructing a line of breastworks, on which they worked for the rest of the day.[11]

Later that evening, regiments from Gibbon's division advanced against the entrenched rebel infantry. The fighting raged until dark, the booming of the cannon mixing with the crash of thunder. In a torrential downpour, the men of the 111th watched as Gibbon's men were repulsed and forced to fall back. By the end of the day's contest, the Union line was shaped like a shallow V. The II Corps held the left of the line opposite Ewell's and Anderson's Confederate corps. The IX Corps was located north of the river at Ox Ford while the V and VI corps held the right of the line south of the river along the Virginia Central Railroad.[12]

The men of the 111th spent June 25 much like the day before, lying behind their works near the railroad. Details from the regiment were sent out on the skirmish line and a lively fire was kept up all day. Wellington Hinman noted, "Sharpshooters skirmished all day, a little cannonading during the day."[13] The hazardous duty caused at least two casualties in the regiment. First Sergeant Hoff was slightly wounded in the shoulder while Charles Webner of Company E received a severe injury that put him out of the regiment.[14]

During his tour on the skirmish line, Sergeant Levi White just missed receiving a wound that would have raised some very embarrassing questions. While dueling with an enemy sharpshooter,

> White took position behind a small pine sapling only eight or ten inches through, which protected only a portion of his body, leaving the residue a fair target for his opponent, twelve rods distant. *Business was brisk*; some ten shots had been exchanged, when a ball struck the edge of the tree behind which White was partially concealed, and came through, just breaking the bark in range of his head. Fearing that in course of time the enemy might miss the tree but not the portion of the U.S. soldier exposed to view, said soldier deemed discretion the better part of valor, and skipped along out of range.[15]

While the regiment remained behind its breastworks near the river, welcome news arrived in the form of promotions for a select group of men. First Lieutenant Marcus Murdock of Company I was promoted to captain and transferred to Company A to take Captain Seeley's place. First Lieutenants Jerome Lattin of Company C and John Lockwood of Company F were each promoted to captain in their respective companies while Second Lieutenant Warren Smith of Company F was promoted to first lieutenant to fill the vacancy left by Lockwood's promotion.[16]

Taking the lessons learned at Spotsylvania to heart, Generals Grant and Meade decided to try once again to get around General Lee's right flank rather than throw the Army of the Potomac against the rebel entrenchments. The move would take the army toward the Pamunkey River and closer to Butler's Army of the James, then bottled up below Richmond. Hancock's II Corps would follow the VI Corps and cross the river near Hanovertown. The V and IX corps would follow on a parallel course and cross the river below Hanovertown.[17]

With a heavy rain still falling, the New Yorkers quietly pulled out of their works around midnight on June 26 and withdrew to the north side of the North Anna River, turned southeast and set off for the Pamunkey.[18] The rain gave way to intense heat the next day, causing the New Yorkers to suffer terribly. Charles White noted in his diary that the "road was strewn with dead horses all the way which was almost sufocating to us when we passed one."[19] However difficult the march may have been, it once again had the desired effect of forcing the Army of Northern Virginia out from behind its formidable entrenchments to stay between Richmond and the Army of the Potomac.

By noon on June 28, the footsore soldiers of the 111th reached the Pamunkey, crossing on a pontoon bridge after the VI Corps. The New Yorkers continued on until reaching the area of Crump's Creek, where they immediately began throwing up a line of entrenchments along the road leading to Haw's Shop. As they labored in the late day heat, the New Yorkers listened as their cavalry battled for control of the important crossroads at Haw's Shop.[20]

The next day, the 111th left the safety of its fieldworks and advanced south with the rest of the First Division to Haw's Shop. General Barlow had been ordered to conduct a reconnaissance to try and locate the main Confederate line. Finding nothing but a few dead troopers from the previous day's fight, the column pressed on until reaching Totopotomoy Creek. Here General Barlow found what he was looking for. He immediately sent word to General Hancock that the Confederates had a strong line of works on the south side of the creek and that it would be no easy task to carry the enemy's position. Word soon came back from the II Corps commander for Barlow to have his men dig in; there would be no attack today.[21]

For the men of the 111th, May 30 was spent much like the previous day, digging in the Virginia dirt and dogging rebel bullets. Union batteries posted to the rear kept up a constant fire throughout the day, pounding the Confederate's position. Wellington Hinman and the rest of the regiment were detailed on the skirmish line. Enemy bullets flew fast and thick, many finding their target. John Sullivan of Company A was killed while William Page of the same company was mortally wounded. Six others were wounded by the intense fire, including 46-year-old Philander Rose and Second Lieutenant Edgar Dudley of Company H.[22] His wounds would eventually force him to resign his commission.

After being treated in a field hospital, the 20-year-old Page was transferred to Carver Hospital in Washington, D.C., where he continued to languish in pain. Lying on his deathbed, Page told the doctors, "Yes, I suffer very much but I am willing to be torn piecemeal, joint from joint while living for my country and for liberty."[23] After more than two months of suffering, Page died on August 3, 1864.

Fighting began in earnest around midmorning on the last day of May. All corps commanders were directed to have their skirmishers move forward and probe the enemy works for a weak spot. It was Meade's intention to consolidate his entire army south of Totopotomoy Creek for one massive assault on the Confederate line. The II Corps moved across the creek and achieved some limited success. While the right-most division of the II Corps, under General Birney, was able to capture a portion of the Confederate line and a number of prisoners, General Barlow's First Division wasn't as fortunate.[24]

The 111th advanced with the rest of the First Division into Totopotomoy Creek and up the steep banks on the other side, all the while subjected to fire from the enemy works. Wallace Fink of Company H was hit and killed instantly. In a desperate display of love and courage, Manning Fink ran to his brother's aid. But Manning was wounded before he could get his dead brother off the field. The New Yorkers pushed on toward the main rebel works. They had not gone far before orders arrived for Captain Husk to halt his regiment and withdraw it back to the north side of the creek. General Barlow had determined that the rebels' works were too strong and could not be carried. The futile effort had cost the regiment three men killed and three wounded.[25]

While the 111th was battling south of the creek, Union cavalry was fighting for control of the valuable crossroads at Old Cold Harbor. After some intense fighting, the Federal troopers managed to drive a combined force of cavalry and infantry from the field. But the cavalry's hold on the crossroads was tenuous at best, as the Confederate First Corps was massing troops to attack the Union cavalry at first light the next morning. The troopers were ordered to hold; the VI Corps was on the way and would be up by morning. Also moving on Old Cold Harbor was the XVIII Corps of the Army of the James, commanded by General W. F. Smith. However, they would not get there in time to save the Federal cavalry from being driven out of Old Cold Harbor.[26]

Since the Confederate works along Totopotomoy Creek proved too strong to capture by frontal assault, Generals Grant and Meade decided on yet another turning movement to the left. Intent on flanking General Lee's army out from behind its works, the Army of the Potomac would pull out of line one corps at a time and march for Old Cold Harbor. General Hancock received orders to vacate the works his corps held on the right flank of the army and move to Old Cold Harbor as soon as it was dark on the night of June 1.[27]

The first day of June found the men of the 111th huddled behind their breastworks, listening to the sound of battle off to their left. The Confederates had launched an attack against the VI Corps front, which, after some fierce fighting, was repulsed. The VI and XVIII corps in turn attacked the Confederates. Elements of both corps managed to breach the enemy position and capture an advance line of works. With part of the enemy line now secure, soldiers from both the VI and XVIII corps began to furiously construct earthworks close to the rebel's main line.[28]

The battle between the skirmishers along the 111th's front continued unabated. Despite being posted behind their earthworks, the regiment took a number of casualties. One of the wounded was Sergeant Levi White of Company I, shot through the right breast. When White was brought off the field, he immediately asked that his brother Charles be brought to him. Charles accompanied his younger brother to the hospital where he ensured Levi was comfortable and well cared for.[29]

During the day, Captain Husk was directed to have the regiment ready to march that night with the rest of the II Corps. General Grant wanted Hancock's men in position at Old Cold Harbor early the next morning to spearhead the attack on the Confederate works. The men were ordered to move all the wounded to the rear, pack their knapsacks, and cook rations. At the appointed hour, the regiment quietly withdrew from their works along Totopotomoy Creek and marched off into the night.[30]

To screen the movement of the regiment, Captain Husk left behind a line of skirmishers, whose number included Wellington Hinman. Around 4:00 A.M. on the morning of June 2, "the Rebels had passed around on our left and surrounded our Picket line," recalled Hinman. "Myself, [Asahel] Fuller and others from the 111 were among those captured. We marched inside the line toward Richmond." After a brief stay in Libby Prison, where men were "so thickly stowed away that we cannot all lie down at a time," Hinman and six others from the regiment began the long journey to Andersonville.[31]

One of those taken prisoner was Franklin Roberts of Company B. Deciding that the life of a prisoner was not for him, Roberts found a way out of his dire situation by enlisting in the Tenth Tennessee Infantry, C.S.A. His service for the Confederacy was short-lived as Roberts was captured at Egypt, Mississippi, three days after Christmas. When he was paroled in April 1865, the enigmatic New Yorker once again switched sides and enlisted in the Fifth United States Infantry.[32]

The night of June 1 was exceedingly hot and humid, and clouds of dust choked the New Yorkers as they marched along the backcountry roads. The engineer officer sent by General Meade to guide Hancock's men decided to conduct the column by a shortcut, which quickly turned into a nightmare for the column. The trail chosen by the officer gradually began to narrow and soon the column was backed up as the corps' artillery became stuck. Confusion reigned while men were separated from their commands and became lost in the darkness. A halt was finally called to allow officers to untangle the mass of men and turn them around, and the column redirected along a different road. The exhausted New Yorkers arrived south of Old Cold Harbor as the sun was rising on the morning of June 2. What was supposed to be an easy nine-mile march turned into a grueling 15-mile test of patience and endurance.[33]

By early afternoon, the 111th was in position along Dispatch Station Road, about half a mile southeast of Old Cold Harbor. Captain Husk immediately posted a strong line of skirmishers to the front and put his men to work constructing a line of fieldworks. Due to the II Corps' late arrival on the field, the attack scheduled for early that morning was postponed until 5:00 P.M. that evening. General Barlow positioned his brigades for the attack, with Miles and Brooke, from left to right, in the front line while Byrnes was behind Miles and MacDougall was positioned behind Brooke. Shortly before 3:00 P.M., the attack was again put off, this time until early the following morning. Generals Grant and Meade believed that Hancock's II Corps soldiers were far too fatigued from the previous night's march for any type of offensive operations.[34]

To the regiment's front was a slight eminence known as Turkey Hill and, for some reason, General Hancock believed that no Confederate troops were present on the hill. With this in mind, the II Corps commander ordered Barlow to advance two of his brigades and occupy the ground. The men of the 111th watched as Miles and Brooke led their brigades out of the works and moved them toward the hill. What was thought to be a hill turned out to be a series of ridgelines, with the Confederates occupying the final ridge. The two brigades pushed forward but were unable to take possession of the hill and quickly returned to their works under a hail of bullets. There was a sense of unease in the regiment as the men knew they would have to return to that same hill the next morning and face an entrenched enemy ready to give them a warm reception. As evening settled over the field, a steady rain began to fall.[35]

The Army of the Potomac occupied a line of works that was well over seven miles long. The right of the army, held by the V Corps, was anchored at Bethesda Church. Posted in reserve behind the V Corps was the IX Corps. Next in line came the XVIII Corps, whose left flank connected with the VI Corps. Finally, holding the left flank of the army was the dependable Hancock. General Hancock posted his II Corps with Gibbon on the right and Barlow on the left. General Birney's division was held in reserve.[36]

The Confederate line was formidable indeed. Over six miles in length, the rebels took full advantage of the numerous low ridges, creeks and swamps so that their line almost disappeared into the landscape. The works were intersected in several places by creeks and marshes. The section of works facing the regiment was fronted by an open plain that sloped gently upward to the enemy earthworks, which were manned by the regiments of Breckinridge's and Mahone's divisions. Running across the field was a sunken road hidden from the New Yorkers' view. Atop the hill was a second line of works that had a commanding view of the fields below. The failed attempt to take Turkey Hill by Barlow's men afforded the Confederates another day to improve and strengthen their works.[37]

General Meade's plan of attack for June 3 was simple; the entire Army of the Potomac would assault the Confederate line. A small force of cavalry and infantry would attack the enemy's left flank while the rest of the army threw itself against the entrenched rebels. The commanding generals believed that sheer numbers alone would carry the day. But they had failed to learn the lessons of Spotsylvania and North Anna, and now many Union soldiers would lose their lives due to such shortsightedness.[38]

The men of the 111th were up early on the 3rd, preparing for the day's attack. General Barlow positioned his brigades in the same formation as the day before, with Miles's and Brooke's brigade in the front line and Byrne and MacDougall in the second line. Promptly at 4:30 A.M., Union artillery opened a furious barrage on the Confederate works, prompting a quick response from the rebel gunners. While the cannons boomed, the New Yorkers were able to get a good view of the enemy works. The sight of the imposing log and earth battlements across the field weakened the knees of even the most stalwart soldier. Quite a few in the regiment were determined not to fill an unmarked grave. So just as at Mine Run the previous December, they attached pieces of paper to their coats on which were written their name and hometown.[39]

When the signal was given, the New Yorkers watched as Miles's and Brooke's regiments stepped off and began to advance toward the rebel line. Moving at the double, the First Division soldiers passed over the sunken road and quickly overpowered the Confederates in the first line of works. The two brigades captured 300 prisoners, three cannons and one stand of colors. But the initial success of Miles and Brooke didn't last long. Although reinforced by Byrnes' brigade, Miles was forced out of the trenches with tremendous loss. For some reason, the 111th and the rest of the Third Brigade never advanced to the support of Brooke, whose soldiers were also driven out of the trenches. When the 111th finally did move forward, the rest of the division was already digging in no less than 100 yards from the enemy's line. The failed attack was over in less than 20 minutes. In fact the fighting had ended so quickly that some portions of the rebel line did not even know there had been a major attack.[40]

Rumor soon spread through the Union ranks that another attack was ordered and the entire army was against it. In 1884, General Grant wrote to Myron Failing of Company E about the order for a second attack: "I will say that I did make an order for a final charge but before the hour arrived for it, I considered that it would be a failure, with much loss to ourselves and without compensating results, and I quietly sent verbal messages to the corps commanders to withhold."[41]

General Meade's army suffered over 5,000 casualties in just about 20 minutes. The II Corps alone lost over 3,000 men, including both Colonels Byrnes and Brooke. Standing in stark contrast to these numbers is the list of casualties suffered by the 111th. On a day when other units were being cut to pieces along the rebel parapets, the regiment had only two men wounded, John Bull of Company F and Samuel Gould of Company G.[42]

The men of the 111th dug furiously with whatever they had available. Some used bayonets and tin cups while others used plates. Those who were not hastily throwing up a line of works were keeping up a constant fire on the enemy. Before long, the entrenchments were sufficiently deep enough for the New Yorkers to crouch down and hide. By

Nelson Skinner, Company F. Enlisted March 1864, he was wounded at Cold Harbor on June 6, 1864, and transferred to the Fourth New York Heavy Artillery (Massachusetts Commandery Military Order of the Loyal Legion and the USAMHI).

6:30 A.M., the major fighting had all but stopped along the regiment's front. The men worked throughout the day improving their position, digging deeper to escape the incessant fire from the enemy's sharpshooters. As evening approached, the Union line erupted in gunfire as the Confederates made an attempt to carry General Gibbon's section of the line. But like the II Corps attack earlier in the day, the enemy was easily repulsed. Night brought no relief from the skirmishing, as soldiers from both sides fired at anything that moved, or appeared to move. Piteous cries for help could be heard coming from the wounded laying between the lines. Further adding to the misery, a steady rain set in turning the New Yorkers' trenches into a sea of knee-deep mud.[43]

June 4 began much as the previous day ended, with heavy skirmishing along the whole line. The New Yorkers dared not show their heads above the trenches for fear of falling victim to a sharpshooter's bullet. Throughout the day, Union artillery pounded the rebel works, drawing in return a heavy fire. Fortunately, most of the shells fell to the rear and not in the trenches. Late in the evening, Southern regiments again tested the II Corps line. The attack was beaten back with no loss of life in the regiment.[44]

By June 7, the stench emanating from the bodies in front of the regiment's line was unbearable. The dead and wounded had been laying exposed to the elements since the attack of June 3, subjected the whole time to sun and rain. Those among the wounded who were not killed by Confederate sharpshooters or who had not died of exposure and neglect, were lucky to be alive. A two-hour truce was called for that evening to allow the Federals to remove their dead and wounded. When the appointed hour arrived, soldiers from both sides climbed over their works to view the carnage. For most, it was the first opportunity they had in four days to stand up and walk around without fear of getting shot. Although orders had been issued forbidding fraternization with the enemy, the men talked and traded freely. The work details buried the soldiers where they had fallen, turning the no-man's land between the works into a massive cemetery. When the truce expired, the two sides returned to their works and started the deadly skirmishing all over again.[45]

While the regiment languished in the trenches at Old Cold Harbor, Colonel MacDougall was visited by his friend and business partner, William H. Seward Jr. Seward, commander of the Ninth New York Heavy Artillery, had just been promoted and came to see MacDougall about securing a pair of colonel's shoulder straps. "MacDougall told Seward he had plenty of eagles, but was looking for stars himself and hadn't succeeded in lighting any yet." After exchanging pleasantries, the two sat down to breakfast, complete with fresh milk from MacDougall's cow.[46]

Over the next couple of days, the men of the 111th labored tirelessly on a new line of entrenchments to the rear of their position. The New Yorkers suffered in the June heat all the while dodging shot and shell coming from the Confederate line. According to Corporal Geer, "the bullets fly thick from morning till night." While writing a letter home, Geer complained about the incessant fire: "The sharpshooters do pick away at us for certain. Occasionally the bullets whistle rather close to me as I sit here writing. If I make any crooked marks you must lay it to that."[47] At least three men fell victim to the enemy sharpshooters. Casper Mandie of Company B was shot and killed while Nelson Skinner of Company F and Theron Dudley of Company H were wounded.

The inability to leave the trenches put a considerable strain on the men. Charles White left the relative safety of the hospital to visit the regiment at the front and was appalled by what he saw. In his diary he wrote, "The boys up to the Regt look pretty tough. They have been now 5 weeks continuly behind the rifle pitts or on the march so they have not had time to wash there shirts."[48]

The reason for digging the new line of works was not simply to keep the men busy. Generals Grant and Meade intended to pull the army out of its lines at Old Cold Harbor and cross to the south side of the James River, where the army would move rapidly to seize the city of Petersburg and its important rail lines. Under cover of darkness, each corps would leave a strong line of skirmishers in the front line while main body occupied the second line of works to the rear. Here, the men would be prepared for one more march to the left.[49]

As usual, the Confederate commander was not sitting idly by waiting for his counterpart to make the next move. General Lee had already sent Breckinridge's division back to the Shenandoah Valley, and now he was ready to deplete his army further to drive the enemy from the all-important valley. The Second Corps under Jubal Early was dispatched to the valley to stop Union general Hunter, who was then driving on Lexington.[50]

When the new line was completed early on June 11, General Meade issued orders for the evacuation of the Union lines to begin the next evening. At dusk on June 12, the 111th fell back to the new position as bands played to mask the noise of the army's withdrawal. Close to midnight, the regiment pulled out of reserve line and began the march toward the James River. Although tired and filthy, the New Yorkers' spirits were high as they left the trenches behind them.[51]

CHAPTER 10

The Cockade City

> There is a rumor today that Grant has notified the Johnnies that Petersburg is in a state of siege and advised them to remove the women and children for safety.[1]

The night was incredibly hot as just over 100 officers and men of the 111th plodded along toward the Chickahominy River. The regiment arrived at Long Bridge at daybreak on June 13 and promptly crossed the Chickahominy, continuing the advance. Clouds of dust shrouded the regiment, covering the New Yorkers uniforms and turning them from dark blue to a dusty gray. By later afternoon, the regiment arrived at Wilcox Landing on the James River. The men were immediately set to work building a line of works to protect the crossing site. Laboring into the night, the men were finally able get a few hours of much needed sleep before they would have to take their turn in crossing the river to the southern shore.[2]

The New Yorkers spent the entire day manning the works around the crossing site. Sometime after midnight, the lead elements of the II Corps began to cross the river. Every type of boat and river craft was pressed into service to ferry the soldiers to Windmill Point. As Barlow's division was the rear element of the corps, it was the last to cross. Dawn was breaking on June 15 by the time the 111th was ready to cross the river.[3]

The move across the James River was going better than expected. The Federal withdrawal from the lines at Old Cold Harbor on June 12 was conducted with such silence that General Lee had no idea they were gone until the next morning. In the early morning hours of June 15, William F. Smith's XVIII Corps and General Augustus Kautz's cavalry brigade of the Army of the James stood poised to attack and capture Petersburg. The II Corps would soon be within supporting distance and would add its weight to the attack. The only obstacle standing between them and their prize was a force of about 10,000 Confederate infantry and artillery, known as the Petersburg Defense Forces, manning the works at Petersburg and Bermuda Hundred.[4]

Before they left the trenches around Old Cold Harbor, the men were issued three days rations. Now, over three days later, the New Yorkers were completely without food. Word was received that rations would be issued prior to the move on Petersburg, but by midmorning the rations still had not arrived. General Hancock could wait no longer and ordered his generals to move their commands. His men tired and hungry, Captain Husk led the regiment away from the James River with the rest of the division, heading for Petersburg.[5]

While the II Corps divisions of Gibbon and Birney marched directly to Petersburg, the 111th marched with the rest of the First Division escorting the corps' wagon train along a different route. The day quickly turned hot and the lack of water and rations caused the men to suffer, many falling out along the line of march from sheer exhaustion. The column was to take up a position just east of the city. But due to some mix-up, the 111th

Albert Rice, Company G. Wounded at Petersburg, June 16, 1864, and died of his wounds January 22, 1865 (courtesy Archive of Michigan).

found itself marching with the rest of the division on the road to City Point, in the opposite direction from Petersburg. The error was eventually discovered but not until the column arrived at the outskirts of City Point. Exhausted, the New Yorkers were turned around and directed back toward Petersburg.[6]

Smith's XVIII Corps and the cavalry attacked the fortifications around Petersburg and after some severe fighting, breached the Confederate line. The door to Petersburg was wide open and ready for the taking, if only Smith could be reinforced. General Hancock received urgent messages from both Smith and General Meade, pleading with him to reinforce Smith as quickly as possible and move into the city. But when the II Corps did not show until after 9:00 P.M., and with only two of his three divisions, Smith wired General Grant that the hour was getting late and he had gained enough for one day. He would rest his troops and resume the attack at first light.

When the advance did resume the next morning, Smith and Hancock would face more than just the Petersburg Defense Forces. As Smith sat idle, portions of the Army of Northern Virginia arrived in the city to bolster the weak defenses. The failure to capture Petersburg on June 15 would haunt the army for the next ten months.[7]

It was close to daylight on June 16 when the 111th finally arrived outside the city. The original point designated for the regiment, the intersection of Harrison's Creek and the City Point Railroad, was actually a half mile behind the Confederate lines. Much time using faulty maps and local guides had been spent searching in vain for this spot. Eventually, the regiment was directed to take up a position with the rest of the First Division on the extreme left of the II Corps line. The New Yorkers filed into the works captured the day before by the XVIII Corps. With skirmishers out, the men were able to get some much-needed rest. Rations soon arrived and were distributed. The regiment's line was soon marked by cooking fires as the New Yorkers fried salt pork and boiled coffee.[8]

The booming of cannon and crackle of small arms fire was heard all morning as patrols were sent forward from the II Corps line to probe the enemy's position. Orders arrived in the afternoon for Captain Husk to begin preparing the regiment to move with the rest of the Third Brigade in an assault of the Confederate line. The area over which the 111th was supposed to attack was an open plain that sloped upward to the enemy's works and was intersected by a number of ravines. After the XVIII Corps' attacks of the previous day, the rebels had begun constructing a new line on the western side of Harrison's Creek. While this position constituted the main Confederate line, some of the original fortifications east of the creek were still manned.[9]

The object of the day's attack was the capture of the works around the Hare house. Birney would advance his division on the right of the II Corps line toward the right of the Hare house while, on the left of the line, Barlow would advance directly on the works at the Hare house. General Gibbon's division would advance behind and in support of the other two divisions. Two brigades of the IX Corps would lend their support to Hancock's infantry. The XVIII Corps was ordered to make a demonstration in their front to keep the enemy from reinforcing the point of attack.[10]

At 6:00 P.M., Union batteries began a furious shelling of the rebel works. Knapsacks were stacked in piles, and the men readied themselves for the coming battle. When the fire from the guns slackened, the regiment moved out of its entrenchments and quickly formed into line of battle. The 111th was on the left of the brigade, with the 126th to its right. Bayonets were fixed, rifles were held at right shoulder shift, and the order to advance was given. With General Barlow at the head of the division, the regiment stepped off, moved through a finger of woods and began to advance toward the rebel works.[11]

In the fading evening light, the 111th moved over fields swept with shell and canister. One of the first to fall was Sergeant Allen Hoxie of Company I. Writing to Hoxie's family days after the battle, Colonel MacDougall described the sergeant as being "shot through the body in the left side just above the hip bone and passing entirely through his body."[12] In the last letter he wrote to his mother, Hoxie expressed his desire to see the day when the "blackest of all crimes — slavery" is eradicated and the Union preserved. Yet he ended his letter with these words: "I hope to see them, but if I do not, I have sisters and brothers and dear friends who will see and enjoy them ... I will thee good by."[13]

Small arms fire was soon added to the artillery already cutting through the New Yorkers' ranks, their line of advance marked by a path of dead and wounded. Company F was particularly hard hit. Sergeants Edward Van Dervere and Artemus Stewart were killed while Sergeant Richard Warren was hit in the leg. In Company K, Second Lieutenant Samuel Bradley fell to the ground wounded.[14]

In a letter written after the battle, Sergeant Warren informed his sister of his wound: "My leg is getting along very well the wound is healing up very fast but it leaves my foot very numb so that I have no use in it at all and when it hangs down there is such a rush of blood in it that it makes it very painful. I am satisfied that I got off as luckey as I did some poor fellows got a great deal worse wounds than I did some of them had both legs taken off and some their arms."[15] Despite his wish to return to the regiment, Warren would sit out the rest of the war in a Washington hospital.

Moving at the double, the 111th passed through a number of ravines and came to a fence line. Here the line seemed to momentarily falter before the men scrambled over the fence and resumed the charge. They pressed on with a yell and rushed right up to the Confederate works. Not to be denied, they swarmed over the earth and log battlements, forcing the defenders out at the point of the bayonet. Officers and sergeants forced their men into some semblance of a line and ordered them to commence firing. They sent volley after volley into the retreating enemy, but when it became apparent that no further advance on the fortifications west of Harrison's Creek was possible, Captain Husk ordered his men to take up a position along the rebel works.[16]

Capturing a portion of the Confederate entrenchments near the Hare house had cost the regiment dearly. Fifteen men were killed outright, another 35 were wounded, and one man was reported as missing. The regiment had suffered almost 50 percent casualties. Captain Lockwood's Company F seemed to have borne the brunt of the casualties with four men killed and eight wounded.[17]

The men spent the night fortifying their trenches, replenishing their ammunition, and skirmishing with the rebels, who were less than a quarter of a mile away. Heavy firing continued unabated all during the night, the rebels making several attempts to retake the works they lost during the day. As the crackle of musketry and pounding of artillery filled the air, a little piece of home arrived in camp in the form of mail. With the army constantly on the go since leaving the trenches around Old Cold Harbor, it had been some time since the New Yorkers received news from home. The letters were distributed and for a while the horrors of war faded away, replaced with thoughts of family and friends.[18]

Sunrise on the morning of June 17 brought the men of the 111th back to reality. Captain Husk was directed to advance what was left of his regiment along with the rest of the brigade to occupy the ground just south of the Hare house hill. Once in position, the men quickly went to work building a line of breastworks. They spent the rest of the day listening to the battle raging to their left, skirmishing and fending off half-hearted attempts by the rebels to retake some of their captured entrenchments. As always, skirmishing with the enemy was not without cost. While taking its turn on the line, the 111th lost Robert Buchanan of Company B and John Duly of Company F was wounded.[19]

Up early the next day, the New Yorkers began to prepare for another attack of the Confederate works. General Meade ordered the entire army to make a coordinated attack before the rest of the Army of Northern Virginia could reinforce the lines surrounding the city. The XVIII Corps held the right of the line, with its right resting near the Appomattox River north of the city. Next came the VI Corps, its right connecting with the XVIII Corps and its left resting on the City Point Railroad. The II Corps connected with the VI Corps on the right and ranged south where it connected with the IX Corps. The V Corps held the left of the line, its regiments stretching south from the IX Corps to the Petersburg and Norfolk Railroad. The II Corps was formed for the attack with Gibbon's Second Division on the right, Mott's Third Division in the center and Barlow's First Division on the left.[20]

Ranks were formed, bayonets fixed, and skirmishers placed to the front. When the signal was given, the men stepped off and moved toward the Confederate line. The going was tough as numerous ravines and thick woods broke the regiment's formation. The New Yorkers were puzzled by the fact that they were not being fired upon. They were even more surprised when they mounted the enemy parapets only to find the trenches empty. What they did not know was that just after midnight, the rebels had pulled back and formed a new line closer to the city.[21]

Precious time was wasted as skirmishers were sent forward to try and find the new Confederate line. When it was located, the corps attacked in piecemeal fashion and not as Meade had ordered. Out of disgust, the army commander ordered the corps commanders to attack immediately. He sent a pointed letter directly to General Birney, who had assumed command of the II Corps from the ailing General Hancock: "I beg you will at once, as soon as possible, assault in a strong column. The day is fast going, and I wish the practicality of carrying the enemy's lines settled before dark."[22] But no coordinated attack was made by the II Corps. The New Yorkers watched as one division after another threw itself against the rebel earthworks, only to be repelled. General Meade finally ordered a halt to active operations for the day and had the men dig in close to the enemy works. The siege of Petersburg had begun.[23]

Digging trenches was becoming a way of life for the Wayne and Cayuga men. The longer they remained in one position, the more elaborate the trench line became. As the earthworks were being dug, dirt would be thrown up in front of the trench. Logs or gabions, baskets made of sticks filled with dirt, were used to reinforce the walls. As the trench line was dug deeper, firing steps were added to allow the men to shoot over the walls of the trench. The depth of the trenches varied, ranging from 10 to 15 feet. In front of the works was placed fraise, sharpened stakes that angled out of the ground at a 45-degree angle used to break up attacking formations. Well in advance of the main trench were picket posts. These posts were typically just holes dug in the ground with some type of protection placed in front.[24]

Placed at intervals along the line were rooms dug deep into the walls of the trench called bombproofs. These structures were typically made of logs and earth, large enough to house a number of soldiers and designed to protect the occupants from the constant pounding of the enemy artillery. Zigzag shaped communication trenches were dug to connect the front lines with the second line of works. Supplies were brought to the front lines through the use of covered roadways, which offered protection from artillery and sharpshooter fire.[25]

As the use of trenches and earthen forts was perfected, so too was the employment of certain types of weaponry. One of those weapons was the mortar. As the opposing armies began to burrow deeper into the ground, conventional field artillery just wasn't effective enough against an entrenched enemy. The mortar had seen use throughout the war but never on such a large scale as at Petersburg. This weapon fired a projectile at a high angle, causing it to fall straight down into the trenches. At night, the men could look up into the sky and see the fuses of the shells burning. Surgeon Benton wrote, "I can sit in the door of my tent and see the shells go through the air and in the night the long curves of the mortar shells go through the air like comets on a fandango."[26]

Soldiers on both sides became experts at predicting where a mortar shell would fall. If the slow-moving projectile was going to land near them, they would hurry to the bombproof until the shell exploded. If the shell headed for another part of the line, the men would simply stay where they were and watch the impact. The constant shelling and sharpshooter fire made living in the trenches unbearable. It was not uncommon for the sentry to be the only person visible in the trenches during the day.

Musketry and artillery on June 20 was quite heavy all along the line. Those not taking their turn on the skirmish line were forced to stay as low as possible behind the works. Company F lost two men wounded on skirmish duty while it dueled with the enemy in the opposite trenches. After dark, Captain Husk led his men out of the trenches and moved them to the safety of a reserve position behind the IX Corps, near the center of the Union line. Early the next morning, the 111th moved with the entire II Corps south behind the main line of works.[27] Lewis Clark wrote in his book, *Military History of Wayne County*, that on the day's march "expectation took the place of dread, and the marching orders were [un]usually welcomed."[28]

The objective of the day's movement was the Petersburg and Weldon Railroad, a vital link between the city and a base of supplies in North Carolina. The II Corps was ordered to join the V Corps, then holding the extreme left of the Union line, and advance on the railroad in an attempt to stretch the army's lines to the left and severe the railroad line. The VI Corps would follow Birney's soldiers and take up a position on their left flank. Moving in concert with the infantry were two divisions of cavalry under General James Wilson. They were ordered to make a dash around the right flank of the Confederate trenches and cut the lines of the South Side Railroad, which entered the city from the south. If these two rail lines could be captured or destroyed, Lee's ability to supply his besieged army would be severely handicapped.[29]

The New Yorkers crossed the Norfolk and Petersburg Railroad and continued marching southwest until they hit Jerusalem Plank Road, a major artery leading into Petersburg from the south. Crossing the road, the column continued a short distance before taking position on the left flank of the V Corps, about two miles short of the Weldon Railroad. When the halt was called, Captain Husk posted skirmishers to the front, and the rest of the men began to throw up a crude line of earthworks. As the skirmishers battled with Confederate infantry of General Cadmus Wilcox's Third Corps Division, the VI Corps arrived on the field and moved in on the II Corps' left. The exchange between the opposing skirmishers became quite severe and the outnumbered New Yorkers were forced back to the main line, with three men wounded and three captured in the process. One of those lost was Captain Jerome Lattin of Company C. He would succumb to his wounds on July 15.[30]

The plan of attack for the next day called for the II Corps and the VI Corps to move together and strike the Confederate works east of the railroad. General Birney formed his corps with Gibbon's Second Division on the right, connecting with the V Corps, Mott in the center and Barlow's First Division on the left. Gibbon was to maintain a close connection with the left of the V Corps while Barlow was to make contact with the VI Corps on his left. The entire line would advance west toward the railroad and then swing north, hoping to strike the flank and rear of the Confederate line.[31]

Early on the morning of June 22, the 111th began to advance. The movement was hampered by dense woods and thick underbrush. After the regiment advanced a short distance, a halt was called to allow time for the VI Corps to move in on Barlow's left. But Wright's men were not moving at all. While the II Corps was makings its way slowly toward the railroad, the VI Corps was bogged down in a battle with a heavy line of enemy skirmishers and was way behind Barlow's First Division. There was no way Barlow could maintain his contact with both the VI Corps on his left and Mott's division to his right. The rest of the II Corps had already turned north and was quickly throwing up a line of works as the First Division continued to wait for the slow-moving VI Corps. Barlow was finally ordered to leave Wright behind and join the rest of the II Corps, even though the move would create a huge gap between the II and VI corps.[32]

It was close to 3:00 P.M., and General Lee was watching the Federals move against the Weldon Railroad with great concern. He commented to General William Mahone, who was standing nearby, that the movement must be stopped. Mahone, a civil engineer who had surveyed this same ground before the war, asked the Confederate commander to let him advance with three brigades and attack the left flank of the Union II Corps. When Lee gave his

George Remington, Company B. Wounded at Petersburg, June 22, 1864, Remington returned to the regiment just before it mustered out in June 1865 (Massachusetts Commandery Military Order of the Loyal Legion and the USAMHI).

approval, Mahone pulled his men out of their trenches and led them through a ravine that led directly to the gap between Barlow and the VI Corps.[33]

After reaching the rest of the II Corps, General Barlow posted his brigades with Miles connecting with the Third Division on the right. The remaining three brigades were thrown back at right angles, facing west, to protect the flank of the division. No sooner had Barlow finished deploying his regiments than Mahone launched his attack on Barlow's unprotected left flank.[34]

The men of the 111th were just settling into position when a thunderous rebel yell rang out from their left. The next thing they knew, bullets began to fly in all directions, coming from the front, left and rear. Corporal Geer remembered that the "trees were so thick we could not see far and the rebels got us nearly surrounded before we knew it."[35] Confusion reigned as troops posted to the New Yorkers' left broke and ran to the rear. Bullets slammed into the trees and shells exploded overhead. Unable to withstand the pressure, the 111th joined the rest of the brigade in what soon deteriorated into a mad dash for safety. There was no order to the retreat as all formation was lost in the dense woods. Geer recalled, "I tell you the way we got up and got out of the woods was a caution. The rebs tried to halt us. They sayed hold on yanks, we wont hurt you, but we couldn't see it. They came very near capturing the whole division."[36]

Charles White, not with the regiment, was told that the men "took leg bail ... for dear life and did not stop untill they got safely behind our rear line of works."[37] After gaining the protection of the hastily built battlements of the previous day, the officers struggled to reform ranks under a tremendous shelling from the enemy guns. Once a rough line was thrown together, Captain Husk posted a skirmish line to the front and waited for the rebels to renew their attack, which never came.

When Barlow's division was routed and fled to the rear, the rest of the II Corps was forced to give way as well. All three divisions were forced to retire to the earthworks along Jerusalem Plank Road. Meanwhile, the VI Corps never advanced close to the railroad. Its progress was stymied by the rugged terrain and the stubborn resistance offered by Wilcox's Confederates. General Wright was content to let his men remain in place for the day.[38]

For its part in the rout of the II Corps, the 111th had 2 men mortally wounded and 7 men wounded, with 14 reported as missing. Wounded were the Perkins brothers of Company A, 18-year-old Charles and 24-year-old George.[39] Of the 14 men captured, 10 would die at Andersonville, most before year's end. One of those to fall victim of the Confederate prison was Charles Todd of Company A. Todd had deserted from the ranks when the regiment was camped at Uniontown, Maryland, the previous June but had returned to the regiment in December under the president's proclamation of amnesty.[40]

As Corporal Geer saw it, the regiment could not afford many more days like this. "I begin to think that we have all got to be either killed soon or missing before this is over."[41] George Peckham of Company I agreed. In a letter to the mother of his friend, Allen Hoxie, he wrote, "It is hard to look back over the last two months & see what we have passed through & then to look around & see the number that have left us since then. We left camp with 45 men in the Co. but 9 of us are here now. The rest are numbered with the died others are suffering with wounds in the hospital & still others are in the hands of the rebels. Oh this is a cruel thing."[42] The constant fighting had reduced the regiment's numbers to just 45.

Early the next morning, the 111th received orders to advance back to the scene of the previous day's battle. But when they arrived, the New Yorkers were pleasantly surprised to find that the rebels had pulled back closer to the city during the night. Captain Husk immediately set his men to work building a line of trenches. The New Yorkers labored for days improving the earth and log fortifications, all the while fighting the intense summer heat and dodging bullets and shells.[43]

By the end of the month, the ranks had swelled to almost 90. The regiment received a batch of new recruits and saw the return of a number of men wounded during the previous month's fighting. Captain Husk was rewarded for his hard work in leading the regiment with a well-deserved promotion to major.[44] Due to the number of casualties suffered by the two brigades since the beginning of the campaign, the Second and Third brigades of the First Division were consolidated into one brigade under the command of Colonel MacDougall. Added to MacDougall's command were the 63rd, 69th and 88th New York regiments, the once mighty Irish Brigade. The new command was known simply as the Consolidated Brigade.[45]

At the beginning of July, General Lee decided that he needed to do something drastic to take the pressure off his beleaguered army languishing in the trenches around Petersburg. Lee made up his mind to send General Jubal Early and his Second Corps into Maryland. Early was already in the Shenandoah Valley, where he had been since the fighting ended at Old Cold Harbor. The Confederate commander hoped that if Early could wreak enough havoc and threaten the vital B & O Railroad, the Union commander would have to weaken his lines at Petersburg by sending reinforcements from the Army of the Potomac north to stop Early. With this in mind, Lee unleashed Early and by July 6, the Confederate Second Corps was across the Potomac River. Just as Lee had hoped, General Grant was quick to react. The same day that Early crossed into Maryland, Grant ordered one division of the VI Corps to move north as quickly as possible.[46]

On July 9, Early attacked a force commanded by General Lew Wallace along the banks of the Monocacy River, south of Frederick City, Maryland. After some intense fighting, the Federals were forced from the field. When word of the Union defeat reached Petersburg, the remaining two divisions of the VI Corps were immediately dispatched to the nation's capital. When the veterans from the Army of the Potomac arrived, they manned the defenses north of the capital and helped defeat the Confederate's half-hearted attempt to attack the city. Early then withdrew his soldiers and led them back to the Shenandoah Valley, with the Union VI Corps following close behind.[47]

The New Yorkers spent most of July digging trenches behind the main Union line. Near the end of the month, the regiment found itself in a reserve position to the rear of the V Corps. It was here that the men learned that they were loosing Colonel MacDougall. Suffering from fever and severe dysentery for more than two weeks, Colonel MacDougall was granted a 30-day leave of absence to travel to Auburn to recuperate. When the colonel left for home, the command of the Consolidated Brigade passed to Colonel Levin Crandell of the 125th New York.[48]

While the men of the 111th were sweating in the intense summer sun that Corporal Geer described as "hot enough to boil coffee," Generals Grant and Meade were devising a plan much like the one their counterpart had already set into motion.[49] First, the II Corps, along with two divisions of cavalry under the command of General Philip Sheridan, would be sent to the north side of the James River in hopes of breaching the Confederate defenses around Deep Bottom. If the opportunity presented itself, the cavalry was to advance as rapidly as possible and attack the Confederate capital. With an entire Federal corps and two divisions of cavalry threatening to march on Richmond, the Confederates were sure to weaken their lines at Petersburg and send troops north in order to meet the threat.

With Lee focused on the II Corps and Sheridan's cavalry, Meade would send the IX Corps, supported by the V and XVIII corps, against the rebel earthworks. They were to drive into Petersburg and split the rebel army in two. The ambitious plan called for the corps commanders to exercise their own initiative and move their soldiers as quickly as possible, something that had yet to be done in any of the fighting at Petersburg.[50]

Just after 4:00 P.M. on July 26, the 111th began marching with the rest of the II Corps on the road toward City Point. Despite the heat, spirits were high as "the general impression was that we were to go to Washington to repell the invasion there." But, as surgeon Benton remarked, "all our fond anticipations were doomed to be crushed for on nearing City Point we turned sharp to the left" and headed for the Appomattox River.[51] The New Yorkers arrived at Point of Rocks late that evening promptly crossing to the north side of the river.[52] The men were allowed a few minutes' rest before setting off for the James River, where the regiment arrived early the next morning.

The II Corps was supposed to cross the river at the upper bridge and head for Chapin's Bluff, about five miles to the west. But when it was learned that the Confederates had constructed a strong line of works near the crossing site, General Hancock was instructed to take his men to the lower bridge site and attempt to turn the left flank of the Confederate line. The New Yorkers made their way onto the long bridge spanning the river which, according to surgeon Benton, was "covered with hay and pine boughs to muffle the sound" of thousands of tramping feet.[53]

Once across the river, the II Corps was deployed at Deep Bottom with Gibbon's Second Division on the left, Barlow occupying the center and Mott's Third Division holding the right. Major Husk quickly formed the 111th into line of battle in a stand of trees. To the front was an open field bordered on the far side by another lines of trees, inside which the Confederates had constructed a strong line of trenches. To the rear of the works was Bailey's Creek, and behind that was another line of works along the crest of Spring Hill. The rebel fortifications, manned by soldiers of Kershaw's division and Wilcox's division, were built to cover the New Market and Malvern Hill roads. These forces were joined later on July 27 by the Third Corps Division of Henry Heth.[54]

At 6:30 A.M., skirmishers from Miles's First Brigade were sent across the field toward the Confederate works. Moving with great vigor, Miles was able to capture the first line, a number of prisoners and four pieces of artillery. Surgeon Benton was quite impressed by the whole affair: The move "was done so dextrously that the Johnnies had to fall back leaving in our hands four twenty pound rifled Parrot guns of the best sort."[55] The four field pieces were brought back to the main line to great cheering from the rest of the division.

But the First Division could not rest on its laurels as there was more fighting to be done before the day was over. The 111th was ordered to fall in and fix bayonets. With skirmishers out in front, the New Yorkers advanced with the rest of the division northwest along New Market Road toward Bailey's Creek and the main Confederate line beyond. The enemy's position, posted behind the creek, took advantage of the natural strength of the ground along Spring Hill. As the New Yorkers advanced in line of battle, huge shells from Union gunboats on the James River screamed overhead and landed atop Spring Hill, sending columns of dirt high into the air. The battle line pushed toward the creek but did not make a concerted effort to cross and assault the works. The New Yorkers were content to post a line of skirmishers to the front and settle into position for the night.[56]

Skirmishing began early the next day along the regiment's front and lasted throughout the day. Added to the crackle of musketry was the shriek of the massive shells as the James River gunboats continued their deadly shelling of the rebel works. General Hancock was ordered not to risk a frontal assault against the Confederate works across Bailey's Creek. Instead, he was to hold his troops in position while the cavalry maneuvered around the enemy's left flank. In a spirited attack, the Union troopers drove the rebels back to a second line of works, capturing a number of prisoners and several battle flags.

While the Confederate line had not been completely broken, the move north of the James River had its desired effect; Lee had weakened his lines at Petersburg to reinforce his lines north of the James River. Besides the three divisions already there, General Lee dispatched two divisions of cavalry and another division of infantry, leaving his siege lines around Cockade City defended by only three divisions of infantry. The Union commander was now ready to set in motion the second part of his plan.[57]

Near the end of June, a regiment from the IX Corps began digging a tunnel leading from their works to a position under the Confederate fortifications. This effort was nothing new to the men of the 48th Pennsylvania whose regiment was composed mainly of coal miners. The tunnel ended just beneath a formidable line of trenches and fortifications known as Elliott's Salient, a little over 100 yards from the Union lines. The tunnel had a key part to play in the Meade's plan. When the tunnel was complete, it was packed with over 8,000 pounds of black powder, which would be exploded to create a huge breach in the Confederate line. The entire IX Corps would rush through the breach caused by the explosion and split the enemy's line in two. The attackers were ordered to drive straight for Jerusalem Plank Road and Cemetery Hill beyond. When the IX Corps made its attack, the V Corps on the left and the XVIII Corps on the right would advance in support.[58]

Friday, July 29 found the 111th holding the same line as the day before. The New Yorkers remained idle as the cavalry sparred with the enemy, and regiments from other divisions in the II Corps maneuvered to test the Confederate earthworks. That night, orders arrived for the II Corps to make a night march back to Petersburg and be ready to add its weight to the attack scheduled for July 30. Shortly before midnight, the regiment crossed back over the James, and after an exhausting march, arrived in the rear of the XVIII Corps before dawn. From their position on the extreme right of the Union line, the men of the 111th were witnesses to one of the greatest blunders of the entire campaign.[59]

Just before dawn, the earth heaved and shuddered as the mine exploded under the Confederate line. Surgeon Benton watched as "up goes a rebel fort and a Regt of rebs and sixteen guns fifty feet in the air and a hundred and twenty guns open the bombardment of Petersburg."[60] The explosion obliterated Elliott's Salient and almost 300 infantrymen and artillerymen were killed or wounded in an instant. The scene defied description but the good doctor imagined "the infernal regions may bear somewhat of a resemblance."[61]

The men of the 111th watched as the IX Corps infantry advanced toward the crater formed by the explosion, which soon became a sea of blue-clad soldiers. They were amazed by the result of the explosion, and many stopped to look at the gaping hole in the line. Officers tried desperately to get their commands into some semblance of a formation and moving forward. The road to Cemetery Hill and the Confederate rear was open if only the attack could be pressed. But the Union ranks lacked any real leadership from their commanders, and the attack sputtered to a stop.[62]

The Confederates, on the other hand, recovered quickly from their shock and launched a devastating counterattack bent on destroying the attackers and retaking their lines. The battle ragged until early afternoon, when the IX Corps divisions were finally repulsed, with the loss of almost 3,800 men. The whole affair was besieged with incompetent leadership, and as usual, the soldiers paid the ultimate price. Benton summed up the whole affair of the march north of the James and explosion of the mine when he wrote to his father: "We have lost a golden opportunity which I am fearful we shall not meet with again."[63]

As darkness settled over the field that night, the men of the 111th fell into ranks and were ordered forward. The regiment moved with the rest of the II Corps back to the trenches they occupied near Jerusalem Plank Road prior to the move north of the James River. Once in place, the exhausted foot soldiers threw themselves to the ground to get a little rest. They knew that in the morning, the deadly game of skirmishing and dodging shells would begin again.[64]

Chapter 11

Routed at Reams Station

> Our Corps was engaged in a heavy fight this afternoon and according to all accounts got badly whipped.[1]

While the move to Deep Bottom fell short of the intended goal, that being the destruction of any large portion of the enemy's lines, it did accomplish one thing. General Meade's advance north forced General Lee to strip his lines at Petersburg in order to send reinforcements north. That partial success emboldened Generals Grant and Meade to again send the II Corps, along with part of the X Corps and some cavalry, to Deep Bottom hoping that Lee would once more bolster his lines below Richmond and halt the reinforcing of General Jubal Early's army in the Shenandoah Valley. And as before, if the opportunity presented itself, Richmond was to be taken.[2]

However, a little deception was added to this plan in hopes of catching the rebels unaware. The Union force would board troop transports and sail down the James River, toward Chesapeake Bay, where the ships would drop anchor. Then, under cover of darkness, the ships would steam back up the river and move on Deep Bottom. The troops would quickly disembark at Jones Neck and make a rapid march around the left flank of the rebel works along Bailey's Creek.[3]

As they boarded the transports at City Point on the morning of August 13, the men of the 111th were certain they were headed for the defenses of Washington. When the transports were finally loaded and the ships set sail for Chesapeake Bay, the New Yorkers were jubilant. The joy and celebration turned to concern when the ships steamed a short distance down the James and dropped anchor in the middle of the river. Their concern turned to utter despair when, around midnight, the ships weighed anchor, turned around and steamed back toward City Point. The disappointed New Yorkers watched the lights of the city pass by as their ship continued its winding course up the river.[4]

Not everyone in the II Corps was traveling to Deep Bottom on the troop transport. The corps' artillery, wagon trains and supporting cavalry were marching to Jones Neck. Moving with the II Corps wagons was Charles White, who left camp the same time as the rest of his comrades but turned to the northwest with the wagons as the 111th continued its march to City Point. The going was difficult and White admitted, "I was about tuckered out and used up but I managed to keep up all night. It was hard work."[5] By the morning of August 14, White reached Jones Neck and crossed the river.

The plan of attack for the II Corps and the accompanying cavalry was simple. Once his soldiers disembarked, General Mott was to rapidly advance his Third Division and assault the enemy works along the New Market and Malvern Hill roads, driving the rebels back beyond Bailey's Creek. General Barlow, commanding both the First and Second divisions, was to take position on Mott's right and assault the rebels in the vicinity of the Jenning's house. General Gregg, with his cavalry division, would screen the right of the II Corps and be ready to make a dash for Richmond once the roads were open and the rebels were in full retreat. But as is usually the case, the simplest of plans often go awry.[6]

As the sun rose on the morning of August 14, the men of the 111th watched as their ship dropped anchor at Deep Bottom. The wharves located at the landing site were severely dilapidated and it had taken most of the night for the engineers to effect repairs. To compound the delay, the transport carrying the Fourth Brigade of Barlow's division ran aground and the men could not disembark until later in the morning. It was 9:00 A.M. before the New Yorkers were on shore and pushing toward New Market Road. The advance was continued until the column neared the rebel works at Fussell's mill. General Barlow quickly deployed part of the Consolidated Brigade and ordered it forward to take the rebel works. But the feeble attack was easily beaten back, and the Union regiments were forced to retreat.[7]

Major Husk was then directed by Colonel Crandell to move to the right with the rest of the brigade and take possession of a hill to the right of the Fussell's mill, close to the intersection of New Market and Darbytown roads. The 111th moved in line of battle, with skirmishers posted to the front. But General Barlow had the regiments move farther to the right than intended, and the men of the 111th found themselves north of Darbytown Road instead of south.[8]

Brigadier General Alfred Terry's division of the X Corps was supposed to assist in the assault on the works along New Market Heights, facing the left of the Union line. With the combined pressure of the II and X corps, the Confederate defenders would easily be overpowered and the line captured. But Terry's infantry quickly got bogged down in the dense underbrush at the base of New Market Heights and, coupled with the fire coming from the formidable rebel works, stopped far short of their objective.[9]

The regiment was on the heights east of Bailey's Creek, over looking Fussell's mill, about five miles northeast of the morning's disembarking site. Hopelessly out of position, the New Yorkers were now destined to be bystanders in the coming fight. Just after 5:00 P.M., the New Yorkers watched as part of the Second Division moved out to attack the rebel works on the opposite bank of Bailey's Creek. Even though carried out with far more spirit than the attack made earlier in the afternoon, it, too, was repulsed. One lone brigade was not enough to crack the enemy's position.[10]

While the II Corps' attacks were faltering against the rebel works, General Terry was finally able to get his division moving. The X Corps infantry sprinted up the slopes of New Market Heights and breached the Confederate line in a number of places. The fighting was at close quarters, often hand-to-hand. Under tremendous pressure, Terry was obliged to pull his men out of the captured works and move them back down to the base of the heights. With the failure to capture any significant portion of the enemy's line, the fighting ended for the day.[11]

That night, the X Corps marched from the left flank of the line and massed in the rear of the II Corps at Fussell's mill. The X Corps would be in position to assist in the next day's attack on the rebel works. General Birney spent most of the day scouting the enemy's position for a weak point to attack and by the time a suitable place was found, it was too late in the day for offensive operations. The attack would have to be put off until the next day.[12]

August 16 seemed to hold the promise of a great victory for the Union. The cavalry under General Gregg had forced its way up Charles City Road toward Richmond and was hell-bent on reaching the Confederate capital. General Birney's X Corps soldiers advanced and quickly overran the first line of works in the woods near the mill. After regrouping, they emerged from the woods onto an open plain and headed straight for the Confederate's second line. But things began to quickly unravel. Heavy fighting stopped the Union troopers a mere seven miles from Richmond, forcing Gregg's saddle-worn troopers to retreat back down Charles City Road. After advancing into the open ground separating the two lines of works, the X Corps soldiers were hit from the front and both flanks with a devastating fire. When the Union line began to waver, the rebels charged over their works, driving Birney's men from the field and recapturing the lost fieldworks.[13]

As the X Corps and Greg's cavalry were engaged with the enemy, the New Yorkers remained in position overlooking Fussell's mill, sparing with enemy skirmishers across the creek. The next day fighting again broke out all along the line, and Union gunboats on the James adding their noise to the din of battle. The day's contest ended with no advantage being gained by either side. On the evening of August 20, Major Husk received orders from General Nelson A. Miles, who had assumed command of the First Division two days earlier, to be ready to move back to Petersburg. The II Corps had once again failed to breach the enemy's defenses north of the James and had failed to lure any reinforcements away from their main works around Petersburg. As dusk settled over the field, the New Yorkers withdrew from their lines at Fussell's mill and headed south for the pontoon bridges at Jones Neck. After crossing the James, the regiment marched for Point of Rocks, where they crossed the Appomattox River and continued the exhausting retreat for the siege lines.[14]

Daylight on the morning of August 21 found the worn-out men of the 111th holding the same line of works they had occupied before the move to Deep Bottom on the 12th. At once they set about boiling coffee and eating what little rations they had in their haversacks. But the brief respite soon ended when, around noon, the regiment was directed to proceed to Jerusalem Plank Road. The 111th, along with two divisions of the II Corps, was being sent southwest to the Weldon Railroad. On this march Captain Marcus Murdock of Company G would lead the regiment. Wracked with fever and at the point of exhaustion, Major Husk was examined by surgeon Benton and found to be totally unfit for duty. The major was granted a 20-day leave of absence in which to recover.[15]

As the New Yorkers were sitting idle in their works at Deep Bottom, General Warren's V Corps was engaged in a desperate struggle south of Petersburg along the Weldon Railroad at Globe Tavern. Warren's soldiers were tasked with cutting the railroad and destroying the tracks as far south as possible. Confederate General Heth was ordered to save the railroad and attacked Warren on August 18. After some severe fighting, the V Corps commander was able to beat off the attacks and hold his own. But on the 19th, Mahone's division of infantry and two divisions of cavalry reinforced Heth, and the battle began anew. The Confederates launched one last attack on the morning of the 21st, which was stopped with severe loss. To bolster Warren's isolated corps, General Hancock was ordered to march the First and Second divisions of his corps south and assume the work of destroying the railroad as far as Reams Station, which was about ten miles south of Petersburg.[16]

By the afternoon of August 22, the New Yorkers were toiling in the hot August sun tearing up tracks and burning ties. The destruction of a railroad was no easy task. The rails first had to be loosened from the ties with long pry bars. With the rails removed, the ties were lifted from the roadbed and stacked one on top of another, forming a hollow square. The piles were then fired and the rails set on top the burning mound. The intense heat melted the middle section of the rails, causing the ends to droop down to the ground. When the twisted rails cooled, they would be useless to anyone attempting to rebuild the railroad. This work went on all-day long; huge plumes of black smoke filled the sky marking the soldiers' progress south.[17]

Despite a steady rain that threatened to extinguish the fires, work continued through August 23. As the New Yorkers continued destroying the railroad, they could hear the sound of skirmishing to the south as their cavalry pickets battled with the enemy. By late afternoon, the regiment worked its way to Reams Station, which had been burned to the ground when General Wilson and his Federal cavalry rode through two months before. The only thing remaining was a rough line of works left behind by the VI Corps who had occupied the area as reinforcements to Wilson. The men of the 111th took possession of a portion of the works and lay on the ground to get some well-deserved sleep.[18]

On the 24th, General Gibbon's Second Division arrived to man the works so the First Division could continue to destroy the railroad. Soon fires were blazing south of Reams Station and columns of black smoke filled the air. The day's objective for the First Division was Malone's Crossing, where the railroad crossed Rowanty Creek about three miles below the station. Troopers of Colonel Samuel Spear's cavalry brigade covered the work parties while General David Gregg patrolled the roads leading west to Dinwiddie Court House with his cavalry division. By nightfall, the 111th reached Malone's Crossing; the road was now destroyed all the way from Globe Tavern. As the sun began to set, Captain Murdock ordered the regiment back to the works at Reams Station.[19]

General Lee was not about to let the threat to one of the two remaining rail lines leading into Petersburg go unchallenged. So on the afternoon of the 24th, the Confederate commander directed A. P. Hill to take three divisions of infantry and a battalion of artillery and linkup with General Wade Hampton and his cavalry west of Reams Station. The combined force would drive east and attack Hancock's isolated force. Lee instructed Hill to "do everything in your power to punish the enemy."[20]

Work began early on the morning of the 25th. General Gibbon marched his men south to continue the destruction of the railroad while the men of the First Division remained at the station to work on the breastworks. The trenches left behind by the VI Corps were worn by two months of rain and neglect and desperately needed improving. They were filled with stagnant water and the walls were not high enough to shelter the occupants. The fieldworks themselves were laid out very poorly. Constructed in a rough U shape, with the bottom of the "U" facing west, the works were intersected in many places by roads and did not take advantage of the railroad bed as a natural breastwork.[21]

The top, or north face, of the works was anchored on Jones Hole Swamp and ran west for about 700 yards before hitting Halifax Road and the railroad, each running north and south. Here a gap existed in the line to allow the two avenues to pass through the works. About 50 yards on the other side of the tracks, the works turned south and ran for a few hundred yards, paralleling the railroad, before crossing Depot Road, where another gap in the line existed. On the other side of the road, the works began to turn gradually back to the east, forming the bottom of the U shape. Crossing over the railroad and Halifax Road again, the works ran another 700 yards back to the northeast before terminating at the edge of a woodline.[22]

The 111th and the rest of the Consolidated Brigade occupied the portion of the breastworks directly in front of the destroyed railroad, with the right of the brigade resting on the northern angle near the railroad bed. The old Third Brigade formed the left of the Consolidated Brigade, while the rest of the brigade made up the right. To the left was the Fourth Brigade and to the right, running along the northern face of the works, was the First Brigade. There was a gap between the Consolidated Brigade and the First Brigade of almost ten yards where the railroad intersected the works. With just over 100 officers and men, the 111th did not present a very imposing sight.[23]

Colonel Crandell was placed in charge of the First Division skirmishers on the night of August 24 and command of the Consolidated Brigade passed to Major John Byron of the 88th New York. The command of the old Third Brigade, in turn, was given to Captain Nelson Penfield of the 125th New York.[24]

Detachments from the 111th joined the division pioneers in chopping down trees in front of the works west of the railroad, clearing fields of fire. Tree branches were used to form a slashing in front of the works, creating an obstacle any attacking force would have to negotiate before reaching the trenches. As they worked under an intense August sun, the men could see pillars of black smoke from the burning railroad ties as work destroying the railroad continued.[25]

By midmorning, firing could be heard coming from the south. The crackle of musketry and the pop of the carbine continued to grow in intensity as the Confederate cavalry drove in Spear's and Gregg's cavalry pickets. These troopers were tasked with screening the work parties from the Second Division. Without the protection of the cavalry, Gibbon had no choice but to cease the work on the railroad and quickly march his soldiers back to the safety of the trenches. After arriving at the station around noon, Gibbon's brigades were assigned positions on the left, or southern, side of the works.[26]

About the time the fighting south of Reams Station broke out, General Hancock had sent an urgent message to General Meade, stating that he was facing a large force of cavalry and infantry, and that they might try to get in between his men at Reams Station and the V Corps at Globe Tavern. Meade was thinking the same thing, so around 1:00 P.M., he ordered the last of Hancock's divisions to Reams. Rather than proceeding straight down the Weldon Railroad, General Mott was directed to march his division south along Jerusalem Plank Road and then west toward the station. This oversight would prove costly as Mott would not make it to Reams in time to help Hancock.[27]

Driving the Union troopers and infantry back to Reams Station, the Confederate cavalry began advancing north along Halifax Road toward the II Corps position. Meanwhile, Hill's infantry moved on the station from the west. When his lead brigades arrived just outside the Union position, they were immediately deployed for battle. McGowan moved his brigade south of Depot Road, while Anderson, Scales, and Conner positioned theirs north of the road. Each brigade sent out a strong line of sharpshooters well in advance of the main battle line to feel for the Union position. It was close to 2:00 P.M. when Hill gave the order to attack.[28]

Under the command of Captain Penfield, the 111th, 125th and 126th advanced out of the works and into the fields west of their position. Penfield was directed to form a skirmish line to cover the Consolidated Brigade's front. Once in position, the remnants of the old Harpers Ferry brigade were to linkup with the 148th Pennsylvania from the Fourth Brigade on its left and the skirmishers of the First Brigade to the right. The men of the 111th advanced with a loud cheer through a thick stand of pines before entering an open field and taking possession of an advance line of rifle pits. No sooner had the New Yorkers clambered into the trenches than the four Southern brigades began to advance right toward them.[29]

Suddenly, gunfire broke out to the regiment's left, coming from McGowan's South Carolinians and aimed at the Fourth Brigade skirmishers. Union guns posted behind the Fourth Brigade sent their shot and shell screaming down Depot Road as McGowan's men came into view. When the firing started, the skirmishers on either side of Penfield's soldiers fell back to the main line. Finding his flanks exposed, the captain ordered the skirmishers to leave their rifle pits and retreat back to the main line of works. Moving at the double, the New Yorkers ran back through the woods and took up a position at the gap in the line caused by the railroad, between the right of their brigade and left of the First Brigade.[30]

The rebels pressed on, crossing the open field and entering the trees at the eastern edge of the field. With a tremendous yell, the rebel battle lines charged. They emerged from the woods directly in front of the Consolidated Brigade and were met with a thunderous volley. Struggling forward while trying to return fire, the Confederates were stopped short of the works. They were unable to withstand the fire cutting into their ranks and retreated to the safety of the woods, leaving the ground covered with their dead and wounded. Even though four brigades had initially been ordered to advance, only Anderson's Georgia brigade and the North Carolina regiments under Scales actively participated in the attack.[31]

No sooner had the attack been beaten back than a rider from General Meade arrived at Hancock's headquarters. The courier delivered a message that stated a division from the IX Corps was on its way to Reams. Despite the objections of its commander, General Meade ordered the reinforcements to march by the same route that General Mott had taken just hours before. Meade's decision sealed Hancock's fate. No help would arrive in time to save the II Corps.[32]

Just after 3:00 P.M., Captain Penfield was ordered by Major Byron to reestablish the picket line in the brigade's front. The captain once again led the three regiments out of the works and into the woods to the right front of the Consolidated Brigade. This time, the captain established his line inside the woods instead of in the rifle pits farther to the front. When the regiments were in position, Penfield sent a detachment of about 25 men to the edge of the woods, near the clearing, with orders to give warning when the Confederates renewed their attack. Back at Reams, the brigade of Lieutenant Colonel Samuel Rugg was ordered to take up a position in the railroad cut behind the Consolidated Brigade.[33]

While the men of the 111th were straining their eyes forward, trying to catch any glimpse of movement in the distant woods, the Confederates were preparing to renew

11. Routed at Reams Station 157

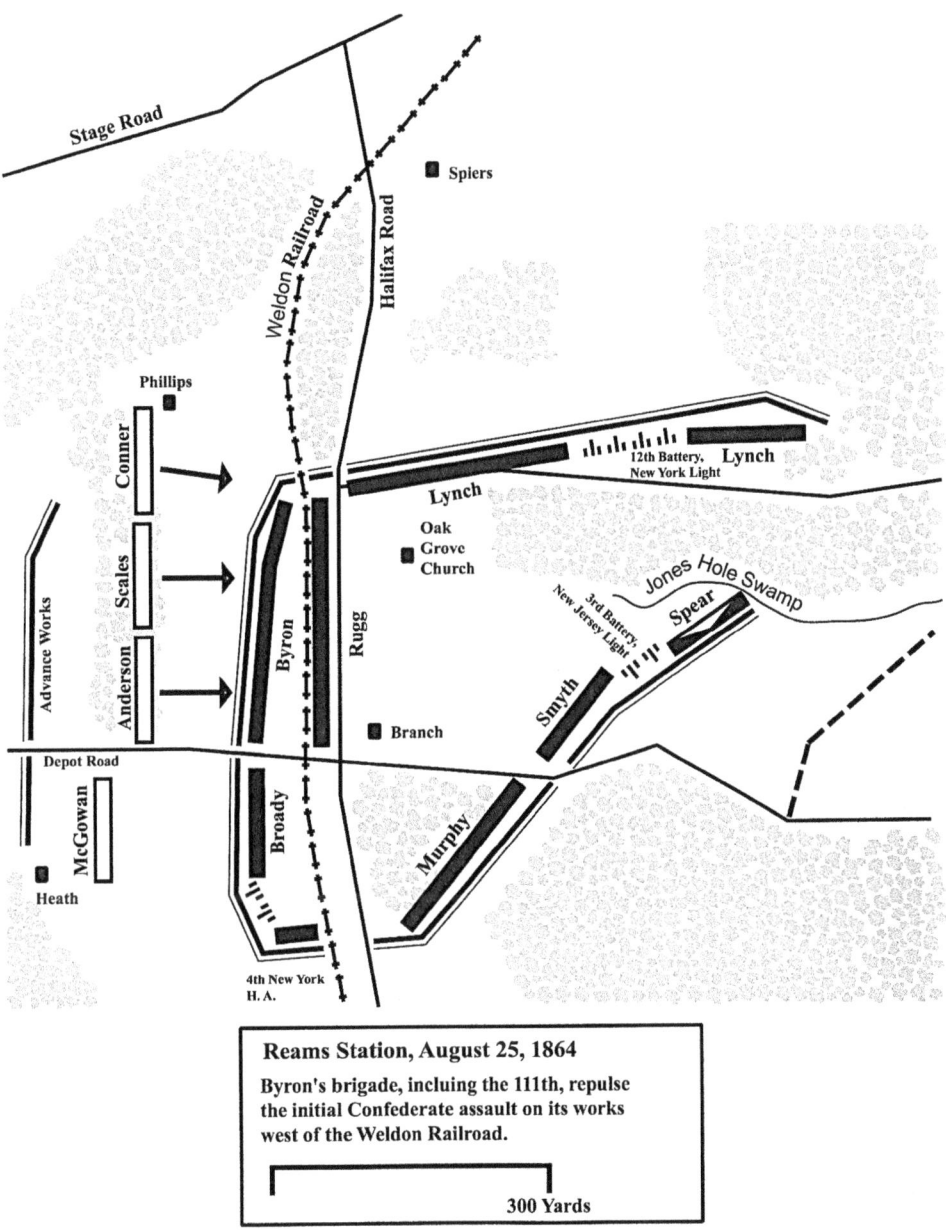

Byron's brigade, including the 111th, repulse the initial Confederate assault on its works west of the Weldon Railroad (map by the author).

their attack. General Heth arrived on the field with his division and was forming his ranks for the attack. He placed Cooke's brigade opposite the left of the Consolidated Brigade and MacRae's brigade to the right rear of Cooke's Tar Heels. To the right of Cooke was Lane's brigade, commanded by General James Conner. Cooke's Carolinians were the same troops the 111th defeated at Bristoe Station almost a year before. As the fresh regiments were taking their place in line, skirmishers were thrown forward to probe the Union works. Each time they came within sight of the earthworks, they were forced to retreat under a hail of bullets.[34]

Sensing that the fighting was not yet done for the day, General Miles took steps to strengthen his weak lines. He placed one gun of the 12th New York Battery in position to cover the gap in the line to the right of the Consolidated brigade. Miles also placed the 152nd New York from Colonel Rugg's brigade in position north along the railroad to attack the enemy in the flank and rear if they advanced on the Consolidated Brigade. Feeling somewhat better about the disposition of his division, Miles waited for the rebels to attack.[35]

At 5:30 P.M., Confederate artillery began a furious bombardment of the Union works. Federal artillery was quick to respond and the noise became deafening. The 111th, stuck out on the skirmish line, was caught in the middle as shells from both sides screamed overhead. The detail sent forward to the edge of the woods by Penfield ran back to the main skirmish line to report that the rebels were advancing. Penfield ignored the warning and kept his men in place. Suddenly Cooke's Tar Heels were right on top of them. Ordered not to fire or cheer until close to the enemy works, the Confederates caught the skirmishers completely by surprise.[36]

It was as if the woods were alive with Confederates; they seemed to spring up from right out of the ground. If the New Yorkers remained in place they would all either be killed or captured. The only thing they could do was to run as fast as their legs could carry them, and run they did. There was no order; the New Yorkers simply sprinted to the rear. With the Confederates right on their heels, the main line had to withhold its fire until the skirmishers were clear. The New Yorkers ran through the works and Captain Murdock rallied his small command in the trenches near the gap to the left of the First Brigade. Once ranks were formed, the men prepared to fire. To the right of the New Yorkers were the 126th and 125th, while the rest of the brigade occupied the works to the left.[37]

With flags flying, the gray-clad infantry came streaming out of the woods with a mighty rebel yell and ran straight into the slashing. The Union line erupted in a wall of flame, temporarily halting the Confederate advance. Not to be denied, the rebels slowly struggle forward, cheering as they advanced. They were subjected to volley after volley from the Union line, and just as the attack began to falter, the unexpected happened. The regiments to the left of the 111th panicked and broke for the rear. With renewed energy at seeing the Union line give way, the rebels pressed forward. Bounding over the works and overrunning the Tenth Massachusetts Light Artillery, posted to the left of the Fourth Brigade, they turned the guns around and began firing into the backs of fleeing Union regiments.[38]

The 37th North Carolina of Conner's brigade advanced straight for the gap in the line between the right of the Consolidated Brigade and the left of the First Brigade. The 111th was now faced with Confederates to its front and on its right flank. The 125th and 126th were the next to break, making for the rear and out of harm's way. The New Yorkers were now all alone in the trenches.[39]

Carolinians from Conner's brigade began to pour through the gap and drop into the trenches on the right of the 111th. With the prospect of spending the rest of the war in a Southern prison running through his mind, Captain Murdock gave the order for his men to abandon the trenches and get to the rear as fast as they could. The New Yorkers scrambled out of the works and joined the rest of the brigade in a headlong flight to safety. Those unlucky enough not make it out of the trenches in time were taken prisoner. One of those captured was the color-bearer, Color Sergeant Aaron Chase of Company I. As he was about to leave the trenches, the national colors were wrestled from his hands. He and the regiment's flag were taken as prisoners of war. Another New Yorker taken prisoner was Thomas Jenkins of Company E. Jenkins would languish in Libby Prison, Belle Island and Salisbury before the war was over.[40]

While the men of the 111th were locked in a desperate struggle with the 37th North Carolina to the front, they had no idea that the rest of Conner's brigade had penetrated the breastworks to their right and were working to cut off the regiment's line of retreat. When the New Yorkers finally gave way and began to make their way to the rear, they were forced to run a gauntlet of shot and shell from their left, right and rear.[41]

General Miles watched with concern as the Consolidated Brigade broke for the rear, and he immediately ordered Lieutenant Colonel Rugg's brigade to move forward into the railroad cut. But these men either fell to the ground and refused to fire or ran to the rear. A similar situation occurred when the 152nd New York was called upon to attack the flank and rear of Conner's brigade. The entire regiment, almost to a man, ran to the rear without firing a shot.[42]

By now the entire line was giving way. The enemy rushed forward with fierce determination, bent on capturing or destroying General Hancock's entire force. Only the stubborn efforts of regiments from the First Brigade on the right and the left-most regiments of the Second Division saved the day. General Hancock was seen riding among his fleeing men, screaming, "Come on, we can beat them yet. Don't leave me for God's sake."[43] His cries were in vain as men from every regiment continued the disorganized dash to safety. General Miles personally led the 61st New York in an attempt to take back the First Brigade works while a rough line was formed in the cornfield to the rear of Oak Grove Church. The fire from this line was able to momentarily halt the Confederate advance.

Through the extraordinary efforts of officers and noncommissioned officers from every regiment in the Consolidated Brigade, the retreating mob was rallied and formed into a rough battle line at the far end of the cornfield. The 111th was able to move forward with the rest of the brigade and occupied a small portion of the works once held by the First Brigade. General Miles launched a counterattack aimed at recapturing the northern line of trenches all the way up to the railroad. The First Brigade was able to fight its way there before being forced to retreat in the face of over ten fresh Confederate regiments. The battle continued to rage as darkness settled over the field, muzzle flashes stabbing forward in the growing dusk.[44]

That evening, General Hancock made the decision to retreat. His command was too badly disorganized and his men too badly shaken to make any further attempt to retake the captured works. When he finished issuing the orders for retreat, Hancock turned to one of his aides and said, "Colonel, I do not care to die, but I pray to God I may never leave this field."[45]

Captain Murdock received orders to have his men proceed by the right flank and fall in behind the Fourth Brigade. Once in position, the 111th marched east until striking Jerusalem Plank Road, then turned north toward Petersburg. The misery of the day was compounded by a heavy rain that soaked the men and turned the roads into thick mud. All night, the men plodded along, moral sinking lower as the mud grew deeper.

Finally, in the early morning hours of August 26, the 111th was halted to the rear of the V Corps.[46]

When Captain Murdock called roll that morning, it was discovered that, despite the intensity of the battle, the regiment had only one man killed and two men wounded. But a quarter of the men were listed as missing. Captured were two officers, Captain John Lockwood and the regimental adjutant Adolphus Capron, and 25 enlisted men.[47] Among the missing enlisted was Daniel Lombard. The 37-year-old from Moravia mustered in with the regiment two years before as a sergeant but was discharged that December for disability. When the opportunity presented itself, Lombard again enlisted in the 111th in February 1864 as a private.[48]

However, the most painful loss of all was the regiment's flag. It was given to them almost two years ago to the day, had been safeguarded at Harpers Ferry and was flown high at Gettysburg and on every field of battle since then. Now it was in the hands of the enemy. Some were critical of Color Sergeant Chase's attempts to defend the flag. First Sergeant Hoff, who returned to the regiment at the end of August after recovering from a wound received at North Anna, was distressed to hear of the loss. The rebels "took some cannon from us and what is worse they took our old battle flag, which is not very well liked. It could have been brought off if the color sergeant had tried to do so."[49] It would take a long time for the men to live down this second stain on their honor.

No one felt the shame of the day's events more keenly than General Hancock. His soldiers held at Gettysburg, fought through the inferno of the Wilderness, stormed the works at Spotsylvania and Old Cold Harbor, and captured large portions of the works in the initial fighting around Petersburg. But for the first time, reduced by tremendous losses in both officers and men, the II Corps failed its commander. Hancock received a message from General Meade aimed at easing his mind over the day's setback: "No one sympathizes with you more than I do in the misfortunes of this evening.... I am satisfied you and your command have done all in your power, and though you have met with a reverse, the honor and escutcheon of the old Second is as bright as ever.... Don't let this matter worry you, because you have given me every satisfaction."[50]

Chapter 12

The Siege Continues

> There is no hour of the day nor of the night but that I hear the report of cannon and firearms. Just at this moment the sound salutes my ears, in fact the sound has become so frequent that I think no more of it than I would of the sound of the ticking of a clock.[1]

With just four officers and close to 70 men, the 111th took up a reserve position behind the Second Division. A skirmish line was established in front of the regiment's position and the exhausted New Yorkers were immediately put to work digging fieldworks in the wet Virginia soil.[2]

Charles White was at the division hospital when he received word that his younger brother Levi was not with the regiment when it returned from Reams Station. He immediately "went back about three quarters of a mile to the Divis[ion] to see the boys about it but could learn nothing of the particulars."[3] The only thing anyone knew was that Levi was captured with a number of other members of the regiment. Indeed, by the time Charles was inquiring as to his brother's whereabouts, the younger White was on his way to Richmond as a prisoner of war. For the third time since he enlisted, it was up to Charles to write to his mother to inform her that something had happened to Levi.

Digging and building works continued until August 27, when Captain Murdock received orders to march the 111th about a mile north with the rest of the brigade and set up camp west of Jerusalem Plank Road. But a new camp meant digging a new line of trenches. This new line of works would stretch back east and connect to Jerusalem Plank Road.[4]

September 4 was a day of great celebration throughout the entire north. The day before, General William T. Sherman wired President Lincoln that he had captured Atlanta. Months of fighting had culminated in Sherman's capture of the vital Confederate city. At midnight on the 4th, General Grant marked the occasion of Sherman's victory by ordering every gun along the entire line at Petersburg "double shotted and fired I do not know how many times,"[5] recalled First Sergeant Hoff. The bombardment left a distinct impression on surgeon Benton: "The way Grant celebrated the fall of Atlanta was a caution. It was ahead of all the pyrotechnic displays I ever witnessed. If the John Henry's over the lines were not astonished they must be very dull of comprehension."[6]

As the 4th was a Sunday, "a catholic meeting was helde hear in the Irish Brig and all the Generals of Corps were preasant from Gen. Hancock down." One of those in attendance was First Sergeant Hoff. In a letter to his wife, he wrote, "They had some wine and refreshments and all went well. There were speeches from all of them and a great many cheers also. For then after the close of Hancock's speech some one in the crowd proposed three cheers ... and there was a spontaneous answer."[7]

Work on the new line continued despite the constant rain of bullets and shells. When they were finally pulled off the line near the middle of September, the 111th left behind two forts they helped construct, Forts Davis and Hays. Both forts were connected by a long series of entrenchments to Fort Sedgwick, about a mile to the north.[8]

While the regiment was toiling in the Virginia clay, Colonel MacDougall was spending his days in Auburn.

Benjamin Hartman, Company D. Enlisted at the age of 19, he was transferred to the Veteran's Reserve Corps in September 1864 (courtesy of R. L. Murray).

Recovered sufficiently from his illness, the colonel immediately set about trying to recruit some desperately needed soldiers for his regiment. His first action was to order all officers and enlisted men from the 111th in the district on furlough or sick leave to report to him at Auburn. These men would provide MacDougall with the staff needed to carry out his work.[9]

Yet recruiting alone was not going to fill the vacant ranks of all the Union armies in the field. The Army of the Potomac was greatly depleted after four months of almost constant fighting. The II Corps alone had lost almost 14,000 men since the beginning of May. The Lincoln administration had been thinking for some time about instituting another draft and now seemed like the right time. President Lincoln had made the call for an additional 500,000 men in mid–July and those states that had not filled their quota would be subjected to a new draft starting September 5.[10]

The criteria for this draft were similar to those held in the past. Those between the ages of 18 and 45 were candidates for military service. A list of the community's eligible men, excluding those already under arms, was created and submitted to the War Department. But there was also a chance that men within this age range could be excluded from service. Exempt were all those not citizens of the United States; anyone that served at least two years in a state militia and was honorably discharged; and all those incapable of performing their duty due to a mental or physical disability. The one difference from the drafts of the past was that the commutation clause was dropped from this draft act.

Commutation allowed a drafted man to pay the government $300 to get out of serving. This time, everyone was expected to serve.[11]

A certain stigma was attached to a soldier who entered the service through the draft. No town in the 25th Military District wanted to have its quota raised in this manner. In response to the latest call for recruits, local papers began running editorials extolling the benefits of enlisting as opposed to being drafted. The papers appealed to the pride of the young men, making it clear that the veterans of the regiment would hold them in higher esteem if they volunteered. When he heard that New York would not suffer much from the draft, surgeon Benton commented that "it is a source of great gratification to those in the field to know they are not forgotten by the loyal population of the north."[12]

Along with the feeling of pride associated with not being drafted, there were more tangible benefits to volunteering. Any man who joined of his own free will for a term of three years would receive a total of $1,000 bounty. Those volunteering for two years would receive $850, while those signing the rolls for one year would get $700. Those who were drafted received nothing. Besides the money, a volunteer could pick the branch of service in which he wanted to serve. The conscript was assigned to a unit with no opportunity to state his preference.[13]

The bounty system instituted early in the war had created a new type of soldier called the "bounty jumper." As the size of bounties increased in an effort to entice more men to enlist, so too did the number of undesirable characters who answered the call. These individuals would enlist in a regiment, receive their bounties, then desert when the first opportunity presented itself. Later, they would enlist again under an assumed name and repeat the process over again.[14]

No regiment was immune from these individuals, not even the 111th. Private William Smith enlisted in Company G and was mustered in along with the rest of the regiment in August 1862. When the New Yorkers were awaiting their exchange at Camp Douglas, Smith deserted. Using the alias "Jones," Smith enlisted two more times in two other regiments for the bounty money. But before receiving the bounty from his third enlistment, he was arrested by a detective from Auburn.[15]

At the beginning of September, a detachment of 167 men left the Depot for Drafted Men at Elmira, New York, bound for the 111th. Under guard of a company from the 83rd Pennsylvania, commanded by Captain J. H. Borden, the detachment reached Baltimore on the 9th and was put in barracks at the Soldier's Rest. Due to the length of the trip and the fatigued condition of the guard, the Pennsylvanians were soon replaced with a company of local militia.[16]

During the night, some of the draftees convinced their guards to help them get out of the barracks. A hole was cut in the floor, through which a number of the substitutes and a few guards passed. The group made its way into the city, visiting, according to Borden, "drinking houses, houses of ill fame and other low resorts."[17] The next morning, when the Pennsylvanians returned to relieve the militia company, the hole in the floor was discovered. They also found that 15 of the substitutes had deserted, taking a few of the militiamen with them.

Despite such incidents, groups of men began to arrive at the front to take their place in the ranks of the 111th. In a letter to his parents, surgeon Benton noted, "It is wonderful to see how fast the army is filling up by returning convalescents and recruits. Every train from City Point brings up a load and they are distributed to their various regiments."[18]

The raw recruits were immediately issued their equipment, assigned to a company, and indoctrinated in the school of the soldier. By the end of September, the ranks of the 111th had swelled to almost 300 men.

Many of the men who arrived as recruits had enlisted together with the expectation that they would remain together when assigned to a company. One such group consisted of six men, four of whom were assigned to Company K while the other two were sent to another company. The four assigned to Company K approached First Sergeant Hoff and "said that they would give me $10 if I would get them together in one company. I thought no more of it, but done so when one came around and slipped in my hand $15."[19] Hoff saw an opportunity to make himself some money since the new men seemed to have piles of greenbacks. "One man got $3000 to come as a substitute."[20]

While the enlisted ranks continued to grow, the number of officers in the regiment increased as well. During the months of September and October, a number of men were promoted to officers, while officers were brought in from other regiments. In Company A, Lafayette Mumford was commissioned as a captain, Roland Dennis was made first lieutenant, and Abner Seeley was promoted to second lieutenant. All three of these men were new to the regiment and had enlisted during the month of September. While not promoted to an officer rank, Corporal Geer received a much-deserved promotion to sergeant.[21]

In Company B, Second Lieutenant John Smith was transferred from Company A and promoted to first lieutenant. Company C received a new commander in Captain David Taylor. He was a veteran who had served with the 16th New York Cavalry and would add needed leadership to the company. Along with Taylor came Second Lieutenant Silas Belding, also new to the regiment. Company D finally received a new commander when Edwin Burnham was commissioned a captain. Burnham had enlisted in the 15th Vermont in 1862 and fought with that regiment before being honorably discharged in late 1863. After graduating from Albany Law School, Burnham moved to Wayne County where he practiced law. But the pull of war was too strong and three months after moving to Wayne County, he enlisted as a private in the 111th.[22]

Two veterans from other regiments were added to Company E. Charles Furman, a first sergeant from the 138th New York, was promoted to first lieutenant and given command of the company. Stephan Pyatt, formerly a first sergeant with the 17th New York, was promoted to second lieutenant. First Lieutenant Daniel Sterling was promoted to captain and took over Company F, where he replaced the captured John Lockwood. In Company H, First Lieutenant Reuben Myers was promoted to captain and First Sergeant George Moore of Company I was promoted to second lieutenant. In Company K, First Sergeant Hoff received his long sought-after promotion to second lieutenant.[23]

The joy of promotion for many was bittersweet, for it meant bidding a fond farewell to those who were leaving the regiment for good. Captain Perry of Company B, Second Lieutenant Welch of Company C, and First Lieutenant August Green of Company D were all discharged for disability due to wounds received in battle. Second Lieutenant George Brown received a general discharge to accept a commission with the 194th New York Infantry.[24]

One of the new soldiers arriving in camp was Chauncey Smith. The 44-year-old farmer had enlisted on August 29 in the town of Ira and was sent to Auburn for his physical exam. According to Smith, the doctor who examined him thought that "my teeth did not look as though I could masticate hard-tack." The doctor offered to "secure me a berth as guard over rebel prisoners" at Elmira prison camp, but Smith declined.[25] He made up his mind to join a number of other men from his town and enlist in the 111th.

On September 20, Smith and his comrades traveled to Baltimore, where they boarded a steamer for the trip down Chesapeake Bay. At Fortress Monroe, Smith changed ships and sailed up the James River to City Point. He recalled, "All along the river I could see towns and the homes of the soldiers who were guarding the rear of Grant's army."[26] As soon as he arrived at City Point, Smith could hear the booming of artillery coming from the front lines around Petersburg. As he listened to the incessant rumble from the heavy siege guns, Smith began to wish he had accepted the position as a prison guard: "My patriotism had cooled off considerable since I left Auburn and Elmira. At the impulse of the moment I began to feel as though I would rather shoot rebel prisoners over the dead line at Elmira, than to be shot at by treacherous rebels."[27]

Smith and about 20 other men were added to Captain Sterling's Company F. When the recruits arrived, the one-time drum major put the men in formation and gave them the following speech: "Boys, I am glad to see you here as recruits of Company F. Some of you are a great deal older than your Captain. I would say to you that in the army in front of the enemy there is neither respect for the younger man nor the older man, it is valor, patriotism and fighting qualities that we admire on the battlefield. When you were at home you were civilians, now that you are in the army you are soldiers and I hope that you will all prove true to your country's flag and do your duty as good soldiers, on the day of trial."[28]

Two others new to the regiment were Newton Ferris and John Howard. These two men were also assigned to Company F and according to Chauncey Smith, "Newton Ferris is tenting with me and I find his company very agreeable. John Howard remains with me yet, he seems like a brother. We three will keep together through the whole year if we can."[29]

"September 15th two years ago today, we were prisoners of war at Harper's Ferry," wrote newly promoted Esek Hoff to his wife. The unhappy anniversary was spent huddling behind earthworks as the "picket firing and cannonading are kept up most of the time."[30] Lost to the sharpshooter's bullet that day was Solomon Dow of Company F. According to the lieutenant, Dow had just come from fatigue duty when along "came a ball popping through the tent entering his left side above the nipple."[31]

On September 20, news arrived in camp of another Union victory. Charles White recalled that there was "great excitement this eavening and cheering all along the lines. Telegraph dispatch of Sheridans Victory in the Valley."[32] What White was referring to was the news of the Northern cavalier's victory over Jubal Early at the battle of Winchester. And just as he did after the fall of Atlanta, Grant ordered every gun along the line to bombard the rebel works in a salute to General Sheridan and his men.

As the New Yorkers continued their exhausting work of digging and dodging the ever-present bullets and shells, Generals Grant and Meade were formulating a third plan for taking the rebel works north of the James River. The attempts made by the II Corps in July and August never brought about the desired results of breaching the enemy's lines and opening a route to Richmond. They were, in fact, merely sideshows for the real attacks on the lines around Petersburg. This time, things would be different. As the X and XVIII corps were attacking north of the James, the V and IX corps would move and capture the South Side Railroad. It was hoped that with both flanks pinned down, no reinforcements could be sent to the aid of the other.[33]

In preparation for the upcoming attack on the enemy lines, the II Corps was ordered to relieve the X Corps in the front lines on September 24. "We started about 7 o'clock in the morning and the first mile was very muddy, as there had been a very heavy rain just before starting," Lieutenant Hoff wrote to his wife. "After the first mile the winds were better and we got along rather better."[34] Hoff and his comrades were astonished to see whose place they were taking in the trenches. "In the night they looked like any white soldier but come to get near the fire they looked black enough. And no wonder. They were the so much despised colored soldiers. When we came up to where they were encamped they said to some of our men, 'They will not fire on you. But they hate us fellows like the debbil.'"[35]

General Edward Ord's XVIII Corps and General David Birney's X Corps, accompanied by General August Kautz's cavalry division, crossed the James River on September 28 and moved along parallel courses toward the Confederate works. On the morning of the 29th, the colored regiments of General Paine's X Corps Division made a series of assaults on the enemy's lines atop New Market Heights before carrying the works. The rest of the X Corps followed, moving west along the ridgeline.[36]

The leading elements of the XVIII Corps reached the open fields of the Childrey farm in the early morning. Before them lay the largest of the southernmost forts guarding the approaches to Richmond, Fort Harrison. No sooner had General Ord's infantry deployed in the fields when they were taken under fire from the fort's guns. The charge was sounded and the Union battle lines surged forward. After intense fighting, the Federals managed to capture the fort. Ord's men spent the rest of the night fortifying their position, waiting for the attacks they knew would come in the morning.[37]

On the last day of the month, divisions from the V and IX corps were marching southwest toward Boydton Plank Road and the South Side Railroad. The column, led by V Corps commander General Warren, was to strike toward the railroad and sever the important supply artery leading into Petersburg. Around 1:00 P.M., Warren's men quickly attacked and overwhelmed an unfinished line of works around Peeble's farm. Pushing on, the attack was stopped by the Confederates posted behind a strong line of works along Boydton Plank Road. The rebels counterattacked and managed to roll up the left flank of the Union line before being forced to retire to the safety of their works. Warren's infantry had captured a large section of enemy trenches and put the Union left flank that much closer to totally encircling Cockade City.[38]

About the time that Warren's men were pressing their attack toward Boydton Plank Road, the Confederates were launching a series of attacks aimed at retaking Fort Harrison. Uncoordinated and ill planned, the attacks were repeatedly beaten back with great slaughter. Fort Harrison was firmly under Union control.[39]

The beginning of October found the men of the 111th occupying the same reserve position about three miles northeast of Fort Davis as they did prior to the move to relieve the X Corps. Away from the immediate danger of the front lines, the New Yorkers turned their attention to the topic gripping the rest of the nation, the presidential election. The camp was alive with the talk of politics. Officers and enlisted alike had their own opinions about the candidates. They debated the merits of each candidate, and in the end, thought surgeon Benton, the men "will favor Father Abraham by a large majority."[40]

12. The Siege Continues

Fort Davis. One of the many forts guarded by the 111th during the siege of Petersburg (Massachusetts Commandery Military Order of the Loyal Legion and the USAMHI).

The election of 1864 saw three candidates competing for the office of the president. General George B. McClellan, the Democrats' candidate, stood for peace. He believed that four years of war had failed to unite the country and that it was time to stop the fighting and bring about peace. The one-time commander of the Army of the Potomac hoped to ride his popularity among the troops to victory. Lieutenant Esek Hoff was at the headquarters of the Irish Brigade when "someone in the crowd proposed three cheers for McClellan and there was a spontaneous answer.... And I would not be surprised if the majority of the army voted for him at election. Although I do not think I shall."[41]

John C. Frémont, the failed Union general, was the champion of the Radical Republicans. This faction believed that the war effort should be pressed, and once the South was defeated, it should be punished for its crime of insurrection, and the leaders of the rebellion should be tried and executed.[42]

The Republican Party candidate was none other than the current president, Abraham Lincoln. The president favored seeing the war through to the end and then welcoming the seceded states back into the Union with a generous offer of peace. While some felt that McClellan would get a large share of the soldier's vote, surgeon Benton felt otherwise: "If the election of Abraham depends on the soldier vote he might as well look up a boarding place in Washington for four years more. There is no doubt of his triumph."[43] When the surgeon cast his vote, he intended it to contain "a bullet for the Rebels and a ballot for Honest Old Abe."

From his bed at the St. John's College Hospital in Annapolis, an unidentified soldier from the 111th wrote a letter with his observations of the coming election. That letter was published in the *Auburn Daily Advertiser and Union*. The soldier writes that he "had a vote here in the hospital yesterday, and out of about 240 votes cast, McClellan got 42, Fremont 1, and Father Abraham the rest ... so I think if you do as well at home, Uncle Abraham will be elected by a large majority. But it is in the north that McClellan will poll his vote. The copperheads stay at home and grumble about peace, taxes, etc., they ought to be made to go into the army and eat hard tack, pork and do a little fighting, then when they got home they would not grumble so much."[44]

The Southern soldiers believed they had a champion in McClellan. A few days before the election, the Confederates in the works opposite the New Yorkers position could be heard giving repeated cheers for the Democratic candidate. On one occasion, seven rebels from a Florida regiment deserted into the lines of the 111th. According to surgeon Benton, these war-weary soldiers openly admitted that the election of McClellan was the "last and only hope of the Confederacy."[45] They wanted peace and believed that only the Young Napoleon could give it to them.

Robert Drummond, Company H. He enlisted in the regiment in 1864, was captured at Petersburg, October 30, 1864, and paroled as a prisoner of war in March 1865 (Massachusetts Commandery Military Order of the Loyal Legion and the USAMHI).

On October 13, the agent from the 25th Senatorial District arrived from New York with the election ballots for the men of the 111th. Three days later, Captain Murdock ordered all detachments of the regiment to return to camp so the men could cast their votes. Officers from each company prepared the ballots and distributed them among the men. Once completed, they were deposited in a box and the agent and the ballots returned to New York where the votes were counted on Election Day, November 8. Lieutenant George Moore of Company I stated that he was very tempted to complete more than one ballot to ensure his candidate would win. In the end, it was not necessary as his candidate, Abraham Lincoln, was reelected by a wide margin.[46]

The voting did not occur without incident. As Robert Drummond of Company H was depositing his ballot in the box, a large shell came flying in from the Confederate line and hit the ground near him. The projectile exploded, showering Drummond with dirt and debris. Once the noise had died down, the sound of cheering could be heard coming from the Confederate line. The first cheer went up for Jefferson Davis. The second cheer was for George McClellan.[47]

12. The Siege Continues

With the election over, life in the trenches returned to normal. The men of the 111th continued to labor building trenches and forts in the rear of the main line of works. They also held regular drills, posted pickets, and performed the usual camp duties. Day and night, the regiment was subjected to shelling from the enemy's line. At times the shelling was so heavy, the earth shook. Chauncey Smith wrote to his wife that the enemy "throw some shell amongst us every day and night, causing us all to be constantly on the lookout for such unwelcome visitors."[48]

New to the regiment, Henry Jeffery of Company A excitedly wrote to his parents after his first time on the skirmish line: "Well father I have had the pleasure of shooting at the Johny Rebs[.] wee are within a half mile of the city of Petersburg and I went out to the front on the picket line. They have got forts and brest work all along the lines. And I had a good view of the rebs and the city last night[.] ther was hevy firing all along the lines we could see the shells burst in the rebs lines from where we are and we can here the pickets fire all day long."[49]

Officers tried to impress upon the new soldiers the importance of not flinching or dodging when under fire. During one such lecture, rebel guns opened on the formation. A shell exploded next to the group of officers, showering them with dirt and debris. According to Chauncey Smith, "such running and dodging, I, nor anyone else ever saw."[50] The recruits had a good laugh as they watched the officers scatter in every direction. From that day forward, no one was reprimanded for dodging an incoming shell.

The shelling seemed to go on unabated. It made such an impression on Charles White that he made note of it in his diary almost every day for a week. Henry Jeffery, too, was amazed by the spectacle of flying and bursting shells. In a letter to his parents, he related what it was like to be in the trenches during a cannonade: "Well you ought to have been here last night to have seen the fire works[.] ther was some of the sharpest fireing that you ever hird[.] wee could see about a dozen shells in the are [air] at a time[.] it is about as much fire works as I ever saw and we could here them wosh just as plane as could be[.] they sound like a beeze sound agoing through the are [air] when one of them mortors go of[f] they make the erth sore all around for a mile[.] wee can go up on the hill back of our camp and see the shells fall in the Johnnys works every time."[51]

As the siege continued, the distance between the opposing lines of works began to shrink. At some points, the trenches were separated by no more than a quarter of a mile, and the pickets were even closer. One evening, Robert Drummond was in camp boiling coffee when orders arrived for his company to take its turn on the picket line. No sooner had one of his comrades made the mistake of stepping in front of the fire when Drummond heard the hiss of a ball go flying past his head. Seconds later he heard a dull thud as the bullet found its target. He turned to see a member of his company lying on his back. Together with Captain Sterling, Drummond lifted the wounded man "tenderly to a stretcher while his life blood spouted from his mouth and nostrils like water gurgling from a spring."[52]

October 22 saw the return to camp of Colonel MacDougall. His time spent at home in Auburn had done wonders for his health, and he was once again ready for duty in the field. Arriving with the colonel was Lewis Husk, newly promoted from major to lieutenant colonel. He too had been able to regain his strength while at home with his wife and children.[53]

Replacing Lieutenant Colonel Husk as major was Joseph Corning. The new major, once lieutenant colonel of the 33rd New York, was already acting in the capacity of a provisional second lieutenant with the 111th when he accepted the promotion. He brought extensive combat experience with him, something that was sorely needed in the regiment. At the battle of Williamsburg in May 1862, Corning led three companies of the 33rd in a desperate charge against two regiments and drove the enemy from the field.[54]

About this time news arrived in camp that the Consolidated Brigade was being disbanded and the various regiments would be returned to their old commands. With the recent influx of so many conscripts, the ranks were again full and it made no sense to keep the regiments consolidated under one command. The old Third Brigade, under the command of Colonel MacDougall, would once again consist of the 7th, 39th, 52nd, 57th, 111th, 125th and 126th New York regiments.[55]

Lieutenant Colonel Husk issued orders on October 24 for the regiment to prepare to leave camp. "I had just got my supper and was putting some hard tack and meat in my haversack for lunch when the orders came to pack our knap sacks and pull tent and hold ourselfs in reddiness for a march," recalled Henry Jeffery. "We had to wait about one hour when the order came to sling knap sacks."[56] The 111th was to march with the rest of the First Division to the front lines and occupy the trenches held by the rest of the II Corps.

Once it was dark, the order to advance was given and the New Yorkers headed for the front. "Just as we commenced our march it began to rain and a darker night I never saw. Our march was around lots and through wood and underbrush and fallen timber and rifle pits, with no light to guide our footsteps," recalled Chauncey Smith. He wrote to his wife that "if it had been light I should have seen a good many stumble but as it was I could only hear the grunts and falls of the poor soldiers."[57] Normally, fires would have illuminated the line of march, but due to the close proximity of the enemy works, fires were prohibited.

After advancing about two miles through the rain and mud, "we came in front of the rebels pickets, they mistrusting our whereabouts sent a volley of blue pills ... but as it so happened that they went whistling in the air over our heads, to our great satisfaction, no one being hurt but a great scare,"[58] remembered Smith. A number of men dropped out of line along the way and did not return to the regiment until the next day, cursing the very day they had enlisted in the army. Lieutenant Colonel Husk's regiment manned a portion of the line between Fort Davis and Fort Hays. The 69th New York of the Second Brigade was to the right of the regiment, the rest of its brigade stretched to the left of the 111th, connecting with the right of the V Corps pickets.

Still enjoying the success of the operations of September 30, General Meade went to his commander with a plan intended to break the Boydton Plank Road line and capture the South Side Railroad once and for all. The plan called for Major General John Parke's IX Corps to initiate the attack against an unfinished line of works near Hacher's Run from its new line at the Peeble farm. Elements of Warren's V Corps would take position on Parke's left flank while the Second and Third divisions of the II Corps would fall in to the left of the V Corps. Hancock's men would cross Hatcher's Run and head straight for the South Side Railroad. Guarding Hancock's exposed flank would be almost an entire division of cavalry under General Gregg. Once the railroad was in Union hands, trenches would be built to connect it to the rest of the Federal works at Peeble's farm.[59]

As with the operations at the end of September, there would once again be a demonstration north of the James to ensure no help was sent to the beleaguered lines south of the city. Butler's Army of the James was to make a feint and threaten the right flank of the Confederate works between the Williamsburg and Nine Mile roads. He was instructed that under no circumstances was he to engage in a frontal assault against an entrenched enemy. Henry Jeffery offered his opinion of the upcoming operation when he wrote his parents: "They are ataking all of the olde troops from here and a sending them to the rite and left, there aint a gointo be eny fighting where we are stationed to amount to eny thing."[60]

By 4:00 A.M. on October 27, Butler's soldiers were underway, marching through a heavy rain. The X Corps infantry encountered the enemy line north of the James around dawn and a spirited skirmish was soon underway. Meanwhile, the XXV Corps was ordered to drive north in an attempt to turn the right flank of the rebel works. Contrary to orders, the Confederate main works were attacked, resulting in great loss of both men and colors. By nightfall, Butler's men were straggling back to their lines, having accomplished absolutely nothing, other than disobeying orders.[61]

As the Army of the James was advancing, soldiers from the V and IX corps were stumbling through the darkness, heading for the Confederate works along Boydton Plank Road. Feeble attempts were made by regiments of both corps to breach the heavily manned works, but each attack failed. With no hope of breaking the Confederate line, the V Corps commander sent one division west to link up with the right of the II Corps.[62]

General Hancock's II Corps soldiers were having a little more luck than their counterparts in the V and IX corps. After meeting slight resistance along Vaughan Road, a detachment from the Second Division charged across Hatcher's Run and captured the rebel works on the opposite bank. Once across the creek, the column turned west and headed straight for Boydton Plank Road. By late morning, Hancock's two divisions reached the area where White Oak Road intersected Boydton Plank Road. With his left anchored on White Oak Road, the rest of the II Corps regiments stretched back to the east, toward the left of the V Corps. The division sent by Warren to linkup with the II Corps never arrived and a gap existed between the two units.[63]

The Confederate commander was not about to let two divisions of Union infantry sit on his right flank unmolested. In response, Lee sent three brigades under Generals Henry Heth and William Mahone south with the intent of destroying Hancock's divisions and rolling up the left flank of the Union position.[64]

As dusk began to settle over the field, rebel infantry came splashing across Hatcher's Run with a deafening yell, pouring into the gap between the II and V corps. The intensity of the attack overwhelmed the right flank of the Third Division, causing it to collapse and fall back. The fighting was so severe that Charles White remembered that "nothing but the roar of artillery and musketry can be heard" in the regiments lines near Fort Davis.[65] Driving deeper into the Union position, the rebels created a bulge in the Union line as they advanced. But in the growing darkness, compounded by a heavy rain, the attackers soon found themselves surrounded. Unable to withstand the pressure of a furious counterattack, the Confederate infantry fell back across Hatcher's Run and returned to the safety of their own lines.

With his chances of easily driving on to the South Side Railroad gone, Hancock reformed his lines and had his men prepare to leave the field. Around 10:00 P.M., with a heavy rain still falling, the II Corps soldiers began to withdrawal from the Boydton Plank

Road line and head toward Dabney's mill. From there, the wet and tired soldiers began to slowly make their way back to the rear of the First Division in the works outside of Petersburg. The Third Division was given no time to rest as its soldiers were ordered to replace the First Division on the picket line.[66]

While the rest of the II Corps was fighting along Boydton Plank Road, Henry Jeffrey and his comrades were spending their time "laying close to the fort (Hays) and all we have to do is drill."[67] When not drilling, the men took their turn on the picket line, which was only about "twenty-five rods from that of the enemy and our only protection from their fire a low line of rifle pits."[68] Bullets from the enemy pickets were not the only danger to the New Yorkers. Shells continuously fell in the regiment's lines, causing Chauncey Smith to comment that "we hold the forth of July here every day and night."[69] While a fatigue party from the regiment was working on the trenches, a shell "dropped down between the two mules and exploded, sending them to their destruction."[70]

A steady stream of Confederate soldiers, disillusioned with life in the trenches, came into the lines of the 111th. Henry Jeffery remembered, "The johneys ceep a coming in every knight from three to eight every knight and they are the sauciest lot of looking fellows and as ragged as a jew."[71] Yet the rebels were not the only soldiers deserting their regiments. During the month of October, the 111th lost ten men to desertion. Three of these men, Isaac Clemens, Valentine Conners, and Michael Conners, went over to the enemy on the night of October 2.

October 30 started like any other day. Except for those on picket duty, the New Yorkers stayed low in their trenches to escape the intermittent picket firing and the occasional artillery shell sent their way. Just like their counterparts across the distant fields, they would fire at anything that moved. From the time the regiment occupied the picket line on the 25th, three of its men were lost to enemy fire.[72]

A detachment of 162 officers and men from the 111th waited anxiously to be relieved from their front-line duty by soldiers of the Third Division. These men occupied the picket line about 200 yards in front of the main line. Along with pickets from the 69th New York on their right, the New Yorkers covered the distance between Fort Davis on the right and Fort Hays on the left.[73]

Lieutenant Colonel Husk was appointed brigade officer of the day and commanded all the soldiers on the picket line, while Captain Lafayette Mumford of Company A commanded the detachment from the 111th. The right section of the regiment's picket line (post one) was commanded by Second Lieutenant Hoff while the left section (post two) was commanded by Second Lieutenant Andrew Camp of Company D. A deep ravine separated the left of Lieutenant Camp's post and the right of the V Corps pickets. Colonel Husk established the picket relief post just in front of Fort Hays, along a road that lead from the fort to the picket line.[74]

As the sun began to set on another day, Chauncey Smith remembered, "A deathlike stillness prevailed along the line."[75] Some of the New Yorkers struck up conversations with the rebels on the other side of the field until Colonel Husk rode along the line and put an end to it. Others took advantage of the relative quiet and wrote letters to loved ones at home. Chauncey Smith sat on a log in the woods, composing a letter to his wife. He told her that he occupied a picket post with John Howard and Newton Ferris and that life on the picket line was not all that bad.

Henry Jeffery penned a few lines to his parents "to pass the time of day on the picket line." He explained his duties and what it was like to be so close to the enemy: "Every six hours i half to go out in the vidst about a rod in advance of the picket. A vidst is a small brestwork thrud up about half as high as a man and they are about two rods apart and a man is put in them to ceep watch and if he sees enythring of a Johny and if haint to far off he has to halt him but if he is to far off to halt then we have to shoot at him and that puts the rest of the picket on there guard." Ending his letter, Jeffery expressed his love to all those at home and asked his parents to write "a little oftiner."[76]

Robert Drummond wrote to his brother, telling him that "before this reaches you, I hope to be among the first of Grant's army that enters the City of Richmond." Finishing his letter, Drummond made his way to the rear to place it in the company mailbag. On the way back to his post, he saw Captain Reuben Myers. The captain, accompanied by his "large white dog that had deserted from the enemy," told Drummond that as soon as it was dark, the pickets would be relieved and sent to the rear.[77] With happy news in hand, Drummond ran back to take his place on the picket line.

About 9:00 P.M. the sound of moving troops could be heard to the right of post one. Believing it to be the picket relief, Second Lieutenant Hoff ordered his men to pack their knapsacks and prepare to move to the rear. Hoff then stepped out of the trench and prepared to meet the officer of the relief to obtain the appropriate number of men for his section. Suddenly, the trenches were filled not with soldiers from the Third Division, but with men wearing blue overcoats and gray pants, pointing rifles. They were soldiers of General Mahone's Confederate division. The New Yorkers at Lieutenant Hoff's post were quickly disarmed, ordered out of the rifle pits and pushed along the trench line. Somehow, the rebels missed Hoff, who ran as fast as he could back to Third Brigade headquarters to report what was happening along the picket line.[78]

Then James Doane heard what he thought was the relief moving behind his position. "They went past my post without relieving me. They went past out of hearing. After they had been gone some time, I went back to the pits to find out what the matter was. I saw the pits were deserted and things strewn around, then I went back to my post."[79] Doane waited about 20 minutes to be relieved when he again heard the sound of troops moving through the brush, this time coming from the left. Thinking that it might be the enemy, Doane ran back toward Fort Hays to inform Colonel Husk of what was happening along the picket line.

Robert Drummond was at his post when "our rifle pit was surrounded from the rear by about thirty or forty Confederate soldiers, who, with cocked rifles in their hands and fixed bayonets, demanded an *unconditional surrender*." Drummond had once sworn with much bravado that he would never be taken prisoner, "but as I looked at the particular individual who held the muzzle of his rifle close to my eye, as I saw the cap glistening under the raised hammer and realized that the finger of the foe was on the trigger, I at once concluded that it is not always safe to tell beforehand what we will or will not do under unforeseen circumstances."[80]

Chauncey Smith and his comrades were looking to the front for the enemy, not the rear, and "consequently we were taken by surprise and were not prepared to defend ourselves" when the rebels appeared behind their position. Smith recalled,

> The front ranks ... were in blue clothes that they had gotten from deserters and this too threw us off our guard as they approached us. When they came up to our post they had some five or six big lusty fellows outside of their ranks to disarm us and shove us into their

trap with a rush. When a big Johnnie snatched at my gun I braced myself and held on to it the best I knew. Two other Johnnies put their bayonets close to my face and with a yell "git in you damb yank or we will stop your breathing." I saw that the majority was against me so I obeyed orders and away they went.[81]

The Confederates formed a hollow square around their prisoners and moved down the line from post to post, "and served them in a similar manner," recalled Drummond. When the Confederates bagged enough prisoners, they "started for their lines acting as though they felt jolly over the game they had played."[82] Once inside the rebel works, the captors quickly herded their prisoners to the rear.

Yet not all were content to be taken as prisoners of war. Several, including Captain Mumford, Lieutenant Camp, and Chauncey Smith were able to slip away in the darkness and make their way back to friendly lines. Smith's escape from his captors was daring, if not foolhardy. Keeping as close to the left side of the square "as I possible could and as near to the guards for I well knew that if I ran the gauntlet of the four guards successfully I would have to use all of the physical force that my body possessed. As the raiders were passing a large pine tree the auspicious moment came I made a desperate jump passed the guards. I passed three of them very quickly without touching, but the outside one I struck and knocked off his feet, he went sprawling to the ground on top of his musket, and the next jump I made I heard the expression 'shoot the damb yank.'"[83]

Smith ran back toward friendly lines as fast as his legs could carry him. Encountering the picket line, he found the fires still burning, but the trenches were empty. He remained on the picket line until relief arrived, when "I went back to camp with a sad heart not knowing the fate of my comrades. I was lonesome for Ferris and Howard and my tent seemed desolate."[84]

Second Lieutenant Camp was attending to his post when the rebels approached. The lieutenant "did fallback from the line without firing a shot or giving any alarm a distance of about 300 yards and formed a new line taking with him all the men on his section that escaped capture by the enemy as they came down the line, remaining there until daylight when he, with the balance of his detail, returned to Fort Hays."[85]

Lieutenant Colonel Husk was at his headquarters when he "heard the tramp of men and the rattling of canteens."[86] He sent one of his aides, an officer from the 69th New York, to investigate the noise. No sooner had the officer disappeared into the woods when he came running back saying that the trenches were empty. Husk mounted his horse and rode to the front to see for himself. Arriving at the picket line, he found the trenches as his aide described, and the ground strewn with guns, knapsacks and all types of equipment. As fast as he could, Husk rode to headquarters to see Colonel MacDougall and give him the sad news. Husk found Lieutenant Hoff with the brigade commander and learned what happened on the picket line.

All night, stragglers from the 111th returned to the regiment. They came in alone and in groups, but in each case without arms or equipment. One man from the regiment encountered General Samuel Crawford of the V Corps and related the tale of his capture and subsequent escape. On hearing the story, Crawford put his entire picket line on alert. When role was called in the morning, it was discovered that of the 160 men standing guard on the picket line, 83 were made prisoners of war.[87]

The incident set off a series of courts-martial of the officers involved. Lieutenant Colonel Husk and Lieutenants Camp and Hoff were each charged with neglect of duty while on picket. The three officers were placed under arrest and confined to quarters. Colonel MacDougall was certain that deserters from the 69th New York were responsible for the incident. Several of their number went over to the enemy while on picket duty, and the colonel believed they gave the enemy valuable information about the picket line.[88]

MacDougall's ire wasn't reserved for just the deserters from the 69th. He was quick to lay the lion's share of the blame squarely at the feet of Lieutenant Hoff. MacDougall reported,

> As soon as he discovered the color of the pants, he immediately started to tell the officer of the picket that the enemy were capturing his men. This seems the most disgraceful affair of the whole. Had this officer attended properly to his duties and informed post No. 2, he might have opened fire upon the enemy and scattered the whole party. Instead of that he ran away to tell the officer in command and let the enemy pass on; and post No. 2, supposing it was the relief, was captured, and so on down nearly along the whole line occupied by the one hundred and eleventh.[89]

The presiding boards for the courts-martial were made up of officers from the various regiments of the First Division and one by one the officers were tried. The charges were read and testimony given. Lieutenant Hoff submitted a written statement to the board in his defense. In part it read, "This being the first time in my military experience ever having been placed in arrest or charges perfered against me. It has been my aim to do my duty to the best of my ability, and if I have erred, it has not been intentionally."[90] Eventually, all three officers were found not guilty of the charges brought against them, but they would not be released from arrest and returned to duty until early December.

Yet no matter what the board decided, the affair weighed heavy on the mind of Lieutenant Hoff. He was well aware that many in the regiment blamed him for the loss of 83 of their comrades. On November 6, he penned a letter to his wife where he contemplated resigning his commission: "We can borrow some consolation from my going out of the service.... I can have enough to pay our debt and we can go and live somewhere in peace."[91] While his wife wanted him to come home right away, Hoff was at least hoping to be honorably discharged as a result of the court-martial. In the end, Hoff decided to remain with the 111th.

November 5 found the 111th manning Fort Stevenson, located in the second line of works ringing Petersburg. The men had prepared "fat pork and beef for supper and sat down turk fashion on the ground and ate our rations like hungry pigs," recalled Chauncey Smith. That evening, quiet reigned in camp as most of the men were sound asleep in their tents, hoping that nothing more "would be wanted of us until the next morning."[92] Unfortunately, this was not to be.

Just after 10:00 P.M., the regiment was ordered to pack knapsacks and fall into ranks. The enemy was pressing the main picket line and the regiment was needed at the front. Major Corning rode to the head of the 111th and led the regiment out of camp. Just as the column was within a mile of the front, the New Yorkers began to "smell gunpowder and some sneaked out [of line] thinking it would not be very safe to get in range of rebel bullets." One of those to leave the ranks was Dennis Mainard of Company F. According to Chauncey Smith, Mainard "fell out for fear of getting into a fight and is now under arrest."[93] Smith had other ideas for himself: "All was dark and nothing was seen but the flash of the fire-arms.... I guess that I felt somewhat timid but made up my mind that I would rather die on the battle ground than to be called a coward."[94]

Major Corning deployed the 111th in line of battle and called a halt. In plain view of the enemy, Corning rode to the head of the regiment and issued his orders. The regiment was to advance on a battery that was inflicting heavy casualties among the Union pickets and either capture it or drive it from the field. When the order to advance was given, the men surged forward, firing as they advanced. It did not take long for the battery to limber up and retreat to the rear, leaving over 100 of its men on the field as killed, wounded or captured. The 111th, by contrast, lost just over ten men in what, according to Chauncey Smith, "will be called only a light skirmish and hardly worth anything."[95]

Returning to Fort Stevenson just as the sun was rising, Major Corning dismissed the men and allowed them to return to their tents. The New Yorkers took advantage of the relative quiet to clean their equipment, get some sleep and catch up on writing letters. Many of the men wrote home requesting special items to be sent to them. Chauncey Smith wrote home asking his wife to send him a "nice pair of woolen mittens."[96] He also asked that she be ready to send him a barrel full of provisions once the regiment entered permanent winter quarters.

A reminder of the awful carnage suffered by the regiment at Gettysburg arrived in camp on November 6. It came in the form of boxes of extra clothes and equipment left in Centerville before that awful campaign started. With so many of the 1862 men gone, there was plenty of extra clothing to be distributed to the men. Lieutenant Hoff was able to retrieve his old coat while Sergeant Geer got an overcoat and a "better woolen blanket than I sent away." Geer retrieved the items left behind by his best friend, Judson Hicks. He sold "Juds overcoat for three dollars" with the intention of sending the money to Hick's family.[97]

Drill soon became the order of the day. Sergeant Geer lamented that "we have drill every day. Company drill from ten to twelve in forenoon. Officers and noncommissioned officers from one to two and company drill again from two to four. That keeps us rather busy."[98] Since some of the companies were composed almost entirely of recruits, many of the veteran soldiers were transferred from their companies to others to help drill and train the "greenies." In a letter Sergeant Geer wrote, "Our regiment is not very well drilled. There are too many men in it that came for *money*." He summed up the feelings of many old soldiers when he said, "I hope we shall not have to do any fighting until this regiment is better drilled. I do not think they would *stand fire*. It is not the original 111th by a long shot."[99]

Some of the sergeant's feelings toward the new men may have stemmed from his loneliness. "I shall have to tell who my tent mates are. Four of us tent together ... they are all good boys but then they are not my old tent mates. There are but two of the old boys present in Company A."[100] While melancholy for his lost friends, Geer was at least pleased with his new company commander. "I like Capt. Mumford better than any officer we have ever had in Company A before. He is a gay looking officer but he is not very *airy*. Anything he can do for the boys he always seems to be willing *to do*."[101]

Near the end of November, Major Corning gave the order for the men to build winter quarters. For Chauncey Smith, it was time indeed: "When we got out of our nest this morning the ground where we lay was all water and we all looked like chickens that had just come out of a swill pot."[102] By the end of the day, Charles White and his tent mates had finished their quarters, complete with fireplace and chimney. Laboring in the freezing temperatures was worth it to White. His diary entry for this day ended with, "Well, here I am this evening sitting by my fire which I have just built in my new fireplace."[103]

November 26 was a sad day for the 111th as the regiment lost its beloved corps commander, Winfield Scott Hancock. He had continued to suffer immensely from a wound he received at Gettysburg over a year before and was granted a 20-day leave of absence in hopes that he would recovery sufficiently and return to the army. But this was not to be. After turning over command of the corps to General Humphreys, Hancock penned a farewell address to his beloved II Corps, acknowledging that "whatever military honor has befallen me during my association with the Second Corps has been won by the gallantry of the officers and soldiers I commanded, I feel that in parting from them I am severing the strongest ties of my military life."[104]

A few weeks after Hancock left the army, Colonel MacDougall penned a letter to his old commander. News that Hancock was asked to raise a corps of veteran troops had reached MacDougall and he wanted a command: "I am very desirous of having a command under you in the new corps. You know what I have done for the service in the way of recruiting and fighting. If you consider me worthy I would like very much to be with you."[105] Hancock never returned to the army and MacDougall would have to be content with remaining at the head of the Third Brigade.

In the early morning hours of November 30, the men of the 111th left the safety of Fort Stevenson behind and marched southwest. Their destination was the works on the extreme left of the Union line around Peeble's farm. The movement was made without incident, and the men once again took their place in the front line. The regiment's pickets were within speaking distance of the rebels, and an informal truce between the two sides was agreed upon, even though orders strictly forbid talking to the enemy. The band from each side could be heard playing at all hours of the day, "one side playing the tune of dixie and the other side yankee doodle."[106]

Work on winter huts began anew. The New Yorkers were becoming experts at constructing quarters in very little time, although it made them very cynical about the prospects of remaining in them for too long. Sergeant Geer remarked, "We may stay here all winter and we may not stay twenty four hours ... we are building winter quarters but may not winter in them."[107]

Geer's words rang true, for Major Corning was directed to have the regiment ready to advance with the rest of the First Division at daylight on December 9. The 111th would take part in a reconnaissance of the Confederate line at Armstrong's mill, near the scene of the fighting at the end of October. Just after sunrise, the New Yorkers stepped off with the rest of the brigade, minus the 57th and 126th which were ordered to remain in the works. The weather had turned bitterly cold and the men were half frozen before they even made it out of camp.[108]

The main thrust of the operation was to stop railroad transportation on the Weldon Railroad for good. Even though the railroad was useless to the Confederates from Stony Creek Station to Petersburg, a distance of almost 20 miles, the resourceful rebels were able to bring much needed supplies by rail as far as the station and then haul them by wagon, through Dinwiddie Court House, into the besieged city. The job of destroying this line from Stony Creek Station to Hicksford fell to General Warren and three divisions of his V Corps. Accompanying Warren would be a division of cavalry under General Gregg. His troopers would screen Warren's column and protect the working parties. By the time the 111th broke camp on the 9th, the V Corps infantry had already been hard at work for two days destroying the rail line just south of Jarret's Station, about five miles short of Hicksford.[109]

The 111th marched at the rear of the division as the column advanced down Vaughan Road toward Hatcher's Run. Firing could be heard coming from the head of the column as elements of the First Brigade battled with Confederate infantry trying to block the ford where Vaughan Road crossed Hatcher's Run. The II Corps Infantry forced its way across the ford, making way for Greg's troopers. Major Corning positioned his men along the east bank of Hatcher's Run, establishing a picket line and making camp for the night.[110]

Operations south of the city were going surprisingly well. Warren's infantry was busy destroying the railroad and Gregg's cavalry rode farther south to clear the way toward Hicksford. But here, he found the bridge over the Meherrin River destroyed and the enemy posted along the opposite bank. Not wanting to bring on a general engagement, Warren decided that he had fulfilled his orders and directed the cavalry to pull back and be prepared to return to the lines at Petersburg the next day. However, Warren had not done as he was told. While a stretch of the railroad was destroyed, the vital supply line into Petersburg remained in operation.[111]

Just after midnight on the morning of the 10th, sleet and rain began to fall, and the New Yorkers woke the next morning in half-frozen blankets. The men were ordered to act as rear guard for the division as it made its way through ankle-deep mud back to the lines around Peeble's farm. Although sparring with the enemy the entire way, there were no casualties among the men. Arriving in camp around midday, the regiment took its place in trenches filled with ice and mud.[112]

With no more offensive operations scheduled for the rest of the year, the regiment settled back into the routine of drill, inspections and posting pickets. Lieutenant Colonel Husk, assuming command of the regiment around the middle of the month, began to hold training classes for all officers in the regiment. "The officers of every company on dress parade are drilled and trained by the lieutenant colonel and have to give a strict account of all of their doing through the day,"[113] recalled Chauncey Smith. Like Colonel MacDougall before him, Lieutenant Colonel Husk took great pains to maintain the morale and discipline of the men.

To that end, Husk issued Special Order No. 5. In it he chided the company commanders for allowing the appearance of their men to deteriorate. The order stated that all men must have their hair cut short, beards neatly trimmed and their hands and faces washed clean at all times. "If any soldier neglects to wash or has dirty hands or face he is at once transferred to what is called the dirty brigade and then he is drilled and taught how to keep himself clean and decent."[114] The lieutenant colonel knew, as many in the regiment did, that the next campaign could very well be the last, and he wanted his men ready.

Chapter 13

The Last Campaign

> On the sixth day of our march Old Lee was surrounded and taken prisoner with all of his whelps.[1]

The first days of 1865 found the 410 men of the 111th huddled in their winter quarters, fighting off the cold. A fresh blanket of snow covered the ground and helped to hide the scars of war that marred the landscape for as far as the eye could see. Those unlucky enough to be detailed for picket duty had to endure one of the coldest winters on record.[2]

When the weather permitted, the New Yorkers spent most of the time drilling, at least five hours a day. Colonel Husk was determined to make the recruits as proficient on the parade ground as the veterans. On one particularly cold day, the men were called out of their warm huts for company drill. Company F "took a few right and left flanks on the march of double quick in order to keep warm but the air was too keen and cutting,"[3] recalled Chauncey Smith. After less than an hour of maneuvers, the men were ordered back to their quarters to sit by the fire and get warm.

The cramped conditions of the winter quarters were just as dangerous to the men as the frigid temperatures outside. In a letter Chauncey Smith wrote, "There is now a great deal of sickness in camp, the most prevalent disease is jaundis, some four or five of company F here have got this complaint."[4] During the first two months of 1865, nine men of the 111th died of disease, while many more were confined to the division hospital at City Point.

In addition to subzero temperatures, the pickets also had to contend with Confederate deserters who made their way into the Union lines every night. One evening, almost 20 rebels came into the picket line held by the Third Brigade. They regaled the New Yorkers with tales of horrible privations, and they said that their pickets were ordered to shoot anyone caught deserting. A few weeks into the new year, every regiment in the Third Brigade was ordered to march in plain view of the Confederate works. According to Chauncey Smith, the intent was to "intimidate the rebs by our great numbers" and encourage more to desert.[5]

On one particularly cold January evening, Smith and other members of Company F were standing guard in front of the regiment's position. In a letter to his wife, Smith wrote, "There were two boys that came over to our side from the rebels, they got into us

Sergeant Wager Remington, Company B. Wounded at the Wilderness, May 5, 1864, he later served as a lieutenant and then captain of Company G (Massachusetts Commandery Military Order of the Loyal Legion and the USAMHI).

about nine o'clock and they stayed with us until morning before we escorted them into camp, they appeared to be first rate good fellows and were very talkative and social, looking for something to eat." Smith shared some of the food his wife sent from home, and his newfound friends were very thankful. "They looked as though they were almost starved, they say the whole Rebel army is waiting for a chance to come over to our side."[6]

With the new year came a new round of promotions. First Lieutenant Philip Ira Lape was promoted to captain in Company B while Second Lieutenant George Moore of Company I was promoted to first lieutenant and transferred to Company D. New to the regiment, Franklin Deuel was assigned as a second lieutenant in Company F, while Second Lieutenant Wager Remington of Company G was elevated to the rank of first lieutenant. After recovering from wounds received in the Wilderness, Sergeant Major John Fishback returned to the regiment and received a promotion to first lieutenant in Company H. Sergeant Minard McDonald received a promotion to second lieutenant in the same company. Paroled after his capture at Ream's Station the previous August, Sergeant Levi White of Company I was rewarded with a much-deserved promotion to first lieutenant.[7]

The receipt of bad news in camp tempered the celebrations. With their time of enlistment over, the men of the 57th New York were mustered out of Federal service and returned home to New York. After joining the Harpers Ferry brigade in the spring of 1864, these men had shared the hardships of campaign life and charged side by side with the 111th into the burning tangles of the Wilderness. These fighting men would be sorely missed in the campaign to come.[8]

Even more heartfelt than the loss of the 57th was the loss of Colonel MacDougall. A partner in a bank back home in Auburn, MacDougall asked for a 15-day leave of absence to see to his business. The leave was granted in mid–January and the colonel left his beloved regiment and returned home. In his absence, Brevet Brigadier General Henry Madill was assigned to command the Third Brigade. Leaving the same time as MacDougall was Major Corning. Corning accepted a promotion to colonel in the 194th New York and tendered his resignation and left the 111th.[9]

As January gave way to February, Generals Grant and Meade became increasingly concerned by the thought that General Lee would evacuate the Richmond and Petersburg defenses and slip unmolested through their grasp. Once free of the siege line, the Confederate army would be free to march south and join forces with General Joseph Johnston's army. With their combined strength, the two armies could attack and destroy General William Sherman's army, then drive north through the Carolinas and turn their attention to the Army of the Potomac.[10]

To prevent such an event from happening, the two Union commanders devised a plan designed to keep Lee's attention focused on the army to his front. Part of Meade's army would march west in yet another attempt at severing the vital supply line running from Hicksford to Petersburg. This was the same artery that the army failed to sever the previous December. Grant gave explicit orders for the Southern wagon trains bringing supplies into the beleaguered city to be destroyed. If the lifeline could not be cut, the army could at least continue to stretch its trenches west and tighten the grip on Cockade City. As surgeon Benton saw it, "every stroke here is just as good as if it was executed directly on the Rebel capital."[11] The date for the start of the operation was February 5.

Before sunrise on the appointed day, Smyth's Second Division and Mott's Third Division of the II Corps, along with the entire V Corps, broke camp and began marching through the frigid morning air. Warren's V Corps was headed south toward Dinwiddie Court House to assist Gregg's cavalry division in cutting Boydton Plank Road and capturing as many of the enemy's supply wagons as they could. The two divisions of the II Corps were ordered to march west toward the Confederate works at Hatcher's Run and intercept any force sent south to attack Warren's and Gregg's soldiers. The First Division was ordered to man the trenches once held by the entire II Corps. The Third Brigade was posted in the works with the 125th and 126th in garrison at Fort Seibert and the 39th at Fort Emory. The 111th, 7th and 52nd were placed in a reserve position between the two forts.[12]

By early morning, both infantry columns reached their objective and began to construct fieldworks. The II Corps line ran from Armstrong's mill back toward the main line of works held by the First Division. After placing his regiments in line, General Humphreys noticed a gap in the line between the right of Smyth's line and the left of Mott and immediately took steps to close the breach. Unfortunately, the Confederates also saw the gap in his line and moved to attack.[13]

It was close to 4:00 P.M. when Confederate battle lines appeared in front of the II Corps works. Regiments from Gordon's Second Corps and Hill's Third Corps attacked with the intent of exploiting the opening in the Union line. But the intensity of the fire coming from the Union works, coupled with blasts of canister from their artillery, drove the rebels back with severe loss. Darkness brought an end to the contest and the gray-clad infantry withdrew from the field.[14]

General Warren's V Corps arrived at the Vaughan Road crossing of Hatcher's Run early on the morning of February 6. He had been ordered there the night before in fear that his command, isolated near Dinwiddie Court House, might be attacked and destroyed. Warren placed his regiments in position on the southwest side of Hatcher's Run, along Dabney's Mill Road. Later that afternoon the V Corps was attacked near Dabney's mill by elements of the Confederate First Corps and driven back. Only the timely arrival of reinforcements from the VI Corps and heroic fighting by some of Warren's regiments saved the V Corps from being totally routed.[15]

As was usually the case, the 111th did not remain in position for too long. With operations against the Confederate right flank over for now, the 111th and the rest of the First Division were ordered to march south and take possession of the newly constructed works near the Vaughn Road crossing of Hatcher's Run. The actions on February 5 and 6 fell far short of the commanding general's expectations. General Gregg's troopers only captured a handful of wagons and did not make a permanent break in the Boydton Plank Road line. The only bright spot was the continuation of the siege lines farther to the west, continuing the stranglehold on Petersburg.[16]

The beginning of March found the 111th occupying trenches with the rest of the II Corps south of where Vaughn Road crossed Hatcher's Run. The return of springlike weather saw an increase in drill and inspections. The New Yorkers held daily company and battalion drills and ended every day with a dress parade. New uniforms were issued, excess clothing and blankets were packed and sent to City Point, and sutlers ordered out of camp. All indications pointed to the resumption of active campaigning.[17]

Despite the rumors of an impending advance, drills and inspections continued unabated. To Sergeant Geer, there was too much drilling for his taste: "I marched my company out had them fix bayonets stack arms and lie down. I dislike to drill and this drilling five hours every day to learn these new men I don't go much on. I get excused every day when there is any show for it."[18] Part of Geer's dislike for drill probably stemmed from the fact that he was responsible for drilling the "awkward squad," soldiers who had problems learning the movements of the soldier.

On March 8, the regiment bid farewell to surgeon James Dana Benton. The doctor mustered out of service to accept a position as chief surgeon with the 98th New York.

For over two and a half years, Benton had marched with the regiment in every campaign, endured every privation, and suffered every hardship. His presence and faithful ministration would be deeply missed.[19]

In appreciation for their hard work, the men of the 111th were rewarded with a break from their daily routine. According to the editors of the *Auburn Daily Advertiser and Union*, the 111th was "an honor to the 25th District. [The regiment] has been enjoying a week's respite from duty as reward for building the best line of breastworks in the Division, near Hatcher's Run, and complimented for its fine appearance in review."[20] It was a rest well deserved.

Near the end of March, a welcome yet unexpected visitor arrived in the regiment's camp, Sidney Mead. Captured along with 30 other members of the regiment at Mine Run more than a year before, Mead managed to escape from his captors. He arrived in Knoxville, Tennessee, around the beginning of January 1865, with a number of other escaped officers and was sent home to convalesce before being ordered to report to the regiment. As hollow consolation for his trials and travails, Mead was promoted to major.[21]

On the night of March 24, General Grant began to formulate a plan intended to breach the lines around Petersburg and end the siege. It called for a concentrated thrust along the entire front by the II, V and IX corps and Sheridan's cavalry. His force would break the siege lines and, if all went as planned, destroy Lee's army. But before Grant could put his plan in motion, the enemy struck first.[22]

Advancing before dawn on March 25, Confederate general John Gordon led the four divisions of his Second Corps across the no-man's land separating the opposing lines of works. The target of the attack was Fort Stedman and its IX Corps defenders. General Lee hoped that the Union line could be split in two, causing great confusion among the Federals and buying time for the Confederate commander to pull his army away from Petersburg. The gray tide swept over the fields, penetrated the works and captured the fort. Fighting raged back-and-forth in the trenches and along the ramparts of the fort before the Federals were finally able to mount a counterattack and drive Gordon and his men back to their lines.[23]

Word of the attack on Fort Stedman spread like wildfire through the Union defenses. It was believed that the rebels must have depleted other parts of their line to mount such an impressive attack. With this in mind, General Meade ordered the entire Union line to be on alert and ready to move at a moment's notice. If the enemy's lines were weakened as he had hoped, one of his corps should be able to punch a hole in the rebel defenses.[24]

With General Madill absent, Colonel Augustus Funk of the 39th took charge of the brigade and led the New Yorkers out of camp in the early afternoon. After the halt was called, the 111th, along with the rest of the Third Brigade, was posted in reserve to the rear of the First Division. The remaining three brigades quickly attacked and overran the enemy's picket line, then readied themselves for the attack on the main Confederate works to their front.[25] The day wore on to the crackle of musketry as each side's skirmishers trading shots over the trench lines. Colonel Funk was ordered to move his brigade out of reserve and place it on the left flank of First Division.[26]

As the New Yorkers waited in line, General Miles directed Funk to leave the 111th in place and position the rest of his regiments to the right of the Second Brigade. The general then rode over to Lieutenant Colonel Husk and, according to Chauncey Smith, instructed Husk to "move your regt [regiment] right to the front of our picket line in double quick and hold it at all events and save our pickets from being killed or taken prisoner." Asked if the enemy was close at hand, Miles responded, "they were just over the hill ready for the charge."[27] No time was wasted getting the 111th into position and ready to move.

Lieutenant Colonel Husk led his men at the double to the skirmish line in front of the right flank of the Third Division. No sooner was the regiment in position when they began receiving fire from enemy sharpshooters. Husk ordered the men to lie down to escape the deadly fire. Luckily, most of the deadly missiles either sailed harmlessly to the rear or impacted into the dirt in front of the men.[28]

Close to 6:30 P.M., "the rebs made their appearance at the top of the hill," charged with a tremendous yell and headed straight for the right flank of Mott's Third Division. As the enemy line swept forward, it was met with a well-delivered volley from the 111th. "The order was fire and we did in good earnest, such a stream of death I never saw before," recalled Chauncey Smith. "It seemed as though every shot killed."[29] When the gray battle line began to slow, the New Yorkers delivered another volley that stopped it dead in its tracks. The third volley "made them skeedaddle in confusion and the field was ours to the joy of the scared pickets and the whole regiment."[30]

No sooner had the first attack been beaten back when a second line emerged from the wood line to the regiment's left and charged straight for Mott's line. Husk immediately ordered the 111th to shift to the left and open fire. Even though the New Yorker's volleys caught the rebels in the flank, the gray battle line bravely pushed forward, overwhelming Mott's soldiers and forcing them to fall back. The New Yorkers rate of fire increased, and the Confederate attack ground to a halt. The well-placed volleys coming from the ranks of the 111th allowed the Third Division regiments to reform and begin to fight back. Combined with the fire from Mott's reformed battle line, the 111th drove the enemy back up the hill.[31]

The sun had set by the time the fighting ended and a skirmish line was sent out into the darkness to guard against any further attacks. Despite the severe casualties inflicted upon the enemy, the losses suffered by the regiment were incredibly light. Charles Anstead of Company F was wounded in the hand while Marcus Berge of Company H was missing, presumed killed. Chauncey Smith admitted to his wife, "It looks to me almost like a miracle to think that no more of us were hurt, for bullets whistled like hail all around us."[32] Sergeant Geer felt he was very lucky: "I got one pretty close call but a miss is as good as a mile."[33]

Both Lieutenant Colonel Husk and General Madill had high praise for the New Yorkers' actions. The regimental commander was impressed by how the men acquitted themselves, despite the fact that over two-thirds of them had never fired their muskets in combat before.[34] Even though he was not present at the battle, Madill filed an official report on the action performed by his brigade. The general felt that Lieutenant Colonel Husk and the 111th New York saved the Third Division and behaved "as though they had been in a score of battles." For his part in directing the regiment, Husk was awarded a brevet promotion for bravery to the rank of colonel.[35]

The night was quiet, except for the occasional crack from the picket's rifle, each side firing at the other's muzzle flashes. A few deserters came into the regiment's picket line with stories of the afternoon's fight and how their side was soundly beaten. Just after midnight on the morning of March 26, Husk received orders to join the rest of the Third Brigade as it marched back to camp south of Vaughn Road. Once again the army had failed to punch a hole in the Confederate works and the siege would continue.[36]

The New Yorkers had little time to rest before resuming the offensive. Sergeant Geer figured, "We shall have a chance to try them again soon,"[37] and he was right. On the morning of March 29, the men were again loaded down with four days rations and 50 rounds of ammunition. Generals Grant and Meade planned to shift the II and V corps around the right flank of the Confederate army, while sending a formidable force of cavalry to capture Dinwiddie Court House, the Confederates last line of supply and communication into Petersburg. If the Confederates concentrated on the infantry moving around their right flank, they would loose Dinwiddie and be forced to lengthen already thinly manned trench lines. If, on the other hand, General Lee challenged the cavalry, he stood a good chance of having his army flanked out from behind their works.[38]

The regiment broke camp for what the men hoped would be the last time and headed west with the II Corps. With General Madill back in command of the Third Brigade, the 111th crossed Hatcher's Run at Vaughan Road. The 126th deployed out in front of the brigade as skirmishers and the march continued until the head of the column reached Gravelly Run, a tributary of Hatcher's Run. Here the column was halted and the regiment's deployed in line of battle. As Colonel Husk posted skirmishers in front of the regiment's position, the rest of the men were put to work constructing earthworks. Darkness descended over the field and a heavy rain began to fall, quickly drenching the men.[39]

Around noon on the 30th, General Miles ordered the advance to continue. With a detachment from the regiment under Lieutenant John Fishbeck deployed as skirmishers, the regiment advanced in line of battle northwest toward White Oak Road. The lieutenant's skirmishers soon encountered enemy videttes and drove them back across Boydton Plank Road to their main line of works. The advance was halted and, like the day before, digging began in earnest. Sergeant Geer and others from the regiment were ordered to "fell the timber in front of the breastworks,"[40] clearing fields of fire. Skirmishers continued to trade shots with the enemy as night descended on the field. Despite the constant exposure to enemy bullets, the regiment only suffered two men wounded.[41]

The last day of March came early and by 4:00 A.M., and with rain still falling, the New Yorkers continued their march west, following the Fourth Brigade. After advancing a short distance, the men were deployed behind works recently vacated by the V Corps, with Boydton Plank Road on their right. Skirmishers were deployed in front of the works and the men immediately began improving their position.[42]

Not long after midday, fighting began to intensify at the front. The V Corps was ordered to advance on White Oak Road to determine the strength of the Confederate works. Two divisions sent by General Warren met with stiff resistance and were driven back in disorder. General Lee was on hand to personally direct the movements of his forces in fending off the Union advance. The V Corps commander then sent in his last division to steady his forces. Close to 2:30 P.M., the line was reformed and was ready to advance once again.[43]

As the V Corps soldiers were rallying, General Humphreys ordered two brigades from the First Division to fall in on the right of Warren's line. General Madill's brigade was one of those selected. Colonel Husk called the regiment to attention, had the men fix bayonets and ordered the advance. No sooner had the regiment stepped over the works then it was met by a devastating volley from the enemy. One of the first to fall was George Andrews of Company B. Andrews received a mortal wound to the stomach and died the next day.[44] The 111th continued to advance despite the withering fire slicing through its ranks. Captain Edgar Hueston went down wounded while William Bennett, Thomas Jarvis, James Jones, and Orlando Robins, all of Company D, were killed. Humphrey Davenport of Company I was shot through the right side, the bullet "cutting off two ribs, and lodged in his left side, where it still remains."[45]

Posted as the left guide of the regiment, Corporal Franklin Lutes of Company D looked across the field to see the "rebel color-guard, proudly waving the flag of the 41st Alabama Infantry."[46] Recently paroled from a Confederate prisoner of war camp where he languished since his capture at Ream's Station, Lutes was ready to exact revenge. He yelled to the men around him that they should capture the flag. The corporal ran out ahead of the regiment and took up a position behind some fence rails stacked between two trees. At the right moment, Lutes jumped out from behind his cover, grabbed the flag, its color-bearer and one other soldier from the Color Guard. In a single act, the corporal bagged a Confederate flag, two prisoners and his nation's highest honor, the Medal of Honor.

The New Yorkers helped recapture the advance line of works and push the Confederates back to their main works on the north side of White Oak Road. They pressed the attack along the front of the Confederate works but the entrenchments were found to be too strong to carry. However, the left-most V Corps regiments were able to gain a small foothold on the right flank of the rebel line, thwarting any chance of reinforcements being sent to their comrades near Dinwiddie Court House.[47]

Unable to carry the position, the combined II and V corps line fell back and began to dig in, with the V Corps on the left and the II Corps on the right. A strong skirmish line was posted in front of the brigade, the detachment from the 111th under the command of Lieutenant Esek Hoff. Fighting between the two sides lasted long into the night. When roll was called that evening, it was discovered that the regiment had suffered 4 men killed, 23 wounded and 1 man missing during the day's battle.[48]

Among the killed was 17-year-old Charles Hosey of Company A, considered to be the "pet and pride of the regiment." Hosey was "as usual, among the first men when a bullet struck him in the neck and he fell upon his face, killed instantly and when we went for his body, he lay there as if asleep." According to his comrades, Hosey exhibited some peculiar traits while in battle. "When the minie bullets came too near, he would make a quick motion with his hand as though to brush away an impertinent fly. When an unusually large shell burst over our heads, he would say, 'that was a bad one, wasn't it,' and would simply hug the soil of the Old Dominion a little closer."[49]

Before the sun rose on the first day of April, the regiment was once again under arms, occupying the trenches it vacated the day before west of Boydton Plank Road. Skirmishers were posted while the rest of the New Yorkers dropped down in the mud to get some much-deserved rest. The men were roused after a few hours and told to be ready to move. Around 11:00 A.M., General Miles ordered Colonel Husk to deploy the regiment as skirmishers and advance toward the enemy works along White Oak Road. Husk was instructed to reconnoiter the enemy's line and "if possible, carry them by assault."[50]

The men were ordered into ranks and at 1:00 P.M., crossed their works and advanced in line of battle toward the enemy battlements. The rain of the past few days had turned the woods and fields into quagmires of thick mud, slowing the advance of the regiment. Suddenly, the rebel line erupted with the sound of a thunderclap, sending a wall of lead hurtling toward the 111th. Luckily, the volley was fired high and caused only a few slight wounds among the men. Colonel Husk quickly determined that the enemy works were still heavily defended and could not be easily taken. Wanting no part of a direct assault on an entrenched enemy, Colonel Husk gave the order for the regiment to return to its works west of Boydton Plank Road.[51]

Shortly after the 111th returned to their entrenchments, the men were formed in ranks and marched to the left of the Union line. The New Yorkers pulled out of line and followed the rest of the First Division west, toward Dinwiddie Court House. They were supposed to take up a position along Clairborne Road to keep any reinforcements from reaching Confederate general George Pickett's division at Five Forks. When just within a few miles of Dinwiddie, the regiment was directed to turn around and march back to the works they had just left. As the frustrated New Yorkers tramped along the muddy roads, their comrades in the cavalry and the V Corps were routing General Pickett's rebels at Five Forks, taking close to 3,000 prisoners. They arrived back at their works close to 4:00 P.M. and were allowed a few hours' rest. Some took the trouble to light fires and boil coffee while others simply wrapped themselves in their blankets and quickly went to sleep.[52]

That evening, Generals Grant and Meade issued orders for a general assault to take place along the entire front the next day. Both knew that the enemy's lines were stretched to the limit and it would not take much effort on their part to make them break. Their plan called for the IX Corps, on the right of the Union line, to attack the enemy works around Fort Mahone. The VI Corps, to the left of the IX Corps, was to launch their assault on the lines near Fort Fisher. The Army of the James, which recently joined Meade's army from Bermuda Hundred, would move against the enemy to the left of the VI Corps. Finally, the II Corps was to attack beyond Dabney's mill, just west of where the Confederate line was anchored on Hatcher's Run. If all went as planned, Petersburg would be in Union hands by nightfall.[53]

Just before dawn on April 2, the 425 men of the 111th were once again ready to move. With the regiment posted in front of the brigade as skirmishers, the final push to capture Petersburg began. As they anxiously moved forward, the New Yorkers could hear the booming of artillery and crackle of musketry off to the east. The main assault had begun at 4:30 A.M., and heavy fighting was taking place all along the line. The regiment pressed forward toward the works along White Oak Road. Many were worried about their chances of success, the thought of the previous day's encounter of heavily defended works fresh on their minds. But to their surprise, the men from Wayne and Cayuga counties encountered little resistance. According to Sergeant Geer, the regiment "drove the enemy from his works" and easily mounted the trenches along White Oak Road.[54] Most of the defenders had fled north during the night to where a new line was being formed closer to the city.

Colonel Husk quickly dressed the ranks and the pursuit of the fleeing enemy began anew. General Humphreys had the entire II Corps on the move toward Sutherland Station, a stop on the South Side Railroad about five miles west of Petersburg. The New Yorkers splashed across Hatcher's Run and, after advancing almost a mile, struck Clairborne Road, which they followed north. Around 10:00 A.M., the men stopped inside a wood line within sight of the railroad. Forming in line of battle along the edge of a wood line, everyone in the regiment readied themselves for the order to charge.[55]

The line to their front was formidable indeed. The enemy works sat along Cox Road; the left was anchored on Ocran Methodist Church, while the right rested at Sutherland Tavern. To the rear of the works was the South Side Railroad and Sutherland Station. Four brigades of battle-tested veteran infantry under General Heth manned the works. The men of the 111th had faced these men before and knew they were in for a rough go of it.[56]

At 11:00 A.M., General Madill led his brigade forward. The 111th held the right flank of the brigade, with the 125th to its left. No sooner had the regiment stepped forward from the safety of the wood line when it was met with a terrible volley of artillery and musketry. Second Lieutenant Silas Belding of Company C was hit and killed instantly. The men advanced into a perfect hail of bullets and were halted short of the works. Unable to advance, General Madill ordered the brigade to return to the woods. But before the maneuver was complete, Madill fell with a serious wound. The command of the brigade fell to the regiment's own Clinton MacDougall. He had just returned days earlier from leave with a well-deserved promotion to brevet brigadier general and he was ready for a fight.[57]

General Miles brought the Second Brigade forward, placed it to the left of MacDougall's brigade and ordered them both forward. Again the fields were swept with a terrific fire from the enemy lines. A bullet hit Colonel Husk in the shoulder, causing a slight wound and ripping the rank insignia from his uniform coat. Soon after, he was thrown to the ground when his horse was hit by enemy fire. The colonel was helped to his feet by some nearby soldiers, and he led the regiment on foot for the rest of the day.[58]

General MacDougall rode in front of the charging battle lines and, according to Sergeant Geer, "cheered the men by his presence and example of personal bravery, going before them in the charge, and receiving a flesh wound in the right arm. He still keeps his saddle and attends to his duties notwithstanding his wound."[59] But just like the first assault, this one also failed, and the New Yorkers were forced for the second time to fall back to the safety of the wood line.

Close to 3:00 P.M., the regiment was once again ready to assault the enemy works. This time, the Fourth Brigade was brought forward and placed in position to the right of the 111th. The New Yorkers stepped out of the woods and advanced toward the railroad under a perfect hail of bullets. As they got closer to the earthworks, the New Yorkers could see the left of the enemy line giving way under the weight of the Fourth Brigade's flank attack. Not to be denied, the New Yorkers surged forward with a yell, scaling the works into the Confederate position and forcing the rebels to retreat up Namozine Road. With the railroad secure and the rebels on the run, the regiment quickly reformed and advanced about a mile and camped for the night.[60]

A heavy price was paid for the railroad. In the three charges against the enemy works, 1 officer and 4 enlisted men were killed, 1 officer and 40 men were wounded, and 2 officers and 16 men were missing from the regiment. Lieutenant Belding, the 41-year-old blacksmith from Canandaigua, has the unfortunate distinction of being the last officer of the regiment killed in action. The two officers captured were Captain Reuben Myers of Company H and Captain Edwin Burnham of Company D.[61]

The day's actions could not have gone better for the army. Starting on the right of

Brigadier General Clinton MacDougall (Massachusetts Commandery Military Order of the Loyal Legion and the USAMHI).

the Union line northeast of the city, the IX Corps had punched a hole in the Confederate line and after some of the most tenacious fighting of the siege, had captured Fort Mahone and put its defenders to flight. In the center of the line, the VI Corps had also gained a measure of success. After breaking through the rebel earthworks, the VI Corps infantry cut Boydton Plank Road and drove on to the South Side Railroad. The regiments of General Ord's Army of the James scaled the works to their front, marched by the right flank and began driving on the city. By midafternoon, Ord's soldiers had assaulted and captured Forts Gregg and Whitworth. Finally, on the left of the Union line, the II Corps had broken through along its entire front and Humphreys' men were driving the rebels back at all points. By nightfall, the entire rebel army had evacuated the Petersburg and Richmond lines, and triumphant Union soldiers marched into both cities early on the morning of April 3.[62]

The pursuit of the rebel army began again the next day. Deployed in front of the division as skirmishers, the 111th made its way west along the muddy back roads of Dinwiddie County. The crackle of rifle fire could be heard all day as the regiment advanced. The line of march took the men past Namozine Church, where troopers of General George Custer's cavalry division had attacked and defeated Southern cavalry, forcing their retreat to the west. Here, the regiment turned southwest along Cousin's Road. After a rather uneventful day, the New Yorkers camped on the Coleman farm, along Winticomack Creek.[63]

Early on the morning of April 4, the drums beat the long roll, and the men of the 111th grabbed their rifles and took their place in line. With knapsacks slung across their backs, the New Yorkers began to advance with the rest of the division. The column had only proceeded about three miles when orders arrived recalling the regiment. Colonel Husk turned the men around and marched them back to their camp of the night before. The rains at the end of March, coupled with the thousands of men and wagons passing over them, had turned the roads into quagmires. Husk's men were to be put to work corduroying the roads.[64]

Captain Reuben Myers, Company H. Captured at Sutherland Station, April 2, 1865 (courtesy of David Mohr).

The backbreaking labor continued all day. By nightfall, the exhausted men were relieved of their duty and made camp along side of the road. Most of the New Yorkers simply fell to the ground in exhaustion. They needed what little sleep they got for at midnight, the men were awakened to draw three days' rations. By 2:00 A.M. on April 5, the regiment was on the move again. After escorting the wagons of the II, V and cavalry corps on the day's march, the 111th was able to join the rest of the First Division at Jetersville by midmorning.[65]

April 6 came early for the New Yorkers as the pursuit of Lee's dwindling army continued. The line of march took the regiment west, in the direction of the Appomattox River. The sound of gunfire could be heard all morning as the skirmishers of their corps' First Division tangled with the rear guard of Confederate general John Gordon's Second Corps. By early afternoon, it was once again the regiment's turn on the skirmish line, and it wasn't long before they were trading shots with Gordon's men.[66]

Littering the Confederate line of retreat were equipment, abandoned wagons, tents and everything a soldier trying to escape in haste might throw away. At Holt's Corner, Gordon and his soldiers followed their wagon train as it turned north and then back to the west. The road the Confederate column was following began to dip down toward a marshy bottomland where Little Sailor's and Big Sailor's creeks came together. The road passed over two bridges spanning the creeks before continuing on to Rice's Station and Farmville beyond. As the head of the wagon train reached the creek, the formation began to slow down. When one of the bridges collapsed, the entire column came to a halt. Gordon formed a battle line on the east side of the two creeks and prepared for battle. While the ragged line prepared to meet the enemy, others fought desperately to repair the downed bridge and get the wagons rolling to safety.[67]

The 111th came over the rise and was confronted with General Gordon's battle line. The rest of the division formed in line and began to trade volleys with the Confederates. The New Yorkers watched as the First Brigade advanced and easily pushed the rebels to the west side of the creeks, where they formed another battle line. Under orders from General MacDougall, Colonel Husk advanced his regiment with the rest of the brigade down to the double creeks. The men waded through the chest-deep water with rifles and cartridge boxes held above their heads, under heavy rifle and artillery fire. Moving at the double, the 111th helped drive off the enemy batteries and break the weak line of infantry, which retreated west. After marching a short distance away from the creek, the men camped for the night. The day's operations had netted the II Corps 13 battle flags, 4 pieces of artillery, over 1,700 prisoners and close to 140 wagons. The cost of the day's fighting to the regiment was one man wounded.[68]

On the morning of April 7, the chase began anew. Before long, the regiment came within sight of the Southside Railroad bridge over the Appomattox River, known locally as High Bridge. Two forts on the eastern end of the span and two on the western end protected the bridge. Below the lofty span was a wagon bridge that crossed the river.[69]

When the Third Brigade arrived, fighting was already raging for control of the bridge. The regiment formed under heavy artillery fire and stood ready to join the action. The New Yorkers watched as the enemy was forced to retire, but not before setting fire to both the railroad and wagon bridges. As soldiers from the Second Division rushed to put out the flames, the 39th and 52nd were deployed as skirmishers along the edge of the river. Once the flames were extinguished, the 111th crossed on the still-smoldering wagon bridge and continued on toward Farmville, where the enemy was trying to reform its ranks. The Confederate commander hoped to concentrate his forces, then push south to meet up with Joe Johnston, who was at that moment retreating north through the Carolinas with General Sherman hot on his heels.[70]

But General Lee was not alone in using the sleepy Appomattox River town to concentrate his soldiers. Both the Army of the Potomac and the Army of the James were converging on the city. Two divisions of the II Corps were advancing on the town from the southeast while the remaining division under General Barlow was approaching from the south. The VI Corps, along with the Army of the James, quickly forded the river and occupied Farmville. With the Union army's disposition complete, Lee's route south was blocked. The only hope now for the rebels was to reach Lynchburg, located at the foot of the Blue Ridge Mountains.[71]

Traveling along Jamestown Road, the New Yorkers encountered the enemy in a strongly entrenched position around Cumberland Church, just north of Farmville. Colonel Husk formed his men in a line of woods and waited for the order to attack. But much to their relief, the New Yorkers watched as the First Brigade launched an attack against the left flank of the enemy position, which was easily beaten back. As darkness settled over the area, the men from Wayne and Cayuga counties busied themselves throwing up a line of earthworks in the woods facing the church.[72]

Sensing the hopelessness of further resistance on the part of the Confederate army, Grant sent a note under a flag of truce to Lee as the fighting around Cumberland Church was winding down. He asked that, in order to prevent further loss of life, Lee surrender his army at once. While noting he was not yet prepared to surrender his army, Lee did ask what terms Grant was prepared to offer his men. This note reached the Grant just after midnight the next day.[73]

At sunrise on the morning of April 8, the men of the 111th were relieved to discover that the enemy had vacated the works to their front sometime during the night. Along with the 125th and 126th, Company A from the 111th was placed out in front of the brigade as skirmishers. The New Yorkers were once again following the general route taken by General Gordon's Second Corps, along the Lynchburg-Richmond Stage Road. After a march of about 20 miles, Colonel Husk halted the regiment just west of New Store. The men were allowed to rest for about two or three hours before renewing the chase. The column pushed on for about seven more miles before the men were allowed to stop for the night.[74]

The messages that began to pass between the two army commanders on the evening of the 7th continued on the 8th. After reading Lee's letter asking what terms would be granted to the Confederate army, Grant at once drafted a reply. He stated that peace being his ultimate goal, all surrendered soldiers could not take up arms against the United States government until exchanged.[75] When General Lee received the response to his letter of the previous day, he read the note and hurried off his reply. In the letter he agreed to meet with Grant at 10:00 A.M. the next day along Stage Road to discuss the terms of surrender of the Army of Northern Virginia.

The situation for the Confederate army was indeed hopeless. During the day, the Union cavalry under General George Custer had stormed into Appomattox Station, capturing the vital rail center with its trainloads of provisions for the hungry and weary rebel foot soldiers. The V Corps, along with the Army of the James, took up positions southwest of Appomattox Court House, blocking the direct line of march to Lynchburg. The II and VI corps were positioned behind the Confederate army, which was entrenched near New Hope Church, while the cavalry under General Phillip Sheridan was positioned to the southeast and southwest of the village.[76]

By 7:00 A.M. on April 9, the 111th was again advancing west along the Lynchburg-Richmond Stage Road. All along the route, the men encountered debris of the fleeing Confederate army. Around midday the New Yorkers encountered the rearguard of the Confederate army under General James Longstreet entrenched around New Hope Church. To the sound of rifle fire coming from the skirmish line the men prepared to assault the breastworks. Presently, an officer carrying a white flag could be seen riding along the line. The message was that a cease-fire had been arranged, and all hostilities would be suspended until further notice. As the firing died down, the men began to talk wildly amongst themselves. They had been speculating about this day from the moment they broke through the siege lines at Petersburg, and now the day of surrender seemed to be at hand.[77]

The hours passed slowly as an eerie silence enveloped the field. It was strange for men used to the constant rattle of musketry to be so close to the enemy without hearing the familiar whiz of the sharpshooter's bullet or the telltale thud of its impact. The New Yorkers had no idea that as they sat facing the enemy on the other side of the breastworks, General Grant sat facing General Lee across a table as the Confederate commander signed the formal surrender agreement. By 3:00 P.M. it was all over.[78]

General MacDougall, II Corps officer of the day, was at army headquarters when the news of the surrender arrived. MacDougall at once mounted his horse and raced back to his old regiment to inform Colonel Husk of the surrender, waving his hat in the air with his good arm as he rode. When they heard the news, the men of the 111th went wild with joy, many firing their guns in celebration. When General Meade rode along the line, the men offered their commander cheer after cheer, until they yelled themselves hoarse. One who did not celebrate was Sergeant Geer. In a letter to a friend, he wrote, "I could not cheer. I thought of the many brave boys we have lost."[79] Excitement over the day's events kept the men awake for most of the night. With their part of the war over, thoughts quickly turned to home.

Almost as if to capture the mood of the vanquished foe, April 10 dawned to a cold, drizzling rain. The New Yorkers spent most of the day helping to bury the dead and tend to the wounded of the previous day's skirmishing. Those captured since the start of the campaign returned to camp, including Captains Burnham and Myers. The next day the II Corps started north for Washington, marching over muddy roads. But the men of the 111th did not seem to mind for they knew that at the end of this march there was no enemy waiting for them, only the safety of their homes back in New York. As the march continued on April 12, their counterparts in the Army of Northern Virginia were stacking arms for the last time, furling their beloved banners and preparing to make their way home.[80]

The column arrived at Burkville on April 13 and remained there until the end of the month. Here the New Yorkers received the first mail from home since the beginning of the campaign. They set up a permanent camp, drew rations and new clothing. Daily drills and inspections were held. In a letter to friends, Sergeant Geer wrote, "I suppose the officers begin to think they can not get us killed off in battle anymore, so they mean

General MacDougall and staff. MacDougall is seated at the center. Seated at the far right is First Lieutenant John Lockwood. Standing on the left is Edgar Hueston (Massachusetts Commandery Military Order of the Loyal Legion and the USAMHI).

to drill us to death. We have to polish boots and brass again now. Everything has to look just so."[81] Chauncey Smith liked the change in the regiment's routine: "All is quiet in camp, the sound of fire arms is heard in our camp no more, a few weeks ago the talk amongst the soldiers and officers was all fight, how changed the scene, now the talk is all peace, how we soldiers all like the change."[82]

News arrived in camp on April 16 of President Lincoln's death at the hands of John Wilkes Booth. Sergeant Geer made a simple entry in his diary to mark the passing of the president: "Got news that president Lincoln is dead."[83]

At the end of April, the regiment received orders to pack knapsacks and be ready to march. Colonel Husk led the men out of camp and marched them about 20 miles south toward the Roanoke River where they were ordered to guard a VI Corps supply train. The regiment remained on duty until May 2, when it returned to the camp at Burkville. With no time to rest, tents were struck and the 111th left camp in the early afternoon, heading for Richmond. What was left of the city came into view three days into the march as the New Yorkers arrived in Manchester, on the south side of the James River from the city. For some reason, the men were pushed very hard on the march from Burkville to Richmond. A number of men in the II Corps died due to the heat and extreme exhaustion, which caused Chauncey Smith to remark, "This is very hard indeed after they had lived and passed through the spring campaign and had braved all kinds of dangers and hardships on the field of strife and then after all this to be killed on a foolish march."[84]

When the men entered the one-time Confederate capital, they were amazed at the sight that greeted them. When the city was evacuated on the night of April 2, all warehouses and military stores were set to the torch. But in the confusion that reigned, looters set fire to other buildings and large portions of the city had burned to the ground. The men continued on through the ruins and reached Fredericksburg by May 10. Three days later, the 111th reached Bailey's Cross Roads, within sight of Washington, and went into camp.[85]

The New Yorkers passed long, boring days in camp. No one was allowed to leave the regimental area unless they had a signed pass from an officer. Most spent their time writing letters to loved ones or speculating when they would be allowed to go home. Others, like Chauncey Smith, wondered what it would be like to eat food not infested with worms, cook something other than salt pork, or sleep in a real bed instead of on the cold, wet ground.[86] The only excitement in camp occurred when it was read in a hometown paper that the regiment was going to be mustered out of service in Albany and not in Auburn as expected. Rumors ran rampant through camp and most, like Sergeant Geer, heard "so much we do not believe anything we hear."[87]

To show its appreciation for the victory over the Confederacy and the hardships endured by the soldiers, the new administration planned a grand review of both General Sherman's and General Meade's armies. Both bands of soldiers would parade from the Capitol down Pennsylvania Avenue to the White House. The day set for the Army of the Potomac was May 23.[88]

In preparation for the event, Colonel Husk ordered equipment cleaned and polished, and uniforms washed and mended. As the sun rose in the east on the 23rd, Husk formed the regiment, marched it out of camp, and led it over Long Bridge into the nation's capital. The entire army was forming along Capitol Hill for its triumphant march through the city. At the appointed hour the signal guns rang out and the parade began.[89]

The men moved down Pennsylvania Avenue toward the White House, with the swagger of battle-hardened veterans. Their lines were perfectly dressed, moving as if they were one. Streets were lined with thousands of waving and cheering spectators, buildings were decorated with red, white and blue bunting, bands played and people threw flowers at their feet as they passed.[90]

Three years of war had exacted a terrible price. In total, the 111th suffered 191 killed and mortally wounded, 501 wounded, with 241 being taken captive. Almost half of those captured perished while languishing in Southern prisons. But despite it all, those who survived had stood the test of battle and were rewarded for their sacrifice with victory. They had faced death at places whose names would forever be venerated: Gettysburg, Bristoe Station, the Wilderness, Spotsylvania, Petersburg.[91]

But on this day they were not alone, for marching with them were the spirits of those left behind. There was Martin Van Buren Moore, the first of the regiment to be killed in battle. Lieutenant John Drake was there, as were Judson Hicks and that cross-eyed Dutchman Gustavus Ritter, all killed at Gettysburg. Joining the victory march were Horace Hill, the gallant officer who fell while rallying his men in the horrors of the Wilderness, and Artemus Stewart, killed before the gates of Petersburg. Not to be forgotten were those, like Daniel Grandin, who suffered beyond words and died at Andersonville.

The 111th made its way down Pennsylvania Avenue with the rest of the II Corps. A massive reviewing stand had been erected in front of the White House to hold

Victory Arch located on Auburn's Genesee Street to welcome the returning soldiers (from the collection of the Cayuga Museum).

13. The Last Campaign

Casper Wallace, Company G. Mustered in with the regiment in August 1862 and mustered out with the regiment in June 1865, never having been wounded (author's collection).

dignitaries, civilians and military alike. When they passed the reviewing stand, the New Yorkers saw President Andrew Johnson and Generals Grant, Meade and Sherman. Offering a salute to the new president, the column continued on, through Georgetown, over the Aqueduct Bridge spanning the Potomac River, and back to quiescence of camp life.[92]

At the beginning of June, Colonel Husk gave the order the men had been waiting for; strike tents, pack knapsacks and prepare to go home. There was an air of celebration as the men marched into Washington and boarded a train to begin the trip north. The train passed through many of the same cities the regiment encountered on its way to war almost three years earlier, before arriving in Albany on June 4. Here the men relinquished their arms and equipment and were mustered out of the service. Those who enlisted the previous September for three years were transferred to the Fourth New York Heavy Artillery. Their term of service would end in September when that regiment was mustered out of service.[93]

When word reached the citizens of Auburn that their soldiers were finally coming home, the townspeople set about at once to prepare a celebration worthy of their returning heroes. Auburn was decked in banners, and evergreen arches were placed over Genesee Street that read, "Wel-

Photograph of the veterans at the dedication of the regimental monument at Gettysburg, June 26, 1891 (Don Chatfield Collection).

come Victorious Conquerors." The train carrying the battle-scarred men of the 111th pulled into town on the morning of June 8 to the ringing of the city's church bells and the cheers of a jubilant crowd. Colonel Husk formed the men on Chappel Street and marched them down Genesee Street to the Western Exchange Hotel, where the regiment had received its colors almost three years before.[94]

Only 134 members of the original regiment stood in the ranks, a testament to the hard fighting endured. Their number included Corporal John Grinnell of Company I, wounded at Gettysburg, Petersburg, and Sutherland Station, and Casper Wallace who had never been wounded. Just five of the officers who mustered with the regiment in 1862 were present. They were Colonel Lewis Husk, Captains Sidney Mead, Edgar Hueston and Reuben Myers, and First Lieutenant Adolphus Capron.[95]

After a song by the Auburn Quartette Club, General MacDougall was asked to speak to the crowd. He declined, saying that he and Colonel Husk were fighting men and not speakers. He asked that Chaplain Brown address the people. The chaplain gladly related the heroic work performed by the regiment, and the many sacrifices the men endured in the name of their country and their loved ones back home. At the end of his speech, the townspeople cheered the regiment for its deeds, who in turn cheered their friends and family.[96]

As the city clock rang out 12 times, Colonel Husk called the men to attention and marched them through the city streets, escorted by the Auburn Coronet Band and the Auburn Fire Department. The New Yorkers were treated to a wonderful lunch at the various hotels and dining rooms throughout the city. When the meal ended, the regiment marched back to the railroad depot for the trip to Syracuse. Here they were paid for the last time as soldiers before returning to Auburn on Wednesday, June 14. Before throngs of anxious onlookers, the men were dismissed from service once and for all.[97]

No longer needed, many of the soldiers of the 111th New York went back to the lives they led before the war, while others moved on to different pursuits. Clinton MacDougall became a senator for New York and turned down a number of appointments from President Rutherford B. Hayes only to become a United States marshall. He died in Paris, France, in 1914. In later life, Lewis Husk moved to Wisconsin where he became a prominent businessman. He returned to Auburn around the turn of the century and died in 1911, surrounded by family and friends. As a testament to the love and respect the men had for their commander, the pallbearers at Husk's funeral included Roland Dennis, Reuben Myers, Robert Drummond and Henry Clark, along with three former members of Company G.

The prolific letter writer Thomas Geer returned to Marion, got married, raised a family and eventually became the town's postmaster. He would suffer the rest of his life from the sickness he contracted during the Gettysburg campaign. Reunited with his wife and four children, Esek Hoff settled back into the quiet life of a brick mason. After his release and recovery from his horrible ordeal at Salisbury prison, one-time farmer Robert Drummond gave up his plow to become a lawyer, opening a thriving practice in Auburn. He went on to be elected district attorney for Cayuga County. Reuben Myers became sheriff of Cayuga County while Henry Clark, the beloved aide to General MacDougall, went back to making hats.

Mustered out of the 98th New York, surgeon James Dana Benton returned home and opened a private practice. But the war years had exacted a heavy toll on his health,

The veterans, along with wives and children, at the dedication of the regimental monument at Gettysburg, June 26, 1891 (collections of Seward House Museum, Auburn, NY).

and he died at the young age of 59. Philip Ira Lape tried his hand at a number of businesses before moving to Kansas where he lived out the remainder of his days. The Angel of Salisbury, Thomas Jenkins, returned to Newark and opened a meat market. He and his wife Annie had five children. It took a long time for Daniel Hutchins to fully recover, both mentally and physically, from the horrors of Andersonville. He eventually made his way to Michigan and went back to school. Richard Warren once again made Port Byron his home and resumed making wagons. Five years later, Richard married Elizabeth Day, with whom he had eight children.

George Salisbury and his new bride, married just three days before the regiment departed Auburn in 1862, had four children. He opened a drug store in Ledyard with his friend and comrade Johnson McDowell, the sergeant who had lost a leg at Gettysburg. The White brothers, Charles and Levi, went into business together in their hometown of Moravia. German-born Augustus Donk got married and had three children. He worked 43 years for the New York Central and Hudson River Railroad. And Chauncey Smith went home to his beloved Fanny and their four children, to once again take up the life of a gentleman farmer.

They would gather many times in the coming years, recounting deeds of valor, wandering long quiet battlefields, and remembering with reverent pride the names of fallen comrades. They would again share laughs and shed many tears. But no matter where they were, these men carried with them what they did and what they saw in the war. For many, the years of the Civil War were the defining years of their lives. Indeed, they were soldiers.

Appendix A

"We Left Him at Salisbury"

I felt his hand slip from my grasp. I felt that his heart had ceased to beat and realized that my noble friend and comrade prisoner was dead.[1]

Eighty-three men stood facing the diminutive General William Mahone on the last day of October 1864. They had been captured the night before as they manned their posts along the picket line between Forts Hays and Davis. Now they found themselves prisoners of the Confederacy. The majority of the men from Wayne and Cayuga counties were new to the 111th, having only joined the regiment a month or so before.[2]

The general quickly ordered the bewildered men stripped of all overcoats, blankets, hats, and in some cases, shoes. Despite many protests, the New Yorkers were even relieved of all treasured mementos from loved ones back home. Some of the Confederates protested the order to loot the prisoners, but in the end followed their superior's commands. One of them told the group, "Boys, it's hard, but I must obey orders."[3] Scared and uncertain of the fate awaiting them, the New Yorkers were surrounded by armed guards and hurried along on their way to Richmond.

Arriving in the capital later that day, the prisoners were paraded through the city streets, much to the joy of the local populace. When asked by a resident who they were, one of the New Yorkers quipped, "Madam, we are General Grant's advance on Richmond."[4] Indeed, Robert Drummond's prediction to his brother of being one of the first to enter Richmond had come true, "but under far different circumstances than [he] had anticipated." The march ended when the prisoners arrived "before a building in whose identity we could not be mistaken; it was the notorious Libby Prison."[5]

The captives found themselves reunited with comrades from the 111th who had been captured on other battlefields. It was in Libby Prison where they received their first real taste of the hell that awaited them as prisoners of war. According to Robert Drummond, "here commenced the process of starvation that was soon to swell our death roll."[6] The small warehouse-turned-prison was already filled to capacity with underfed, sick Federal soldiers, so Drummond and his comrades would have to be moved to another prison.

Remaining in the Richmond hellhole for less than a week, the 83 prisoners, along with soldiers from other regiments, were marched to the city's railroad depot and packed like cattle into boxcars. The train steamed out of the station and headed south. Finally, after a dreary ride on the North Carolina Railroad, the New Yorkers found themselves at Salisbury Prison in Salisbury, North Carolina.[7]

Established during the winter of 1861 out of a dire need for more facilities to house captured Union soldiers, the prison occupied roughly six acres of land. A 12-foot high stockade fence surrounded the compound, atop which sat more than a dozen sentry posts. Along the outside of the stockade ran a raised platform upon which the guard could keep an eye on the prisoners. On the inside of the stockade was the dead line. It was located six feet from the wall and ran the entire length of the fence. Any prisoner who happened to get too close or cross it would be shot, no questions asked.[8]

The main structure inside the prison area was the four-story brick Maxwell Chambers Factory, an abandoned cotton manufacturing plant. The factory had originally been used to house the prisoners, but as more captives arrived, it became the camp's main hospital. Other structures located inside the stockade fence included nine wells, almost a dozen hospitals, the dead house, and a number of smaller buildings that acted as kitchens. The sinks, or latrines, were located along the southwest wall of the stockade and drained into a creek located about a half mile from the rear wall of the prison.[9]

When the New Yorkers arrived at the beginning of November 1864, the conditions inside the prison were deplorable. Roughly 9,000 men were crammed inside the yard designed to hold only 2,000. Even Brigadier General John H. Winder, the commissary general of prisons for the Southern government, had little good to say about the prison: "There was a shortage of water both for drinking and for flushing away the accumulated filth of the prison. As a result the sinks produced a stench insupportable both to the prisoners and people of the vicinity. The soil was considered to be unfit for a prison because it was a stiff, stickey clay, and after a slight rain is over shoe top in mud."[10]

To make matters worse, only 300 tents had been issued to shelter the men. Those not lucky enough to have one were forced to seek shelter underground for protection against the elements. One of the preferred methods was to dig under one of the many buildings inside the compound. A second type of shelter constructed by the men was made by digging a trench big enough for a number of men to lie down in and covering it with a shelter half or blanket. But the most common type of shelter used at Salisbury was a simple hole in the ground. The men would dig an entrance into the ground and then burrow down about five feet. A chamber would then be dug at right angles with the entrance large enough for at least one person and sometimes two. A fireplace was usually located at the far end of the chamber to provide warmth during the frigid winter months.[11]

Robert Drummond and his newly arrived comrades found themselves in dire circumstances. They had to choose whether "to remain out doors or dig holes in the ground in which to stay. To adopt the former course was sure death at no distant day; the latter was just as sure, but the process of dissolution was not quite so rapid. In company with four others of my own regiment, it was my lot to make choice between the two methods just mentioned, and we went into the ground as our choice of the two terrible evils." Drummond described how the subterranean dwelling was built: "We built that tenement with a piece of broken case knife and the hands that Nature had given us. The process was slow, but the emergency was great and in due time the work was accomplished."[12]

One of Drummond's fellow subterranean dwellers was Charles Green, also of Company H. Green was among the many new recruits to join the 111th in early September. Instead of fighting along the siege works of Petersburg, the 23-year-old college student now found himself digging with his hands into the hard North Carolina clay in a desperate race against the elements.[13]

In December, the prison's quartermaster succeeded in procuring a supply of lumber for the prisoners to build themselves barracks. Construction started but was soon stopped by order of General Winder. The Southern government planned to move the camp's occupants to another location and did not want to waste precious wood on barracks that would not be inhabited long. Instead, the prisoners were forced to survive with what little shelter they had for the remainder of their stay at Salisbury.[14]

Besides the squalid conditions in which the men were expected to live, they were subjected to starvation rations. The typical fare was about three pints of corn meal, usually eaten raw. In the middle of November, an oven was constructed within the stockade, and the corn meal was baked into bread before being issued. But whether raw or baked, it was still vile to the taste. Meat was sometimes issued but not on a regular basis. A substitute for the meat ration was offal. This specific item consisted of the "heart, liver, lungs, and intestines of slaughtered animals."[15]

Ramps were constructed along the sentry's walkway to allow the guards to dump loads of meat scraps into the prison yard. It was not uncommon for the guards to stand and laugh as starving prisoners scrambled to collect pieces of intestine and hungrily devour them on the spot. When meat was not available, molasses was issued in its place.[16]

Robert Drummond felt the lack of rations contributed greatly to the sickness that swept through camp: "The rations, issued very irregularly, were insufficient to support life. Men grew feeble before living upon them a week. Prisoners eagerly devoured the potato skins from our table." Any animal that dared stray into camp was fair game. Drummond recalled his comrades eating rats, dogs, and cats.[17]

Sickness was a death sentence at Salisbury. Very few that entered the hospitals ever left under their own power. They were usually wheeled out on the dead cart. The main hospital was in the bottom floor of the Maxwell Chambers building, where the sick and dying were laid upon the floor in rows so compact that the doctors could not even pass between the men. Robert Drummond remembered that straw was initially provided for the sick but it quickly wore away, leaving the afflicted to lie "upon the cold, naked, filthy floors, without even the degree of warmth and cleanliness usually afforded to brutes."[18] According to a fellow prisoner, "the rebel surgeons seem to give little attention to the sick. They go about the rounds in a cold perfunctory manner. Very little medicine is given. Nearly as many died inside the stockade, without having received any medical attention whatsoever, as in the hospitals."[19] Conditions were the same in the other, smaller hospital buildings throughout the prison.

The main cause of sickness among the men was the lack of food and adequate shelter. Drummond felt "little, if anything, could be done for them medically. Hunger and exposure could not be remedied by the material media. What advantage was quinine and opium when they could get neither bread nor raiment? The sending of physicians to the prison limits was a ghastly farce." Drummond watched as his comrades were stricken with "pneumonia, catarrh, diarrhea, and dysentery.... The weakened men were powerless to resist disease and they were carried to the dead house in appalling numbers."[20]

Drummond did what he could for the sick, regardless to what regiment they belonged. "We could not get cold water to wash the hands and faces of those sick and dying.... The wasted forms and sad, pleading eyes of those sufferers, waiting wearily for the tide of life to ebb away — without the commonest comforts, without one word of sympathy, or one tear of affection — will never cease to haunt me."[21]

Another member of the regiment worked tirelessly to help the infirm and dying. Captured at Reams Station in August 1864, Thomas Jenkins of Company E was confined at Libby Prison and Belle Island before being transferred to Salisbury Prison. Here he spent most his time in the various hospitals of the prison, doling out as much care and compassion as he could. Jenkins ministered "as far as it was in his power to do, for the sick and starving fellow prisoners, caring for forty from the town of Arcadia, burying them when they died, taking their last messages to their friends at home."[22]

Captured along with Drummond was Sergeant Henry Hoagland of Company K. The highest-ranking soldier from the regiment at Salisbury, Hoagland was in charge of the group of prisoners from the 111th, and it was his duty to keep the men together and make sure they were cared for. Everyday he would call the roll and hand out, "piece by piece that scanty morsel of food for the day."[23]

In December, the Confederates offered a way out for many prisoners, a way to end their suffering and leave the horrors of prison life behind. Robert Drummond describes what was offered to the prisoners: "A Confederate officer enters the enclosure, followed by a well dressed, well fed soldier from the army. Following him comes a colored man with a loaf of bread and some piece of well cooked meat. The officer points out the fact that to remain here is to *starve* and to *die*; that to desert the old flag and swear allegiance to the Confederacy is to eat such rations as the sample on exhibition, to wear such clothing as are worn by the Confederate soldier by his side; in short to desert is to *live*, not to desert is to *die*."[24]

Some Union prisoners thought enlisting in the Confederate army was the only way of avoiding certain death. There are three documented cases of members of the 111th who chose to join the enemy's ranks rather than languish in the prison pen. Of the three, Jeremiah Hayes and Malone Kilmer deserted soon after taking their oath of allegiance to the South.[25]

While each day brought new suffering, there were moments when the enemy showed kindness. One such example was Reverend Adolphus Mangum, chaplain of the Sixth North Carolina. Drummond recalled that despite being an ardent Confederate, the reverend's "heart was so great and his sympathy so tender that he came in among us day after day and preached the word of life to us and sang sacred hymns to those suffering and dying men. I remember ... that same reverend ... breaking the bread of life to an audience of 14000 ragged, hungry and despondent men and boys."[26]

As 1864 gave way to a new year, no end to the daily misery and anguish appeared in sight. Snow fell several times during the winter, compounding the suffering. "It was piteous beyond description to see the poor fellows, coatless, hatless and shoeless, shivering about the yard," recalled Drummond. Along with the cold, lack of food was a constant concern. "Almost daily one or more divisions was without food for twenty-four hours. Several times some of them received no rations for forty-eight hours."[27]

At the beginning of February, Drummond watched as his friend Charles Green began to weaken. "I used every art at my command to buoy him up. I pictured to him our return after having endured to the end; I talked to him of the olden times and of my loneliness should he be taken from me. I urged him by the love we bore each other to rouse himself for another struggle, but all in vain. The *spirit* was willing but the *flesh* was *too* weak, and I saw with a beating heart that his days were nearly numbered."[28]

Green, too, knew his time was near and asked Drummond to be forthright about his condition. Drummond recalled, "I told him in plain words that he must die. He said my judgement agreed with his own and asked me, 'how long before the final struggle?' And I told him that before the morning he would be in the Eternal City."[29]

Drummond lay down beside his friend in the earthen hovel they shared and read "some of the consoling words of the Master. I did so, and, in a feeling prayer, such as only a Christian can offer, he commended his soul to his God." The two talked quietly for some time. Green asked Drummond to break the news to his family back home and to tell them that his last thoughts were of them. After a short while, Green fell silent and "he too was numbered among the unrecorded heroes. All night long I sat by his body and gave way to my grief."[30]

In the morning, Drummond was faced with the unpleasant task of burying his friend. He recalled,

> I asked the aid of a fellow prisoner and we carried him tenderly to the dead house, where, with a bit of cloth, (I had no handkerchief) wet with my own tears, I wiped his face, which was calm and serene as though in sleep, and arranged his stiffening limbs for burial. He had no shroud, no coffin, no change of apparel, but was clothed only in his manhood, his loyalty and his Christian fortitude, all of which had been severely tested but all of which *had withstood the test*. I could not see him thrown into the dead cart, so calling him tenderly by name, I bade him "good-bye" and went back to my lonely habitation.[31]

By the middle of February, welcome news arrived that the prisoners were going to be paroled. On the 21st, the prisoners were ordered to assemble at the front gate and told that the sick would be sent on to Richmond while those able to make the journey would be marched northeast about 50 miles to Goldsboro, where rail transportation awaited them. Throughout his confinement, Drummond had not allowed himself think of home. But on the night before his release, the New Yorker "gave my thoughts full play as to home and home scenes and that night in my dreams I was again in old Cayuga and sitting by my Mother's side in the home of my boyhood."[32]

On the second day of March, a day of liberation longed for during many sleepless, lonely nights, almost 3,000 destitute soldiers tramped through the gates of Salisbury Prison, grateful to have endured what many would consider hell on Earth. According to Drummond, "we made little progress the first day, and that night camped in a piece of woods." For many it was the first time in almost a year they had slept above ground.[33]

The next day, Drummond and a few others found themselves too weak to continue their journey. But as luck would have it, a group of Confederate officers rode by and helped the group secure passage on a train bound for Goldsboro. Here all of those released from Salisbury gathered to receive their formal parole as prisoners of war. By March 4, 1865, Drummond and his fellow prisoners were safely behind Union lines in Wilmington.[34]

Of the 83 men of the 111th taken along the picket line on that fateful October night, only 29 remained to be paroled. Thirty-eight died in captivity while seven died soon after receiving their paroles. Many died horrible deaths, their suffering prolonged by the unimaginable conditions surrounding them. David Contant died of diarrhea; John Horton died from "lack of shelter and clothing"; Bela Curtis died of pneumonia; Adam Truax died of starvation; Orin Woodworth died of typhoid fever. It is fair to say that the words used by Robert Drummond to describe his departed comrade, Charles Green, could be applied to these men as well; they, too, are numbered among the unrecorded heroes.[35]

Drummond eventually made his way home and began the long journey back to health, under the loving care of his mother. Every day people from across the county came to see him, hoping to learn the fate of their loved ones imprisoned with him at Salisbury. Drummond's mother tried to send them away, but "they beg me the poor privilege of sitting by your bedside and looking at a prisoner of war, at one who was with their husbands, their sons and their brother when they died."[36]

It wasn't long before Drummond received the visitor he had been dreading the most: "My prisoner friend with his dying breath asked me to break the news of his death tenderly to his aged father ... my heart sank within me as I saw the well known form and features of this same aged father before me."[37] The father slowly approached the bedside, knelt down and took Drummond by the hand. He asked, almost pleaded, "Where's Charlie?" Barely able to utter a word, his eyes filled with tears, Drummond said, "We left him at Salisbury."[38]

MEN CAPTURED ON OCTOBER 30, 1864, ALONG THE PICKET LINE AT PETERSBURG, VIRGINIA

Name	*Company*	*Comments*
Baker, Charles	E	Died—no date
Blakeley, Alexander	A	Paroled—no date
Blanchard, Earl	D	Died February 3, 1865
Blowers, Peter	I	Died December 10, 1864
Bohn, Charles	K	Paroled March 11, 1865
Bolton, Noble	K	Died February 25, 1865
Boorman, Albert*	E	Transferred to Fourth New York Heavy Artillery while prisoner
Britt, John	K	Paroled March 10, 1865
Brown, James	E	Died January 6, 1865
Cavender, John	K	Paroled March 3, 1865
Connors, John	K	Died March 20, 1865
Contant, David	D	Died January 26, 1865
Cox, Thomas*	K	Paroled March 16, 1865
Culver, Ambrose	K	Died January 29, 1865
Culver, Horace	G	Died January 31, 1865
Curtis, Bela	K	Died December 14, 1864
Drummond, Robert	H	Paroled March 2, 1865
Ennis, Edward	K	Paroled March 2, 1865
Ferguson, James	K	Paroled March 11, 1865
Ferris, Newton	F	Died January 31, 1865
Fisk, Daniel	E	Died January 16, 1865
Gilbertson, James	K	Paroled March 10, 1865, and died in U.S. General Hospital in Annapolis, Maryland, March 19, 1865

Name	Company	Comments
Glinn, Thomas	K	Escaped and reached Union lines March 11, 1865
Green, Amos	H	Paroled — no date
Green, Charles	H	Died February 15, 1865
Hackett, William	E	Died — no date
Hampshire, George	A	Died January 1, 1865
Haney, James	E	Paroled February 28, 1865
Hanie, Franklin	E	Joined rebel army
Harris, William	H	Paroled February 28, 1865, and died March 10, 1865
Hart, Horace	E	Died — no date
Hartnutt, Patrick	E	Died — no date
Hayes, Jeremiah	K	Joined Company B, Second Foreign Legion, C.S.A, escaped April 7, 1865
Hoagland, Henry	K	Paroled March 15, 1865
Hoff, John	K	Paroled — no date
Horton, John	K	Died December 31, 1864
Howard, John	F	Died January 31, 1865
Hudson, Joel	E	Died January 9, 1865
Hyser, Isaiah	K	Paroled March 11, 1865
Impson, Gilbert	I	No further record
Jackson, David	K	Paroled March 1, 1865
James, Frank	E	Died February 17, 1865
Jeffery, Henry	E	Died January 26, 1865
Johnson, Emery	D	Paroled March 10, 1865
Johnson, Levi*	E	Transferred to Fourth New York Heavy Artillery while prisoner
Johnston, William	I	No further record
Jones, William	K	Paroled and died March 28, 1865, at Annapolis, Maryland
Kays, Thomas	E	Died December 16, 1864
Keller, Delevan	K	Died — no date
Kelly, George	K	Paroled March 2, 1865
Kelly, Patrick	E	Paroled — no date
Kenney, Auburn	E	Paroled — no date
Kilmer, Malone	E	Joined rebel army and escaped April 12, 1865
Kramm, Frederick	E	Paroled — no date
Lewis, Robert	F	Died November 27, 1864
McMahon, James*	K	Paroled — no date
Miles, William	K	Died — no date
O'Brien, John*	F	Paroled March 2, 1865
Owens, William*	K	Paroled — no date
Pitcock, Howard	K	Paroled — no date

Name	Company	Comments
Pitkin, Lucius	K	Paroled — no date
Probasco, Myron	K	Paroled and died at home in Marbletown, New York
Reamer, Isaac	K	Died — no date
Richmond, Edwin	D	Paroled February 28, 1865
Rounds, William	K	Died December 28, 1864
Rush, Charles	K	Died — no date
Samson, Levi	H	Paroled March 2, 1865
Sebring, Alfred	D	Died January 23, 1865
Shuster, Philip	K	Paroled — no date
Smith, George*	K	No further record
Smith, Zenas	K	Died — no date
Somhofe, Henry	F	Died December 28, 1864
Sturgis, Nathan	K	Died February 10, 1865
Tabor, Benjamin	K	Died November 19, 1864
Tinney, Madison	K	Paroled and died April 1, 1865, at home in Palmyra, New York
Tousey, George	A	Died January 20, 1865
Truax, Adam	H	Died January 21, 1865
Van Dyne, George	K	Died December 30, 1864
Van Dyne, William	K	Paroled and died at home in Phelps, New York, March 30, 1865
Will, Jacob*	K	Transferred to Fourth New York Heavy Artillery while prisoner
Wissmuller, George	K	Died — no date
Wolf, John	K	Paroled — no date, died March 23, 1865, at Annapolis, Maryland
Woodworth, Orin	D	Died January 2, 1865

*These men were reported to have deserted to the enemy during their captivity at Salisbury.

APPENDIX B

Regimental Strength

The following table shows the number of men actually present with the regiment during the month and year specified. It does not include those reported as sick or on detached service. From June 1863 through March 1864, the total does not include Companies B and C, as they were on detached service.[1]

1862

Month	Officers / Men Present
August	37 / 932
September	32 / 791
October	27 / 700
November	30 / 662
December	33 / 504

1863

Month	Officers / Men Present
January	26 / 504
February	26 / 479
March	27 / 499
April	32 / 544
May	29 / 529
June	26 / 450
July	10 / 136
August	14 / 131
September	15 / 144
October	18 / 125
November	15 / 127
December	17 / 138

1864

Month	Officers / Men Present
January	15 / 123
February	13 / 121
March	12 / 205
April	17 / 422
May	11 / 188
June	8 / 87
July	7 / 79
August	8 / 66
September	6 / 232
October	16 / 505
November	16 / 399
December	16 / 408

1865

Month	Officers / Men Present
January	15 / 397
February	15 / 395
March	15 / 410
April	12 / 352
May	11 / 373

Chapter Notes

Chapter 1

1. *Auburn Daily Advertiser and Union* (*ADAU*), July 3, 1862.
2. *ADAU*, August 22, 1862; Thomas Geer to friends, August 23, 1862.
3. *ADAU*, July 8, 1862.
4. *Ibid.*; Donald Dale Jackson, *The Civil War: Twenty Million Yankees; The Northern Home Front*. Alexandria, VA: Time Life, 1985, p. 87.
5. *Ibid.*
6. *ADAU*, July 8 and 17, 1862; Jackson, *The Civil War*, p. 87.
7. *Courier-Journal*, May 2, 1973; Office of the County Historian, Wayne County, New York. *Wayne County: A Brief History*, p. 4. Hereinafter referred to as *Wayne County*; The canal was given the nickname "Clinton's Big Ditch" for DeWitt Clinton, the mayor of New York City who authorized the construction of the canal.
8. *Courier-Journal*, May 2, 1973; *Wayne County*, pp. 1–2.
9. *Courier-Journal*, May 2, 1973; *Wayne County*, p. 4.
10. Henry M. Allen, *A Chronicle of Early Auburn 1793–1860*, Auburn, NY: 1953, sec. 3, p. 1.
11. Allen, *Chronicle of Early Auburn*, sec. 3, p. 1; James Hardenbergh is also listed in many publications and official documents as "Hardenburgh."
12. Henry Hall, *The History of Auburn*. Auburn, NY: Dennis Bro's, 1869, pp. 302–431.
13. *ADAU*, July 8 and 17, 1862.
14. *ADAU*, July 28, 1862; New York (State), Adjutant General's Office. *Annual Report of the Adjutant General of the State of New York for the Year 1903*. Albany, NY: Oliver Quayle, 1904, p. 835. Hereinafter referred to as Adjutant General's Report; Borne on the rolls as Isaac Mullie, Mulligan served with the regiment until being wounded at Sutherland Station on April 2, 1865.
15. *ADAU*, August 5, 1862; Sensebaugh served with the regiment until mustering out with the regiment on June 4, 1865, only suffering one wound.
16. Military service record for Simeon Sensebaugh, National Archives, Washington, D.C.
17. *ADAU*, August 5 and 9 1862.
18. *ADAU*, July 29 and 30, 1862.
19. *Ibid.*
20. *ADAU*, July 30 and 31, 1862.
21. *ADAU*, July 26 and August 5, 1862.
22. Newman Eldred, "Newman Eldred's Account of Service in the Civil War," *Yesteryears* 22, no. 88 (Summer 1979): 77; Adjutant General's Report, p. 843.
23. *ADAU*, July 15, 1862.
24. *Auburn Bulletin*, "Death of Colonel Segoine," August 14, 1895.
25. *Ibid.*; Frederick Phisterer, comp, *New York in the War of the Rebellion*, vol. 4, Albany, NY: F. B. Lyon, 1912. p. 3314; Adjutant General's Report, p. 807; Military service record for John Knapp, National Archives, Washington, D.C.
26. *ADAU*, August 7, 1862.
27. Military Service and Pension records of Clinton D. MacDougall, National Archives, Washington, D.C.; Arabella Willson, *Disaster, Struggle, Triumph: The Adventures of 1000 Boys in Blue*. Albany, NY: Argus, 1870, pp. f287–88; Joel H. Monroe, *Historical Records of a Hundred and Twenty Years*, Geneva, NY: W. F. Humphrey, 1913, p. 213.
28. *ADAU*, August 2, 13, and 29, 1862.
29. *ADAU*, August 2, 1862.
30. James Dana Benton to father, October 4, 1862.
31. *ADAU*, July 19, 1862.
32. *ADAU*, July 19 and August 22, 1862; Temple Hollcroft, *The Town of Ledyard in the Civil War*, unpublished manuscript, p. 13.
33. Lewis Clark, *Military History of Wayne County*, Sodus, NY: Clark, Hulett, and Gaylor, 1884, p. 381.
34. *ADAU*, July 30, 1862.
35. Clark, *Military History of Wayne County*, p. 383.
36. John Coe to Major Sprague, October 7, 1862, RG 94, National Archives, Washington, D.C.; Phisterer, *New York in the War of the Rebellion*, p. 3311.
37. Lape family history provided graciously by Jeff Lape.
38. Hollcroft, *Town of Ledyard*, p. 14.
39. Loyal Legion of the United States, Headquarters Commandery of the State of Wisconsin, May 11, 1911, circular no. 11, ser. 1911, whole no. 487.
40. No. 198 Quartermaster General SNY 1863 (for 1862) pp. 122–40; The initial uniform issue consisted of a nine-button, dark-blue frock coat; one pair of sky-blue trousers; one great coat; one four-button sack coat; one forage cap with regimental numbers and company

letter; one blanket; two shirts; two pair of drawers; two pairs of socks and one pair of shoes; one haversack; one knapsack; and one canteen.
41. *ADAU*, August 5, 1862; According to the *ADAU*, the uniforms arrived at Camp Cayuga on August 5 and "were first rate"; Geer to friends, August 23, 1862.
42. Benton to father, August 14, 1862.
43. *ADAU*, August 20, 1862; Hollcroft, *Town of Ledyard*, p. 16.
44. Original Muster Roll of the 111th New York, RG 94, National Archives, Washington, D.C.; *ADAU*, August 20, 1862; Phisterer, *New York in the War of the Rebellion*, pp. 3306–20.
45. Phisterer, *New York in the War of the Rebellion*, p. 3305; *ADAU*, July 17, 22, 24, 25, 26, and 29, 1862; Monroe, *Historical Records of a Hundred and Twenty Years*, p. 210.
46. Adjutant General's Report, pp. 671–930; Clark, *Military History of Wayne County*, p. 380; *ADAU*, May 15, 1894; The four students were Henry Gifford, Samuel Halstead, Ansel Smith, and Horace Smith. All four would die during the war.
47. Adjutant General's Report, pp. 671–930; Research conducted by author R. L. Murray indicates that several of the men were 14 and 15 years old.
48. Original Muster Roll of the 111th New York, RG 94, National Archives, Washington, D.C.; Adjutant General's Report, pp. 671–930; *Newark Courier*, May 1905.
49. Military service record of Isaac Lusk, National Archives, Washington, D.C.; Phisterer, *New York in the War of the Rebellion*, pp. 3310–20.
50. Benjamin Thompson, "Flight from Florida," *Civil War Times Illustrated*, August 1973, pp. 13–21.
51. *ADAU*, August 20, 1862.
52. *Ibid*.
53. *Ibid*.; Geer to friends, August 23, 1862.
54. *ADAU*, August 22, 1862; *Advertiser-Journal*, August 22, 1916.
55. *ADAU*, August 22, 1862; Geer to friends, August 23, 1862.
56. *ADAU*, August 22, 1862.
57. *ADAU*, August 21 and 22, 1862.
58. Clark, *Military History of Wayne County*, pp. 383, 575.
59. *ADAU*, August 22, 1862.
60. *Ibid*.; Regimental Return for September 1862, RG 94, National Archives, Washington, D.C.; Twenty-two cars were provided to the regiment for its trip to Albany.

Chapter 2

1. Benton to father, October 14, 1862.
2. *ADAU*, August 23, 1862; Esek Hoff to wife, August 22, 1862; Michael Barton, "I Begin to Know What Hard Times Is," *Manuscripts* 30, no. 2, (Spring 1978): 93.
3. Barton, "I Begin to Know," p. 93; Hoff to Captain Carr, August 27, 1862.
4. *ADAU*, August 29 1862; "Reduced to the ranks" means that a soldier, of whatever rank, is reduced to the grade of private.
5. Benjamin Thompson, "Into This Hell of Destruction," *Civil War Times Illustrated*, October 1973, p. 14.
6. Hoff to Carr, August 27, 1862; Geer to friends, August 23, 1862; Eldred, "Newman Eldred's Account," vol. 22, no. 88 (Summer 1979): 77.
7. Eldred, "Newman Eldred's Account," vol. 22, no. 88 (Summer 1979): 77; Thompson, "Into This Hell of Destruction," p. 14; Hoff to Carr, August 27, 1862; Geer to friends, August 23, 1862.
8. Eldred, "Newman Eldred's Account," vol. 22, no. 88 (Summer 1979): 77.
9. *ADAU*, August 29, 1862.
10. Paul Teetor, *A Matter of Hours*, Associated University Presses, 1982, pp. 42–43.
11. Eldred, "Newman Eldred's Account," vol. 22, no. 88 (Summer 1979): 77; Thompson, "Into This Hell of Destruction," p. 19; Time Life, *Spies, Scouts and Raiders: Irregular Operations*, Alexandria, VA: Time Life, 1985, p. 12; Hoff to Carr, August 27, 1862; Hoff was referring to the fact that Baltimore had become a city firmly under Union control. When Union general Benjamin Butler took control of the city soon after a mob attacked the Massachusetts men, he had the guns atop Federal Hill turned on the city, homes of Confederate sympathizers searched, and citizens vocal in their opposition to the Federal government arrested and imprisoned at Fort McHenry.
12. Eldred, "Newman Eldred's Account," vol. 22, no. 88 (Summer 1979): 77–78.
13. Hoff to Carr, August 27, 1862.
14. Teetor, *Matter of Hours*, p. 167; Hoff to wife, August 30, 1862; Eldred, "Newman Eldred's Account," vol. 22, no. 88 (Summer 1979): 78.
15. William C. Davis, *The Civil War: First Blood; Fort Sumter to Bull Run*, Alexandria, VA: Time Life, 1983.
16. Thompson, "Into This Hell of Destruction," p. 14.
17. Barton, "I Begin to Know," p. 94; Hoff to wife, August 30, 1862.
18. *ADAU*, September 6, 1862; Hoff to wife, September 11, 1862.
19. *ADAU*, September 6, 1862.
20. *Ibid*.
21. Adjutant General's Report, p. 753.
22. Simeon Cooper to father, August 27, 1862.
23. No. 66 State New York Comm. General Order 1863 (for 1862) pp. 60–61; According to the quartermaster general reports for New York, the original issue for the regiment took place between July 28 and August 23, 1862. Most of the equipment listed as issued August 23 was probably issued to the regiment when it arrived at Harpers Ferry. Newman Eldred, Benjamin Thompson, and John Nostrant all mention getting their equipment after the regiment arrived at Harpers Ferry; Francis A. Lord, *Civil War Collector's Encyclopedia*, Castle Books, 1963, pp. 243–44.
24. On August 26, Colonel Segoine received a letter from Colonel Miles offering the assistance of eight drill officers for the following day. On September 10, Colonel Segoine issued General Order (GO) 22, stating that the regiment would receive the assistance of eight drill officers from the 39th New York. GO 22 also stated that the heavy infantry drill would be dropped in favor of the light infantry drill; Regimental Order Books, 111th New York, RG 94, National Archives, Washington D.C.; W. J. Hardee, *Rifle and Light Infantry Tactics*, vol. 1, reprint, Philadelphia, PA: J. B. Lippincott, 1861, pp. 17–18.
25. *ADAU*, September 6, 1962.

26. Hoff to wife, September 4, 1862.
27. Thomas Dadswell to "Dear Father," n.d., Thomas Dadswell Papers, RG 308, Special Collections and Archives Department, RBD Library, Auburn University, Alabama.
28. Ronald H. Bailey, *The Bloodiest Day: The Battle of Antietam*, Alexandria, VA: Time Life, 1984, pp. 18–21; Michael Bacarella, *Lincoln's Foreign Legion: The 39th New York Infantry, The Garibaldi Guard*, Shippensburg, PA: White Mane, 1996, pp. 90–91.
29. Record of Events, Company Muster Rolls, Company F, 111th New York, National Archives, Washington, D.C.; The order to make the move to Bolivar Heights was received by Colonel Segoine on September 5 and according to Company F's record of events, the regiment did not move until September 6.
30. Teetor, *Matter of Hours*, p. 58; RG 94 to Assistant Adjutant General, Harpers Ferry, National Archives, Washington, D.C.
31. Gary W. Gallagher, ed., *Antietam: Essays on the 1862 Maryland Campaign*, Kent, OH: Kent State University Press, 1989, pp. 19–21; U.S. War Department, *The War of the Rebellion: The Official Records of the Union and Confederate Armies*, 128 vols., Washington, D.C.: U.S. Government Printing Office, 1890–1901, ser. 1, vol. 19, pt. 1, p. 575. Hereinafter referred to as *War of the Rebellion*.
32. *War of the Rebellion*, ser. 1, vol. 19, pt. 1, p. 575.
33. *Ibid*.
34. Gallagher, *Antietam*, p. 19.
35. Stephen Sears, *Landscape Turned Red: The Battle of Antietam*, Ticknor and Fields, 1983, pp. 90–91; Gallagher, *Antietam*, p. 15; Jay Luvaas and Harold W. Nelson, eds., *The U.S. Army War College Guide to the Battle of Antietam: The Maryland Campaign of 1862*, Carlisle, PA: South Mountain Press, 1987, pp. 8–9.
36. Teetor, *Matter of Hours*, pp. 124–25.
37. Frank Moore, ed., *The Rebellion Record: A Diary of American Events*, vol. 5, New York: Putnam, 1863, p. 445; John Paylor, diary entry, September 13, 1862.
38. Bailey, *The Bloodiest Day*, pp. 58–59.
39. Teetor, *Matter of Hours*, pp. 144–45.
40. Paylor, diary entry, September 14, 1862; Eldred, "Newman Eldred's Account," vol. 22, no. 88 (Summer 1979): 78; Hoff to wife, September 17, 1862.
41. Paylor, diary entry, September 14, 1862; Hoff to wife, September 17, 1862; Eldred, "Newman Eldred's Account," vol. 22, no. 88 (Summer 1979): 79.
42. Harry Smith to parents, September 23, 1862.
43. Eldred, "Newman Eldred's Account," vol. 22, no. 88 (Summer 1979): 79.
44. Paylor, diary entry, September 14, 1862; *War of the Rebellion*, ser. 1, vol. 19, pt. 1, p. 683; *ADAU*, October 8, 1862.
45. Benton to father, October 4, 1862.
46. Hoff to wife, September 17, 1862.
47. Military service record of Martin Van Buren Moore, National Archives, Washington, D.C.; Adjutant General's Report, p. 832.
48. Thompson, "Into This Hell of Destruction," p. 14.
49. Teetor, *Matter of Hours*, p. 167.
50. *War of the Rebellion*, ser. 1, vol. 19, pt. 1, pp. 683–84.
51. *Ibid*.
52. *Ibid*.
53. *Ibid*.

54. Paylor, diary entry, September 15, 1862; Manley Stacey to father, October 1, 1862; *War of the Rebellion*, ser. 1, vol. 19, pt. 1, p. 684; Adjutant General's Report, p. 746.
55. Hollcroft, *Town of Ledyard*, p. 18.
56. Eldred, "Newman Eldred's Account," vol. 22, no. 88 (Summer 1979): 79; Thompson, "Into This Hell of Destruction," p. 14.
57. Hoff to wife, September 17, 1862.
58. *ADAU*, September 19, 1862.
59. Eldred, "Newman Eldred's Account," vol. 22, no. 88 (Summer 1979): 79.
60. *Ibid*.; *War of the Rebellion*, ser. 1, vol. 19, pt. 1, p. 684.
61. Thompson, "Into This Hell of Destruction," p. 14.
62. *War of the Rebellion*, ser. 1, vol. 19, pt. 1, p. 683; Teetor, *Matter of Hours*, pp. 184–85, 190–94.
63. *Ibid*.; Teetor, *Matter of Hours*, p. 186; Thompson, "Into This Hell of Destruction," p. 14.
64. Eldred, "Newman Eldred's Account," vol. 22, no. 88 (Summer 1979): 80.
65. Thompson, "Into This Hell of Destruction," p. 14.
66. Eldred, "Newman Eldred's Account," vol. 22, no. 88 (Summer 1979): 80; Hoff to wife, September 17, 1862.
67. *War of the Rebellion*, ser. 1, vol. 19, pt. 1, p. 666.
68. *War of the Rebellion*, ser. 1, vol. 19, pt. 1, pp. 552–53.
69. *Ibid*.; Bacarella, *Lincoln's Foreign Legion*, pp. 100–101.
70. Thompson, "Into This Hell of Destruction," p. 14; Hoff to wife, September 17, 1862.
71. George E. David to D. S. Titus, October 5, 1862.
72. Eldred, "Newman Eldred's Account," vol. 22, no. 88 (Summer 1979): 80.
73. *Ibid*.; Paylor, diary entry, September 16, 1862; Thompson, "Flight from Florida," p. 14.
74. *ADAU*, September 18 and October 21, 1862.

Chapter 3

1. Smith to parents, September 23, 1862.
2. Thompson, "Into This Hell of Destruction," p. 14; Smith to parents, September 23, 1862; *ADAU*, September 26, 1862.
3. Paylor, diary entry, September 16, 1862.
4. *ADAU*, September 18 and 22, 1862.
5. Hoff to wife, September 17, 1862.
6. Sears, *Landscape Turned Red*, pp. 184–205, 216–54, 262–97.
7. Pension Record of Jesse Segoine, National Archives, Washington, D.C.; *ADAU*, October 7, 1862.
8. Smith to parents, September 23, 1862; Pension records for Colonel Jesse Segoine, National Archives, Washington, D.C.
9. Eldred, "Newman Eldred's Account," vol. 22, no. 88 (Summer 1979): 81.
10. *Ibid*.; Hoff to wife, September 28, 1862.
11. Benton to Maggie, September 22, 1862; John A Garraty, and Robert A. McCaughey, *The American Nation: A History of the United States to 1877*, 6th ed., vol. 1, New York: Harper & Row, 1987, p. 423.
12. Eldred, "Newman Eldred's Account," vol. 22, no. 88 (Summer 1979): 82; Record of events, company muster rolls, Company F, entry for September and October 1862, National Archives, Washington, D.C.; James

H. Clark, *The Iron Hearted Regiment: Being an Account of the Battles. Marches and Gallant Deeds Performed by the 115th N.Y. Vols.*, Albany, NY: Munsell, 1865, p. 33.

13. Eldred, "Newman Eldred's Account," vol. 22, no. 88 (Summer 1979): 82; The railroad charged the government the passenger car rate of two cents a mile even though the regiment was transported in freight cars.

14. *Ibid.*; Benton to father, October 4, 1862; Clark, *The Iron Hearted Regiment*, pp. 34–35; Hoff to wife, September 26, 1862.

15. Eldred, "Newman Eldred's Account," vol. 22, no. 88 (Summer 1979): 82.

16. Benton to father, October 4, 1862; Clark, *The Iron Hearted Regiment*, pp. 34–35; Hoff to wife, September 26, 1862.

17. George Levy, *To Die in Chicago: Confederate Prisoners at Camp Douglas*, Evanston IL: Evanston Publishing, 1994, pp. 11–12.

18. Levy, *To Die in Chicago*, pp. 11–12.

19. Francis T. Miller, ed., *The Photographic History of the Civil War in Ten Volumes, Part Seven: Prisons and Hospitals*, New York: 1957, pp. 22–23, 68; Willson, *Disaster, Struggle, Triumph*, pp. 111–12; Benton to father, November 4, 1862; Smith to father, October 3, 1862; Hoff to wife, September 28, 1862.

20. Benton to father, November 4, 1862; Willson, *Disaster, Struggle, Triumph*, p. 108; *ADAU*, October 16, 1862; Military service record of Ansen (Austin) Legg, National Archives, Washington, D.C.

21. Pension record for Elizabeth Nichols, National Archives, Washington, D.C.; Elizabeth Nichols was in a protracted fight with the Bureau of Pensions to secure a pension for her service during the war. Many veterans whom she treated came to her aid and testified as to her service.

22. Levy, *To Die in Chicago*, pp. 71, 97; Hoff to wife, October 19, 1862.

23. Smith to father, October 3, 1862.

24. Paylor, diary entry, October 20, 1862; Sebastian Holmes to sister, October 16, 1862.

25. Benton to father, November 4, 1862.

26. Hoff to wife, October 19, 1862.

27. *Ibid.*; Levy, *To Die in Chicago*, p. 93; Paylor, diary entry, October 17, 1862; Geer to Julia, October 22, 1862.

28. Geer to Julia, October 2, 1862; Levy, *To Die in Chicago*, p. 93.

29. Hoff to wife, October 19, 1862; Paylor, diary entry, October 21, 1862.

30. Levy, *To Die in Chicago*, p. 93; Paylor, diary entry, October 20, 1862; Eldred, "Newman Eldred's Account," vol. 23, no. 89 (Fall 1979): 9.

31. Benton to father, October 3, 1862; Cooper to father, October 24, 1862.

32. General Order No. 16, Headquarters, Camp Douglas. Transcript of the General Courts-Martial of Privates Jeremiah Collins and Samuel Adams, RG 94, National Archives, Washington, D.C.

33. *Ibid.*

34. General Orders, Headquarters of 111th, Camp Douglas, RG 94, National Archives, Washington, D.C.

35. Adjutant General's Report, pp. 671–930.

36. Regimental Order Books, RG 94, National Archives, Washington, D.C.; These punishments were intended to both punish and humiliate the soldier. The wooden overcoat was simply a barrel with both ends removed and straps attached so the soldier could wear it like a coat.

37. Hoff to wife, November 12, 1862; Adjutant General's Report, p. 902.

38. Geer to Julia, October 2, 1862.

39. Eldred, "Newman Eldred's Account," vol. 23, no. 89 (Fall 1979): 8–9.

40. Hoff to wife, September 28, 1862.

41. Hoff to wife, November 9, 1862.

42. Eldred, "Newman Eldred's Account," vol. 23, no. 89 (Fall 1979): 9.

43. Smith to father, dated October 3, 1862; Paylor, diary entry, November 3, 1862; Eldred, "Newman Eldred's Account," vol. 23, no. 89 (Fall 1979): 8; Hoff to wife, November 12, 1862.

44. Regimental Order Books, RG 94, National Archives, Washington, D.C.

45. Levy, *To Die in Chicago*, p. 93.

46. Paylor, diary entry, November 9, 1862; Warren to sister, October 13, 1862.

47. Hoff to wife, September 28, 1862.

48. Geer to Julia, October 22, 1862; Benton to father, October 4, 1862; Levy, *To Die in Chicago*, pp. 92–93; Eldred, "Newman Eldred's Account," vol. 23, no. 89 (Fall 1979): 9.

49. Hoff to wife, October 3, 1862.

50. Cooper to father, October 24, 1862.

51. Benton to father, October 27, 1862.

52. *Ibid.*; Cooper to father, October 24, 1862.

53. Paylor, diary entry, November 20, 1862; Phisterer, *New York in the War of the Rebellion*, pp. 3306–09.

54. Military service record of Hasseltine Moore, National Archives, Washington, D.C.

55. Paylor, diary entry, November 20, 1862.

56. Hoff to wife, November 19, 1862.

57. *ADAU*, November 20 and 21, 1862.

58. Regimental Order Books, RG 94, National Archives, Washington, D.C.; Hoff to wife, November 19, 1862.

59. Regimental Order Books, RG 94, National Archives, Washington, D.C.

60. Paylor, diary entry, November 26, 1862; Hoff to wife, November 26, 1862; Adjutant General's Report, pp. 671–930.

61. Hoff to wife, November 30, 1862.

62. Paylor, diary entries, November 27, 28, and 29, 1862.

63. Eldred, "Newman Eldred's Account," vol. 23, no. 89 (Fall 1979): 10.

64. Paylor, diary entries, November 29 and 30, 1862.

65. Hoff to wife, November 30, 1862.

66. Paylor, diary entry, November 30, 1862.

Chapter 4

1. Benton to father, January 26, 1863.

2. Benton to father, December 7 and 23, 1862; General Order No. 1, RG 94, National Archives, Washington, D.C.; Regimental Return for November 1862, RG 94, National Archives, Washington, D.C.

3. Lord, *Civil War Collector's Encyclopedia*, p. 280; John D. Billings, *Hard Tack and Coffee or the Unwritten Story of Army Life*, 4th ed., Williamston, MA: Corner House, 1987, pp. 46–47; Hoff to wife, December 6, 1862; James I. Robertson, *Tenting Tonight: The Soldier's Life*, Alexandria, VA: Time Life, 1984, p. 49; Gregory A. Coco, *The Civil War Infantryman*, Gettysburg, PA: Thomas Publications, 1996, p. 22; When properly

stockaded, the Sibley, or "bell," tent could comfortably hold 20 men and their equipment.
4. Paylor, diary entries, December 4 and 8, 1862.
5. Hoff to wife, December 9, 1862.
6. Benton to father, December 7, 1862.
7. Paylor, diary entry, December 10, 1862.
8. Hoff to wife, December 9, 1862.
9. *ADAU*, December 23 and 27, 1862; Military service record for John Johnson, National Archives, Washington, D.C.; Regimental Return for December, RG 94, National Archives, Washington, D.C.; Varioloid is a form of smallpox that strikes those who previously had smallpox or those who were vaccinated against the disease.
10. *ADAU*, December 11, 1862.
11. Benton to father, December 7, 1862; Geer to Jule, December 13, 1862; Hoff to wife, December 14, 1862.
12. Holmes to sister, December 21, 1862.
13. Paylor, diary entry, December 25, 1862; Benton to father, December 7, 1862; Geer to Jule, December 13, 1862; Hoff to wife, December 14, 1862.
14. *Ibid.*
15. Paylor, diary entry, December 13, 1862.
16. Geer to Orrin, December 28, 1862; Jay Luvaas and Harold W. Nelson, eds., *The U.S. Army War College Guide to the Battles of Chancellorsville and Fredericksburg*, Carlisle, PA: South Mountain Press, 1988, p. 116.
17. Paylor, diary entry, December 25, 1862; Lord, *Civil War Collector's Encyclopedia*, p. 108.
18. Geer to Orrin, December 28, 1862.
19. Hoff to wife, December 28, 1862.
20. Paylor, diary entry, December 28, 1862.
21. *Ibid.*
22. Paylor, diary entries, December 28–31, 1862; Phisterer, *New York in the War of the Rebellion*, p. 3305.
23. Manley Stacey, diary entries, January 1 and 2, 1863.
24. Thompson, "Into This Hell of Destruction," p. 15.
25. Hoff to wife, January 5, 1863.
26. Stacey, diary entry, January 6, 1863; Hoff to wife, January 5, 1863; Paylor, diary entry, January 6, 1863.
27. Thompson, "Into This Hell of Destruction," p. 15; Regimental Returns, National Archives, entry for Company C, December 1862 and January–February 1863; George Davis, Leslie Perry, and Joseph Kirkley, *The Official Military Atlas of the Civil War*, New York: Fairfax Press, 1983, plate 7.
28. Cooper to father, January 26, 1863.
29. Hoff to wife, December 14, 1862.
30. Eldred, "Newman Eldred's Account," vol. 23, no. 89 (Fall 1979): 11; Adjutant General's Report, p. 727.
31. Russell K. Brown, *Fallen in Battle: American General Officer Combat Fatalities From 1775*, Westport, CT: Greenwood Press, 1988, p. 59; Stacey, diary entry, January 17, 1863.
32. Phisterer, *New York in the War of the Rebellion*, pp. 3306–09; Military service records of Jesse Segoine, Henry Segoine, John Coe, Edward Thomas, Ezra Northrop[EH1], Silas Tremain, Ezra Hibbard, Jacob Van Buskirk, John Tremper, and Andrew Soverill, National Archives, Washington, D.C.; Dadswell to father, January 24, 1863.
33. Military service record of John Tremper, National Archives, Washington, D.C.
34. *Ibid.*

35. Richard Warren, letters, January 20, 1863.
36. Phisterer, *New York in the War of the Rebellion*, pp. 3306–09; Military service records of James Haggerty, Irving Jacques, Horace Hill, Ira Jones, John Laing, Augustus Proseus, John Brown, Frank Rich, Rueben Myers, Edgar Dudley, George Smith, Adolphus Capron, and Samuel Bradley, National Archives, Washington, D.C.; Adjutant General's Report, pp. 671–930.
37. Geer to Al, February 19, 1863.
38. Phisterer, *New York in the War of the Rebellion*, p. 3312; Military service record of Ezra Hibbard, National Archives, Washington, D.C.
39. Resignation letters from various officers dated January 1863, RG 94, National Archives, Washington, D.C.; Phisterer, *New York in the War of the Rebellion*, pp. 3306–09.
40. Willson, *Disaster, Struggle, Triumph*, pp. f287–88; After the war, MacDougall served in the U.S. House of Representatives from 1873 to 1877, and as a U.S. marshal, Northern District of NY from 1877 to 1885 and from 1901 to 1910.
41. General Order No. 7, January 5, 1863, RG 94, National Archives, Washington, D.C.; Muster roll for January 1863, National Archives, Washington, D.C.; Military Service and Pension records of Clinton D. MacDougall, National Archives, Washington, D.C.
42. General Order No. 7.
43. Smith to mother, January 28, 1863.
44. Stacey, diary entry, January 13, 1863; Paylor, diary entry, January 13 1863.
45. Stacey, diary entry, January 23, 1863.
46. *ADAU*, March 20, 1863; *ADAU*, March 21, 1863.
47. *ADAU*, March 21, 1863; Hoff to wife, March 17, 1863.
48. Stacey, diary entry, March 1, 1863; Hoff to wife, March 3, 1863; Spencer Langdon to mother, March 1, 1863; Smith to father and mother, March 3, 1863.
49. David Pease to father, March 1, 1863; Stacey, diary entry, March 1, 1863; Hoff to wife, March 3, 1863; Langdon to mother, March 1, 1863; Smith to father and mother, March 3, 1863.
50. Pease to Solomon Pease, April 10, 1863.
51. *Ibid.*
52. Warren to sister Mary, March 30, 1863; Instead of using the long roll to order the regiments into line, General Hays ordered the guard to yell "turn out quickly." This way the beat of the drum would not indicate that the garrison was forming ranks.
53. Benton to father and mother, April 5, 1863.
54. Eldred, "Newman Eldred's Account," vol. 23, no. 89 (Fall 1979): 12–13.
55. Paylor, diary entries, February 17 and 25, 1863; Stacey, diary entry, February 25, 1863.
56. Paylor, diary entries, February 17 and 25, 1863; General Order No. 12, May 9, 1863, National Archives, Washington, D.C.; Stacey, diary entry, May 9, 1863; Adjutant General's Report, p. 737.
57. Benton to father and mother, February 28, 1863.
58. *ADAU*, March 23, 1863; Smith to brother Charles, January 28, 1863.
59. Thompson, "Into This Hell of Destruction," p. 15; Stacey, diary entry, March 9, 1863; Time Life, *Spies, Scouts and Raiders*, pp. 117–18.
60. Military Service and Pension records of Seneca Smith, National Archives, Washington, D.C.; Stacey, diary entry, March 24, 1863.
61. Stacey, diary entry, April 29, 1863.

62. Stacey, diary entries, January 20, February 13, and May 20, 1863.
63. Langdon to folks at home, April 19, 1863.
64. *ADAU*, April 7, 1863; Warren to sister, April 7, 1863; Phisterer, *New York in the War of the Rebellion*, p. 3313; Military service record of Charles Frisbee, National Archives, Washington, D.C.
65. *ADAU*, April 7, 1863; Phisterer, *New York in the War of the Rebellion*, p. 3313; Warren to sister, April 7, 1863.
66. Military service record of James Haggerty; Philthsis pulmoralis is a disease of the lungs.
67. Phisterer, *New York in the War of the Rebellion*, pp. 3306–09; Military service records of Robert Perry, Howard Servis, Jerome Lattin, Adolphus Capron, and John Drake, National Archives, Washington, D.C.
68. Hoff to wife, March 17, 1863.
69. Dadswell to father, April 12, 1863.
70. *Ibid.*
71. Paylor, diary entry, May 4, 1863.
72. Benton to father, May 31, 1862; Smith to father, March 15, 1863.
73. Benton to father, May 31, 1862; *ADAU*, March 9, 1863; *ADAU*, April 14, 1863.
74. Geer to Jule, May 22 and June 14, 1863.
75. *ADAU*, June 13, 1863; Regimental Returns, National Archives, Washington, D.C., entry dated June and August 1863; Stacey, diary entry, June 5, 1863; David Gibbs, diary entry, June 5, 1863.
76. Smith to father, June 20, 1863.
77. Stacey, diary entry, June 15, 1863.
78. Eldred, "Newman Eldred's Account," vol. 23, no. 89 (Fall 1979): 14; Because his father was a shoemaker, Eldred had the nickname "wax" because of his penchant for playing with the wax on his father's cobbler bench; Smith to father, June 20, 1863; Hoff to wife, June 22, 1863.
79. Stacey, diary entry, June 19, 1863.
80. Hoff to wife, June 18, 1863.
81. Thompson, "Into This Hell of Destruction," p. 16.
82. Smith to father, June 20, 1863; Stacey, diary entry, June 20, 1863.
83. Hoff to wife, June 22, 1863.
84. Champ Clark, *Gettysburg: The Confederate High Tide*, Alexandria, VA: Time Life, 1985, p. 12; A. L. Long, *Memoirs of Robert E. Lee*, reprint, Secaucus, NJ: Blue and Grey Press, 1983, pp. 267–68.
85. Hoff to wife, June 23, 1863.
86. Stacey, diary entry, June 22, 1863.
87. Willson, *Disaster, Struggle, Triumph*, pp. 150–51; Paylor, diary entry, June 24 1863; Stacey, diary entry, June 21, 1863.
88. Hoff to wife, June 24, 1863.
89. *Ibid.*
90. Paylor, diary entry, June 25, 1863; Stacey, diary entry, June 25, 1863; Hoff to wife, June 28, 1863; Due to the frantic conditions under which the regiment joined the army and the nature of the campaign, there was no time for corps badges to be sewn on by members of the 111th. The appropriate corps badge would have been a blue trefoil, indicating the regiment was part of the Third Division, II Corps. General Hays was given command of the Third Division when its commander, General French, was transferred to Harpers Ferry. General Abercrombie should have been given command but he was away on a leave of absence.

91. Thompson, "Into This Hell of Destruction," p. 16.
92. *ADAU*, July 6, 1863; Gibbs, diary entry, June 27, 1863.
93. Paylor, diary entry, June 26, 1863; Stacey, diary entry, June 27, 1863; Thompson, "Into This Hell of Destruction," p. 16.
94. Smith to mother, July 1, 1863.
95. Paylor, diary entry, June 28, 1863.
96. Hoff to wife, June 22, 1863.
97. Thompson, "Into This Hell of Destruction," p. 16.
98. Eldred, "Newman Eldred's Account," vol. 23, no. 89 (Fall 1979): 14.
99. Thompson, "Into This Hell of Destruction," p. 16.
100. Thompson, "Into This Hell of Destruction," p. 16.
101. Smith to mother, July 1, 1863; Sergeant Marcellus Mosher had a horse because he was temporarily assigned to the ambulance corps.
102. Smith to mother, July 1, 1863.
103. Thompson, "Into This Hell of Destruction," p. 16.
104. New York Monument Commission, *New York at Gettysburg: Final Report on the Battlefield of Gettysburg*, Albany, NY: J. B. Lyon, 1900, p. 802; The strength of the regiment was reported as 476 men in the muster roll at the end of June, which was completed before the regiment left Centerville. The difference between this number and the number mustered on June 30 can be attributed to the following factors: a large number of men were left behind when the regiment left Centerville and at least one man deserted at Union Mills, several men were sent to Washington on June 28th, several more deserted along the line of march, and a large number of men were incapacitated during the march on June 29th.

Chapter 5

1. Edward Holcombe, diary entry, July 3, 1863.
2. Thompson, "Into This Hell of Destruction," p. 17; Stacey, diary entry, July 1, 1863.
3. Thompson, "Into This Hell of Destruction," p. 17; Today, the hill referred to by Thompson is called Little Round Top. But during the battle, it was known locally as Sugar Loaf Hill.
4. New York Monument Commission, *New York at Gettysburg*, p. 800; Military service record for First Sergeant James Allen, National Archives, Washington, D.C.; Allen survived the wound and later served in the 16th New York Heavy Artillery; Eldred, "Newman Eldred's Account," vol. 23, no. 90 (Winter 1979): 37.
5. Eldred, "Newman Eldred's Account," vol. 23, no. 90 (Winter 1979): 38; Military service records of Charles Todd and Robert Johnson, National Archives, Washington, D.C.
6. Warren W. Hassler Jr., *Crisis at the Crossroads*, reprint, Ron R. Van Sickle Military Books, 1988, pp. 28–29.
7. New York Monument Commission, *New York at Gettysburg*, p. 800; Military service record of Henry Walker, National Archives, Washington, D.C.
8. New York Monument Commission, *New York at Gettysburg*, p. 800; Today the area is changed markedly from its 1863 appearance. The national park's cyclo-

rama now occupies much of what was once the Brien orchard and Zeigler's grove, while numerous monuments stand on the site of the Bliss farm. Much to the credit of the National Park Service, it has undertaken an ambitious campaign to return much of the battlefield to its 1863 appearance, including the replanting of the Brien orchard.

9. New York Monument Commission, *New York at Gettysburg*, p. 800; *War of the Rebellion*, ser. 1, vol. 27, pt. 1, p. 475.

10. *War of the Rebellion*, ser. 1, vol. 27, pt. 1, p. 368; Thompson, "Into This Hell of Destruction," p. 18; George T. Fleming, *Life and Letters of Alexander Hays*, Gilbert Adam Hays, 1919, p. 431.

11. Thompson, "Into This Hell of Destruction," p. 18.

12. Hoff to wife, July 5, 1863.

13. Thompson, "Into This Hell of Destruction," p. 17.

14. *Ibid.*; Eldred, "Newman Eldred's Account," vol. 23, no. 90 (Winter 1979): 38.

15. Harry W. Pfanz, *Gettysburg: The Second Day*, University of North Carolina Press, 1987, p. 137; Thompson, "Into This Hell of Destruction," p. 18.

16. *Ibid.*

17. New York Monument Commission, *New York at Gettysburg*, p. 884; Eldred, "Newman Eldred's Account," vol. 23, no. 90 (Winter 1973): 39; Thompson, "Flight from Florida," p. 18.

18. Eric Campbell, "Remember Harpers Ferry: The Degradation, Humiliation and Redemption of Col. George L. Willard's Brigade," *Gettysburg Magazine*, no. 7 (July 1, 1992): 64.

19. W. G. Lightfoote, *Proceedings of the Reunion of the Veterans of the 111th and the 126th Regiments N.Y. Vols.*, Times Book and Job Printing House, 1886, p. 36; Stacey, diary entry, July 2, 1863.

20. Willson, *Disaster, Struggle, Triumph*, p. 168; Campbell, "Remember Harpers Ferry," p. 65; Thompson, "Into This Hell of Destruction," p. 18.

21. Willson, *Disaster, Struggle, Triumph*, p. 168; *War of the Rebellion*, ser. 1, vol. 27, pt. 1, p. 475; Clark, *Gettysburg*, p. 108; Thompson, "Into This Hell of Destruction," p. 19; Pfanz, *Gettysburg*, p. 405.

22. Campbell, "Remember Harpers Ferry," p. 65; David L. Ladd and Audrey J. Ladd, eds., *The Batchelder Papers*, 3 vols., Dayton, OH: Morningside House, 1994, vol. 1, p. 339; *War of the Rebellion*, ser. 1, vol. 27, pt. 1, p. 476.

23. Pfanz, *Gettysburg*, pp. 347–49; J. S. McNeily, *Barksdale's Mississippi Brigade at Gettysburg*, reprint, Olde Soldier Books, 1987, p. 245; Clark, *Gettysburg*, p. 102.

24. Chaplain Ezra Simons, *A Regimental History: The One Hundred and Twenty Fifth N.Y.S.V.*, Judson, 1888, p. 111; Thompson, "Into This Hell of Destruction," p. 18.

25. Thompson, "Into This Hell of Destruction," p. 18.

26. Eldred, "Newman Eldred's Account," vol. 23, no. 90 (Fall 1979): 39; Thompson, "Into This Hell of Destruction," p. 19; Campbell, "Remember Harpers Ferry," p. 67.

27. Pfanz, *Gettysburg*, p. 362.

28. Eldred, "Newman Eldred's Account," vol. 23, no. 90 (Fall 1979): 40; John W. Busey, *These Honored Dead*, Longstreet House, 1988, p. 142.

29. *War of the Rebellion*, ser. 1, vol. 27, pt. 1, pp. 475–76.

30. Thompson, "Into This Hell of Destruction," p. 19.

31. Stacey, diary entry, July 2, 1863.

32. Eldred, "Newman Eldred's Account," vol. 23, no. 90 (Winter 1979): 40.

33. Clark, *Military History of Wayne County*, p. 576.

34. *War of the Rebellion*, ser. 1, vol. 27, pt. 1, p. 475.

35. Thompson, "Into This Hell of Destruction," p. 19.

36. Lightfoote, *Proceedings of the Reunion of the Veterans of the 111th and the 126th Regiments N.Y. Vols.*, p. 38.

37. Busey, *These Honored Dead*, pp. 141–42; R. L. Murray, *The Redemption of the "Harper's Ferry Cowards,"* Wolcott, NY: Benedum, 1994, pp. 106–108; Adjutant General's Report, p. 731; Geer to friends, July 6, 1863; Hoff to wife, July 5, 1863; Busey, *These Honored Dead*, p. 142; Hicks was buried on July 5, but not before his best friend Thomas Geer retrieved his pocket bible and a set of keys. All other items belonging to the color sergeant were already removed by scavengers; While the September 13, 1863, edition of the *ADAU* states that Corporal Derby was wounded on July 3, numerous other sources, including his military service record, list Derby as being wounded on July 2.

38. Murray, *The Redemption of the Harper's Ferry Cowards*, p. 110; Busey, *These Honored Dead*, pp. 141–44; Military service record of Alfred Miller, National Archives, Washington, D.C.

39. *ADAU*, July 11, 1863; *War of the Rebellion*, ser. 1, vol. 27, pt. 1, p. 476; James A. Wright, *Historical Sketches of the Town of Moravia from 1791 to 1918*, Auburn, NY: Benton and Reynolds, 1874, p. 119; Military service records of George Smith and Alfred Miller, National Archives, Washington, D.C.

40. Hoff to wife, July 14, 1863; Clark, *Military History of Wayne County*, p. 577; Monroe, *Historical Records of a Hundred and Twenty Years*, p. 214; Fleming, p. 426.

41. Hollcroft, *Town of Ledyard in the Civil War*, p. 33.

42. Cooper to father, July 21, July 31, and August 31, 1863.

43. Chaplain John Brown to George Cooper, December 10 and December 12, 1863.

44. Willson, *Disaster, Struggle, Triumph*, p. 177; Thompson, "Into This Hell of Destruction," p. 19; Stacey, diary entry, July 2, 1863.

45. Thompson, "Into This Hell of Destruction," p. 19; *War of the Rebellion*, ser. 1, vol. 27, pt. 1, p. 476.

46. Thompson, "Into This Hell of Destruction," p. 19; Pfanz, *Gettysburg*, p. 404; John Brinkerhoff to C. D. MacDougall, July 9, 1890, John Batchelder Papers, New Hampshire Historical Society, Concord, microfilm copy, G.N.M.P. Historians Office; Hoff to wife, July 5, 1863.

47. Thompson, "Into This Hell of Destruction," p. 19.

48. Simons, *A Regimental History*, p. 112; Thompson, "Into This Hell of Destruction," p. 18; Campbell, "Remember Harpers Ferry," p. 73.

49. Campbell, "Remember Harpers Ferry," pp. 73–74; *War of the Rebellion*, ser. 1, vol. 27, pt. 1, p. 476.

50. Pfanz, *Gettysburg*, p. 407; John M. Pellicano, *Conquer or Die: The 39th New York Volunteer Infantry; Garibaldi Guard*. Flushing, NY: John Pellicano, 1996, pp. 100–101.

51. Wayne Mahood, *Written in Blood: A History of the 126th New York Infantry in the Civil War*. Hightstown, NJ: Longstreet House, 1997, p. 133; Campbell, "Remember Harpers Ferry," p. 74.
52. Thompson, "Into This Hell of Destruction," p. 19.
53. Campbell, "Remember Harpers Ferry," p. 74; *War of the Rebellion*, ser. 1, vol. 27, pt. 1, p. 476; Thompson, "Into This Hell of Destruction," p. 19; The reason for Sherrill's arrest seemed to stem from a misinterpretation of the phrase "original position." Apparently, Sherrill assumed that Willard meant the brigade's original position at Zeigler's grove, and was in the process of carrying out this order when Hancock approached MacDougall.
54. *War of the Rebellion*, ser. 1, vol. 27, pt. 1, p. 476; In his official report, Colonel MacDougall reported the regiment's loss on the second day's battle at 185 men. Extensive research by the author has determined that the regiment suffered 155 casualties on this day.
55. New York Monument Commission, *New York at Gettysburg*, p. 800.
56. *War of the Rebellion*, ser. 1, vol. 27, pt. 1, p. 476.
57. New York Monument Commission, *New York at Gettysburg*, pp. 800, 803.
58. *ADAU*, December 12, 1863.
59. Thompson, "Into This Hell of Destruction," pp. 19–20.
60. Hoff to wife, July 5, 1863.
61. Eldred, "Newman Eldred's Account," vol. 23, no. 90 (Winter 1979) 40.
62. *War of the Rebellion*, ser. 1, vol. 27, pt. 1, p. 476; Stacey, diary entry, July 3, 1863.
63. John Michael Priest, *Into the Fight: Pickett's Charge at Gettysburg*, Shippensburg, PA: White Mane, 1998, pp. 9–11; Stacey, diary entry, July 3, 1863; Thompson, "Into This Hell of Destruction," p. 20; Lewis W. Husk to General C. D. MacDougall, June 25, 1890, Batchelder Papers; John I. Brinkerhoff to General C. D. MacDougall, July 9, 1890, Batchelder Papers.
64. New York Monument Commission, *New York at Gettysburg*, p. 800; John I. Brinkerhoff to General C. D. MacDougall, July 9, 1890, Batchelder Papers.
65. Thompson, "Into This Hell of Destruction," p. 20.
66. *Ibid.*
67. Priest, *Into the Fight*, pp. 16–17; Sebastian Holmes to General MacDougall, July 10, 1890, Batchelder Papers.
68. S. D. Holmes to General MacDougall, July 10, 1890, Batchelder Papers.
69. Charles A. Hitchcock to John Batchelder, January 20, 1886, Batchelder Papers; Fleming, pp. 431–32.
70. *Ibid.*
71. *Ibid.*; Before leaving the Bliss farm, Hitchcock picked a flower from the garden to give to General Hays. The flower remained pressed in the Hays' family bible for many years after the war.
72. Eric Campbell, "Remember Harper's Ferry: The Degradation, Humiliation and Redemption of Colonel George Willard's Brigade, Part 2," *Gettysburg Magazine*, January 1, 1993, Issue 8, p. 99.
73. Thompson, "Into This Hell of Destruction," pp. 20–21; Eldred, "Newman Eldred's Account," vol. 23, no. 90 (Winter 1979): 41; "Bummer" was the nickname given to those who were adept at foraging, or stealing, supplies.
74. Thompson, "Into This Hell of Destruction," pp. 20–21.
75. *Ibid.*
76. Robert U. Johnson and Clarence C. Buel, eds., *Battles and Leaders of the Civil War*, 4 vols., reprint, Secaucus, NJ: Castle,1983, vol. 3, p. 362; Pfanz, *Gettysburg*, pp. 416–17; George R Stewart, *Pickett's Charge*, Morningside, 1980, reprint, p. 114.
77. Thompson, "Into This Hell of Destruction," p. 21; New York Monument Commission, *New York at Gettysburg*, p. 801; David Shields to General C. D. MacDougall, August 26, 1890, Batchelder Papers; Fleming, p. 453.
78. Lewis W. Husk to General MacDougall, June 25, 1890, Batchelder Papers; Campbell, Issue Eight, January 1993, p. 94.
79. Eldred, "Newman Eldred's Account," vol. 23, no. 90 (Winter 1979): 42.
80. *Ibid.*; Eldred, "Newman Eldred's Account," vol. 23, no. 99 (Spring 1980): 54.
81. Thompson, "Into This Hell of Destruction," pp. 21–22; S. B. McIntyre to General MacDougall, June 27, 1890, Batchelder Papers.
82. Charles A. Hitchcock to John Batchelder, January 20, 1886, Batchelder Papers; *War of the Rebellion*, ser. 1, vol. 27, pt. 1, p. 476.
83. Thompson, "Into This Hell of Destruction," pp. 21–22; Priest, *Into the Fight*, p. 66.
84. Eldred, "Newman Eldred's Account," vol. 23, no. 90 (Winter 1979): 40.
85. New York Monument Commission, *New York at Gettysburg*, p. 801; Ladd and Ladd, *Batchelder Papers*, vol. 3, p. 1399.
86. Thompson, "Into This Hell of Destruction," p. 22.
87. S. D. Holmes to General MacDougall, July 10, 1890, Batchelder Papers.
88. Stacey, diary entry, July 3, 1863; McIntyre to MacDougall, June 27, 1890, Batchelder Papers; Ladd and Ladd, *Batchelder Papers*, vol. 3, p. 1754; Priest, *Into the Fight*, p. 66; Hoff to wife, July 5, 1863.
89. Wright, *Historical Sketches of the Town of Moravia from 1791 to 1918*, p. 119.
90. New York Monument Commission, *New York at Gettysburg*, p. 801.
91. *War of the Rebellion*, ser. 1, vol. 27, pt. 1, p. 476; New York Monument Commission, *New York at Gettysburg*, p. 802; McIntyre to MacDougall, June 27, 1890; Fleming, p. 433; Ladd and Ladd, *Batchelder Papers*, vol. 3, p. 1763.
92. *War of the Rebellion*, ser. 1, vol. 27, pt. 1, p. 476; New York Monument Commission, *New York at Gettysburg*, p. 802; McIntyre to MacDougall, June 27, 1890.
93. *War of the Rebellion*, ser. 1, vol. 27, pt. 1, p. 476.
94. McIntyre to MacDougall, June 27, 1890.
95. *War of the Rebellion*, ser. 1, vol. 27, pt. 1, p. 651; Lance J. Herdegen and William J. K. Beaudot, *Into the Bloody Railroad Cut at Gettysburg*, Morningside House, 1990, pp. 180–83.
96. Thompson, "Into This Hell of Destruction," p. 22; Pension Records of Henry Clark, National Archives, Washington, D.C.; Holmes to MacDougall, July 10, 1890; Ladd and Ladd, *Batchelder Papers*, vol. 3, p. 1762; Several postwar accounts report that one shell exploded near the colors, killing seven men. Colonel MacDougall refuted this claim stating, "I have never heard of the destruction named by the explosion of this shell but the

facts are four color bearers were killed in the action of July 3rd, and all by bullets, none by shells"; MacDougall's aide, Henry Clark, must have endeared himself to the colonel for he served in that capacity for most of the war. Clark did spend some time in the Quartermaster's Department until returning to act as "Col. MacDougall's servant" and as a brigade orderly after MacDougall was promoted to brigade command.

97. New York Monument Commission, *New York at Gettysburg*, p. 907.

98. New York Monument Commission, *New York at Gettysburg*, p. 801; Walter Clark, comp., *Histories of Several Regiments and Battalions from North Carolina*, vol. 2, reprint, Avera Press, 1982, p. 565; Priest, *Into the Fight*, pp. 132–34.

99. J. N. Thomas to General MacDougall, July 7, 1890, Batchelder Papers.

100. New York Monument Commission, *New York at Gettysburg*, p. 801; Clark, *Histories of Several Regiments and Battalions from North Carolina*, p. 565; Hollcroft, *Town of Ledyard in the Civil War*, p. 33; Sebastian Holmes to General C.D. MacDougall, June 27, 1880, Batchelder Papers; Priest, *Into the Fight*, pp. 132–34.

101. Johnson and Buel, *Battles and Leaders*, vol. 3, p. 392; Mahood, *Written in Blood*, pp. 154–55.

102. Eldred, "Newman Eldred's Account," vol. 23, no. 91 (Spring 1980): 55.

103. McIntyre to MacDougall, June 27, 1890, Batchelder Papers; Thompson, "Into This Hell of Destruction," p. 22; Willson, *Disaster, Struggle, Triumph*, p. 186; Priest, *Into the Fight*, p. 158.

104. *War of the Rebellion*, ser. 1, vol. 27, pt. 1, p. 476; Thompson, "Into This Hell of Destruction," p. 22; McIntyre to MacDougall, June 27, 1890, Batchelder Papers.

105. Eldred, "Newman Eldred's Account," vol. 23, no. 91 (Spring 1980): 55.

106. Fleming, p. 463.

107. Thompson, "Into This Hell of Destruction," p. 23.

108. *ADAU*, July 11, 1863; List of casualties developed by the author; The one soldier reported as missing was Frank Saxton of Company G. He deserted from the ranks sometime on July 3.

109. Extensive research conducted by the author has found the casualty figures reported on the monument are basically correct. The numbers used here were arrived at through research of records at the National Archives, casualty lists published in the *ADAU* after the battle, the Adjutant General's Report, along with dozens of other sources. Both Lieutenants Edgar Hueston and Merrill Murdock were listed as slightly wounded but still on duty. There is no indication of when they received their wounds or to what extent they were wounded.

110. Adjutant General's Report, pp. 915–16, 923; Busey, *These Honored Dead*, pp. 144–45; *ADAU*, July 11, 1863.

111. Eldred, "Newman Eldred's Account," vol. 23, no. 91 (Spring 1980): 60.

112. *War of the Rebellion*, ser. 1, vol. 27, pt. 1, p. 453.

113. *Ibid.*, p. 455.

114. Fleming, *Life and Letters of Alexander Hays*, p. 433.

115. *Ibid.*

116. John I. Brinkerhoff to General C. D. MacDougall, July 9, 1890, Batchelder Papers.

117. Eldred, "Newman Eldred's Account," vol. 23, no. 91 (Spring 1980): 56; Thompson, "Into This Hell of Destruction," p. 23; Stacey, diary entry, July 4, 1863; *Advertiser-Journal*, August 22, 1916; During a postwar reunion of the 111th, a member of the regiment approached Henry Segoine and presented him with a pocketknife containing his name. The man told Segoine he found it in the haversack of a dead Confederate soldier at Gettysburg. Segoine stated that the knife was located with the officer's baggage when the regiment was captured at Harpers Ferry in 1862, and he was unable to retrieve it before the rebels took the baggage away.

118. Stacey, diary entry, July 4, 1863.

119. Eldred, "Newman Eldred's Account," vol. 23, no. 91 (Spring 1980): 58; Adjutant General's Report, p. 841; Thompson, "Into This Hell of Destruction," p. 23.

120. Eldred, "Newman Eldred's Account," vol. 23, no. 91 (Spring 1980): 59.

121. Thompson, "Into This Hell of Destruction," p. 23.

122. Geer to friends, July 6, 1863.

Chapter 6

1. Benton to father, August 16, 1863.
2. Hoff to wife, July 7, 1863.
3. Stacey, diary entry, July 8, 1863.
4. Holcombe, diary entry, July 4, 1863.
5. Paylor, diary entry, July 9, 1863; Stacey, diary entry, July 9, 1863.
6. Eldred, "Newman Eldred's Account," vol. 23, no. 91 (Spring 1980): 61.
7. *Ibid.*, pp. 86–89.
8. *Ibid.*
9. *Ibid.*, p. 61; Eldred, "Newman Eldred's Account," vol. 23, no. 92 (Summer 1980): 86–89; The VRC was made up of soldiers were no longer fit for field service but who could still perform certain duties of the soldier. VRC. soldiers often served as guards for prisons or fort garrisons.
10. Paylor, diary entry, July 10 and 11, 1863; Gary Gallagher, ed., *The Third Day at Gettysburg and Beyond*, University of North Carolina Press, 1994, pp. 165, 170; Stacey, diary entry, July 11, 1863.
11. Gallagher, *Third Day at Gettysburg*, pp. 164, 170; Johnson and Buel, *Battles and Leaders*, p. 424.
12. Davis, Perry, and Kirkley, *The Official Military Atlas of the Civil War*, plate 42.
13. Gallagher, *Third Day at Gettysburg*, pp. 165, 171.
14. *ADAU*, July 11 and 17, 1863.
15. Entry for Company C, July 1863, Company Returns, National Archives, Washington, D.C.; Paylor, diary entry, July 12, 1863; Stacey, diary entry, July 12, 1863.
16. Paylor, diary entries, July 12 and 13, 1863.
17. Stacey, diary entry, July 13, 1863.
18. Gallagher, *Third Day at Gettysburg*, p. 172; Clark, *Gettysburg*, p. 156.
19. Stacey, diary entry, July 14, 1863.
20. Paylor, diary entry, July 15, 1863; Frank Welcher, *The Eastern Theater*, vol. 1, *The Union Army 1861–1865*, Bloomington: Indiana University Press, 1989, p. 761; Stacey, diary entry, July 15, 1863.
21. Military service record of Frank Rich, National Archives, Washington, D.C.
22. Paylor, diary entry, July 18, 1863.
23. Stacey, diary entry, July 18, 1863.

24. Hoff to wife, July 18, 1863.
25. Willson, *Disaster, Struggle, Triumph*, p. 207; Paylor, diary entry, July 25, 1863; Stacey, diary entry, July 25, 1863; Hoff to wife, July 27, 1863.
26. Hoff to wife, July 27, 1863.
27. Stacey, diary entry, July 26, 1863.
28. *Ibid.*
29. Benton to father, February 28, 1863.
30. Stacey, diary entries, July 27–29, 1863.
31. Paylor, diary entries, July 30, 31, and August 1, 1863; Francis A. Walker, *History of the Second Army Corps of the Army of the Potomac*. New York: Scribner's, 1891, pp. 310–11; Mahood, *Written in Blood*, p. 174.
32. Benton to parents, August 16, 1863.
33. *Ibid.*
34. Mahood, *Written in Blood*, p. 174; Paylor, diary entries, August 8 and 15, 1863.
35. Mahood, *Written in Blood*, p. 174; Paylor, diary entries, August 8 and 15, 1863; Geer to Jule, August 17, 1863; Thompson, "Into This Hell of Destruction," p. 23.
36. Ladd and Ladd, *Batchelder Papers*, vol. 3, pp. 1736–37; Phisterer, *New York in the War of the Rebellion*, p. 3312; Adjutant General's Report, p. 784.
37. Regimental Return for August 1863, RG 94, National Archives, Washington, D.C.
38. Mahood, *Written in Blood*, p. 175; Walker, p. 318; Davis, Perry, and Kirkley, plate 29, no. 3.
39. Hoff to wife, September 1 and 4, 1863.
40. *Ibid.*
41. Adjutant General's Report, p. 884; Military service record of George Smith, National Archives, Washington, D.C.; Phisterer, *New York in the War of the Rebellion*, pp. 3311–12.
42. Regimental Returns for August 1863, National Archives, Washington, D.C.
43. William D. Henderson, *The Road to Bristoe Station; Campaigning with Lee and Meade*, H. E. Howard, 1987, p. 29; Glenn Tucker, *Chickamauga: Bloody Battle in the West*, Konecky and Konecky, 1961, p. 87.
44. Willson, *Disaster, Struggle, Triumph*, p. 308; Paylor, diary entries, September 12, 1863; Henderson, *The Road to Bristoe Station*, p. 31; Regimental Return for August 1863, RG 94, National Archives, Washington, D.C.
45. Willson, *Disaster, Struggle, Triumph*, p. 308; Paylor, diary entries, September 12–13, 1863; Mahood, *Written in Blood*, p. 177; Henderson, *The Road to Bristoe Station*, p. 31.
46. Paylor, diary entries, September 15 and 16, 1863.
47. *Ibid.*
48. *Ibid.*; Mahood, *Written in Blood*, pp. 177–78; Welcher, *Eastern Theater*, p. 323.
49. Paylor, diary entry, September 18, 1863; Mahood, *Written in Blood*, p. 178; Benton to parents, September 25, 1863.
50. Adjutant General's Report, p. 890.
51. Benton to parents, September 25, 1863; Ague is similar to the flu, the symptoms being fever, chills, and a cough.
52. Henderson, *The Road to Bristoe Station*, p. 68.
53. Paylor, diary entries, September 29 and October 3, 1863; Henderson, *The Road to Bristoe Station*, p. 71; Welcher, *Eastern Theater*, p. 323.
54. Gibbs, diary entry, October 2, 1863.
55. Regimental Returns, National Archives, entry for Detachment Companies B and C, October 1863; Frank M. Myers, *The Comanches: A History of White's Battalion, Virginia Cavalry*, reprint, Stonewall House, 1985, pp. 231–32; *ADAU*, October 7, 1863; Adjutant General's Report, pp. 671–930; Regimental Returns for October 1863, National Archives, Washington, D.C.; While Company C suffered only one attack during the month, Company B fended off three assaults.
56. *ADAU*, October 7 and 8, 1863; Regimental Returns, National Archives, entry for Detachment Companies B and C, October 1863; Adjutant General's Report, pp. 671–930.
57. Henderson, *The Road to Bristoe Station*, pp. 74–78; Welcher, *Eastern Theater*, p. 323; Pellicano, *Conquer or Die*, p. 110.
58. Henderson, *The Road to Bristoe Station*, p. 85; Paylor, diary entry, October 10, 1863.
59. *War of the Rebellion*, ser. 1, vol. 29, pt. 1, p. 235–36; Henderson, *The Road to Bristoe Station*, pp. 133–34, 138; Mahood, *Written in Blood*, p. 181; Walker, *History of the Second Army Corps*, p. 362.
60. *Ibid.*
61. *War of the Rebellion*, ser. 1, vol. 29, pt. 1, pp. 235–36; Henderson, *The Road to Bristoe Station*, pp. 133–34, 138; Walker, *History of the Second Army Corps*, p. 324.
62. Benton to father, October 21, 1863.
63. Henderson, *The Road to Bristoe Station*, p. 155; *War of the Rebellion*, ser. 1, vol. 29, pt. 1, pp. 236–37; Welcher, *Eastern Theater*, p. 324.
64. Henderson, *The Road to Bristoe Station*, p. 155; *War of the Rebellion*, ser. 1, vol. 29, pt. 1, pp. 299–300.
65. *War of the Rebellion*, ser. 1, vol. 29, pt. 1, p. 303; Henderson, *The Road to Bristoe Station*, pp. 157–58; *ADAU*, October 19, 1863.
66. Henderson, *The Road to Bristoe Station*, p. 158; , ser. 1, vol. 29, pt. 1, pp. 301–302; Mahood, *Written in Blood*, p. 184.
67. Benton to father, October 21, 1863.
68. Walker, *History of the Second Army Corps*, p. 341.
69. *War of the Rebellion*, ser. 1, vol. 29, pt. 1, pp. 300, 302; Walker, *History of the Second Army Corps*, p. 336.
70. Henderson, *The Road to Bristoe Station*, pp. 168–71.
71. Henderson, *The Road to Bristoe Station*, p. 177; *War of the Rebellion*, ser. 1, vol. 29, pt. 1, p. 302.
72. *Ibid.*; Pellicano, *Conquer or Die*, p. 112.
73. *Ibid.*; Willson, *Disaster, Struggle, Triumph*, p. 215; David G. Martin, *Confederate Monuments at Gettysburg*, Vol. 1, Longstreet House, 1986, p. 199; Dean Thomas, *Cannons*, Thomas Publications, 1985; Poague's battalion was composed of four batteries, with four guns each, and was a mix of rifled and smoothbore pieces. Although it is not clear whether all of his guns were engaged in the fight, it is doubtful that Poague used his smoothbores from his initial position to shell the 111th.
74. *War of the Rebellion*, ser. 1, vol. 29, pt. 1, pp. 301–302; *ADAU*, October 19, 1863.
75. Benton to father, October 21, 1863.
76. Hoff to wife, October 24, 1863.
77. Based on the official records and a letter written by Captain Charles A. Richardson to John Bachelder, the regiments were probably ordered in the following manner: from left to right was the 111th, 125th, 39th, and 126th; Ladd and Ladd, *Batchelder Papers*, vol. 1, p. 319.
78. Today, the area around Bristoe Station is still largely undeveloped. The open fields through which Heth's division advanced are now filled with scrub brush and are slowly being reclaimed by heavy woods. Although some accounts refer to the railroad bed as a "cut,"

the tracks sat atop an elevated embankment. Unfortunately as the town of Manassas continues its unchecked growth, the area may soon fall victim to developers.
  79. *War of the Rebellion*, ser. 1, vol. 29, pt. 1, p. 302; Henderson, *The Road to Bristoe Station*, p. 177; Walker, *History of the Second Army Corps*, p. 342n.
  80. Benton to father, October 21, 1863.
  81. *War of the Rebellion*, ser. 1, vol. 29, pt. 1, p. 302.
  82. Wright, *Historical Sketches of the Town of Moravia from 1791 to 1918*, p. 103; *ADAU*, October 19, 1863; Adjutant General's Report, p. 856.
  83. *War of the Rebellion*, ser. 1, vol. 29, pt. 1, pp. 302, 431, 435; Henderson, *The Road to Bristoe Station*, pp. 180–81; James I. Robertson, Jr., *General A. P. Hill: The Story of a Confederate Warrior*, Random House, 1987, p. 238.
  84. Henderson, *The Road to Bristoe Station*, pp. 181–82; *War of the Rebellion*, ser. 1, vol. 29, pt. 1, pp. 298–99.
  85. *War of the Rebellion*, ser. 1, vol. 29, pt. 1, p. 300; *ADAU*, October 19, 1863; Walker, *History of the Second Army Corps*, pp. 354–55; Benton to father, October 25, 1863.
  86. *War of the Rebellion*, ser. 1, vol. 29, pt. 1, p .302; *ADAU*, October 19, 1863; Pension Record of Isaac Lusk, National Archives, Washington, D.C.; Lusk received a slight wound in the foot; Company Muster Rolls, Company K, entry dated October 1863, National Archives, Washington, D.C.
  87. Clark, *Military History of Wayne County*, p. 100f; Adjutant General's Report, p. 730; Deming was also carried on the regimental rolls as "Denning."
  88. *War of the Rebellion*, ser. 1, vol. 29, pt. 1, p. 301; Walker, *History of the Second Army Corps*, p. 361; Benton to father, October 21, 1863.
  89. General Order No. 17, October 15, 1863, RG 94, National Archives, Washington, D.C.

Chapter 7

  1. Paylor, diary entry, December 31, 1863.
  2. *War of the Rebellion*, ser. 1, vol. 29, pt. 1, p. 302; Adjutant General's Report, p. 915; Bacarella, *Lincoln's Foreign Legion*, pp. 143–44; Hoff to wife, October 21, 1863.
  3. Martin Graham and George F. Skoch, *Mine Run: A Campaign of Lost Opportunities: October 21, 1863–March 1, 1864*, H. E. Howard, 1987, pp. 2–5; *War of the Rebellion*, ser. 1, vol. 29, pt. 1, p. 302; Hoff to wife, October 21, 1863.
  4. Gregory Jaynes, *The Killing Ground: Wilderness to Cold Harbor*, Alexandria, VA: Time Life, 1986, p. 26.
  5. Paylor, diary entry, October 19, 1863; Walker, *History of the Second Army Corps*, pp. 365–66.
  6. Hoff to wife, October 21, 1863.
  7. *Ibid*.
  8. Benton to father, October 23, 1863.
  9. Hoff to wife, October 21, 1863.
  10. *Ibid*., October 28, 1863.
  11. Paylor, diary entry, October 25 and 27, 1863.
  12. Adjutant General's Report, pp. 709, 713, 811; Military service record of John Lockwood, National Archives, Washington, D.C.
  13. Graham and Skoch, *Mine Run*, pp. 9–10; Walker, *History of the Second Army Corps*, pp. 366–67.
  14. Benton to father, November 16, 1863.
  15. Graham and Skoch, *Mine Run*, pp. 15, 101; Paylor, diary entry, November 7, 1863; Walker, *History of the Second Army Corps*, p. 366; Stacey, diary entry, November 7, 1863.
  16. Stacey, diary entry, November 8, 1863.
  17. *Ibid*., November 10, 1863.
  18. Hoff to wife, November 10, 1863.
  19. *Ibid*., October 24, 1863.
  20. *Ibid*., November 18, 1863.
  21. Graham and Skoch, *Mine Run*, pp. 40–41; Walker, *History of the Second Army Corps*, p. 368; Welcher, *Eastern Theater*, p. 789.
  22. Graham and Skoch, *Mine Run*, p. 42; Walker, *History of the Second Army Corps*, p. 367.
  23. Walker, *History of the Second Army Corps*, p. 368.
  24. Stacey, diary entry, November 26, 1863.
  25. Graham and Skoch, *Mine Run*, p. 47; Long, *Memoirs of Robert E. Lee*, p. 313.
  26. Paylor, diary entry, November 27, 1863; Graham and Skoch, *Mine Run*, pp. 45, 48; *War of the Rebellion*, ser. 1, vol. 29, pt. 1, p. 695; Welcher, *Eastern Theater*, p. 790.
  27. Paylor, diary entry, November 27, 1863; Graham and Skoch, *Mine Run*, pp. 45, 48; *War of the Rebellion*, ser. 1, vol. 29, pt. 1, p. 695; Welcher, *Eastern Theater*, p. 790; Walker, *History of the Second Army Corps*, pp. 372–73; Stacey, diary entry, November 27, 1863.
  28. *Ibid*.
  29. Graham and Skoch, *Mine Run*, p. 69.
  30. *Ibid*.; Paylor, diary entry, November 28, 1863; *War of the Rebellion*, ser. 1, vol. 29, pt. 1, p. 696; Phisterer, *New York in the War of the Rebellion*, p. 3306.
  31. Stacey, diary entry, November 29, 1863.
  32. *Ibid*.; *War of the Rebellion*, ser. 1, vol. 29, pt. 1, p. 696; Graham and Skoch, *Mine Run*, p. 74; Walker, *History of the Second Army Corps*, p. 377; Paylor, diary entry, November 29, 1863.
  33. Geer to Albert, December 10, 1863.
  34. *War of the Rebellion*, ser. 1, vol. 29, pt. 1, p. 698; Welcher, *Eastern Theater*, p. 792; Walker, *History of the Second Army Corps*, p. 380.
  35. Benton to parents, December 22, 1863; *War of the Rebellion*, ser. 1, vol. 29, pt. 1, p. 698; Paylor, diary entry, November 30, 1863.
  36. *War of the Rebellion*, ser. 1, vol. 29, pt. 1, p. 698.
  37. Geer to Albert, December 10, 1863.
  38. Stacey, diary entry, November 30, 1863.
  39. *Ibid*., December 1, 1863.
  40. Geer to Jule, December 4, 1863.
  41. RG 94, Regimental Returns for December 1863, National Archives, Washington, D.C.; Adjutant General's Report, pp. 671–930; Paylor, diary entry, December 2, 1863; Simons, *A Regimental History*, p. 185; Dadswell to father, December 19, 1863.
  42. Geer to Jule, December 4, 1863.
  43. Stacey, diary entry, December 2, 1863.
  44. Paylor, diary entry, December 2, 1863.
  45. Benton to father, December 22, 1863.
  46. Stacey, diary entry, December 8, 1863.
  47. Paylor, diary entry, December 6, 1863.
  48 *Ibid*., December 2–5, 25, 26, and 30, 1863.
  49. Stacey, diary entry, December 25, 1863.
  50. Paylor, diary entries, January 2 and 3, 1864; Daniel Hutchins, diary entry, January 2, 1864; Regimental Return for December 1863, National Archives, Washington, D.C.
  51. Paylor, diary entries, January 2 and 3, 1864; Adjutant General's Report, p. 893; Mahood, *Written in*

Blood, p. 211; Charles White, diary entry, January 3, 1864; Hutchins, diary entry, January 2, 1864; Hoff to wife, January 13, 1864.

52. Benjamin Thompson, "Back to the South," *Civil War Times Illustrated*, November 1973, p. 28; Bacarella, *Lincoln's Foreign Legion*, p. 286.

53. Thompson, "Back to the South," p. 28; Adjutant General's Report, p. 752.

54. Hoff to wife, January 3, 1864.

55. *ADAU*, February 5, 1864; Special Order 113, February 2, 1864, RG 94, National Archives, Washington, D.C.; White, diary entry, January 29, 1864; Geer to Jule, February 4, 1864.

56. Special Order 113, February 2, 1864, RG 94, National Archives, Washington, D.C.; *ADAU*, February 4, 1864.

57. Graham and Skoch, *Mine Run*, pp. 87–88; Walker, *History of the Second Army Corps*, p. 394; Pellicano, *Conquer or Die*, p. 117.

58. *War of the Rebellion*, ser. 1, vol. 33, pt. 1, p. 114–17; Graham and Skoch, *Mine Run*, p. 87; Walker, *History of the Second Army Corps*, p. 394.

59. *War of the Rebellion*, ser. 1, vol. 33, pt. 1, p. 135; Hutchins, diary entry, February 6, 1864; Horace Hill, diary entry, February 6, 1864; White, diary entry, February 6, 1864.

60. Graham and Skoch, *Mine Run*, pp. 88, 93; Bacarella, *Lincoln's Foreign Legion*, p. 158.

61. *War of the Rebellion*, ser. 1, vol. 33, pt. 1, p. 133; Geer to Julia, February 12, 1864; Benton to parents, February 8, 1864.

62. *War of the Rebellion*, ser. 1, vol. 33, pt. 1, p. 133; Graham and Skoch, *Mine Run*, pp. 88, 93; Bacarella, *Lincoln's Foreign Legion*, p. 158.

63. *War of the Rebellion*, ser. 1, vol. 33, pt. 1, p. 135; Graham and Skoch, *Mine Run*, p. 92; White, diary entry, February 6, 1864.

64. *War of the Rebellion*, ser. 1, vol. 33, pt. 1, p. 136; Bacarella, *Lincoln's Foreign Legion*, p. 158; Benton to parents, February 8, 1864.

65. Phisterer, *New York in the War of the Rebellion*, p. 3306; White, diary entry, February 7, 1864; Benton to parents, February 8, 1864; Hutchins, diary entry, February 7, 1864.

66. *War of the Rebellion*, ser. 1, vol. 33, pt. 1, p. 136.

Chapter 8

1. Benton to parents, March 6, 1864.
2. Hill, diary entries, January 25 and February 18, 1864.
3. Hutchins, diary entries, February 9 and 19–23, 1864.
4. Geer to Julia, February 11, 1864; White, diary entry, February 11, 1864.
5. Warren to sister, February 27, 1864; White, diary entry, February 22, 1864; Hill, diary entry, February 22, 1864; Hutchins, diary entry, February 22, 1864.
6. Warren to sister, February 27, 1864.
7. Military service record of Charles Frisbee, National Archives, Washington, D.C.
8. *Ibid.*
9. *Ibid.*
10. Robert Garth Scott, *Into the Wilderness with the Army of the Potomac*, Bloomington, IL: Indiana University Press, 1985, p. 7; *War of the Rebellion*, ser. 1, vol. 33, pt. 1, pp. 735–36; The II and III corps were not the only units to be reorganized. The I Corps was also disbanded and its regiments transferred to the VI Corps. Instead of five corps, the army now had three. The IX Corps would be attached to the army as an independent command during the remainder of the war. General Hays would be killed while at the head of his brigade during the battle at the Wilderness. General Owen would be put under arrest for charges of disobedience to orders during the Spotsylvania Campaign.
11. Willson, *Disaster, Struggle, Triumph*, p. 237; Mahood, *Written in Blood*, pp. 221–22.
12. Geer to Willis, March 20, 1864.
13. *Ibid.*; Military service records for Isaac Lusk and James Hinman, National Archives, Washington, D.C.
14. Smith to parents, April 12, 1864.
15. *Ibid.*
16. *Ibid.*
17. Military service record for John Knapp, National Archives, Washington, D.C.; Phisterer, *New York in the War of the Rebellion*, p. 3314; Adjutant General's Report, p. 807.
18. Geer to Julia, February 4, 1864.
19. Joseph B. Mitchell, *The Badge of Gallantry*, Macmillan, 1968, p. 72.
20. *Ibid.*
21. *Ibid.*
22. *ADAU*, April 7, 12, and May 12, 1864.
23. Military service record of Ira Jones, National Archives, Washington, D.C.
24. Wellington Hinman, diary entry, April 22, 1864.
25. Hoff to wife, January 13, 1864.
26. Regimental Return for April 1864, RG 94, National Archives, Washington, D.C.; Phisterer, *New York in the War of the Rebellion*, pp. 3306–09; Geer to Willis, March 20, 1864, and to Julia, April 28, 1864; *ADAU*, April 29, 1864; Hinman, diary entries, April 2 and 25, 1864.
27. Military service record of Sebastian Holmes, National Archives, Washington, D.C.; Phisterer, *New York in the War of the Rebellion*, p. 3313.
28. White, diary entry, April 26, 1864; Hinman, diary entry, April 26, 1864.
29. Horace Porter, *Campaigning with Grant*, reprint, Mallard Press, 1991, pp. 35–36; Scott, *Into the Wilderness with the Army of the Potomac*, pp. 8–9.
30. Bruce Catton, *Grant Takes Command*, Boston, MA: Little, Brown, 1968, p. 153.
31. Scott, *Into the Wilderness with the Army of the Potomac*, p. 13; Jaynes, *Killing Ground*, p. 57.
32. Jaynes, *Killing Ground*, p. 57; Noah Andre Trudeau, *Bloody Roads South: The Wilderness to Cold Harbor May–June 1864*. New York: Fawcett Columbine, 1989, p. 26; Walker, *History of the Second Army Corps*, p. 407.
33. *National Tribune*, March 26, 1896; *War of the Rebellion*, ser. 1, vol. 36, pt. 1, p. 318.
34. *National Tribune*, March 26, 1896.
35. *Ibid.*; Walker, *History of the Second Army Corps*, p. 409; *War of the Rebellion*, ser. 1, vol. 36, pt. 1, p. 318; Andrew A. Humphreys, *The Virginia Campaign 1864–1865*, reprint, Da Capo Press, 1995, p. 422; White, diary entry, May 4, 1864; Hinman, diary entry, May 4, 1864.
36. *National Tribune*, March 26, 1896.
37. *War of the Rebellion*, ser. 1, vol. 36, pt. 1, pp. 318–19; Walker, *History of the Second Army Corps*, pp. 412–13; *National Tribune*, March 26, 1896; Joseph Marshall Fav-

ill, *Diary of a Young Officer*, Chicago, IL: R. R. Donnelly, 1909, p. 287; Trudeau, *Bloody Roads South*, p. 46.

38. Trudeau, *Bloody Roads South*, pp. 45–50; John Michael Priest, *Nowhere to Run: The Wilderness, May 4th and 5th, 1864*, Shippensburg, PA: White Mane, 1995, p. 7; As usual, Meade had to contend not only with the enemy but also with hesitant corps commanders. General Warren failed to ensure that his commander's orders were carried out and the V Corps attack along the Orange Turnpike was over two hours late in getting started.

39. *War of the Rebellion*, ser. 1, vol. 36, pt. 1, p. 400; Hutchins, diary entry, May 5, 1864; White, diary entry, May 5, 1864; Gilbert Frederick, *The Story of a Regiment*, Fifty-Seventh Veteran Association, C. H. Morgan, 1895, p. 220.

40. Priest, *Nowhere to Run*, p. 204; Frederick, *Story of a Regiment*, p. 220.

41. *National Tribune*, April 2, 1896.

42. Adjutant General's Report, p. 884; Military service record of James Snedaker, National Archives, Washington, D.C.

43. *ADAU*, May 16, 1864; Adjutant General's Report, pp. 761, 884; Information pertaining to the wounds received during the battle of the Wilderness was obtained from a Web page devoted to Corporal David Gibbs maintained by Charles Bennett.

44. *National Tribune*, April 2, 1896.

45. Military service records of August Green, George Brown, and Horace Hill, National Archives, Washington, D.C.; Abner Hill, Lieutenant Hill's brother, tried to retrieve his brother's body a few days after the battle but was unable to reach the battlefield. He returned a year later and was able to recover the lieutenant's body from the well-marked grave prepared by the members of Company A.

46. *War of the Rebellion*, ser. 1, vol. 36, pt. 1, p. 400; Frederick, *Story of a Regiment*, p. 221.

47. Jaynes, *Killing Ground*, p. 74; Trudeau, *Bloody Roads South*, pp. 76–83.

48. Jaynes, *Killing Ground*, p. 78; John Michael Priest, *Victory Without Triumph: The Wilderness, May 5th and 6th, 1864*, Shippensburg, PA: White Mane, 1996, p. 77; *War of the Rebellion*, ser. 1, vol. 36, pt. 1, p. 321; Walker, *History of the Second Army Corps*, p. 426.

49. *National Tribune*, April 2, 1896.

50. Scott, *Into the Wilderness with the Army of the Potomac*, p. 129; Priest, *Victory Without Triumph*, pp. 77–78; Frederick, *Story of a Regiment*, pp. 222–23.

51. *National Tribune*, April 2, 1896.

52. Ibid.

53. Hutchins, diary entry, May 6, 1864.

54. Scott, *Into the Wilderness with the Army of the Potomac*, p. 129; *War of the Rebellion*, ser. 1, vol. 36, pt. 1, p. 353; Priest, *Victory Without Triumph*, p. 79.

55. Scott, *Into the Wilderness with the Army of the Potomac*, p. 160; Priest, *Victory Without Triumph*, p. 91; *War of the Rebellion*, ser. 1, vol. 36, pt. 1, p. 323.

56. Trudeau, *Bloody Roads South*, pp. 108–109; Scott, *Into the Wilderness with the Army of the Potomac*, p. 169.

57. Phisterer, *New York in the War of the Rebellion*, p. 3306; *ADAU*, May 21, 1864; Adjutant General's Report, pp. 671–930.

58. Adjutant General's Report, pp. 671–930; Military service record of Albert Snedaker, National Archives, Washington, D.C.

59. Phisterer, *New York in the War of the Rebellion*, p. 3306; *ADAU*, May 21, 1864; Priest, *Victory Without Triumph*, p. 233; While he was away from the regiment recovering from his wound, Captain Aaron Seeley was promoted to the rank of lieutenant colonel. Unfortunately, he was never mustered in under the rank.

60. Benton to parents, March 6, 1864.

61. Hutchins, diary entry, May 7, 1864.

62. Trudeau, *Bloody Roads South*, pp. 121–22; Gordon C. Rhea, *The Battles for Spotsylvania Court House and the Road to Yellow Tavern May 7–12, 1864*, Louisiana State University Press, 1997, p. 14; Walker, *History of the Second Army Corps*, pp. 442–43.

63. Rhea, *Battles for Spotsylvania Court House*, pp. 28–29, 46; Walker, *History of the Second Army Corps*, pp. 442–43.

64. William D. Matter, *If It Takes All Summer: The Battle of Spotsylvania*, University of North Carolina Press, 1988, pp. 77–78; Welcher, *Eastern Theater*, vol. 1, p. 959; Rhea, *Battles for Spotsylvania Court House*, p. 75; White, diary entry, May 8, 1864; Hutchins, diary entry, May 8, 1864.

65. *War of the Rebellion*, ser. 1, vol. 36, pt. 1, pp. 402–404; Frederick, *Story of a Regiment*, p. 223; Part of the detail of escorting the wounded to Fredericksburg included the 22nd New York Cavalry, whose commander was described by Hancock as appearing stupid.

66. Hutchins, diary entry, May 9, 1864.

67. Matter, *If It Takes All Summer*, p. 124; *War of the Rebellion*, ser. 1, vol. 36, pt. 1, pp. 402–404; Walker, *History of the Second Army Corps*, p. 447; Hutchins, diary entry, May 9, 1864.

68. Matter, *If It Takes All Summer*, p. 125; *War of the Rebellion*, ser. 1, vol. 36, pt. 1, p. 404; Walker, *History of the Second Army Corps*, p. 447; Rhea, *Battles for Spotsylvania Court House*, p. 112.

69. Matter *If It Takes All Summer*, pp. 129–30; Rhea, *Battles for Spotsylvania Court House*, p. 113.

70. Rhea, *Battles for Spotsylvania Court House*, pp. 123–25; Walker, *History of the Second Army Corps*, p. 450.

71. *War of the Rebellion*, ser. 1, vol. 36, pt. 1, p. 404; Rhea, *Battles for Spotsylvania Court House*, p. 134; Matter, p. 141; Johnson and Buel, *Battles and Leaders*, vol. 4, p. 166.

72. Rhea, *Battles for Spotsylvania Court House*, pp. 136–37; Walker, *History of the Second Army Corps*, p. 452; *War of the Rebellion*, ser. 1, vol. 36, pt. 1, p. 357; White, diary entry, May 10, 1864.

73. Matter, *If It Takes All Summer*, p. 144; Mahood, *Written in Blood*, pp. 247–48; Favill, *Diary of a Young Officer*, p. 294.

74. Smith to sister, May 17, 1864.

75. Hutchins, diary entry, May 10, 1864.

76. Smith to sister, May 17, 1864; Trudeau, *Bloody Roads South*, pp. 150–51; Walker, *History of the Second Army Corps*, p. 453; Adjutant General's Report, pp. 671–930; Phisterer, *New York in the War of the Rebellion*, p. 3306.

77. *War of the Rebellion*, ser. 1, vol. 36, pt. 1, p. 137; Walker, *History of the Second Army Corps*, p. 426; Mahood, *Written in Blood*, p. 247.

78. Walker, *History of the Second Army Corps*, p. 467; Porter, *Campaigning with Grant*, pp. 99–101.

79. Matter, *If It Takes All Summer*, p. 189; Walker, *History of the Second Army Corps*, p. 469; Trudeau, *Bloody Roads South*, pp. 169–71; *War of the Rebellion*, ser. 1, vol. 36, pt. 1, p. 358; Each regiment was formed with "companies doubled on the center." This means that each

regiment's column was two companies wide, with one company behind the other.

80. Matter, *If It Takes All Summer*, p. 189; Walker, *History of the Second Army Corps*, p. 469; Favill, *Diary of a Young Officer*, pp. 296–97; Smith to sister, May 17, 1864.

81. Davis, Perry, and Kirkley, plate 55.

82. Walker, *History of the Second Army Corps*, p. 469; Matter, *If It Takes All Summer*, p. 192; Favill, *Diary of a Young Officer*, p. 297.

83. Rhea, *Battles for Spotsylvania Court House*, p. 235; Simons, *A Regimental History*, pp. 206–207; Walker, *History of the Second Army Corps*, p. 471; Porter, *Campaigning with Grant*, p. 102.

84. Rhea, *Battles for Spotsylvania Court House*, pp. 238–39; Matter, *If It Takes All Summer*, pp. 198–99.

85. Smith to sister, May 17, 1864.

86. Matter, *If It Takes All Summer*, p. 204; Rhea, *Battles for Spotsylvania Court House*, p. 248; Trudeau, *Bloody Roads South*, p. 178.

87. Matter, *If It Takes All Summer*, p. 210; Humphreys, *Virginia Campaign*, p. 97.

88. Matter, *If It Takes All Summer*, p. 210; Humphreys, *Virginia Campaign*, p. 97.

89. Hinman, diary entry, May 12, 1864.

90. Rhea, *Battles for Spotsylvania Court House*, p. 311; Porter, *Campaigning with Grant*, pp. 111–12; Humphreys, *Virginia Campaign*, pp. 101–102.

91. Military service record of Clinton MacDougall, National Archives, Washington, D.C.

92. *ADAU*, May 16, 1864.

93. Trudeau, *Bloody Roads South*, p. 191; Walker, *History of the Second Army Corps*, p. 482; Humphreys, *Virginia Campaign*, p. 110; White, diary entry, May 15, 1864.

94. Statements of Adrian Content and Silas Gage, Pension Records of Daniel Grandin, National Archives, Washington, D.C. Silas Gage stated that Grandin died on the 28th; Adjutant General's Report, p. 767; The place of capture for all three men on the 15th is listed as the Tar River. Reviews of both current and period maps, as well as discussions with the park historian of the Fredericksburg and Spotsylvania National Battlefield Park, failed to locate any river named Tar in the vicinity of Spotsylvania. It is the opinion of the author that the men were captured along the Ni River while on picket duty. This conclusion is based on the fact that the one man wounded and the three captured were all from the same company, none of them were listed as on detached service, and the regiment was in the vicinity of the Ni River on the 15th.

95. White, diary entry, May 16, 1864; Hinman, diary entry, May 16, 1864; Military service record of Lewis Husk, National Archives, Washington, D.C.; Adjutant General's Report, p. 887.

96. Trudeau, *Bloody Roads South*, p. 191; Walker, *History of the Second Army Corps*, p. 482; Humphreys, *Virginia Campaign*, p. 110; Sometime between the attack on the 12th and the planned assault on the enemy entrenchments on the 18th, General Hancock saw fit to reorganize the II Corps. With the heavy casualties sustained by the Third and Fourth divisions since the opening of the campaign in early May, Hancock decided to consolidate the battered divisions into one, under the command of General Birney.

97. Smith to parents, May 24, 1864.

98. Smith to sister and parents, May 17 and 24, 1864; Walker, *History of the Second Army Corps*, p. 485; Porter, *Campaigning with Grant*, p. 123; White, diary entry, May 18, 1864; Hinman, diary entry, May 18, 1864.

99. Smith to parents, May 2, 1864.

100. *ADAU*, July 6, 1864; Adjutant General's Report, pp. 671–930.

101. Walker, *History of the Second Army Corps*, p. 485; Matter, *If It Takes All Summer*, pp. 310–11.

102. Smith to sister and parents, May 17 and 24, 1864.

103. Robert C. Perry, military service record, National Archives, Washington, D.C.; Phisterer, *New York in the War of the Rebellion*, p. 3306; *ADAU*, June 17, 1864.

104. Welcher, *Eastern Theater*, p. 973; Walker, *History of the Second Army Corps*, p. 486; The exact number of casualties suffered during this campaign is very hard to determine. While the figures for the attack on May 10 and 18 are given in detail, only two men are listed as wounded during the attack on the 12th. The problem is compounded by the fact that no regimental return exists for May 1864.

Chapter 9

1. Warren to sister, May 26, 1864.

2. Matter, *If It Takes All Summer*, p. 348; Catton, *Grant Takes Command*, pp. 248–49; Michael J. Miller, *The North Anna Campaign: Even to Hell Itself, May 21–26, 1864*, H. E. Howard, 1989, p. 12.

3. Hinman, diary entry, May 20, 1864.

4. White, diary entry, May 21, 1864.

5. Ibid.; Walker, *History of the Second Army Corps*, pp. 491–92.

6. Miller, *North Anna Campaign*, p. 27; Walker, *History of the Second Army Corps*, pp. 491–92; Long, *Memoirs of Robert E. Lee*, p. 344.

7. Geer to Jule, May 22, 1864.

8. Miller, *North Anna Campaign*, p. 42; *War of the Rebellion*, ser. 1, vol. 36, pt. 1, p. 363; Humphreys, *Virginia Campaign*, p. 127; Walker, *History of the Second Army Corps*, p. 493; Hinman, diary entry, May 23, 1864.

9. *War of the Rebellion*, ser. 1, vol. 36, pt. 1, p. 363; Miller, *North Anna Campaign*, p. 58; Hinman, diary entry, May 23, 1864.

10. White, diary entry, May 23, 1864; Walker, *History of the Second Army Corps*, p. 494; Miller, *North Anna Campaign*, pp. 57–58.

11. Willson, *Disaster, Struggle, Triumph*, p. 313; Walker, *History of the Second Army Corps*, p. 494; Miller, *North Anna Campaign*, pp. 92–93; Hinman, diary entry, May 24, 1864.

12. Miller, *North Anna Campaign*, pp. 118–20; *War of the Rebellion*, ser. 1, vol. 36, pt. 1, pp. 363–64; White, diary entry, May 24, 1864.

13. Hinman, diary entry, May 25, 1864.

14. Phisterer, *New York in the War of the Rebellion*, p. 3313; *War of the Rebellion*, ser. 1, vol. 36, pt. 1, p. 364; Adjutant General's Report, pp. 784, 918.

15. Wright, *Historical Sketches of the Town of Moravia from 1791 to 1918*, p. 121.

16. Adjutant General's Report, pp. 671–930; Phisterer, *New York in the War of the Rebellion*, pp. 3306–09.

17. Walker, *History of the Second Army Corps*, pp. 497–98; Miller, *North Anna Campaign*, pp. 130–31; *War of the Rebellion*, ser. 1, vol. 36, pt. 3, pp. 214–15.

18. *War of the Rebellion*, ser. 1, vol. 36, pt. 1, p. 364.

19. White, diary entry, May 27, 1864.

20. *Ibid.*, May 28, 1864; *War of the Rebellion*, ser. 1, vol. 36, pt. 1, p. 364; Willson, *Disaster, Struggle, Triumph*, p. 314; Welcher, *Eastern Theater*, p. 983; Louis J. Baltz, *The Battle of Cold Harbor, May 27–June 13, 1864*, H. E. Howard, 1994, pp. 21–22; Hinman, diary entry, May 28, 1864.
21. Walker, *History of the Second Army Corps*, p. 500; Simons, *A Regimental History*, p. 215; *War of the Rebellion*, ser. 1, vol. 36, pt. 1, p. 364 and Pt. 3, p. 299; Baltz, *Battle of Cold Harbor*, p. 29; Humphreys, *Virginia Campaign*, p. 166.
22. *War of the Rebellion*, ser. 1, vol. 36, pt. 1, p. 365 and pt. 3, pp. 328–29; *ADAU*, July 6, 1864; Phisterer, *New York in the War of the Rebellion*, p. 3311; Adjutant General's Report, pp. 671–930; Military service record for Edgar Dudley, National Archive, Washington, D.C.
23. Clark, *Military History of Wayne County*, p. 93f.
24. Baltz, *Battle of Cold Harbor*, pp. 58–60; Walker, *History of the Second Army Corps*, p. 503; Humphreys, *Virginia Campaign*, p. 170.
25. Walker, *History of the Second Army Corps*, p. 503; Benton to parents, June 5, 1864; Hinman, diary entry, May 31, 1864; *ADAU*, July 6, 1864; *War of the Rebellion*, ser. 1, vol. 36, pt. 1, p. 366; Adjutant General's Report, p. 834; If the list of casualties presented in the *ADAU* is any indication, Companies A and H were probably the two companies posted out in front of the regiment as it moved across the creek and were later posted on the skirmish line.
26. Baltz, *Battle of Cold Harbor*, pp. 65–70; Porter, *Campaigning with Grant*, p. 162; Humphreys, *Virginia Campaign*, p. 171; Trudeau, *Bloody Roads South*, pp. 262–63.
27. Walker, *History of the Second Army Corps*, p. 503; Trudeau, *Bloody Roads South*, p. 268; *War of the Rebellion*, ser. 1, vol. 36, pt. 1, p 366; Humphreys, *Virginia Campaign*, p. 176.
28. R. Wayne Maney, *Marching to Cold Harbor: Victory and Failure, 1864*. Shippensburg, PA: White Mane, 1995, p. 18; Welcher, *Eastern Theater*, p. 986; Trudeau, *Bloody Roads South*, pp. 272–73.
29. *ADAU*, July 16, 1864; White, diary entry, June 1, 1864; Hinman, diary entry, June 1, 1864; Wright, *Historical Sketches of the Town of Moravia From 1791 to 1918*, p. 121.
30. Walker, *History of the Second Army Corps*, p. 506; White, diary entry, June 1, 1864; Trudeau, *Bloody Roads South*, p. 275.
31. Hinman, diary entry, June 2, 1864; *ADAU*, July 16, 1864; Adjutant General's Report, pp. 696, 766, 776, 839, 867; The prisoners stayed at Libby Prison until the June 8, when they traveled by rail to Andersonville.
32. Adjutant General's Report, p. 867.
33. Maney, *Marching to Cold Harbor*, pp. 116–17; Walker, *History of the Second Army Corps*, p. 506; Welcher, *Eastern Theater*, p. 989.
34. Trudeau, *Bloody Roads South*, pp. 277–279; *War of the Rebellion*, ser. 1, vol. 36, pt. 1, p. 366; Humphreys, *Virginia Campaign*, pp. 178–79; White, diary entry, June 2, 1864.
35. Maney, *Marching to Cold Harbor*, p. 132; Baltz, *Battle of Cold Harbor*, pp. 130–32; White, diary entry, June 2, 1864.
36. Walker, *History of the Second Army Corps*, p. 507; Baltz, *Battle of Cold Harbor*, pp. 136–38; Davis, Perry, and Kirkley, plate 97, no. 2; Porter, *Campaigning with Grant*, p. 174.

37. Maney, *Marching to Cold Harbor*, p. 126; Baltz, *Battle of Cold Harbor*, p. 134; Davis, Perry, and Kirkley, plate 97, no. 2.
38. Humphreys, *Virginia Campaign*, p.180; Catton, *Grant Takes Command*, p. 261.
39. Walker, *History of the Second Army Corps*, pp. 509–10; Humphreys, *Virginia Campaign*, pp. 182–83; Maney, *Marching to Cold Harbor*, pp. 136–37.
40. Baltz, *Battle of Cold Harbor*, p. 140; Humphreys, *Virginia Campaign*, p. 183; Walker, *History of the Second Army Corps*, pp. 510–11; *War of the Rebellion*, ser. 1, vol. 36, pt. 1, p. 366; Porter, *Campaigning with Grant*, p. 175.
41. Ulysses S. Grant to C. M Failing, February 14, 1884. U.S. Military History Institute, Carlisle Barracks, PA.
42. *ADAU*, July 16, 1864; *War of the Rebellion*, ser. 1, vol. 36, pt. 1, p. 166; Walker, *History of the Second Army Corps*, p. 512; Adjutant General's Report, pp. 671–930.
43. *War of the Rebellion*, ser. 1, vol. 36, pt. 1, pp. 366–67; Trudeau, *Bloody Roads South*, p. 297; Walker, *History of the Second Army Corps*, p. 511.
44. *War of the Rebellion*, ser. 1, vol. 36, pt. 1, p. 367; White, diary entry, June 4, 1864; Walker, *History of the Second Army Corps*, p. 517.
45. Trudeau, *Bloody Roads South*, p. 308; Baltz, *Battle of Cold Harbor*, pp. 184–91; Walker, *History of the Second Army Corps*, p. 518; Humphreys, *Virginia Campaign*, p. 192; *War of the Rebellion*, ser. 1, vol. 36, pt. 1, p. 368; The first letter regarding the collection of wounded was sent to General Lee by General Grant on June 5. Over the next two days, Grant and Lee sent letters back and forth, debating the proper procedures for requesting a flag of truce. General Grant wanted to avoid the appearance of being labeled the battle's loser, and General Lee intended to humble his opponent by making him adhere to the formal procedures. While the two generals debated the finer points of etiquette, many good soldiers who otherwise might have lived, suffered and died from neglect.
46. *ADAU*, October 17, 1901; MacDougall was known to keep a cow, and it was not uncommon for the beast to be tied to the colonel's personal wagon when on campaign.
47. Geer to friend Julia, June 6 and 12, 1864.
48. White, diary entry, June 7, 1864.
49. Baltz, *Battle of Cold Harbor*, p. 205; Humphreys, *Virginia Campaign*, p. 196; Walker, *History of the Second Army Corps*, p. 520.
50. Welcher, *Eastern Theater*, p. 994; B. F. Cooling, *Jubal Early's Raid on Washington, 1864*, Nautical and Aviation, 1989, pp. 10–11.
51. Noah A. Trudeau, *The Last Citadel*, Boston, MA: Little, Brown, 1991, p. 14; Walker, *History of the Second Army Corps*, pp. 520–21; White, diary entry, June 12, 1864; Jacob H. Cole, *Under Five Commanders or the Boys Experience with the Army of the Potomac*. Patterson, NJ: News Printing, 1906, p. 214; Adjutant General's Report, pp. 690–931.

Chapter 10

1. Petersburg was known as the Cockade City because of the Cockade monument erected in honor of its War of 1812 volunteers. Each soldier that enlisted

wore a cockade on the side of his hat; Benton to parents, July 22, 1864.

2. *War of the Rebellion*, ser. 1, vol. 40, pt. 1, p. 180; White, June 12, 1864; Walker, *History of the Second Army Corps*, p. 525; Cole, *Under Five Commanders*, p. 214.

3. Trudeau, *Last Citadel*, p. 22; *War of the Rebellion*, ser. 1, vol. 40, pt. 1, p. 180; Walker, *History of the Second Army Corps*, p. 525.

4. Thomas J. Howe, *The Petersburg Campaign: Wasted Valor, June 15–18, 1864*, H. E. Howard, 1988, p. 27; Trudeau, *Last Citadel*, pp. 11, 19, 501.

5. *War of the Rebellion*, ser. 1, vol. 40, pt. 1, pp. 303–304; Walker, *History of the Second Army Corps*, p. 526; Humphreys, *Virginia Campaign*, p. 205; Trudeau, *Last Citadel*, p. 36.

6. Trudeau, *Last Citadel*, pp. 22, 42; *War of the Rebellion*, ser. 1, vol. 40, pt. 1, p. 305 and pt. 2, p. 437; Humphreys, *Virginia Campaign*, p. 211; Walker, *History of the Second Army Corps*, p. 527; Cole, *Under Five Commander*, p. 214.

7. Williams C. Davis, *Death in the Trenches: Grant at Petersburg*, Alexandria, VA: Time Life, 1986, p. 44; Richard Wayne Lykes, *Campaign for Petersburg*, U.S. Government Printing Office, 1970, pp. 11–12; Trudeau, *Last Citadel*, pp. 41–42; Walker, *History of the Second Army Corps*, p. 527.

8. *War of the Rebellion*, ser. 1, vol. 40, pt. 1, pp. 303–305; Howe, *Petersburg Campaign*, p. 43; Walker, *History of the Second Army Corps*, p. 528.

9. Cole, *Under Five Commanders*, p. 215; Howe, *Petersburg Campaign*, p. 44.

10. Howe, *Petersburg Campaign*, pp. 49–50; Walker, *History of the Second Army Corps*, p. 535; *War of the Rebellion*, ser. 1, vol. 40, pt. 1, p. 306; Cole, *Under Five Commanders*, pp. 214–15; Mahood, *Written in Blood*, p. 280.

11. *Ibid.*; Welcher, *Eastern Theater*, p. 839.

12. Colonel MacDougall to George J. Letchworth, June 25, 1864.

13. Allen Hoxie to mother, n.d.

14. Phisterer, *New York in the War of the Rebellion*, p. 3319; *ADAU*, July 16, 1864.

15. Warren to sister, July 1, 1864.

16. Phisterer, *New York in the War of the Rebellion*, p. 3319; Cole, *Under Five Commanders*, p. 215; *War of the Rebellion*, ser. 1, vol. 40, pt. 1, p. 306; Howe, *Petersburg Campaign*, p. 57; Mahood, *Written in Blood*, p. 280.

17. Howe, *Petersburg Campaign*, p. 57; *ADAU*, July 16, 1864; Phisterer, *New York in the War of the Rebellion*, p. 3306; Adjutant General's Report, pp. 671–930.

18. Warren to sister, July 1, 1864; Howe, *Petersburg Campaign*, pp. 77–78, 101; Simons, *A Regimental History*, pp. 226–27.

19. Howe, *Petersburg Campaign*, pp. 77–78, 101; Simons, *A Regimental History*, pp. 226–27; *War of the Rebellion*, ser. 1, vol. 40, pt. 1, p. 306; Adjutant General's Report, pp. 671–930.

20. Welcher, *Eastern Theater*, p. 840; *War of the Rebellion*, ser. 1, vol. 40, pt. 1, p. 318; Howe, *Petersburg Campaign*, p. 113.

21. *Ibid.*; Howe, *Petersburg Campaign*, pp. 106, 110.

22. Walker, *History of the Second Army Corps*, p. 541; In the early hours of June 18, General Birney assumed command of the II Corps when General Hancock stepped down due to complications with the wound he received at Gettysburg.

23. Welcher, *Eastern Theater*, p. 841; Howe, *Petersburg Campaign*, pp. 120–23; Trudeau, *Last Citadel*, pp. 52–54.

24. Davis, *Death in the Trenches*, p. 127; Billings, *Hard Tack and Coffee*, pp. 380–80.

25. Davis, *Death in the Trenches*, p. 127.

26. Benton to parents, July 22, 1864.

27. Welcher, *Eastern Theater*, p. 844; White, diary entry, June 21, 1864; Adjutant General's Report, pp. 671–930.

28. Clark, *Military History of Wayne County*, p. 579.

29. *War of the Rebellion*, ser. 1, vol. 42, pt. 1, p. 318; Humphreys, *Virginia Campaign*, pp. 226–28; Davis, *Death in the Trenches*, p. 53; Welcher, *Eastern Theater*, p. 844.

30. Welcher, *Eastern Theater*, p. 844; Cole, *Under Five Commanders*, p. 217; Phisterer, *New York in the War of the Rebellion*, p. 3314; Trudeau, *Last Citadel*, p. 68; Adjutant General's Report, p. 812; In *Military History of Wayne County*, author Lewis Clark states that Colonel MacDougall personally led the regiment in a charge upon a battery, which resulted in the capture of "a rebel Colonel and others." It is doubtful that MacDougall, the brigade commander, would have led a skirmish line in any action, let alone a charge upon a battery. This action was not reported by any other regiment in the brigade nor is it reported in the official records.

31. Walker, *History of the Second Army Corps*, p. 544; Humphreys, *Virginia Campaign*, p. 227; Trudeau, *Last Citadel*, p. 69.

32. *Ibid.*; *War of the Rebellion*, ser. 1, vol. 40, pt. 1, p. 319; Welcher, *Eastern Theater*, p. 844.

33. Trudeau, *Last Citadel*, p. 72; Long, *Memoirs of Robert E. Lee*, p. 377; Cole, *Under Five Commanders*, p. 218.

34. Trudeau, *Last Citadel*, p. 72; *War of the Rebellion*, ser. 1, vol. 40, pt. 1, p. 330.

35. Geer to Jule, June 26, 1864.

36. *Ibid.*

37. White, diary entry, June 22, 1864.

38. Trudeau, *Last Citadel*, pp. 78–79; Humphreys, *Virginia Campaign*, pp. 228–29.

39. *ADAU*, July 16, 1864; Adjutant General's Report, pp. 852, 853, 905.

40. Military service record of Charles Todd, National Archives, Washington, D.C.

41. Geer to Jule, June 26, 1864.

42. George Peckham to Mrs. Hoxie, July 10, 1864, courtesy of Ken Hoxie; *ADAU*, July 16, 1864; Regimental Returns for May and June, 1864, RG 94, National Archives, Washington, D.C.

43. Trudeau, *Last Citadel*, p. 80; Humphreys, *Virginia Campaign*, p. 229; Walker, *History of the Second Army Corps*, p. 546; *War of the Rebellion*, ser. 1, vol. 40, pt. 1, p. 319.

44. Military service record for Lewis W. Husk, National Archives, Washington, D.C.; Regimental Returns for July, 1864, RG 94, National Archives, Washington, D.C.

45. Walker, *History of the Second Army Corps*, p. 550.

46. Welcher, *Eastern Theater*, p. 851; Humphreys, *Virginia Campaign*, pp. 243–44.

47. *Ibid.*; Cooling, *Jubal Early's Raid on Washington, 1864*, pp. 75–78; Porter, *Campaigning with Grant*, pp. 237–39.

48. Military service record of Clinton D. MacDougall, National Archives, Washington, D.C.

49. Geer to Jule, June 26, 1864.
50. Porter, *Campaigning with Grant*, pp. 258–59; Humphreys, *Virginia Campaign*, pp. 247–48; Welcher, *Eastern Theater*, p. 852; Johnson and Buel, *Battles and Leaders*, vol. 4, p. 546.
51. Benton to father, August 2, 1864.
52. White, entries dated July 26 and 27, 1864.
53. Benton, letter to father dated August 2, 1864.
54. *War of the Rebellion*, ser. 1, vol. 40, pt. 1, p. 321; Welcher, *Eastern Theater*, p. 852; Walker, *History of the Second Army Corps*, p. 562.
55. Benton to father, August 2, 1864.
56. *War of the Rebellion*, ser. 1, vol. 40, pt. 1, pp. 321–22; Welcher, *Eastern Theater*, p. 852; White, diary entry, July 28, 1864.
57. Walker, *History of the Second Army Corps*, p. 565; *War of the Rebellion*, ser. 1, vol. 40, pt. 1, p. 322; Humphreys, *Virginia Campaign*, p. 248; White, diary entry, July 28, 1864; Benton to father, August 2, 1864.
58. Davis, *Death in the Trenches*, pp. 74–75; Humphreys, *Virginia Campaign*, p. 250; Benton to father, August 2, 1864; Trudeau, *Last Citadel*, pp. 106–107.
59. *War of the Rebellion*, ser. 1, vol. 40, pt. 1, p. 323; Humphreys, *Virginia Campaign*, p. 249; Walker, *History of the Second Army Corps*, p. 566; Benton, to father, August 2, 1864.
60. Benton to father, August 2, 1864.
61. *Ibid.*
62. *Ibid.*; *War of the Rebellion*, ser. 1, vol. 40, pt. 1, p. 324; Trudeau, *Last Citadel*, pp. 117–21, 127.
63. Benton to father, August 2, 1864.
64. *War of the Rebellion*, ser. 1, vol. 40, pt. 1, p. 324; Walker, *History of the Second Army Corps*, p. 568.

Chapter 11

1. White, diary entry, August 25 1864.
2. Davis, *Death in the Trenches*, p. 95; Walker, *History of the Second Army Corps*, p. 569; Trudeau, *Last Citadel*, pp. 143–46.
3. *Ibid.*; Humphreys, *Virginia Campaign*, p. 269.
4. *War of the Rebellion*, ser. 1, vol. 42, pt. 1, pp. 43, 47; White, diary entry, August 14, 1864; Humphreys, *Virginia Campaign*, p. 268.
5. White, diary entries, August 12–14, 1864.
6. Humphreys, *Virginia Campaign*, pp. 269–70; Walker, *History of the Second Army Corps*, p. 571; Trudeau, *Last Citadel*, p. 150; Welcher, *Eastern Theater*, p. 861.
7. John Horn, *Petersburg Campaign: The Destruction of the Weldon Railroad; Deep Bottom, Globe Tavern and Reams Station August 14–25, 1864*, H. E. Howard, 1991, p. 16; Trudeau, *Last Citadel*, p. 151; Welcher, *Eastern Theater*, p. 862; *War of the Rebellion*, ser. 1, vol. 42, pt. 1, p. 241; White, diary entry, August 14, 1864.
8. Walker, *History of the Second Army Corps*, p. 571; Welcher, *Eastern Theater*, 862; *War of the Rebellion*, ser. 1, vol. 42, pt. 1, p. 47.
9. Trudeau, *Last Citadel*, pp. 150–52; Walker, *History of the Second Army Corps*, p. 575.
10. Horn, *Petersburg Campaign*, p. 18; *War of the Rebellion*, ser. 1, vol. 42, pt. 1, p. 241; Walker, *History of the Second Army Corps*, pp. 573–74.
11. Horn, *Petersburg Campaign*, p. 18.
12. Walker, *History of the Second Army Corps*, p. 575; *War of the Rebellion*, ser. 1, vol. 42, pt. 1, p. 241; Trudeau, *Last Citadel*, p. 153; Porter, *Campaigning with Grant*, p. 277.
13. Trudeau, *Last Citadel*, pp. 155–56; Walker, *History of the Second Army Corps*, p. 576; Horn, *Petersburg Campaign*, pp. 28–31; *War of the Rebellion*, ser. 1, vol. 42, pt. 1, p. 242.
14. Willson, *Disaster, Struggle, Triumph*, pp. 316–17; *War of the Rebellion*, ser. 1, vol. 42, pt. 1, p. 244; Walker, *History of the Second Army Corps*, p. 580.
15. Military service record of Lewis W. Husk, Surgeons Certificate, August 24, 1864, National Archives, Washington, D.C.; Although the ranking officer in the regiment after Major Husk, Captain Marcus Murdock had just received his commission May 23, 1864. The only other captain in the regiment, John Lockwood of Company F, received his commission on June 4, 1864; *War of the Rebellion*, ser. 1, vol. 42, pt. 1, p. 244.
16. Trudeau, *Last Citadel*, p. 168; *War of the Rebellion*, ser. 1, vol. 42, pt. 1, p. 244.
17. Walker, *History of the Second Army Corps*, p. 581; Horn, *Petersburg Campaign*, p. 118.
18. Trudeau, *Last Citadel*, pp. 69, 177; *War of the Rebellion*, ser. 1, vol. 42, pt. 1, p. 244; Welcher, *Eastern Theater*, p. 869; Today the only remnant of the station is a water-filled pit located where the station's water tower once stood.
19. *Ibid.*; Horn, *Petersburg Campaign*, p. 118; White, diary entry, August 24, 1864.
20. Trudeau, *Last Citadel*, p. 179; Horn, *Petersburg Campaign*, p. 120; Welcher, *Eastern Theater*, pp. 869–70.
21. Horn, *Petersburg Campaign*, p. 117; Humphreys, *Virginia Campaign*, p. 279; Trudeau, *Last Citadel*, p. 182; Emil Rosenblatt, ed., *Anti-Rebel: The Civil War Letters of Wilbur Fisk*, Croton-on-Hudson, NY: Rosenblatt, 1983, pp. 233–35.
22. Horn, *Petersburg Campaign*, p. 117; Walker, *History of the Second Army Corps*, p. 582; Not much is left of the works that once occupied Reams Station and what little portions that do exist are on private property. The scene of the fighting is overgrown with scrub brush and stands of pine and bears little resemblance to its 1864 appearance. Many of the landmarks have changed location as well. When the Weldon Railroad changed its course, what was once the railroad bed is now Halifax Road. Little remains of the original Halifax Road. One of the last remaining sections, Corn Drive, runs in front of Oak Grove Church. The existing church is not the original structure, although it is located on the same site where the original church was located during the battle. The original church had been moved closer to the current Halifax Road, used for other purposes and has since fallen into disrepair and left to rot.
23. Horn, *Petersburg Campaign*, p. 127; Trudeau, *Last Citadel*, p. 182; Regimental Returns for July and August 1864, RG 94, National Archives, Washington, D.C.
24. Horn, *Petersburg Campaign*, p. 127; Phisterer, *New York in the War of the Rebellion*, pp. 2982, 3493; *War of the Rebellion*, ser. 1, vol. 42, pt. 1, p. 288.
25. Horn, *Petersburg Campaign*, p. 127; Trudeau, *Last Citadel*, p. 182.
26. Davis, *Death in the Trenches*, pp. 105–107; Humphreys, *Virginia Campaign*, p. 279; Horn, *Petersburg Campaign*, p. 129.
27. Trudeau, *Last Citadel*, pp. 185–86; *War of the Rebellion*, ser. 1, vol. 42, pt. 2, p. 468.
28. Horn, *Petersburg Campaign*, pp. 130; Trudeau,

Last Citadel, p. 184; Walker, *History of the Second Army Corps*, pp. 587–88.
  29. Horn, *Petersburg Campaign*, p. 120, 131; Bacarella, *Lincoln's Foreign Legion*, pp. 180–81; *War of the Rebellion*, ser. 1, vol. 42, pt. 1, p. 288.
  30. Horn, *Petersburg Campaign*, p. 131; *War of the Rebellion*, ser. 1, vol. 42, pt. 1, p. 47; Trudeau, *Last Citadel*, p. 184.
  31. *Ibid*.; *War of the Rebellion*, ser. 1, vol. 42, pt. 1, p. 245; Walker, *History of the Second Army Corps*, p. 588.
  32. Trudeau, *Last Citadel*, pp. 185–86; *War of the Rebellion*, ser. 1, vol. 42, pt. 2, p. 468.
  33. Horn, *Petersburg Campaign*, p. 155; *War of the Rebellion*, ser. 1, vol. 42, pt. 1, pp. 252, 288.
  34. Horn, *Petersburg Campaign*, pp. 137–38; Welcher, *Eastern Theater*, p. 871.
  35. *War of the Rebellion*, ser. 1, vol. 42, pt. 1, p. 252; Trudeau, *Last Citadel*, p. 186; Horn, *Petersburg Campaign*, p. 138.
  36. Horn, *Petersburg Campaign*, p. 155; *War of the Rebellion*, ser. 1, vol. 42, pt. 1, pp. 245, 289; Welcher, *Eastern Theater*, p. 871.
  37. Horn, *Petersburg Campaign*, p. 155; *War of the Rebellion*, ser. 1, vol. 42, pt. 1, p. 289; Welcher, *Eastern Theater*, p. 871.
  38. Bacarella, *Lincoln's Foreign Legion*, p. 181; Mahood, *Written in Blood*, p. 308; Trudeau, *Last Citadel*, p. 187; Welcher, *Eastern Theater*, p. 871; Horn, *Petersburg Campaign*, p. 157.
  39. Trudeau, *Last Citadel*, p. 187; Welcher, *Eastern Theater*, p. 871; *War of the Rebellion*, ser. 1, vol. 42, pt. 1, p. 253; Walker, *History of the Second Army Corps*, p. 594.
  40. *War of the Rebellion*, ser. 1, vol. 42, pt. 1, p. 289; *ADAU*, September 8, 1864; Hoff to wife, August 30, 1864; Frederick, *Story of a Regiment*, p. 264.
  41. Horn, *Petersburg Campaign*, p. 159; *War of the Rebellion*, ser. 1, vol. 42, pt. 1, p. 289.
  42. *Ibid*.; Mahood, *Written in Blood*, p. 308; *War of the Rebellion*, ser. 1, vol. 42, pt. 1, p. 226; Walker, *History of the Second Army Corps*, p. 594.
  43. Walker, *History of the Second Army Corps*, p. 594.
  44. *War of the Rebellion*, ser. 1, vol. 42, pt. 1, pp. 277, 289; Horn, *Petersburg Campaign*, p. 165; Trudeau, *Last Citadel*, p. 188.
  45. *Ibid*.
  46. *War of the Rebellion*, ser. 1, vol. 42, pt. 1, p. 289; Horn, *Petersburg Campaign*, p. 170; Walker, *History of the Second Army Corps*, p. 599; White, diary entry, August 25, 1864.
  47. Adjutant General's Report, p. 817; *ADAU*, September 8, 1864; Phisterer, *New York in the War of the Rebellion*, pp. 3306–09; Captain Lockwood was killed while trying to escape from his captors. Unfortunately, the date of his death is not known.
  48. Lombard was later paroled from prison and returned to the regiment. When the war ended and the 111th mustered out of service, Lombard was transferred to the Fourth New York Heavy Artillery.
  49. Hoff to wife, August 30, 1864; The national colors was returned to the State of New York in 1888. It is not known if the regiment ever received new colors to replace the colors captured at Ream's Station. A flag in the collection of Mike Nusbaum of Williamsburg, Virginia, came from the estate of Marcus Murdock and was thought to be a replacement flag for the one captured at Ream's Station. But this flag is made of cotton, is three feet tall by five feet wide and has 36 stars. The number of stars on national colors did not increase to 36 until July 4, 1865. Therefore, it is very doubtful that this flag belonged to the 111th during the war. In Albany, New York, there is one national flag, a regimental flag, and two guidons attributed to the 111th. The regimental flag along with the guidons were sent to Auburn in December 1864 and put on display; General Gibbon was so infuriated by the conduct of some of his regiments that he ordered those that lost their colors would not be allowed to carry new colors until they earned the right.
  50. Walker, *History of the Second Army Corps*, pp. 601–602; *War of the Rebellion*, ser. 1, vol. 42, pt. 2, p. 486; Glenn Tucker, *Hancock the Superb*, reprint, Dayton, OH: Morningside Bookshop, 1980, p. 255; A cause of further despair was the fact that Hancock had just received his promotion to brigadier general in the regular army.

Chapter 12

  1. Chauncey Smith to wife, October 18, 1864.
  2. *War of the Rebellion*, ser. 1, vol. 42, pt. 1, pp. 42, 246; Regimental Returns for August 1864, RG 94, National Archives, Washington, D.C.
  3. White, diary entry, August 27, 1864.
  4. *Ibid*.
  5. Hoff to wife, August 4, 1864.
  6. Benton to parents, September 15, 1864.
  7. Hoff to wife, September 4, 1864.
  8. *War of the Rebellion*, ser. 1, vol. 42, pt. 1, p. 247; White, diary entries, September 6–9, 1864; Benton to parents, September 15, 1864; Fort Hays was named for the regiment's old division commander, Alexander Hays, while Fort Sedgwick was named for the dead VI Corps commander, John Sedgwick.
  9. *ADAU*, August 28 and 31, 1864; Military service record of Clinton D. MacDougall, National Archives, Washington, D.C.
  10. Donald Dale Jackson, *Twenty Million Yankees: The Northern Home Front*, Alexandria, VA: Time Life, 1985, p. 110; Humphreys, *Virginia Campaign*, p. 408; Porter, *Campaigning with Grant*, pp. 279–80; Walker, *History of the Second Army Corps*, p. 612; James Geary, *We Need Men: The Union Draft in the Civil War*, DeKalb: Northern Illinois University Press, 1991, p. 152.
  11. *ADAU*, August 24, 1864; Geary, *We Need Men*, pp. 34–35; Jackson, *Twenty Million Yankees*, p. 95; During the previous drafts, the money raised through commutation helped ease the burden of bounties on the states. But without the commutation fees, the cities and states were forces to shoulder the entire cost of the bounties themselves.
  12. *ADAU*, August 23, 1864; Benton to parents, September 15, 1864.
  13. *Ibid*.; Billings, *Hard Tack and Coffee*, p. 215.
  14. Bell I. Wiley, *The Life of Billy Yank*, Garden City, NJ: Doubleday, 1952, p. 275; Jackson, *Twenty Million Yankees*, p. 89.
  15. *ADAU*, May 31, 1864.
  16. Captain J. H. Borden 83rd PA to Brigadier General L. Thomas, Adjutant General Washington, D.C., September 19, 1864, RG 94, National Archives, Washington, D.C.
  17. Borden to Thomas, September 19, 1864.

18. Benton to parents, September 21, 1864.
19. Hoff to wife, September 14, 1864.
20. *Ibid.*
21. Adjutant General's Report, pp. 731, 835, 877; Phisterer, *New York in the War of the Rebellion*, pp. 3306–10; Military service records of Roland Dennis, Lafayette Mumford, and Abner Seeley, National Archives, Washington, D.C.
22. Adjutant General's Report, pp. 683, 887, 900; Phisterer, *New York in the War of the Rebellion*, pp. 3306–10; Military service records of Silas Belding, John C. Smith, and David Taylor, National Archives, Washington, D.C.; George Cowles, ed., *Landmarks of Wayne County, New York*, Syracuse, NY: D. Mason, 1895, p. 24.
23. Adjutant General's Report, pp. 758, 785, 832, 838, 857, 893; Phisterer, *New York in the War of the Rebellion*, pp. 3306–10; Military service records of Charles Furman, Esek Hoff, George Moore, Reuben Myers, Stephan Pyatt, and Daniel Sterling, National Archives, Washington, D.C.; Stephen Pyatt was discharged from the 17th New York in November 1862, due to illness caused by exposure; There was some controversy surrounding the commission of Charles Furman. According to his service record, he was never officially discharged from the 138th New York (Ninth New York Heavy Artillery). In December, Furman had to submit an official letter requesting his discharge from the 138th. The matter would not be settled until after the New Year.
24. Adjutant General's Report, pp. 769, 853, 919; Phisterer, *New York in the War of the Rebellion*, pp. 3306–10; Military service records of August Green, Robert Perry, and Patrick Welch, National Archives, Washington, D.C.
25. Smith, notes from speech delivered to Grand Army of the Republic, p. 2.
26. Smith, notes from speech, p. 3.
27. *Ibid.*
28. Smith, notes from speech, p. 4; Captain Daniel Sterling was only 29 years old. A number of the new recruits were in their thirties or forties.
29. Adjutant General's Report, pp. 748, 788; Chauncey Smith to Fanny and Little Ones, October 18, 1864; Smith was referring to the fact that the three men enlisted for a term of one year and hoped that they would be able to live through that term together.
30. Hoff to wife, September 14, 1864.
31. *Ibid.*
32. White, diary entry, September 20, 1864.
33. Trudeau, *Last Citadel*, pp. 207–208; Humphreys, *Virginia Campaign*, p. 284; Richard J. Sommers, *Richmond Redeemed: The Siege at Petersburg*, Garden City, NJ: Doubleday, 1981, pp. 21–22; Porter, *Campaigning with Grant*, p. 299.
34. Hoff to wife, September 24, 1864.
35. *Ibid.*
36. Humphreys, *Virginia Campaign*, p. 284; Sommers, *Richmond Redeemed*, pp. 29, 36–37; Porter, *Campaigning with Grant*, p. 300.
37. Humphreys, *Virginia Campaign*, p. 285; Sommers, *Richmond Redeemed*, pp. 39, 46; Welcher, *Eastern Theater*, p. 877.
38. Humphreys, *Virginia Campaign*, p. 291; Trudeau, *Last Citadel*, p. 213; Walker, *History of the Second Army Corps*, p. 607.
39. Trudeau, *Last Citadel*, p. 213; Welcher, *Eastern Theater*, p. 879.
40. *War of the Rebellion*, ser. 1, vol. 42, pt. 1, p. 44; Benton to parents, September 21, 1864; Hoff to wife, October 9, 1864.
41. Jackson, *Twenty Million Yankees*, pp. 152–54; Bruce Catton, *The Army of the Potomac: A Stillness at Appomattox*, Garden City, NJ: Doubleday, 1953, pp. 323–24; Hoff to wife, September 4, 1864.
42. Jackson, *Twenty Million Yankees*, pp. 152–54.
43. Benton parents, October 18, 1864.
44. *ADAU*, September 10, 1864; Copperheads, or antiwar Democrats, were northerners who opposed the war effort. They were vocal opponents of the Lincoln administration and how it ran the war.
45. Benton to parents, September 15, 1864.
46. *ADAU*, October 22, 1864; Captain Marcus Murdock to Lieutenant George Mitchell, A.A.A.G, RG 94, National Archives, Washington, D.C.; Porter, *Campaigning with Grant*, pp. 321–23.
47. Robert L Drummond, "Personal Reminiscences of Prison Life During the War of the Rebellion," speech, Hamilton College, February 22, 1901, p. 4.
48. Benton to parents, October 18, 1864; Henry Jeffery to parents, October 19, 1864; Chauncey Smith to wife and children, October 23, 1864.
49. Jeffery to parents, October 11, 1864.
50. Smith to family, October 18, 1864.
51. Jeffery to parents, October 19, 1864.
52. Drummond, "Personal Reminiscences," p. 7.
53. Military service records of Clinton D. MacDougall and Lewis W. Husk, National Archives, Washington, D.C.
54. Phisterer, *New York in the War of the Rebellion*, p. 3311; Military Service record of Joseph Corning, 111th New York, National Archives, Washington, D.C. According to the service record, Corning was not officially mustered in to the rank of major until October 27; George Contant, *Path of Blood: The True Story of the 33rd New York Volunteers*, Savannah, NY: Seeco, 1996, pp. 137–40.
55. *ADAU*, October 21, 1864; *War of the Rebellion*, ser. 1, vol. 42, pt. 2, p. 240; While the order disbanding the Consolidated Brigade was issued on October 2, the reformations of the Second and Third brigades were not officially approved until November 3, 1864.
56. Jeffery to parents, October 26, 1864.
57. Smith to wife and children, October 30, 1864.
58. *Ibid.*
59. Trudeau, *Last Citadel*, pp. 222–23; Humphreys, *Virginia Campaign*, p. 294; Walker, *History of the Second Army Corps*, pp. 613–15; Davis, *Death in the Trenches*, p. 154.
60. Jeffery to parents, October 26, 1864.
61. Trudeau, *Last Citadel*, pp. 228–29; Welcher, *Eastern Theater*, pp. 892–93.
62. Davis, *Death in the Trenches*, p. 154; Trudeau, *Last Citadel*, p. 232; Welcher, *Eastern Theater*, pp. 894–95.
63. Davis, *Death in the Trenches*, p. 155; Porter, *Campaigning with Grant*, pp. 309–10; Welcher, *Eastern Theater*, p. 895; Walker, *History of the Second Army Corps*, p. 617.
64. Trudeau, *Last Citadel*, p. 244; *War of the Rebellion*, ser. 1, vol. 42, pt. 2, p. 373.
65. White, diary entry, October 27, 1864.
66. Trudeaul, *Last Citadel*, p. 250; Welcher, *Eastern Theater*, p. 897; Walker, *History of the Second Army Corps*, p. 635.
67. Jeffery to parents, October 26, 1864.

68. Smith to wife and children, October 30, 1864.
69. *Ibid.*
70. *Ibid.*
71. Jeffery to parents, October 26, 1864.
72. Adjutant General's Report, pp. 671–930; Drummond, "Personal Reminiscences," p. 15.
73. *War of the Rebellion*, ser. 1, vol. 42, pt. 2, pp. 437, 486; Lieutenant Colonel Lewis W. Husk to Lieutenant Mitchell, A.A.A.G., II Corps, RG 94, National Archives, Washington, D.C.; Smith to wife and children, October 30, 1864.
74. *War of the Rebellion*, ser. 1, vol. 42, pt. 1, pp. 256–58 and pt. 2, p. 437; Court-martial transcript of Second Lieutenant Esek Hoff, RG 94, National Archives, Washington, D.C.
75. Smith to wife and children, October 30, 1864.
76. Jeffery to parents, October 30, 1864.
77. Drummond, "Personal Reminiscences," pp. 15–16.
78. Drummond, "Personal Reminiscences," p. 17; Court-martial transcript of Second Lieutenant Esek Hoff, RG 94, National Archives, Washington, D.C.; *War of the Rebellion*, ser. 1, vol. 42, pt. 1, p 258.
79. Testimony of Private James Doane, Court-martial transcript of Second Lieutenant Esek Hoff, RG 94, National Archives, Washington, D.C.
80. Drummond, "Personal Reminiscences," p. 17; In a letter written on July 14, 1913, to Miss Juliet Le Roy Mangum of Chapel Hill, North Carolina, Drummond claims it was members of the Eighth Alabama who captured the pickets from the regiment on the night of October 30. Although there is no other direct evidence to support this claim, there is a mention in the official records of an Alabama regiment capturing Union pickets on the night of October 30, 1864.
81. Smith, notes from speech, p. 8.
82. Drummond, "Personal Reminiscences," p. 17; Smith, notes from speech, p. 8.
83. Smith, notes from speech, p. 10.
84. *Ibid.*
85. Charges and specifications forwarded against Second Lieutenant Andrew Camp, military service record for Andrew Camp, National Archives, Washington, D.C.
86. Court-martial transcript of Second Lieutenant Esek Hoff, RG 94, National Archives, Washington, D.C.; *War of the Rebellion*, ser. 1, vol. 42, pt. 1, p. 258.
87. *War of the Rebellion*, ser. 1, vol. 42, pt. 2, p. 440; The final number of men captured was determined through extensive research of the Adjutant General's Report, individual military service records and regimental records from RG 94, National Archives, Washington, D.C. While some modern sources infer that men were captured on both October 30 and 31, all of the pickets were captured on the night of the 30th. None of the author's research of wartime sources indicates that men were taken prisoner on both nights.
88. The courts-martial transcripts of Lieutenant Colonel Lewis W. Husk and Second Lieutenants Andrew Camp and Esek Hoff, RG 94, National Archives, Washington, D.C.; *War of the Rebellion*, ser. 1, vol. 42, pt. 1, 256.
89. *War of the Rebellion*, ser. 1, vol. 42, pt. 1, p. 256.
90. The courts-martial transcripts of Lieutenant Colonel Lewis W. Husk and Second Lieutenants Andrew Camp and Esek Hoff, RG 94, National Archives, Washington, D.C.; Written statement of Esek Hoff, December 6, 1864, RG 94, National Archives, Washington, D.C.
91. Hoff to wife, November 6 and December 10, 1864; *War of the Rebellion*, ser. 1, vol. 42, pt. 1, p. 256; Military service record of Esek Hoff, National Archives, Washington, D.C.
92. Smith to wife and little ones, November 5, 1864; White, diary entry, November 5, 1864.
93. *Ibid.*; Adjutant General's Report, p. 821.
94. *Ibid.*
95. *Ibid.*
96. Smith to wife and children, October 30, 1864.
97. Hoff to wife, November 6, 1864; Geer to friend, November 11, 1864.
98. Geer, letters, November 11 and 18, 1864.
99. *Ibid.*
100. Geer to friend, November 23, 1864.
101. Geer, letters, November 11 and 18, 1864.
102. Smith to wife, November 23, 1864.
103. White, diary entry, November 23, 1864; Around this time the regiment was issued new uniforms, which consisted of a four-button sack, or fatigue, coat and sky-blue trousers.
104. Tucker, *Hancock the Superb*, p. 261; Geer to friend, November 23, 1864; Walker, *History of the Second Army Corps*, pp. 640–41.
105. C. D. MacDougall to General Winfield Hancock, December 17, 1864, RG 94, National Archives, Washington, D.C.
106. *War of the Rebellion*, ser. 1, vol. 42, pt. 1, p. 43; Walker, *History of the Second Army Corps*, p. 641; White, diary entry, November 30, 1864; Smith to wife and children, December 15, 1864; Hoff to wife, December 8, 1864; Geer to friend, December 4, 1864.
107. Geer to friend, December 4, 1864.
108. *War of the Rebellion*, ser. 1, vol. 42, pt. 1, pp. 43, 47; Trudeau, *Last Citadel*, p. 274; Geer to friend, December 11, 1864.
109. Humphreys, *Virginia Campaign*, p. 312; Trudeau, *Last Citadel*, p. 264; Welcher, *Eastern Theater*, p. 902.
110. *War of the Rebellion*, ser. 1, vol. 42, pt. 1, pp. 43, 47; Trudeau, *Last Citadel*, pp. 274–75; Welcher, *Eastern Theater*, p. 903; Humphreys, *Virginia Campaign*, pp. 312–13.
111. Welcher, *Eastern Theater*, p. 902; Trudeau, *Last Citadel*, pp. 276–77; Porter, *Campaigning with Grant*, p. 346.
112. *War of the Rebellion*, ser. 1, vol. 42, pt. 1, pp. 43, 47; Welcher, *Eastern Theater*, p. 903; Walker, *History of the Second Army Corps*, p. 642; White, diary entry, November 10, 1864.
113. Special Order No. 5, Headquarters 111th New York Vols., December 14, 1864, RG 94, National Archives, Washington, D.C.; Smith to wife, December 15, 1864.
114. Special Order No. 5

Chapter 13

1. Smith to wife and children, April 16, 1865.
2. Regimental Return for December 1864, RG 94, National Archives, Washington, D.C.; Smith to wife, January 4, 1865; Thomas Geer, diary entry, January 10, 1865.
3. Smith to wife, January 28, 1865.
4. Smith to wife, January 4, 1864.

5. Geer to Albert, January 13, 1865; Smith to wife, January 16, 1865; Moving a whole brigade forward was also used to advance the picket line closer to the enemy works. When the line was established and work on new entrenchments had begun, the regiments would fall back to their old line; Humphreys, *Virginia Campaign*, p. 311.
6. Smith to wife, sometime in January 1865.
7. Adjutant General's Report, pp. 671–930; Phisterer, *New York in the War of the Rebellion*, pp. 3306–09; John Fishback was temporarily assigned to the staff of General Madill. He was relieved from this duty on March 18, 1865, due to an excess of staff officers. Before the promotions were approved, each man was given a physical examination by the surgeons. It was the job of the doctors to certify that each prospective officer was a "sound and able bodied man and capable of performing all the duties of an officer in active field service."
8. Mahood, *Written in Blood*, p. 327; Priest, *Victory Without Triumph*, p. 198; Walker, *History of the Second Army Corps*, p. 643.
9. Headquarters Third Brigade, First Division, II Corps, letter from Colonel Clinton D. MacDougall to Major Richard A. Brown, January 17, 1864, RG 94, National Archives, Washington, D.C.; Phisterer, *New York in the War of the Rebellion*, p. 3311; The actual date of Major Corning's discharge from the 111th was February 3, 1865.
10. Jerry Korn, *Pursuit to Appomattox: The Last Battles*, Alexandria, VA: Time Life, 1987, p. 27; Long, *Memoirs of Robert E. Lee*, pp. 402–403; Humphreys, *Virginia Campaign*, p. 316.
11. Benton to parents, October 9, 1864.
12. Trudeau, *Last Citadel*, p. 313; *War of the Rebellion*, ser. 1, vol. 46, pt. 1, p. 202; Welcher, *Eastern Theater*, pp. 903–904; Smyth assumed command of the Second Division while General Gibbon was absent on leave. At the end of February, Gibbon was given the command of the XXIV Corps, and the command of the Second Division passed to General William Hays. After General Hancock's wounding at Gettysburg, Hays led the II Corps under General Warren.
13. Trudeau, *Last Citadel*, p. 314; Korn, *Pursuit to Appomattox*, p. 30; *War of the Rebellion*, ser. 1, vol. 46, pt. 1, p. 202.
14. Trudeau, *Last Citadel*, p. 315; Welcher, *Eastern Theater*, pp. 903–904; Walker, *History of the Second Army Corps*, pp. 648–49.
15. Humphreys, *Virginia Campaign*, pp. 314–15; Korn, *Pursuit to Appomattox*, pp. 30–31; Welcher, *Eastern Theater*, p. 906.
16. Trudeau, *Last Citadel*, p. 322; Walker, *History of the Second Army Corps*, p. 649; Welcher, *Eastern Theater*, p. 907; Humphreys, *Virginia Campaign*, p. 315.
17. Smith to wife, March 10, 1865; Geer, diary entries, March 1–10, 1865; Geer to friend, March 17, 1865.
18. Geer to friend, March 17, 1865; Geer, diary entry, March 18, 1865.
19. Military service record for James Dana Benton, National Archives, Washington, D.C.; Adjutant General's Report, p. 685.
20. *ADAU*, March 24, 1865; Mahood, *Written in Blood*, p. 332; Geer to Jule, March 2, 1865.
21. *ADAU*, March 24, 1865; Phisterer, *New York in the War of the Rebellion*, pp. 3306–09; Adjutant General's Report, p. 827.
22. Trudeau, *Last Citadel*, p. 330; Walker, *History of the Second Army Corps*, p. 650.
23. Trudeau, *Last Citadel*, pp. 330–31; Walker, *History of the Second Army Corps*, pp. 650–51; Welcher, *Eastern Theater*, p. 908.
24. Humphreys, *Virginia Campaign*, p. 320; Smith to wife, March 25, 1865; Walker, *History of the Second Army Corps*, pp. 650–51.
25. *War of the Rebellion*, ser. 1, vol. 46, pt. 1, pp. 203, 205; Geer to friend, March 20, 1865; Walker, *History of the Second Army Corps*, p. 651; Welcher, *Eastern Theater*, p. 910.
26. *War of the Rebellion*, ser. 1, vol. 46, pt. 1, p. 203; Geer to Jule, March 26, 1865; Walker, *History of the Second Army Corps*, p. 651; Welcher, *Eastern Theater*, p. 910.
27. Smith to wife, March 28, 1865.
28. *War of the Rebellion*, ser. 1, vol. 46, pt. 1, p. 206; Smith to wife, March 28, 1865; Geer to Jule, March 26, 1865.
29. Smith to wife, March 28, 1865.
30. *Ibid.*
31. *War of the Rebellion*, ser. 1, vol. 46, pt. 1, p. 206; Smith to wife, March 28, 1865; Geer to Jule, March 26, 1865.
32. Smith to wife, March 28, 1865.
33. Geer to Jule, March 26, 1865.
34. *ADAU*, April 4, 1865.
35. Military service record of Lewis W. Husk, National Archives, Washington, D.C.; Phisterer, *New York in the War of the Rebellion*, p. 3313; Adjutant General's Report, pp. 671–930; Husk received his brevet promotion to colonel of regular troops on June 13, 1865, dating back to February 25, 1865. Because of the date of the promotion, Husk mustered out with the regiment before the promotion could take affect and mustered out of the service as a lieutenant colonel.
36. *War of the Rebellion*, ser. 1, vol. 46, pt. 1, pp. 205–206; Geer, diary entry, March 25, 1865; Smith to wife, March 28, 1865.
37. Geer, diary entry, March 29, 1865.
38. Walker, *History of the Second Army Corps*, pp. 656–57; Chris Calkins, *The Appomattox Campaign*, Conshohocken, PA: Combined Books, 1997, pp. 14–17.
39. Calkins, *Appomattox Campaign*, pp. 14–17; *War of the Rebellion*, ser. 1, vol. 46, pt. 1, p. 80; Geer, diary entry, March 29, 1865; Mahood, *Written in Blood*, p. 335.
40. Geer, diary entry, March 30, 1865.
41. *War of the Rebellion*, ser. 1, vol. 46, pt. 1, p. 80; Adjutant General's Report, pp. 671–930.
42. *War of the Rebellion*, ser. 1, vol. 46, pt. 1, p. 733; Geer, diary entry, March 31, 1865; Mahood, *Written in Blood*, p. 335.
43. *War of the Rebellion*, ser. 1, vol. 46, pt. 1, p. 733; Korn, *Pursuit to Appomattox*, p. 85; Walker, *History of the Second Army Corps*, p. 662; Calkins, *Appomattox Campaign*, pp. 25–26.
44. *ADAU*, April 21, 1865; Adjutant General's Report, pp. 671–930.
45. Wright, *Historical Sketches of the Town of Moravia from 1791 to 1918*, p. 127.
46. W. F. Beyer, and O. F. Keydel, eds., *Deeds of Valor: How America's Civil War Heroes Won the Congressional Medal of Honor*, Stamford, CT: Long Meadow Press, 1992, p. 507; Phisterer, *New York in the War of the Rebellion*, p. 3310; Geer, diary entry, March 31, 1865; Robert B. Bradley, *Documenting the Civil War Period Flag Collection at the Alabama Department of Archives and History*, Birmingham: Alabama Department of

Archives and History, January 1997; The flag captured by Lutes was a Department of South Carolina, Georgia, and Florida issue flag manufactured at the Charleston Depot. Poles sleeves of flags from the Charleston Depot usually matched the unit's branch of service; infantry was blue, cavalry was yellow and artillery was red. For some reason, the 41st was issued a flag with a red pole sleeve. After its capture, the flag was forwarded to the War Department through Generals Miles and Meade and was cataloged at Capture Number 259. Returned to the State of Alabama on March 25, 1905, a few veterans of the 41st Alabama claimed that the flag was not captured in battle but was actually being stored in a trunk in Petersburg when the city fell. This claim proved to be false and Lutes was given full credit for the capture.

47. *War of the Rebellion*, ser. 1, vol. 46, pt. 1, p. 733; Walker, *History of the Second Army Corps*, pp. 662–64.
48. *War of the Rebellion*, ser. 1, vol. 46, pt. 1, p. 733; Adjutant General's Report, pp. 671–930; Geer, diary entry, March 31, 1865; *ADAU*, April 21, 1865; Walker, *History of the Second Army Corps*, pp. 662–64.
49. Adjutant General's Report, p. 787; Drummond, "Personal Reminiscences," p. 12.
50. *War of the Rebellion*, ser. 1, vol. 46, pt. 1, p. 734; Geer, diary entry, April 1, 1865.
51. *Ibid.*
52. Calkins, *Appomattox Campaign*, pp. 32–36; Geer, diary entry, April 1, 1865; Mahood, *Written in Blood*, pp. 336–37.
53. Calkins, *Appomattox Campaign*, pp. 43–46; Trudeau, *Last Citadel*, pp. 356–57, 366–67, 378–79, 390–91; Walker, *History of the Second Army Corps*, p. 669.
54. Geer, diary entry, April 2, 1865.
55. Calkins, *Appomattox Campaign*, p. 48; Walker, *History of the Second Army Corps*, pp. 670–71.
56. Calkins, *Appomattox Campaign*, p. 48.
57. *Ibid.*; Walker, *History of the Second Army Corps*, p. 671; Military service record of Clinton D. MacDougall, National Archives, Washington, D.C.; Geer to friend, March 20, 1865; Geer, diary entry, April 2, 1865; *ADAU*, April 22, 1865.
58. Loyal Legion of the United States, Headquarters Commandery of the State of Wisconsin, May 11, 1911, circular no. 11, ser. 1911.
59. Geer, diary entry, April 2, 1865.
60. Calkins, *Appomattox Campaign*, p. 48; *War of the Rebellion*, ser. 1, vol. 46, pt. 1, p. 743; Geer, diary entry, April 2, 1865.
61. *War of the Rebellion*, ser. 1, vol. 46, pt. 1, p. 742; Military service record of Silas W. Belding, National Archives, Washington, D.C.; Clark, *Military History of Wayne County*, p. 581; Adjutant General's Report, pp. 671–930; Geer, diary entry, April 2, 1865.
62. Walker, *History of the Second Army Corps*, p. 672; Calkins, *Appomattox Campaign*, pp. 48–58.
63. *War of the Rebellion*, ser. 1, vol. 46, pt. 1, p. 735; Calkins, *Appomattox Campaign*, pp. 72–74; Phisterer, *New York in the War of the Rebellion*, p. 3317; Geer, diary entry, April 3, 1865.
64. Geer, diary entry, April 4, 1865; Mahood, *Written in Blood*, p. 340; *War of the Rebellion*, ser. 1, vol. 46, pt. 1, p. 735.
65. *War of the Rebellion*, ser. 1, vol. 46, pt. 1, p. 735; Geer, diary entry, April 5, 1865; Mahood, *Written in Blood*, p. 340.
66. Korn, *Pursuit to Appomattox*, pp. 114–15; Noah A. Trudeau, *Out of the Storm*, Baton Rouge: Louisiana State University Press, 1994, p. 107; *War of the Rebellion*, ser. 1, vol. 46, pt. 1, p. 735; Calkins, *Appomattox Campaign*, p. 98.
67. Trudeau, *Out of the Storm*, p. 108; Calkins, *Appomattox Campaign*, pp. 112–14.
68. Trudeau, *Out of the Storm*, pp. 108–110; Humphreys, *Virginia Campaign*, p. 381; *War of the Rebellion*, ser. 1, vol. 46, pt. 1, p. 735; Mahood, *Written in Blood*, p. 341; Adjutant General's Report, pp. 671–930.
69. *War of the Rebellion*, ser. 1, vol. 46, pt. 1, p. 735; Humphreys, *Virginia Campaign*, p. 387f.
70. Trudeau, *Out of the Storm*, pp. 120–21; *War of the Rebellion*, ser. 1, vol. 46, pt. 1, p. 735; Humphreys, p. 387.
71. Trudeau, *Out of the Storm*, pp. 120–22; Walker, *History of the Second Army Corps*, p. 681.
72. *War of the Rebellion*, ser. 1, vol. 46, pt. 1, p. 735; Geer, diary entry, April 7, 1865; Walker, *History of the Second Army Corps*, pp. 682–83.
73. Trudeau, *Out of the Storm*, pp. 124–25; Calkins, *Appomattox Campaign*, pp. 134–35.
74. *War of the Rebellion*, ser. 1, vol. 46, pt. 1, p. 735; Geer, diary entry, April 8, 1865; Walker, *History of the Second Army Corps*, p. 686; Calkins, *Appomattox Campaign*, p. 148.
75. Trudeau, *Out of the Storm*, pp. 125, 130; Walker, *History of the Second Army Corps*, pp. 685–86.
76. Korn, *Pursuit to Appomattox*, p. 138; Calkins, *Appomattox Campaign*, pp. 152–54; Walker, *History of the Second Army Corps*, pp. 686–87.
77. *War of the Rebellion*, ser. 1, vol. 46, pt. 1, p. 735; Humphreys, *Virginia Campaign*, p. 395; Calkins, *Appomattox Campaign*, p. 165.
78. *War of the Rebellion*, ser. 1, vol. 46, pt. 1, p. 735; Smith to wife and children, April 16, 1865.
79. Geer to friend, April 14, 1865.
80. Calkins, *Appomattox Campaign*, pp. 185–88; Smith to wife and children, April 16, 1865; Geer, diary entry, April 10, 1865.
81. Geer to friends, April 27, 1865; Geer, diary entries, April 14–30, 1865.
82. Smith to Fanny, April 30, 1865.
83. Geer, diary entry, April 16, 1865.
84. Smith to Fanny, May 5, 1865.
85. Trudeau, *Out of the Storm*, pp. 68, 75; Mahood, *Written in Blood*, p. 346; Geer, diary entry, May 6, 1865.
86. Smith to wife, May 22, 1865.
87. Geer to friend, May 17, 1865.
88. Richard W. Murphy, *The Nation Reunited: War's Aftermath*, Alexandria, VA: Time Life, 1987, p. 8.
89. Geer, diary entry, May 23, 1865; Walker, *History of the Second Army Corps*, p. 692.
90. Jack Rudolph, "The Grand Review," *Civil War Times Illustrated*, November 1980, pp. 34–42.
91. The final casualty figures were developed through extensive research by the author. They differ somewhat from the normally accepted numbers published in Phisterer's *New York in the War of the Rebellion*. This list omits a number of pivotal events in the life of the regiment, including the capture of pickets before Fort Davis in October 1864, while including the surrender of the regiment at Harpers Ferry.
92. Geer, diary entry, May 23, 1865; Walker, *History of the Second Army Corps*, p. 692.
93. *ADAU*, June 8, 1865; Geer, diary entry, June 8, 1865; Adjutant General's Report, p. 770.

94. *ADAU*, June 8, 1865; Geer, diary entry, June 8, 1865.
95. Adjutant General's Report, pp. 671–930; General MacDougall is not included in the count, since as a general officer, he was no longer considered part of the regiment.
96. *ADAU*, June 8 and 14, 1865; Geer, diary entries, June 8–15, 1865.
97. *Ibid.*

Appendix A

1. Drummond, "Personal Reminiscences," p. 48.
2. Regimental Returns for September and October, 1864, RG 94, National Archives, Washington, D.C.; Adjutant General's Report, pp. 671–930.
3. Drummond, "Personal Reminiscences," p. 18; Drummond admitted after the war that he was no fan of General Mahone as a politician. "When, to the disgrace of the Nation, he occupied a seat in the U.S. Senate, it seems to me highly appropriate that he should belong to a party composed *entirely of himself*, for he was too small in body and in soul to be *associated with men*."
4. *Ibid.*, p. 19.
5. *Ibid.*, p. 19.
6. *Ibid.*, pp. 20–22.
7. *Ibid.*, p. 24; Military service records for those captured on the night of October 30, 1864, National Archives, Washington, D.C.; Asa B. Isham, Henry M. Davidson, and Henry B. Furness, *Prisoners of War and Military Prisoners*, Cincinnati, OH: Lyman and Cushing, 1890, p. 420.
8. Louis A. Brown, *The Salisbury Prison: A Case Study of Confederate Military Prisons 1861–1865*, Wilmington, NC: Broadfoot, 1992, pp. 19–20; Drummond, "Personal Reminiscences," p. 26; Isham, Davidson, and Furness, *Prisoners of War and Military Prisoners*, p. 420.
9. Brown, *Salisbury Prison*, p. fl8, 20; The factory, built in 1839, was already 20 years old when converted into a prison in 1861. Major renovations were needed before the building was able to house prisoners. All of the cotton manufacturing equipment was removed, floors and walls repaired, and bars placed on the windows. The factory was intended to house all of the prisoners, but by the time the men of the 111th arrived, it had been converted to the prison hospital.
10. Isham, Davidson, and Furness, *Prisoners of War and Military Prisoners*, p. 421; Brown, *Salisbury Prison*, p. 23.
11. Isham, Davidson, and Furness, *Prisoners of War and Military Prisoners*, p. 421; Drummond, "Personal Reminiscences," p. 27.
12. *Ibid.*, p. 27.
13. Adjutant General's Report, p. 769; List of captured developed by the author; Military service record for Charles Green, National Archives, Washington, D.C.; Drummond, "Personal Reminiscences," p. 47.
14. Brown, *Salisbury Prison*, p. 35.
15. Brown, *Salisbury Prison*, pp. 110–11; Drummond, "Personal Reminiscences," p. 30.
16. Brown, *Salisbury Prison*, p. 111; Drummond, "Personal Reminiscences," p. 30.
17. Drummond, "Personal Reminiscences," p. 26.
18. *Ibid.*, pp. 35–38.
19. Brown, *Salisbury Prison*, p. 135.
20. Drummond, "Personal Reminiscences," p. 35.
21. *Ibid.*, p. 38.
22. Cowles, *Landmarks of Wayne County*, p. 275; After the war, Jenkins assisted many widows and orphans of those who died at Salisbury.
23. Robert Drummond to Juliet Le Roy Mangun, July 4, 1913, Robert Drummond Papers #1051, Southern Historical Collection, Manuscripts Division, Wilson Library, University of North Carolina at Chapel Hill.
24. Drummond, "Personal Reminiscences," p. 41; Brown, *Salisbury Prison*, pp. 100–101.
25. Brown, *Salisbury Prison*, pp. 102–103; Adjutant General's Report, pp. 671–930; Military service records for Jeremiah Hayes and Malone Kilmer, National Archives, Washington, D.C.
26. Robert Drummond, monument dedication address, Salisbury Prison, Robert Drummond Papers #1051, Southern Historical Collection, Manuscripts Division, Wilson Library, University of North Carolina at Chapel Hill.
27. Drummond, "Personal Reminiscences," p. 37.
28. *Ibid.*, p. 46.
29. *Ibid.*, p. 46.
30. Drummond, "Personal Reminiscences," p. 47; Adjutant General's Report, p. 769; Military service record of Charles Green, National Archives, Washington, D.C.; Brown, *Salisbury Prison*, p. 297.
31. Drummond, "Personal Reminiscences," pp. 48–49.
32. Brown, *Salisbury Prison*, p. 158; Drummond, "Personal Reminiscences," p. 52.
33. Drummond, "Personal Reminiscences," p. 55.
34. Drummond, "Personal Reminiscences," pp. 56–58; Brown, *Salisbury Prison*, p. 160.
35. List of captured compiled by the author; RG 94, National Archives, Washington, D.C.; Adjutant General's Report, pp. 671–930; Drummond, "Personal Reminiscences," p. 48; Drummond Papers, #1051, Southern Historical Collection, Manuscripts Department, Wilson Library, University of North Carolina at Chapel Hill.
36. Drummond, monument dedication address, Salisbury Prison.
37. *Ibid.*
38. *Ibid.*

Appendix B

1. Monthly Returns, 1862–1865, RG 94, National Archives, Washington, D.C.

Bibliography

Letters and Diaries

Benton, Francis. Speech. Courtesy of Frances Benton.

Benton, James Dana. Letters, 111th New York. Courtesy of Francis Benton.

Bradley, S. C. Letter, February 27, 1930, 111th New York. Courtesy of Kurt Kabelac.

Cooper, Simeon. Letters, 111th New York. Includes letter from Chaplain John Brown. Courtesy of Hallie Sweeting.

Dadswell, Thomas. Letters, 111th New York. Thomas Dadswell Papers, Auburn University Libraries, Ralph Brown Draughon Library, Special Collections and University Archives Department.

David, George E. Letter, 111th New York. Courtesy of Michael Reid.

Drummond, Robert. Letter, December 25, 1907. Courtesy of Burke Drummond.

_____. Personal reminiscences of prison life during the war of the rebellion, 111th New York. Courtesy of Burke Drummond.

Geer, Thomas. Diary for 1865, 111th New York. Courtesy of David Crane and George Contant.

_____. Letters, 111th New York. Courtesy of David Crane and George Contant.

Grant, Ulysses. S. Letter to M. C. Failing dated February 14, 1884. Manuscript Collection at U.S. Military History Institute, Carlisle Barracks, PA.

Hill, Horace Gilbert. Diary for 1864, 111th New York. Wayne County Historical Society.

Hinman, Wellington. Diary for 1864, 111th New York. Cortland County Historical Society.

Hoff, Esek. Letters, 111th New York. Courtesy of Ken Harris.

Holcombe, Edward. Diary, Auburn University Libraries, Ralph Brown Draughon Library, Special Collections and University Archives Department.

Holmes, Sebastian. Letters, Gifford/Holmes Family Collection, U.S. Army Military History Institute. Manuscript Division, Carlisle Barracks.

Hoxie, Allen. Diary for 1864, 111th New York. Courtesy of Ken Hoxie.

_____. Letters, 111th New York. Courtesy of Ken Hoxie.

Hutchins, Daniel. Diary for 1864, 111th New York. William L. Clements Library, University of Michigan.

Jeffery, Henry. Letters, 111th New York. Courtesy of Sally Hall and George Contant.

John Batchelder Papers. New Hampshire Historical Society, Concord, microfilm copy, Gettysburg National Military Park, Historian's Office.

Langdon, Spencer. Letters, 111th New York. Courtesy of Bill Holmes and Lela Rose Hergert.

Paylor, John. Diary for 1862 to 1864, 111th New York. Courtesy of Don Chatfield.

Pease, David. Letters, March 1, 1863 and April 10, 1863, microfilm copy, Library of Congress, Washington, D.C.

Smith, Chauncey. Letters, 111th New York. Courtesy of Joe Flynn.

_____. Notes of a speech given before a meeting of the Grand Army of the Republic. Courtesy of Joe Flynn.

Smith, Harry. Letters, 111th New York. Courtesy of Norman and Rosemary Smith.

Stacey, Manley T. Diary for 1863, 111th New York. Pearce Collection Museum, Navarro College, Corsicana, TX.

_____. Letters, 111th New York. Pearce Collection Museum, Navarro College, Corsicana, TX.

Vaughn, Henry. Letter, July 10, 1863, Kennedy's

Independent Battery, First New York Volunteers. Courtesy of Bill Jacobs.

Warren, Richard. Family history, 111th New York. Courtesy of H. Richard Taylor.

———. Letters, 111th New York. Courtesy of George Kimbes.

White, Charles. Diary for 1864, 111th New York. Courtesy of Joe Weaver.

Manuscripts and Records

Ball, Levertt. "History of the Military of Auburn and Vicinity." Read to the April 10, 1883, meeting of the Cayuga County Historical Society.

Company Muster Rolls for the 111th New York, National Archives, Washington, D.C.

Drummond Papers. #1051, Southern Historical Collection, Manuscripts Department, Wilson Library, University of North Carolina at Chapel Hill.

Hollcroft, Temple. *The Town of Ledyard in the Civil War*. Unpublished manuscript.

Military service and pension records for members of the 111th New York, National Archives, Washington, D.C.

Monthly returns for the 111th New York. National Archives, Washington, D.C.

Quartermaster General State of New York 1863 (for 1862), National Archives, Washington, D.C.

Record Group 94, regimental order books and boxed records for the 111th New York. National Archives, Washington, D.C.

Wayne County: A Brief History. Office of the County Historian, Wayne County, New York.

Books and Articles

Allen, Henry M. *A Chronicle of Early Auburn 1793–1860*. Auburn, NY: Allen, 1953.

Bacarella, Michael. *Lincoln's Foreign Legion: The 39th New York Infantry, the Garibaldi Guard*. Shippensburg, PA: White Mane, 1996.

Bailey, Ronald H. *Battles for Atlanta: Sherman Moves East*. Alexandria, VA: Time Life, 1985.

———. *The Bloodiest Day: The Battle of Antietam*. Alexandria, VA: Time Life, 1984.

Baltz, Louis J. *The Battle of Cold Harbor, May 27–June 13, 1864*. Lynchburg, VA: Howard, 1994.

Barton, Michael. "I Begin to Know What Hard Times Is." *Manuscripts*, 30, no. 2 (Spring 1978).

Beyer, W. F., and O. F. Keydel, eds. *Deeds of Valor: How America's Civil War Heroes Won the Congressional Medal of Honor*. Stamford, CT: Long Meadow Press, 1992.

Billings, John D. *Hard Tack and Coffee or the Unwritten Story of Army Life*, 4th ed. Williamston, MA: Corner House, 1987.

Bradley, Robert B. *Documenting the Civil War Period Flag Collection at the Alabama Department of Archives and History*. Birmingham: Alabama Department of Archives and History, January 1997.

Brown, Louis A. *The Salisbury Prison: A Case Study of Confederate Military Prisons 1861–1865*. Wilmington, NC: Broadfoot, 1992.

Brown, Russell. *Fallen in Battle: American General Officer Combat Fatalities from 1775*. Westport, CT: Greenwood Press, 1988.

Brugger, Robert J. *Maryland: A Middle Temperament 1634–1980*. Baltimore, MD: Johns Hopkins University Press, 1988.

Busey, John W. *These Honored Dead: The Union Casualties at Gettysburg*. Hightstown, NJ: Longstreet House, 1988.

Busey, John W., and David G. Martin. *Regimental Strengths and Losses at Gettysburg*. Hightstown, NJ: Longstreet House, 1986.

Campbell, Eric. "Remember Harper's Ferry: The Degradation, Humiliation and Redemption of Colonel George Willard's Brigade." *Gettysburg Magazine*, July 1992.

Catton, Bruce. *The Army of the Potomac: Glory Road*. Garden City, NJ: Doubleday, 1952.

———. *The Army of the Potomac: A Stillness at Appomattox*. Garden City, NJ: Doubleday, 1953.

———. *Grant Takes Command*. Boston, MA: Little, Brown, 1968.

Calkins, Christopher. *The Appomattox Campaign*. Conshohocken, PA: Combined Books, 1997.

Christ, Elwood. *The Struggle for the Bliss Farm at Gettysburg, July 2nd and 3rd, 1863*. Baltimore, MD: Butternut and Blue, 1993.

Clark, Champ. *Gettysburg: The Confederate High Tide*. Alexandria, VA: Time Life, 1985.

Clark, James H. *The Iron Hearted Regiment: Being an Account of the Battles, Marches and Gallant Deeds Performed by the 115th N.Y. Vols*. Albany, NY: Munsell, 1865.

Clark, Lewis. *Military History of Wayne County*. Sodus, NY: Clark, Hulett, and Gaylord, 1884.

Clark, Walter, comp. *Histories of Several Regiments and Battalions from North Carolina*. Vol. 2. Reprint. Newdell, NC: Avera Press, 1982.

Coco, Gregory A. *The Civil War Infantryman*. Gettysburg, PA: Thomas Publications, 1996.

———. *A Vast Sea of Misery: A History and Guide to the Union and Confederate Field Hospitals at Gettysburg July 1–November 20, 1863*. Gettysburg, PA: Thomas Publications, 1988.

Coddington, Edward. *The Gettysburg Campaign:*

A Study in Command. New York: Scribner's, 1968.
Cole, Jacob H. *Under Five Commanders or the Boys Experience with the Army of the Potomac*. Patterson, NJ: News Printing, 1906.
Contant, George. *Path of Blood: The True Story of the 33rd New York Volunteers*. Savannah, NY: Seeco, 1996.
Cooling, B. F. *Jubal Early's Raid on Washington, 1864*. Baltimore, MD: Nautical and Aviation, 1989.
Cowles, George, ed. *Landmarks of Wayne County, New York*. Syracuse, NY: Mason, 1895.
Davis, George, Leslie Perry, and Joseph Kirkley. *The Official Military Atlas of the Civil War*. New York: Fairfax Press, 1983.
Davis, William C. *Death in the Trenches: Grant at Petersburg*. Alexandria, VA: Time Life, 1986.
_____. *First Blood: Fort Sumter to Bull Run*. Alexandria, VA: Time Life, 1983.
Duncan, Louis C. *The Medical Department of the United States Army in the Civil War*. Reprint. Gaithersburg, MD: Olde Soldier Books, 1997.
Dyer, Frederick. *A Compendium of the War of the Rebellion*. Vol. 3. Dayton, OH: Morningside Press, 1978.
Eldred, Newman. "Newman Eldred's Account of Service in the Civil War." *Yesteryears* 22–24, nos. 88–93 (Summer 1979–Fall 1980).
Favill, Josiah Marshall. *Diary of a Young Officer*. Chicago: Donnelly, 1909.
Fleming, George T. *Life and Letters of Alexander Hays*. Pittsburgh, PA: Gilbert Adam Hays, 1919.
Frederick, Gilbert. *The Story of a Regiment*. Chicago, IL: Fifty-Seventh Veteran Association, C. H. Morgan, 1895.
Gallagher, Gary, ed. *The Third Day at Gettysburg and Beyond*. Chapel Hill: University of North Carolina Press, 1994.
Garraty, John A., and Robert A. McCaughey. *The American Nation: A History of the United States to 1877*. 6th ed. Vol. 1. New York: Harper & Row, 1987.
Geary, James. *We Need Men: The Union Draft in the Civil War*. DeKalb: Northern Illinois University Press, 1991.
Graham, Martin, and George F. Skoch. *Mine Run: A Campaign of Lost Opportunities October 21, 1863–March 1, 1864*. Lynchburg, VA: Howard, 1987.
Hall, Henry. *The History of Auburn*. Auburn, NY: Dennis Bro's, 1869.
Hassler, Warren W. *Crisis at the Crossroads*. Reprint, Gaithersburg, VA: Van Sickle Military Books, 1988.
Henderson, William. *The Road to Bristoe Station: Campaigning with Lee and Meade August 1–October 20, 1863*. Lynchburg, VA: Howard, 1987.
Herdegen, Lance J., and William J. K. Beaudot. *Into the Bloody Railroad Cut at Gettysburg*. Dayton, OH: Morningside House, 1990.
History of Wayne County, New York. Philadelphia, PA: Lippincott, 1877.
Horn, John. *The Petersburg Campaign: The Destruction of the Weldon Railroad Deep Bottom, Globe Tavern and Reams Station August 14–25, 1864*. Lynchburg, VA: Howard, 1991.
Howe, John. *The Petersburg Campaign: Wasted Valor June 15–18, 1864*. Lynchburg, VA: Howard, 1988.
Humphreys, Andrew A. *The Virginia Campaign 1864–1865*. Reprint. New York: De Capo, 1995.
Jackson, Donald Dale. *Twenty Million Yankees: The Northern Home Front*. Alexandria, VA: Time Life, 1985.
Jaynes, Gregory. *The Killing Ground: Wilderness to Cold Harbor*. Alexandria, VA: Time Life, 1986.
Jaquette, Henrietta Stratton. *South After Gettysburg: Letters of Cornelia Hancock 1863–1868*. New York: Crowell, 1937.
Johnson, Robert U., and Clarence C. Buel, eds. *Battles and Leaders of the Civil War*. 4 vols. Reprint. Secaucus, NJ: Castle,1983.
Korn, Jerry. *Pursuit to Appomattox: The Last Battles*. Alexandria, VA: Time Life, 1987.
Ladd, David L., and Audrey J. Ladd, eds. *The Bachelder Papers*. 3 vols. Reprint. Dayton, OH: Morningside House, 1994.
Levy, George. *To Die in Chicago: Confederate Prisoners at Camp Douglas*. Evanston, IL: Evanston Publishing, 1994.
Lightfoote, W. G. *Proceedings of the Reunion of the Veterans of the 111th and the 126th Regiments N.Y. Vols. Held at Gettysburg, PA June 10 & 11, 1886*. Canandaigua, NY: Times Book and Job Printing House, 1886.
Long, A. L. *The Memoirs of Robert E. Lee*. Reprint. Secaucus, NJ: Blue and Grey Press, 1983.
Longacre, Edward. *To Gettysburg and Beyond: The Twelfth New Jersey Volunteer Infantry*. Hightstown, NJ: Longstreet House, 1988.
Lord, Francis A. *Civil War Collectors Encyclopedia*. Secaucus, NJ: Castle Books, 1963.
Loyal Legion of the United States, Headquarters Commandery of the State of Wisconsin circular no. 11, series 1911 (May 11, 1911).
Luvaas, Jay, and Harold W. Nelson, eds. *The U.S. Army War College Guide to the Battle of Antietam: The Maryland Campaign of 1862*. Carlisle, PA: South Mountain Press, 1987.
_____. *The U.S. Army War College Guide to the*

Battles of Chancellorsville and Fredericksburg. Carlisle, PA: South Mountain Press, 1988.

Lykes, Richard Wayne. *Campaign for Petersburg.* Washington, D.C.: U.S. Government Printing Office, 1970.

Mahood, Wayne. *Written in Blood: A History of the 126th New York Infantry in the Civil War.* Hightstown, NJ: Longstreet House, 1997.

Makeover, C. M. *Civil War Battle Flags of the Union Army an Order of Battle.* Reprint. New York: Knickerbocker Press, 1997.

Maney, R. Wayne. *Marching to Cold Harbor: Victory and Failure, 1864.* Shippensburg, PA: White Mane, 1995.

Martin, David G. *Confederate Monuments at Gettysburg.* Vol. 1. Hightstown, NJ: Longstreet House, 1986.

Marvel, William. *Andersonville: The Last Depot.* Chapel Hill: University of North Carolina Press, 1994.

Matter, William D. *If It Takes All Summer: The Battle of Spotsylvania.* Chapel Hill: University of North Carolina Press, 1988.

McNeily, J. S. *Barksdale's Mississippi Brigade at Gettysburg: Most Magnificent Charge of the War.* Reprint. Gaithersburg, MD: Olde Soldier Books, 1987.

Menge, W. Springer, and J. August Shimrak. *The Civil War Notebook of Daniel Chisolm.* New York: Ballantine, 1990.

Miller, Francis T., ed. *The Photographic History of the Civil War in Ten Volumes, Part Seven: Prisons and Hospitals,* New York: T. Yoseloff, 1957.

Miller, J. Michael. *The North Anna Campaign: Even to Hell Itself, May 21–26, 1864.* Lynchburg, VA: Howard, 1989.

Mitchell, Joseph B. *The Badge of Gallantry.* New York: Macmillan, 1968.

Monroe, Joel H. *Historical Record of a Hundred and Twenty Years.* Geneva, NY: Humphrey, 1913.

Moore, Frank, ed. *The Rebellion Record: A Diary of American Events.* Vol. 5. New York: Putnam, 1863.

Murphy, Richard W. *The Nation Reunited: War's Aftermath.* Alexandria, VA: Time Life, 1987.

Murray, R. L. *The Redemption of the "Harper's Ferry Cowards": the Story of the 111th and 126th New York State Volunteers at Gettysburg.* Wolcott, NY: Benedum, 1994.

Myers, Frank M. *The Comanches: A History of White's Battalion, Virginia Cavalry.* Reprint. Alexandria, VA: Stonewall House, 1985.

New York (State), Adjutant General's Office. *Annual Report of the Adjutant General of the State of New York for the Year 1903.* no. 34. New York: Quayle, 1904.

New York Monument Commission. *New York at Gettysburg: Final Report on the Battlefield of Gettysburg.* 3 vols. Albany, NY: Lyon, 1900.

Pellicano, John M. *Conquer or Die: The 39th New York Volunteer Infantry; Garibaldi Guard.* Flushing, NY: Pellicano, 1996.

Pfanz, Henry. *Gettysburg: The Second Day.* Chapel Hill: University of North Carolina Press, 1987.

Phisterer, Frederick, comp. *New York in the War of the Rebellion.* Vol. 4. Albany: Lyon, 1912.

Porter, Horace. *Campaigning with Grant.* Reprint. New York: Mallard Press, 1991.

Presentation of Flags of New York Volunteer Regiments. Albany: Weed Parsons, 1865.

Priest, John Michael. *Nowhere to Run: The Wilderness, May 4th and 5th, 1864.* Shippensburg, PA: White Mane, 1995.

_____. *Victory Without Triumph: The Wilderness, May 6th and 7th.* Shippensburg, PA: White Mane, 1996.

Priest, John Michael, ed. *Into the Fight: Pickett's Charge at Gettysburg.* Shippensburg, PA: White Mane, 1998.

_____. *One Surgeon's Private War: Doctor William Potter of the 57th New York.* Reprint. Shippensburg, PA: White Mane, 1996.

Rhea, Gordon. *The Battle for Spotsylvania Court House and the Road to Yellow Tavern May 7–12, 1864.* Baton Rouge: Louisiana State University Press, 1997.

_____. *The Battle of the Wilderness May 5–6, 1864.* Baton Rouge: Louisiana State University Press, 1994.

Robertson, James I. *General A. P. Hill: The Story of a Confederate Warrior.* New York: Random House, 1987.

_____. *Tenting Tonight: The Soldier's Life.* Alexandria, VA: Time Life, 1984.

Rodick, Burleigh Cushing. *Appomattox: The Last Campaign.* Reprint. Gaithersburg, MD: Olde Soldier Books, 1987.

Roe, Alfred Seelye. *The Ninth Heavy Artillery N.Y.* Worcester, MA: Blanchard, 1899.

Rosenblatt, Emil, ed. *Anti-Rebel: The Civil War Letters of Wilbur Fisk.* Croton-on-Hudson, NY: Rosenblatt, 1983.

Roster of Survivors of the 111th Reg't N.Y.S. Vols., August 1899.

Rudolph, Jack. "The Grand Review." *Civil War Times Illustrated,* November 1980.

Scott, Robert Garth. *Into the Wilderness with the Army of the Potomac.* Bloomington, IL: Indiana University Press, 1985.

Sears, Stephen W. *Chancellorsville.* New York: Houghton Mifflin, 1996.

_____. *Landscape Turned Red: The Battle of Antietam.* New York: Ticknor and Fields, 1983.

Simons, Chaplain Ezra. *A Regimental History of the One Hundred and Twenty-Fifth N.Y.S.V.* New York: Judson, 1888.

Sommers, Richard J. *Richmond Redeemed: The Siege at Petersburg.* Garden City, NJ: Doubleday, 1981.

Stewart, George. *Pickett's Charge.* Reprint. Dayton, OH: Morningside Press, 1980.

Stewart, Robert Laird. *History of the One Hundred and Fortieth Regiment Pennsylvania Volunteers.* Regimental Association, 1912.

Teetor, Paul. *A Matter of Hours.* Brunswick, NJ: Associated Press, 1982.

Thomas, Dean. *Cannons.* Arendtsville, PA: Thomas Publications, 1985.

Thompson, Benjamin. "Back to the South." *Civil War Times Illustrated,* November 1973.

———. "Flight from Florida." *Civil War Times Illustrated,* August 1973.

———. "Into This Hell of Destruction." *Civil War Times Illustrated,* October 1973.

Time Life. *Spies, Scouts and Raiders: Irregular Operations.* Alexandria, VA: Time Life, 1985.

Toombs, Samuel. *New Jersey in the Gettysburg Campaign.* Reprint. Hightstown, NJ: Longstreet House, 1988.

Townsend, Thomas. *Honors of the Empire State in the War of the Rebellion.* New York: Lovell, 1889.

Trudeau, Noah Andre. *Bloody Roads South: The Wilderness to Cold Harbor May–June 1864.* New York: Fawcett Columbine, 1989.

———. *The Last Citadel: Petersburg, Virginia, June 1864–April 1865.* Boston, MA: Little, Brown, 1991.

———. *Out of the Storm: The End of the Civil War April–June 1865.* Baton Rouge: Louisiana State University Press, 1994.

Tucker, Glenn. *Chickamauga: Bloody Battle in the West.* New York: Konecky and Konecky, 1961.

———. *Hancock the Superb.* Reprint. Dayton, OH: Morningside Bookshop, 1980.

U.S. War Department, *The War of the Rebellion: The Official Records of the Union and Confederate Armies.* 128 vols. Washington, D.C.: U.S. War Department, 1890–1901.

Wadsworth, John Ogden. *Wolcott, New York, Old and New.* Wolcott, NY: Wadsworth, 1975.

Walker, Francis A. *History of the Second Army Corps of the Army of the Potomac.* New York: Scribner's, 1891.

Welcher, Frank. *The Union Army 1861–1865.* Vol. 1, *The Eastern Theater.* Bloomington: Indiana University Press, 1989.

White, Russell C., ed. *The Civil War Diary of Wyman S. White.* Baltimore, MD: Butternut and Blue, 1991.

Wiley, Bell I. *The Life of Billy Yank.* Garden City, NJ: Doubleday, 1952.

Willson, Arabella. *Disaster, Struggle, Triumph: The Adventures of 1000 Boys in Blue.* Albany: Argus, 1870.

Wright, James A. *Historical Sketches of the Town of Moravia from 1791–1918.* Auburn, NY: Benton and Reynolds, 1874.

Newspapers

Advertiser-Journal, microfilm copies, Auburn-Cayuga County Community College, Auburn, NY.

Auburn Bulletin, microfilm copies, Auburn-Cayuga County Community College, Auburn, NY.

Auburn Citizen, microfilm copies, Seymour Library, Auburn, NY.

Auburn Daily Advertiser and Union, microfilm copies, Auburn-Cayuga County Community College, Auburn, NY.

Courier-Journal, May 2, 1973, courtesy of Office of the Historian, Wayne County, NY.

National Tribune, microfilm copies, Antietam National Military Park, Sharpsburg, MD.

Newark Courier, May 11, 1905.

Index

Numbers in ***bold italics*** indicate pages with photographs.

Abraham Brien farm 56, 65, 67, 69, ***70***, 71, 74–76
Accotink Bridge 50, 52
Acker, Horace 25
Adams, Samuel 33
Alabama Troops: 11th Infantry 40; 41st Infantry 186
Albany, New York 17, 19, 37, 195, 197
Alexandria, Virginia 39, 40–43, 50
Allen, James 55
Anderson, Abraham 82, 83
Anderson, Gen. George T. (CSA) 155, 156
Anderson, Gen. Richard (CSA) 120
Andersonville prisoner of war camp 126
Andrews, George 186
Annapolis, Maryland 28, 29, 43
Anstead, Charles 184
Appomattox Court House 193
Appomattox River 148, 153, 191, 192
Arcadia, New York 11, 206
Archer, Gen. James (CSA) 24
Armstrong's Mill 177; battle of 182
Army of Northern Virginia 20, 39, 81, 85, 94, 110, 111, 119, 132, 141, 143, 192
Army of the Potomac 4, 18, 37, 41, 49–52, 69, 81, 83, 87, 97, 101, 107, 110, 119, 120, 129–135, 141, 162, 167, 181, 195
Auburn, New York 1, 3, 5–7, 9–11, 15, 16, 18, 30, 31, 34, 41, 45, 46, 49, 50, 81, 97, 103, 106, 109, 126, 162, 164, 195, ***196***, 197, 201
Auburn, Virginia 88, 89
Aurora, New York 10, 11, 81

Bailey's Creek 151, 152; battle of 148–149

Baker, Charles 208
Baltimore, Maryland 17, 18, 19, 30, 37, 59, 80, 163
Barksdale, Gen. William (CSA) 21, 22, 58–60, 63
Barlow, Gen. Francis (USA) 107, 116, 117, 121, 122, 124, 126, 127, 130, 132–135, 139, 141–143, 145, 146, 152, 192
Bealton Station 85, 87, 88, 96
Beardsley, William C. 5
Belding, Silas 164, 188
Belle Island prisoner of war camp 159, 206
Bennett, William 186
Bentley, George ***12***
Benton, James D. 8, ***9***, 11, 39, 41, 47, 49, 83, 86, 88, 90, 95, 96, 100, 101, 104, 105, 120, 128, 199; Camp Douglas 33, 35, 36; Gettysburg 70, 71; Harpers Ferry 23; Petersburg 48, 149, 150, 153, 161, 163, 166–168, 181–183
Berge, Marcus 184
Bermuda Hundred 139, 187
Bidlack, DeWitt 87
Birdsall, William 61
Birney, Gen. David (USA) 121, 130–132, 134, 140, 143–145, 153
Blakeley, Alexander 208
Blanchard, Earl 208
Bliss farm 56, 66–68, 72
Block House Bridge 121, 125
Blowers, Peter 208
Bohn, Charles 208
Bolivar Heights 18, 21, 22, 24–26, 28
Bolton, Noble 208
Boorman, Albert 208
Boothwell, William ***69***
Borden, Capt. J.H. (USA) 163
Boydton Plank Road 166, 170, 172, 181, 182, 185–187, 189; battle of 171
Bradley, Samuel 44, 74, 109, 142
Branch, Gen. Lawrence O'Brien (CSA) 27
Brandy Station 85, 96, 102
Breckenridge, Gen. John (CSA) 135, 138
Brinkerhoff, John 64, 77
Bristoe Station battle of 89–95
Britt, John 208
Broad Run 89, 93, 95
Brock Road 111, 112, 115, 116, 118–120, 122
Brooke, Gen. John (USA) 119, 121, 123, 124, 127, 134, 135
Brown, George 12, 114, 164
Brown, Col. Hiram (USA) 123, 125, 126
Brown, James 208
Brown, John 44
Brown, Chaplain John N. 13, 42, 57, 61, 63, 67, 83, 102, 199
Brown, William 61
Brynes, Col. Richard (USA) 127, 134, 135
Buchanan, Robert 143
Buford, Gen. John (USA) 55, 56
Bull, John 136
Bull Hill 18, 24, 26
Bull Run 46, 50, 94, 95, 112
Bump, James 61
Burkville, Virginia 193, 194
Burnham, Edwin 164, 188, 193
Burrad, William 71
Butler, Gen. Benjamin (USA) 103, 110, 171
Byron, Maj. John (USA) 155, 156

Caitlin, Charles 102
Caldwell, Gen. John (USA) 89, 92, 103

243

Camp, Andrew 172, 174
Camp Beckwith 85, 87
Camp Cayuga 10, 15, 30
Camp Douglas 30–37, 84
Camp Hill 19, 24
Camp Pomeroy 39, 42, *43*
Camp Rucker 85
Camp Vermont 40–42
Capron, Adolphus 44, 49, 160, 199
Carroll, Gen. Samuel (USA) 98, 104
Catlett's Station 88, 89
Cato, New York 11, 16, 48, 59
Caulkins, Thomas 23, 28, 52
Cavender, John 208
Cayuga Lake Academy 12, 62
Cemetery Hill (Petersburg) 149, 150
Cemetery Ridge 56–58, 64–67, 69, 77
Centerville, Virginia 42, 43, 47–52, 54, 67, 88, 89, 93, 95
Chase, Aaron 159, 160
Chesterfield Bridge 130, 131
Chicago, Illinois 30, 32–34, 50
Chickahominy River 139
City Point 141, 151, 163, 165, 178, 182
City Point Railroad 141, 148
Clark, Henry 74, 199
Clemens, Isaac 172
Clyde, New York 5, 9–11, 106
Coe, John 10, 12, 44, 45
Collins, Jeremiah 33
Confederate Corps: First 57, 85, 86, 110, 120, 133; Second 88, 94, 98, 103, 138, 147, 182, 183, 191, 192; Third 94, 98, 102, 182
Conley, James 13
Connecticut Troops: 14th Infantry 68
Conner, Gen. James (CSA) 155, 158, 159
Conners, Michael 172
Conners, Valentine 172
Conquest, New York 11
Consolidated Brigade 147, 152, 155–159, 170
Contant, Adrian 126
Contant, David 207, 208
Cooke, Gen. John (CSA) 89, 90, 92, 157, 158
Cookingham, Charles *66*
Cooper, Simeon 19, 33, 35, 43, 62, 63
Corning, Jpseph 169, 170, 175–178, 181
Cox, Thomas 208
Crandell, Col. Levin (USA) 147, 152, 155
Crater, battle of 149–150
Crawford, Gen. Samuel (USA) 174
Culpeper, Virginia 85–87, 101
Culp's Hill 56, 66
Culver, Ambrose 208

Culver, Horace 208
Cumberland Church, battle of 192
Curtis, Albert *114*
Curtis, Bela 207, 208

Dabney's Mill 172, 182, 187
Dadswell, Thomas 20, 44, 49
Darbytown Road 152
Davenport, Humphrey 186
David, George 28
Davis, Pres. Jefferson (CSA) 47, 168
Davis, Martin L. 43, 57
Dearlove, John 122
Deep Bottom 148, 151
Delaware Troops: 1st Infantry 67; 4th Infantry 41
Deming, Joseph 93
Dennis, Roland 164, 199
Depot Road 155, 156
Derby, Payson 61
Deuel, Franklin 181
Dietrick, Henry 13
Dinwiddie Court House 154, 177, 181, 182, 185–187
Disbrow, John 25
Doane, James 173
Donk, Augustus 13, 119, 201
Douglas, Stephen 3, 25
Dow, Solomon 165
Drake, John 49, 71, 95, 195
Drummond, Robert *168*, 169, 173, 174, 199, 203–208
Dryer, Lewis 47
Dubois, Peter 3
Dudley, Edgar 44, 132
Dudley, Theron 137
Duly, John 143
Dumpling Mountain 101, 103, 104, 109, 128
D'Utassey, Col. Frederick (USA) 21, 22, 24, 26, 27, 35

Early, Gen. Jubal (CSA) 138, 147, 151, 165
Eldred, Newman 7, 17 30, 31, 34, 43, 47, 50, 53, 79, 80; Gettysburg 55, 59, 66, 70, 71, 75–77; Harpers Ferry 18, 22, 23, 26, 28
Ellicott Mills, Maryland 29, 30
Elliot's Salient 149
Emmitsburg Road 56–60, 63, 64, 66, 70, 74, 75, 77
Ennis, Edward 208
Evans, Col. Clement (CSA) 125
Ewell, Gen. Richard (CSA) 88, 94, 98, 103, 130

Fahy, John 13
Failing, Myron 135
Fairfax Court House, Virginia 39, 48
Fairfax Seminary 40
Farmville, Virginia 191, 192
Ferguson, James 208
Ferris, Newton 165, 172, 208
Fink, Manning 133

Fink, Wallace 57, 132
Fishback, John 46, 85, 118, 181, 185
Fisk, Daniel 208
Fitzgerald, Nicholas 13
Follett, John 19
Ford, Col. Thomas (USA) 21, 22
Fort Davis 162, 166, *167*, 170–173, 203
Fort Donaldson 3, 31
Fort Emory 182
Fort Fisher 187
Fort Gregg 190
Fort Harrison 166
Fort Hays (Centerville) 51
Fort Hays (Petersburg) 162, 170, 172, 174, 203
Fort Henry 3
Fort Lyon 40
Fort Mahone 189
Fort Pulaski 3
Fort Sedgwick 162
Fort Seibert 182
Fort Stedman 183
Fort Stevenson 175–177
Fort Wayne, Indiana 34
Fort Whitworth 190
Francisco, Byron *101*
Frank, Col. Paul (USA) 107, 110–112, 116, 119, 121–123
Frederick City, Maryland 29, 79, 80, 147
Fredericksburg, Virginia 41, 49, 195
Frisbee, Charles 48, 106, 107
Fuller, Asahel 133
Fuller, Samuel 123
Funk, Col. Augustus (USA) 183
Furnam, Charles 164
Fussell's Mill, battle of 152–153
Fynmore, William 79

Galen, New York 11
Gardner, Isaac 102
Gatesman, George 47
Geer, Charles 41
Geer, Thomas 11, *13*, 15, 17, 41, 44, 99, 101, 107, 108, 109, 130, 137, 176, 177, 182, 184, 185, 187, 188, 193–195, 199; Camp Douglas 34, 35; Gettysburg 59, 62, 72, 74, 78; promoted to corporal 50; promoted to sergeant 164
Genoa, New York 11
Gettysburg 1, 80, 81, 83–85, 90, 94–96, 100, 107; battle of 55–78
Gibbon, Gen. John (USA) 121, 125, 126, 130, 131, 134, 137, 140, 141, 143, 145, 148, 184, 185
Gibbs, David 114
Gifford, Henry, 62, *63*, 75, 82, 83
Gilbertson, James, 208
Glinn, Thomas, 209
Globe Tavern, battle of 153–154
Gordon, Gen. John (CSA) 125, 182, 183, 191, 192

Index

Gould, Benjamin Franklin 118
Gould, Samuel 136
Grandin, Daniel 126, 195
Granger, Erastus 74
Grant, Gen. Ulysses S. (USA) 3, 79, 98, 107, 110, 112, 129, 131, 133–135, 138, 141, 147, 151, 161, 165, 181, 193, 185, 187, 192, 193, 197
Gravelly Run 185
Green, Amos 209
Green, Augustus 36, 114, 164
Green, Charles 204, 206–208, 209
Greenwich Road 89, 90, 92
Gregg, Gen. David (USA) 152–155, 170, 177, 178, 181, 182
Grimshaw, Col. A.H. (USA) 41
Grinnell, John 199
Griswold, James 71
Gum Springs, Virginia 51, 52

Hackett, William 209
Haggerty, James 44, 49
Halifax Road 154–155
Hampshire, George 209
Hancock, Gen. Winfield Scott (USA) 51, 53, 57, 58, 65, 112, 119, 126, 129, 130, 131, 133, 134, 139, 141, 143, 148, 149, 153, 155, 156, 159, 160, 162, 170, 171, 177
Haney, James 209
Hanie, Franklin 209
Hare House, battle of 143
Harmon, Simeon 71
Harpers Ferry, Virginia 18, 19, 20, 21, 29–31, 33–37, 39, 42, 43, 50, 53, 55, 59, 61, 68, 75, 76, 82; siege of 22–28
Harpers Ferry Brigade 52, 55, 84, 107, 122, 156, 181
Harris, William 34, 209
Harrisburg, Pennsylvania 31
Harrison's Creek, battle of 141, 142
Hart, Horace 209
Hart, William 61
Hartman, Benjamin *162*
Hartnutt, Patrick, 209
Hatcher's Run 170, 171, 178, 181–183, 185, 187
Hayes, Jeremiah 206, 209
Hays, Gen. Alexander (USA) 43, 44, 47, 51, 52, 56, 57, 65, 67–69, 75–77, 84, 88, 98, 102, 104, 107
Hays, Gen. William (USA) 84
Heth, Gen. Henry (CSA) 153, 157, 171, 188
Hibbard, Ezra 33, 44
Hicks, Judson, 61, *62*, 78, 176, 195
High Bridge 191
Hilderbrandt, Hugo 21, 67, 68
Hill, Gen. A.P. Hill (USA) 29, 89, 94, 98, 99, 112, 115, 154, 182
Hill, Horace 13, 44, 105, 114, 195
Hinman, James 84, 107, 129

Hinman, Wellington 109, 110, 125, 131, 132, 133
Hitchcock, Charles 17, 68, 71, 84
Hoagland, Henry 206, 209
Hoff, Esek 28–32, 37–43, 49–51, 53, 79, 82, 84, 85, 90, 97, 102, 103, 109, 131, 160–162, 165, 167, 186, 199; Camp Douglas 34, 35; capture of pickets 172–175; Gettysburg 56, 61, 65, 72; Harpers Ferry 18, 19, 23, 25, 26; promoted to second lieutenant 164
Hoff, John 209
Holcombe, Edward 79
Holliday, George 18
Holmes, Sebastian 32, 40, 67, 68, 71, 74, 77, 109
Holt's Corner 191
Hooker, Gen. Joseph (USA) 52, 53
Hopkins, Dickenson 36, 48
Horton, John 207, 209
Hosey, Charles 186
Howard, John 165, 172, 209
Hoxie, Allen 142, 146
Hudson, Joel 209
Hueston, Edgar *20*, 76, 109, 119, 127, 186, *194*, 199
Humphreys, Gen. Andrew (USA) 58, 177, 182, 185, 187, 190
Hunting Creek 40, 41, 43
Husk, Lewis W. 1, 6, 10, *11*, 46, 67, 126–130, 133, 134, 139, 141, 142, 144, 146, 148, 152, 153, 170, 178, 179, 184–188, 190–197, 199; capture of pickets 172–174; promoted to lieutenant colonel 169; promoted to major 147; recruiting duty 103
Hutchins, Daniel 12, 13, 15, 118, 120–122, 201
Hydesville, New York 5
Hyser, Isaiah 209

Illinois Troops: 65th Infantry 21
Impson, Gilbert 209
Indiana Troops: 15th Battery 21
Ira, New York 11, 16, 164
Irish Brigade 147, 162, 167

Jackson, David 209
Jackson, Gen. Thomas "Stonewall" (CSA) 20, 22, 27, 28, 49
Jacques, Irving 13, 44, 65
James, Frank 209
James River 138–140, 147–151, 165, 194
Jarvis, Thomas 186
Jeffrey, Henry 169–173, 209
Jenkins, Thomas 159, 201, 206
Jerusalem Plank Road 144, 146, 149, 150, 153, 155, 159, 161
Johnson, Pres. Andrew (USA) 197
Johnson, Gen. Edward (CSA) 125
Johnson, Emery 209
Johnson, John 40
Johnson, Levi 209

Johnson, Robert 55
Johnston, Gen. Joseph (CSA) 182, 192
Johnston, William 209
Jones, Ira 44, 109
Jones, James 186
Jones, William 209
Jones Neck 151, 153

Kautz, Gen. Augustus (USA) 139, 166
Kays, Thomas 209
Keller, Delevan 209
Kelly, George 209
Kelly, Patrick 209
Kenney, Auburn 209
Kershaw, Gen. Joseph (CSA) 21, 148
Kilmer, Malone 206, 209
Kilmer, Martin *115*
Kirkland, Gen. William W. (CSA) 89, 90
Knapp, John 7, 50, 108
Kramm, Frederick 209

Laing, John 16, 44, 90, 127
Lampson, Theodore 36
Langdon, Spencer 48
Lape, Philip Ira 10, 126, 180, 201
Lape, Samuel 10
Lattin, Jerome *36*, 49, 131, 145
Laurel Hill 120, 121
Lawrence, John 59
Ledyard, New York 11, 81, 124
Lee, Charles 81
Lee, Gen. Robert E. (CSA) 20, 49, 51, 52, 69, 78, 80, 81, 83, 85, 94, 95, 97, 98, 103, 110, 111, 121, 123, 130, 131, 133, 138, 144, 145, 147–149, 151, 154, 181, 183, 185, 192, 193
Legg, Anson 31
Lewis, Robert 209
Libby Prison 133, 203, 206
Lincoln, Pres. Abraham (USA) 3, 4, 30, 94, 97, 161, 162, 167, 168, 194
Locke, New York 11
Lockwood, John 95, 118, 131, 142, 160, 164, *194*
Lombard, Daniel 160
Longstreet, Gen. James (CSA) 57, 85, 86, 115, 119, 120, 193
Loudon Heights 18, 22, 85
Lusk, Isaac 13, 44, 49, 74, 78, 81, 87, 92, 97–101, 104, 107
Lutes, Franklin 108, 186
Lynchburg-Richmond Stage Road 192, 193
Lyons, New York 11, 77

MacDougall, Clinton D. 7, *8*, 13, 28, 37, 40, 84–86, 95–97, 103, 106, 107, 109, 134, 135, 137, 142, 147, 162, 169, 174, 175, 177, 181; Bristoe Station 88–90, 92, 93; Gettysburg 56, 57, 59, 61, 62,

64–72, 75, 76, 78; promoted to brigadier general 188, *189*, 191, 193, *194*, 199; promoted to colonel 44, *45*, 46–48, 50, 52, 54; Spotsylvania 126, 128
Madill, Gen. Henry (USA) 181, 183–185, 188
Mahone, Gen. William (CSA) 121, 134, 145, 146, 153, 171, 193, 203
Mainard, Dennis 175
Maine Troops: 25th Infantry 41; 27th Infantry 41
Malone's Crossing 154
Mandie, Casper 137
Marion, New York 11, 78
Martinsburg, Virginia 20, 21
Maryland Heights 18, 19, 21, 22, 24
Massachusetts Troops: 1st Sharpshooters 75; 6th Infantry 6; 9th Battery 51; 10th Battery 158
McAllister, Col. Robert (USA) 117–119
McClellan, Gen. George B. (USA) 3, 4, 56, 167, 168
McDonald, Minard 111, 112, 114, 116, 118, 181
McDowell, Johnson 41, 61, 201
McGowan, Gen. Samuel (CSA) 155, 156
McIntyre, Samuel 9, 12
McLaws, Gen. Lafayette (CSA) 21, 22
McMahon, James 209
Mead, Sidney 26, 67, 74, 101, 108, 183, 199
Meade, Gen. George G. (USA) 53, 56, 69, 71, 80–82, 85–89, 94–98, 100, 106, 110–112, 116, 119, 123, 126, 127, 129–131, 133–135, 138, 141, 143, 147–149, 151, 155, 156, 160, 165, 181, 183, 185–187, 193, 194, 197
Meyers, Solomon 81
Michigan Troops: 8th Cavalry 108; 9th Infantry 108
Miles, Col. Dixon (USA) 19
Miles, Gen. Nelson (USA) 123, 124, 127, 134, 135, 146, 148, 153, 158, 159, 183–185, 188
Miles, William 209
Miller, Alfred 61
Milton Mills, Virginia 96, 97, 101
Mine Run campaign 98–101, 108
Minnesota Troops: 1st Sharpshooters 59
Mississippi Troops: 11th Infantry 74, 75, 122; 13th Infantry 52; 17th Infantry 58; 18th Infantry 58; 21st Infantry 64
Montezuma, New York 11
Moore, George 164, 168, 181
Moore, Hasseltine 36
Moore, Martin Van Buren 24, 195
Moravia, New York 11, 160, 201
Morgan, Christopher 6
Morgan, Gov. Edmund 3, 14, 15
Morgan, Edward 8, 9
Morton's Ford, battle of 86, 103

Mosher, Marcellus 54
Mott, Gen. Gershom (USA) 125, 143, 145, 148, 151, 155, 156, 181, 182, 184
Mulligan, Isaac 6
Mumford, Lafayette 164, 172, 173, 176
Murdock, Marcus 67, 131, 153, 154, 158–161, 168
Myers, Reuben 44, 125, 164, 173, 188, *190*, 193, 199

New Jersey Troops: 12th Infantry 67, 70
New Market Heights 152
New Market Road 148, 152
New York Troops: 4th Heavy Artillery 197; 7th Infantry 107, 170, 182; 9th Heavy Artillery 108, 137; 12th Battery 158; 13th Infantry 83; 16th Cavalry 87, 164; 17th Infantry 164; 19th Infantry 7; 27th Infantry 112; 33rd Infantry 7, 42, 170; 39th Infantry 21, 33, 42, 46, 56, 58, 64, 67, 70, 74, 89, 94, 102, 103, 119, 170, 183, 191; 52nd Infantry 107, 122, 182, 191; 54th National Guard 9; 57th Infantry 107, 112, 114, 120, 170, 177, 181; 61st Infantry 159; 63rd Infantry 147; 69th Infantry 147, 170, 172, 174, 175; 75th Infantry 7, 28, 84; 88th Infantry 147, 155; 98th Infantry 182, 199; 108th Infantry 70; 115th Infantry 21, 24, 37, 41; 125th Infantry 42, 46, 52, 56, 58, 59, 70, 88–90, 103, 117, 147, 155, 156, 158, 170, 182, 188, 192; 126th Infantry 31, 56, 58, 59, 64, 70, 75, 88, 89, 103, 141, 156, 158, 170, 177, 182, 185, 192; 138th Infantry 164; 147th Infantry 50, 76; 152nd Infantry 158, 159; 194th Infantry 164, 181
Newark, New York 5
Newton, Joseph 101
Nichols, Elizabeth 32
Nichols, William 32
Niles, New York 11
North, Daniel 77
North Anna River, battle of 130–132
North Carolina Troops: 6th Infantry 206; 18th Infantry 112; 28th Infantry 75; 37th Infantry 158, 159; 38th Infantry 112; 46th Infantry 92
Northrop, Ezra 13, 44
Nostrant, John 17

O'Brien, John 209
O'Hara, James 7
Ohio Troops: 60th Infantry 21, 24, 32
Old Cold Harbor, battle of 133–138

Ontario, New York 11
Orange and Alexandria Railroad 42, 83, 87, 89, 94
Orange Plank Road 97, 111, 118, 116, 119, 120
Orange Turnpike 97, 98, 99, 111, 112
Owen, Gen. Joshua T. (USA) 84, 88, 89, 92, 95, 98, 99, 103–105, 107, 110
Owens, William 209

Page, William 132
Palmyra, New York 5, 9, 11
Parke, Gen. John (USA) 170
Patterson, Gen. Robert (USA) 18
Paylor, John 22, *23*, 29, 38, 39, 41, 42, 47, 49, 53, 85, 95, 101, 102; Camp Douglas 32, 35; Williamsport 81, 82
Pease, David 46, 47
Peckham, George 54, 146
Peeble's Farm 166, 170, 177, 178
Penfield, Capt. Nelson (USA) 155, 156
Pennsylvania Troops: 48th Infantry 149; 83rd Infantry 163; 143rd Infantry 50; 145th Infantry 123; 148th Infantry 156
Percy, Edward 12
Perkins, Charles 146
Perkins, George 146
Perry, Robert 13, 46, 49, 50, 52, 120–128, 164
Petersburg, Virginia 1; capture of pickets 172–175; siege of 138–190
Petersburg Defense Forces 139, 141
Philadelphia, Pennsylvania 17, 19, 78
Pitcock, Howard 209
Pitkin, Lucius 210
Pittsburgh, Pennsylvania 31, 34, 37
Platt, Ebenezer 92
Po River 120–123, 128
Pomeroy, Theodore, Rep. 6
Port Byron, New York 5, 7, 11, 201
Probasco, Myron 210
Proseus, Augustus 44, 61
Pyatt, Stephen 164

Rapidan River 86, 87, 96–98, 101, 103, 110, 114
Rappahannock River 80, 84, 85, 87, 95–97
Rappahannock Station 87, 96
Reamer, Isaac 210
Ream's Station 154, battle of 155–159
Remington, George *145*
Remington, Wager *180*, 181
Rice, Albert *140*
Rich, Frank 16, 44, 82, 94, 108, 109
Richmond, Edwin 210
Richmond, Virginia 4, 9, 47, 85,

103, 110, 129, 131, 132, 148, 151, 153, 161, 181, 194, 203
Riley, Edward 61
Ritter, Gustavus 13, 72, 195
Roberts, Franklin 134
Robertson's Tavern 98
Robins, Orlando 186
Rodgers, Luther *116*
Rose, Philander 132
Rose Valley, New York 11
Rounds, William 210
Rowanty Creek 154
Rugg, Lt. Col. Samuel (USA) 156, 158, 159
Rush, Charles 210

Salisbury, George 11, *12*, 61, 201
Salisbury prisoner of war camp 159, 204, 206–208
Samson, Levi 210
Savannah, New York 11
Scales, Alfred, Gen (CSA) 155, 156
Schmidt, Frank 13
Scipio, New York 11
Sebring, Alfred 210
Segoine, Henry 24, *25*, 44
Segoine, Col. Jesse 3, 7, *8*, 10, 13, 15–19, 30, 34, 35, 37, 39, 41, 42; Harpers Ferry 21–27; resigns 43
Seeley, Aaron 41, 44, 84, 109, 111; Gettysburg 58, 59, 61, 65, 74, 76; Wilderness 112, 114–116, 118, 119
Seeley, Abner 164
Seminary Ridge 56, 75, 77
Sempronius, New York 6, 11
Sensebaugh, Simeon 6
Servis, Howard 49
Seward, William Henry 30
Seward, William Henry, Jr. 137
Seymour, Milton 47
School House Ridge 22
Shady Grove Church Road 120, 121, 122
Sharpsburg, Maryland 29
Shenandoah Valley 3, 4, 20, 138, 147
Sheridan, Gen. Philip (USA) 147, 148, 151, 165, 183, 193
Sherman, Gen. William T. (USA) 110, 161, 181, 195, 197
Sherrill, Col. Eliakim 64, 65, 68, 74, 76
Shields, Lt. David 69, 75
Shimer, William 92, 93
Shuster, Philip 210
Sickles, Gen. Daniel (USA) 57, 58
Sielliskowski, Franz 13
Skinner, Nelson *136*, 137
Sloan, John 6, 7
Slocum, Warren 114
Smith, Chauncey 164, 165, 169, 170, 176, 178–180, 183, 184, 193–195, 201; capture of pickets 172–175

Smith, George *10*, 25, 44, 61, 85, 210
Smith, Harry 23, 29, 32, 45, 49, 50, 53, 54, 108, 109, 118, 122, 123, 125, 127, 128
Smith, Horace 61, *63*
Smith, John 127, 164
Smith, Seneca 9, 12, 24, 30, 32, 35, 44, 48, 49
Smith, Gen. W.F. (USA) 133, 139, 141
Smith, Warren 83, 131
Smith, William 163
Smith, Zenas 210
Smyth, Gen. Thomas (USA) 98, 123, 127, 181, 182
Snedaker, Albert 119
Snedaker, James 112, 119
Snow, Benjamin 81
Sodus, New York 11, 40
Solomon's Gap 21
Somhofe, Henry 210
South Side Railroad 144, 170, 171, 187–189, 191; battle of 166
Soverill, Andrew 44
Spear, Col. Samuel (USA) 154, 155
Spotsylvania, battle of 120–126
Spring Hill 148 149
Springport, New York 8, 10, 11
Stacey, Manley 25, 40, 42, 46–48, 50, 51, 79, 81–83, 96, 98, 99; death 101, 102; Gettysburg 59, 72, 77
Sterling, Daniel 164, 165, 169
Sterling, New York 11
Stevens, George 102
Stevens, William *106*
Stevensburg, Virginia 101, 102
Stever, William 40
Stewart, Artemus 142, 195
Stuart, Gen. J.E.B. (CSA) 88
Sturgis, Nathan 210
Sullivan, John 132
Summer Hill, New York 11
Sutherland Station 187, battle of 188
Syracuse, New York 17

Tabor, Benjamin 210
Taneytown, Maryland 55, 79
Taneytown Road 55, 68, 71
Taylor, David 164
Templeton, Thomas 125
Ten Eyck, Barney 13, 34
Ten Eyck, Edwin 13
Tennessee Troops: 10th Infantry 134
Terry, Gen. Alfred (USA) 152
Thomas, Edward 31, 44, 81
Thomas, John A. 74
Thompson, Benjamin 14, 17, 18, 24–28, 33, 48, 52–54, 83; Gettysburg 55, 56, 58, 59, 61, 64, 65, 67, 68, 71, 75, 78; leaves regiment 102
Thoroughfare Gap 43

Tilden, William 61
Tinney, Madison 210
Todd, Charles 55, 146
Tomlinson, Robert *14*
Totopotomoy Creek, battle of 132–133
Tousey, George 210
Travers, William 121
Tremain, Silas 6, 10, 16, 25, 44
Tremper, John 44
Truax, Adam 207, 210
Trulan, James 34
Tyler, Gen. Daniel (USA) 33, 35

Uniontown, Maryland 54
Union Army Corps: I 55, 86, 96, 97, 100, 103; II 50–52, 55, 57, 59, 65, 68, 78, 81, 82, 84, 86–90, 96–98, 100, 101, 103–107, 110, 111, 115, 116, 120, 121, 123, 126–131, 134, 135, 137, 139, 141, 143–149, 151–153, 156, 162, 165, 166, 170–172, 177, 181–183, 185–187, 191–195; III 57–59, 63, 64, 82, 86, 88, 89, 96–98, 100, 107; V 81, 84, 86, 89, 90, 96, 97, 100, 110–112, 115, 120, 126, 127, 130, 131, 134, 143–145, 147–149, 153, 160, 165, 166, 170–172, 174, 177, 178, 181–183, 185–187, 192, 194; VI 81, 86, 96, 98, 100, 110–112, 115, 116, 123, 125–128, 130–134, 143–147, 154, 182, 187, 189, 192; IX 110, 115, 120, 126, 128, 131, 134, 141, 143, 144, 148–150, 156, 165, 166, 170, 171, 183, 187, 189; X 151–153, 165, 166, 171; XI 50, 55, 86; XII 66, 74, 81, 86; XVIII 133, 134, 139, 141, 143, 148, 149, 165, 166; XXV 171
Union Mills, Virginia 42
Union Springs, New York 6, 11, 16
United States Troops: Battery I, First Artillery 70 (1st Veteran Reserve Corps 80; 5th Infantry 134); 32nd United States Colored Troops 102

Van Buskirk, Jacob 44, 45
Van Dervere, Edward 142
Van Dyne, George 210
Van Dyne, William 210
Vaninwager, Leonard 13
Van Winkle, Myron *72*
Vaughan Road 178, 182, 185
Venice, New York 11
Vermont Troops: 9th Infantry 32; 15th Infantry 164
Victory, New York 11, 114
Virginia Troops: 35th Battalion Cavalry 87
Vosburgh, William *28*, 44, 49, 79, 82, 93, 109

Walker, Henry 94
Wallace, Alonzo 76
Wallace, Casper 11, *197*, 199

Wallace, George 76
Wallace, Gen. Lew (USA) 147
Walworth, New York 11
Warren, Gen. Governeur (USA) 84, 89, 90, 99, 100, 106, 112, 120, 126, 153, 154, 166, 171, 177, 178, 181, 182, 185
Warren, Richard 13, 44, 106, 142, 201
Warrenton, Virginia 88, 95–97
Washington, D.C. 1, 34, 37, 48, 52, 83, 94, 193, 194
Webner, Charles 131
Weedsport, New York 11
Welch, Morris 13, 61
Welch, Patrick 87, 118, 164
Weldon Railroad 153, 155; battle for 144–145

Western Exchange Hotel *4*, 199
White, Charles 104, 129, 132, 133, 137, 146, 151, 161, 165, 169, 171, 176, 201
White, John **118**
White, Levi 72, 92, 131, 133, 161, 181, 201
White Oak Road 171, 187; battle of 185–186
Whitemore, Emmet 76
Whitemore, William 76
Wilcox, Gen. Cadmus (CSA) 59, 60, 145, 146, 148
Wilcox Landing 139
Wilderness, battle of 110–112, 120
Will, Jacob 210
Willard, Col. George (USA) 52, 56–60, 64, 68, 76

Williamson, New York 11
Williamsport, Maryland 80, 81, 82, 94
Wilson, Gen. James (USA) 144, 154
Winder, Gen. John H. (CSA) 204, 205
Windmill Point 139
Wishart, George 87
Wissmuller, George 210
Wolcott, New York 5
Wolf, John 210
Wood, John, 33
Woodworth, Orin 207, 210

York, William 120

Zeigler's Grove 56, 65

www.ingramcontent.com/pod-product-compliance
Ingram Content Group UK Ltd.
Pitfield, Milton Keynes, MK11 3LW, UK
UKHW050702160426
5217IPUK00038B/1952